BUSINESS AND GENERAL REFERENCE BOOK SERIES FROM IDG

Bird Watching For Dummies

Tweet Sheet

Bird Watchers' Stuff to Take Along

- ❑ Binoculars and spotting scope (if you have one)
- ❑ Field guide
- ❑ Checklist or notebook for recording sightings
- ❑ Pen, pencil, crayon, hunk of coal — any writing utensil
- ❑ A hat (blocks sun and rain and helps retain heat in cold weather)
- ❑ Comfortable, sturdy footwear
- ❑ Wind/rain-blocking outerwear
- ❑ An extra layer of clothing for your upper body
- ❑ Food, especially snacks

- ❑ Drinkable liquids
- ❑ Camera (and film) if you are a photographer
- ❑ A map (unless you don't mind asking directions)
- ❑ Insect-repellent (not necessary in winter in some areas)
- ❑ Aspirin or other pain medication (in case you just miss seeing an Eskimo curlew)
- ❑ Quarters (or your cellular phone) for a payphone in case you *spot* an Eskimo curlew
- ❑ Champagne (or other celebratory beverage) in case it really *is* an Eskimo curlew

FIELD TIP

BACKYARD TIP

The Most Popular Seeds for Birds

- ✔ **Black-oil sunflower seed** — The hamburger of bird-feeding. Readily eaten by many birds.
- ✔ **Mixed seed** — Containing white proso millet, cracked corn, and sunflower seed.
- ✔ **Sunflower hearts** — Like black oil sunflower seed, but without the shell. Expensive but less messy.
- ✔ **White-striped sunflower seed** — Less popular with birds than black-oil, but preferred by large finches such as evening grosbeaks.

- ✔ **Thistle (Niger) seed** — A favorite among the finch family.
- ✔ **Peanuts, peanut bits** — Devoured by woodpeckers, chickadees, titmice, nuthatches, thrashers, towhees, and wrens, among others.
- ✔ **Safflower seed** — Loved by cardinals and sparrows, disliked by squirrels and blackbirds.

Basic Bird Meal Mix

- 1 cup peanut butter
- 1 cup vegetable shortening, melted beef suet, or bacon drippings
- 4 cups cornmeal (yellow meal is best)
- 1 cup white flour

Mix ingredients together and offer in mesh bags (such as empty onion bags) or smear into holes on a suet log or fence post. Adding softened raisins, grape bits, and nut pieces is optional.

...For Dummies: Bestselling Book Series for Beginners

Bird Watching For Dummies™

BIRDY WORDS
Chirp! Chirp!

Quick Bird Name Pronunciation Guide

Avocet	<u>av</u>-oh-set
Egret	<u>ee</u>-gret
Eider	<u>eye</u>-dur
Grebe	<u>greeb</u>
Grosbeak	<u>grows</u>-beak
Ibis	<u>eye</u>-biss
Jaeger	<u>yay</u>-ger
Junco	<u>junk</u>-oh
Osprey	<u>ahs</u>-pray
Parula	<u>pair</u>-you-luh *or* pah-<u>roo</u>-luh
Phalarope	<u>fal</u>-uh-rope
Pileated	<u>pie</u>-lee-ate-ed *or* <u>pill</u>-ee-ate-ed
Plover	<u>pluh</u>-ver
Prothonotary	pro-<u>thaw</u>-no-tair-ee
Ptarmigan	<u>tar</u>-muh-gin *or* <u>tar</u>-muh-jin
Pyrrhuloxia	peer-hull-<u>ox</u>-ee-uh
Scaup	<u>skawp</u>
Scoter	<u>skoh</u>-tur
Tanager	<u>tan</u>-uh-jer
Towhee	<u>toe</u>-hee
Vireo	<u>veer</u>-ee-oh

Bird-Do's

- Look at the bird, not at the book. The book will always be there; the bird may not be so cooperative.
- Be prepared; know what to expect.
- Birds have wings and they use them: be prepared for surprises.
- When identifying a bird, start at the top of the head and work down.
- Ask yourself: What are the three most prominent features of this bird?
- Don't worry if you can't ID a bird. You'll get it next time!
- Don't be afraid to ask another bird watcher for help.
- Be quiet and courteous; avoid scaring the birds or disturbing fellow bird watchers.
- Respect the habitat; don't trample anything in your path in order to see a bird.
- Learn from your mistakes.
- Stay positive.
- Have fun, relax, and enjoy the view!

BIRDIQUETTE

IDG BOOKS WORLDWIDE™

Copyright © 1997 IDG Books Worldwide, Inc. All rights reserved.

Cheat Sheet $2.95 value. Item 5040-3.

For more information about IDG Books, call 1-800-762-2974.

...For Dummies: Bestselling Book Series for Beginners

Praise For *Bird Watching For Dummies*

"If I'd had *Bird Watching For Dummies* many years ago, my life list would have been much longer."
— Jimmy Carter, Former President of the United States

"Let's hear a rousing cheer for Bill Thompson, III. With wit, wisdom, and a wonderful sense for structure, he has delivered what we've all been waiting for — the complete birder's bible. I can't imagine that even the wisest pro will want to leave home without it."
— John G. Mitchell, former field editor for *Audubon* magazine and author of *Dispatches from the Deep Woods*

"This book is for me — a bird watcher and a dummy! Thank you, Mr. Thompson!"
— Janet Leigh, Actress/Author

"Bill Thompson has made the pleasures of bird-watching too palpable and too accessible to resist . . . even for couch potatoes like us, whose experience was limited to looking at a single parrot strut around our den. Come dawn, we'll be out-of-doors, binoculars in hand. This is a book that will change our life!"
— Jane and Michael Stern, Authors of *Eat Your Way Across The USA*

"Bird watching is enormous fun, and the fun begins here. Bill Thompson's conversational style, humor, and great experience make this book an ideal place to start. I also bow to his great skill in bringing cautionary tales about illicit moonshine stills and his own accident-filled honeymoon into a bird watching book. Incidents such as these make for a rattling read as well as making useful points about the absorbing activity that is bird watching."
— Nicholas Hammond, Former Director of Communications, Royal Society for The Protection of Birds, UK

Praise For Bird Watcher's Digest

"The amateur birder, the professional ornithologist, and the journalist all meet in the pages of *Bird Watcher's Digest;* what their articles have in common is not only the manifestation of the authors' love for birds, but the consummate readability of their prose."
— Kenneth C. Parkes, Curator Emeritus of Birds, The Carnegie Museum of Natural History, Pittsburgh, Pennsylvania

"Bird Watcher's Digest is a marvelous melange of bird identification and birding experiences from the heavy to the hilarious. Like Merlin the Magician, under burning midnight oil, its editor, Bill Thompson, III, deftly works his magic on word and art to create a superlative birding magazine."
— Chuck Bernstein, Author of *The Joy of Birding* and column editor for *Birding* magazine

"North America's premier source for information on birding is *Bird Watcher's Digest.* More than timely popular articles on birds written by the best nature writers around, it's chock-full of information from backyard bird watchers, too."
— Jim Berry, Director, The Roger Tory Peterson Institute of Natural History, Jamestown, New York

"Of all the birding magazines available today, *Bird Watcher's Digest* is the one most likely to be read from cover to cover."
— Lola Overman, Author of *The Pleasures of Watching Birds* and *Dial B for Birder*

"Bird Watcher's Digest proves popular with both beginners and experienced birders alike. Its pages capture the remarkable beauty and fascination of the avian world."
— John Tveten, Nature columnist for *The Houston Chronicle* and author of *The Birds of Texas* and other nature books

BIRD WATCHING FOR DUMMIES™

by Bill Thompson, III

Editor, *Bird Watcher's Digest*

Foreword by John C. Sawhill
President & Chief Executive Officer
The Nature Conservancy

IDG Books Worldwide, Inc.
An International Data Group Company

Foster City, CA ◆ Chicago, IL ◆ Indianapolis, IN ◆ Southlake, TX

Bird Watching For Dummies™

Published by
IDG Books Worldwide, Inc.
An International Data Group Company
919 E. Hillsdale Blvd.
Suite 400
Foster City, CA 94404
www.idgbooks.com (IDG Books Worldwide Web site)
www.dummies.com (Dummies Press Web site)

Library of Congress Catalog Card No.: 97-80179

ISBN: 0-7645-5040-3

Printed in the United States of America

10 9 8 7 6 5 4 3 2 1

1E/RQ/QZ/ZX/IN

Distributed in the United States by IDG Books Worldwide, Inc.

Distributed by Macmillan Canada for Canada; by Transworld Publishers Limited in the United Kingdom; by IDG Norge Books for Norway; by IDG Sweden Books for Sweden; by Woodslane Pty. Ltd. for Australia; by Woodslane Enterprises Ltd. for New Zealand; by Longman Singapore Publishers Ltd. for Singapore, Malaysia, Thailand, and Indonesia; by Simron Pty. Ltd. for South Africa; by Toppan Company Ltd. for Japan; by Distribuidora Cuspide for Argentina; by Livraria Cultura for Brazil; by Ediciencia S.A. for Ecuador; by Addison-Wesley Publishing Company for Korea; by Ediciones ZETA S.C.R. Ltda. for Peru; by WS Computer Publishing Corporation, Inc., for the Philippines; by Unalis Corporation for Taiwan; by Contemporanea de Ediciones for Venezuela; by Computer Book & Magazine Store for Puerto Rico; by Express Computer Distributors for the Caribbean and West Indies. Authorized Sales Agent: Anthony Rudkin Associates for the Middle East and North Africa.

For general information on IDG Books Worldwide's books in the U.S., please call our Consumer Customer Service department at 800-762-2974. For reseller information, including discounts and premium sales, please call our Reseller Customer Service department at 800-434-3422.

For information on where to purchase IDG Books Worldwide's books outside the U.S., please contact our International Sales department at 415-655-3200 or fax 415-655-3295.

For information on foreign language translations, please contact our Foreign & Subsidiary Rights department at 415-655-3021 or fax 415-655-3281.

For sales inquiries and special prices for bulk quantities, please contact our Sales department at 415-655-3200 or write to the address above.

For information on using IDG Books Worldwide's books in the classroom or for ordering examination copies, please contact our Educational Sales department at 800-434-2086 or fax 817-251-8174.

For press review copies, author interviews, or other publicity information, please contact our Public Relations department at 415-655-3000 or fax 415-655-3299.

For authorization to photocopy items for corporate, personal, or educational use, please contact Copyright Clearance Center, 222 Rosewood Drive, Danvers, MA 01923, or fax 508-750-4470.

is a trademark under exclusive license to IDG Books Worldwide, Inc., from International Data Group, Inc.

Dedication

For Phoebe, my favorite little bird.

Author's Acknowledgments

I have spent two-thirds of my life watching birds. I have spent one-third of my life editing a magazine about birds. It is another thing altogether to write a book about birds. I could not have completed this project without lots of help.

My most heartfelt thanks go to my wife and birding-pal-for-life, Julie Zickefoose. She more than anybody helped me crawl back from the cliff's edge numerous times, and prevented me from embarrassing myself in print. This was not made any easier by the fact that our daughter, Phoebe Linnea Thompson, was born just as the idea for this book was hatched. I spent plenty of awful hours in the basement office of our house, staring at the keyboard, wishing I could be upstairs with Phoebe. Julie held the fort, encouraged me, and helped out with several chapters. My two girls were my inspiration all the way.

My parents, Bill and Elsa Thompson, founders of *Bird Watcher's Digest,* were at the genesis of the boom in bird watching in North America. In launching BWD, they created a wonderful place for bird watchers to escape to, and a legacy for us Thompson kids. Mom and Dad, I hope we can live up to your dreams and make you proud of us. In exchange, I expect you to get all of your friends to buy copies of this book. I think that's fair.

I had writing and editing help from many, many sources. Special help came from Scott Weidensaul, who did the technical editing for the entire book; from the aforementioned Julie Zickefoose for many of the book's illustrations and for chapters on bird homes, bird feeding, gardening for birds, and field sketching; from Eirik A.T. Blom for larger-than-life work on chapters on field guides, how to ID, bird clubs, listing, field projects, and birding online; and from Kenn Kaufman, for chapters on advanced bird ID, birding hotspots, and bird tours. Sally Onopa contributed her excellent technical illustrations for the book.

At *Bird Watcher's Digest,* Andy, Catbird, Candi, Carol, Helen, Donna, Kat, John, Sara, Jessica, Marlene, and Dan all got to listen to me whine in staff meetings. Kristen got to listen to the whining and got to make my corrections. Andy and John kept the BWD wheels turning while I went AWOL for days at a time in a Dummies-induced haze. Mary Bowers taught me long ago that if you write something and you think it's great, throw it away and start again because it's probably not great. She's right. Honorary BWDers Rebecca Sterner and Mary Ceynowa made their contributions felt, as did Michael MacCaskey of the National Gardening Association.

Two other people from my life deserve a thank you for their indirect contributions to this book. My grandmother, Margaret Thompson, will be 97 when this book is published. I'd like to think I inherited her abilities in English, but you, the reader, will be the judge of that. Thanks, Gram. I really enjoyed sharing the chapters with you as they were completed. The late Pat Murphy was my first bird-watching guru. She lit the fire in our family for avid bird watching, and she was a longtime associate editor at BWD.

At IDG Books Worldwide: Kathy Welton's initial and ongoing enthusiasm for this project was contagious. Kathy Cox was the project editor for this book, as well as my unofficial psychotherapist. She put a human touch on the text and made my job a lot easier than I was making it. Any errors or omissions in the text are all mine, and no fault of hers. Next time we try bird watching together, I promise we won't miss the short-eared owls.

Others at IDG to whom many thanks are due include Constance Carlisle for her enthusiasm and thorough copy editing; to Debbie Stailey and Shelley Lea for design and production of the color section and for enduring the many headaches such a task can bring; to Beth Jenkins for her sensitivity to the needs of the color insert; to Sherry Gomoll who marshalled it all through Production; and to the layout artists and proofreaders and the indexer, who had a massive task. Thanks also to Jamie Klobuchar and Nickole Harris in Chicago, and to Patti Crane in Foster City for her attention to the cover. It takes a lot of hands to produce a book like this and I'm grateful.

And thanks to all of you reading this book — I hope to meet you on a bird walk some day.

ABOUT IDG BOOKS WORLDWIDE

Welcome to the world of IDG Books Worldwide.

IDG Books Worldwide, Inc., is a subsidiary of International Data Group, the world's largest publisher of computer-related information and the leading global provider of information services on information technology. IDG was founded more than 25 years ago and now employs more than 8,500 people worldwide. IDG publishes more than 275 computer publications in over 75 countries (see listing below). More than 60 million people read one or more IDG publications each month.

Launched in 1990, IDG Books Worldwide is today the #1 publisher of best-selling computer books in the United States. We are proud to have received eight awards from the Computer Press Association in recognition of editorial excellence and three from *Computer Currents'* First Annual Readers' Choice Awards. Our best-selling *...For Dummies*® series has more than 30 million copies in print with translations in 30 languages. IDG Books Worldwide, through a joint venture with IDG's Hi-Tech Beijing, became the first U.S. publisher to publish a computer book in the People's Republic of China. In record time, IDG Books Worldwide has become the first choice for millions of readers around the world who want to learn how to better manage their businesses.

Our mission is simple: Every one of our books is designed to bring extra value and skill-building instructions to the reader. Our books are written by experts who understand and care about our readers. The knowledge base of our editorial staff comes from years of experience in publishing, education, and journalism — experience we use to produce books for the '90s. In short, we care about books, so we attract the best people. We devote special attention to details such as audience, interior design, use of icons, and illustrations. And because we use an efficient process of authoring, editing, and desktop publishing our books electronically, we can spend more time ensuring superior content and spend less time on the technicalities of making books.

You can count on our commitment to deliver high-quality books at competitive prices on topics you want to read about. At IDG Books Worldwide, we continue in the IDG tradition of delivering quality for more than 25 years. You'll find no better book on a subject than one from IDG Books Worldwide.

John Kilcullen
CEO
IDG Books Worldwide, Inc.

Steven Berkowitz
President and Publisher
IDG Books Worldwide, Inc.

Eighth Annual
Computer Press
Awards ≥1992

Ninth Annual
Computer Press
Awards ≥1993

Tenth Annual
Computer Press
Awards ≥1994

Eleventh Annual
Computer Press
Awards ≥1995

About the Author

Bill Thompson, III is the editor of *Bird Watcher's Digest,* the popular bi-monthly magazine which has been published by his family since 1978. He holds a bachelor of philosophy degree from Western College at Miami University of Ohio. An avid bird watcher from the age of eight, Bill knew that birds would someday become the focus of his career, in addition to being his main hobby.

Prior to joining *Bird Watcher's Digest* in 1988, Bill held jobs as a musician, house painter, and lunch chef. He was also a senior account executive at the advertising firm of Ogilvy & Mather in New York. In January 1995, he became *BWD*'s editor.

Pursuing birds, Bill has trekked to the farthest reaches of North America, and to many of the great birding hotspots around the world, including sites in Europe, the Middle East, and Central America. But some of his favorite bird watching is done near home on the old 80-acre farm he shares with his wife and daughter.

In his spare time, when he is not playing with daughter, Phoebe, or watching birds, Bill likes to play guitar with his (locally) popular band, The Swinging Orangutangs, which includes his wife, Julie, and his brother, Andy.

How *Bird Watcher's Digest* Got Started

Bird Watcher's Digest was started in 1978 by Bill's parents, Bill and Elsa Thompson, in their living room in Marietta, Ohio. At the time, there was no popular magazine devoted to birds and bird watchers. The three Thompson kids, Bill III, Andy, and Laura, voted (with a little parental persuasion) to donate their savings (read: college money) to help the folks get the magazine started. Of course, the folks also kicked in every cent of their spare change. All the kids helped in those early years, licking stamps, opening the mail, riding the corporate moped to the bank with the meager daily deposit.

Twenty years later, the magazine is thriving with a circulation near 100,000, the college loans are (nearly) repaid, and bird watching is booming in popularity. Most remarkably, almost all the family members still speak to one another. And they barely wince when people tell them they're really "for the birds."

Publisher's Acknowledgments

We're proud of this book; please send us your comments about it by using the IDG Books World-wide Registration Card at the back of the book or by e-mailing us at feedback/dummies@idgbooks.com. Some of the people who helped bring this book to market include the following:

Acquisitions, Development, and Editorial

Project Editor: Kathleen M. Cox

Acquisitions Editor: Kathleen W. Welton

Copy Editor: Constance Carlisle

Technical Editor: C. Scott Weidensaul

Editorial Manager: Mary C. Corder

Editorial Assistant: Donna Love

Production

Project Coordinator: Sherry Gomoll

Layout and Graphics: Steve Arany, Pamela Emanoil, Maridee Ennis, Elizabeth Cárdenas-Nelson, Mark C. Owens

Special Art: Julie Zickefoose, Sally Onopa, and named Photographers

Proofreaders: Laura L. Bowman, Kelli Botta, Michelle Croninger, Nancy Price, Rebecca Senninger, Robert Springer

Indexer: Sherry Massey

Special Help

Nickole Harris, Ann Miller

General and Administrative

IDG Books Worldwide, Inc.: John Kilcullen, CEO; Steven Berkowitz, President and Publisher

IDG Books Technology Publishing: Brenda McLaughlin, Senior Vice President and Group Publisher

Dummies Technology Press and Dummies Editorial: Diane Graves Steele, Vice President and Associate Publisher; Kristin A. Cocks, Editorial Director; Mary Bednarek, Acquisitions and Product Development Director

Dummies Trade Press: Kathleen A. Welton, Vice President and Publisher

IDG Books Production for Dummies Press: Beth Jenkins, Production Director; Cindy L. Phipps, Manager of Project Coordination, Production Proofreading, and Indexing; Kathie S. Schutte, Supervisor of Page Layout; Shelley Lea, Supervisor of Graphics and Design; Debbie J. Gates, Production Systems Specialist; Robert Springer, Supervisor of Proofreading; Debbie Stailey, Special Projects Coordinator; Tony Augsburger, Supervisor of Reprints and Bluelines; Leslie Popplewell, Media Archive Coordinator

Dummies Packaging and Book Design: Patti Crane, Packaging Specialist; Lance Kayser, Packaging Assistant; Kavish + Kavish, Cover Design

♦

The publisher would like to give special thanks to Patrick J. McGovern, without whom this book would not have been possible.

♦

Contents at a Glance

Table of Contents

Foreword

*W*hile walking behind my farm in Rappahannock County, Virginia, on a recent late-spring morning, I saw a Kentucky warbler step warily from the forest undergrowth a few feet ahead of me. For an instant I saw the bird's characteristic black sideburns and yellow spectacles. Then, as if to keep me guessing his secrets, he flitted away as rapidly as he appeared.

The sighting delighted me for two reasons. I had seen this species for the first time just four months earlier, at a Rio Bravo Conservation and Management Area in northern Belize, where the Nature Conservancy is helping its local partner protect the rain forest habitat of some 392 bird species. I knew that this little bird, like so many others, had flown thousands of miles to find haven in my backyard, where it would hopefully find a mate and raise its young successfully.

Yet equally exciting to me was the fact that I had identified the bird as a Kentucky warbler. There was a time when I could not have done so.

Like most Americans, I enjoy watching birds. As the heralds of spring, the singers of sunrise, and the tireless travelers of our hemisphere, birds give us insight into the wonder of the natural world.

At the Conservancy, we are doing everything we can to protect the wild places birds need to survive. Our Wings of the Americas program, sponsored by Canon U.S.A., employs a staff of ornithologists and conservation professionals who are using the best available science to conserve birds and their habitats throughout the Americas.

Now, all of us can become more knowledgeable about these wonderful creatures, thanks to Bill Thompson and the experts at *Bird Watcher's Digest*. *Bird Watching For Dummies* will help you find the best birding spots, tell the difference between a nuthatch and a gnatcatcher, and choose the right binoculars, field guides, and other gear.

Most important, *Bird Watching For Dummies* reminds us that birds should be enjoyed by experts and amateurs alike. You don't have to know a bird's name to appreciate it — but next time you see a Kentucky warbler or another song bird along your woodland walk, wouldn't it be nice to congratulate him on the many miles he's covered?

John C. Sawhill
President & Chief Executive Officer
The Nature Conservancy

Introduction

● ●

*W*elcome to *Bird Watching For Dummies*. One of the many people who read an early draft of this book told me, "Reading this is just what it's like to go on a bird walk with you, Bill." That comment really pleased me because that's what I was after. You can write all you want about the subject of bird watching, but the very best thing to do, if you want to become a bird enthusiast, is to get outside and watch some birds. This book is designed to get you started in the right direction, and give you a sense of the fascination and joy that birds can bring to your life.

About This Book

I want this book to appeal to bird watchers, or birders, at every level of interest and expertise. But the majority of the information that I include is aimed at encouraging the beginner to take up the hobby of bird watching, and encouraging the intermediate bird watcher to explore the fringes of advanced birding. Advanced birders can find something of value in here, too, even if it's only that the text produces an occasional smile of recognition.

Think of this book as a reference. As such, it will serve you for the rest of your bird-watching days. You can come back to it time after time and search its pages for answers to your most nagging questions and for advice on getting better as a birder.

A few things about this book make it different from other books on bird watching or birding.

- First, it's both fun to read and funny to read. I hope I give you a few laughs along the way.
- Second, it's written from my personal perspective (with some help from a few friends who also lent their perspectives) so you benefit from my own real-life experiences and mistakes, rather than from a generic editorial "we" voice.
- Third, this book is designed so that each chapter can stand alone content-wise, sort of like a giant buffet table of food. You can skip whole chapters that don't interest you at present, and read the juicy bits that seem appetizing. You can always come back later to sample the parts you skipped (but please remember to get a clean plate each time).

As you read through this book, you will notice the names of lots of different birds. We have chosen not to capitalize these names, except when they include a proper noun or name, such as Henslow's sparrow, as opposed to song sparrow. Although some bird folks claim that all bird names should be capitalized, I believe (and the rules of proper English language usage concur) that to "cap" all the first letters of every bird name is not only improper, it's overkill. And too much capitalization can result in a bumpy ride for your eyeballs as you read through a sentence chock-full of bird names. I've tried to make it clear when I'm writing about the species yellow warbler, and a warbler that's colored yellow. I hope I've succeeded.

I don't mention brand names of products very often in this book, except in the Appendix. The market for bird watching products is huge, constantly growing and ever-changing. It would be folly (not to mention impossible) to try to do justice to all the companies, products, and people who are out there trying to make a living in the bird-watching world. Nuff said!

Why You Need This Book

When I was a young lad and just starting out as a bird watcher, I was fortunate to be able to follow in my mom's footsteps. I got to tag along with her bird club on outings and field trips and, in doing so, I learned a lot about how to watch birds. If you don't know the basics of bird watching, you've come to the right place. I love teaching people about birds. One of my favorite things is to lead beginners on a bird walk.

Before I really found out how to be a bird watcher, I made all the rookie mistakes — not knowing how to focus binoculars properly, not knowing how to find the bird in the binoculars, not knowing where to find birds! Sometimes I was lucky if I could even find my binoculars! And I repeatedly made the classic beginner mistake of not taking my binoculars when my family went on a trip to another part of the continent. (How could I have thought that I wouldn't see many birds in Florida in winter!) If I'd only had a book like this. . . .

When you first venture out in search of birds to watch, you may have a frustrating experience. You may even have some of the beginner's misfortune I described. Don't worry! Bird watching or birding (I consider the terms interchangeable) is just like any other activity. The more you practice, the better you get. What's great about bird watching is that the practicing part is incredibly fun. The most important thing you can do to become a really good bird watcher (other than buy this book) is to relax and enjoy the birds you see. Without even trying to absorb information, you're gaining knowledge about the birds you watch simply by watching. How painless can it get?

When you positively identify your first bird species, all by yourself, and without lots of hints from a fellow birder, you realize the thrill of victory. It's that kind of experience that has kept me bird watching for all these years.

How to Use This Book

This book is designed to be read in pieces and parts (though if you decide to read it from cover to cover, that's fine too, and I'll be flattered). If you're a total beginner, read the Tweet Sheet (yellow card), and the initial three chapters at first. If you're already a bird watcher, you may wish to read the chapters on advanced bird identification, providing housing for birds, or taking a field trip or birding tour.

I've included all kinds of information to help you become a better bird watcher, no matter where you are now, skillwise. If you become more interested in watching birds after reading this book, I've done my job.

How This Book Is Organized

This book is organized to help you ease into bird watching, and then to help you follow your specific interests as you become more acquainted with the world of birds. The beginning bird watcher has a lot of questions, but may feel sheepish about asking these questions of another, more experienced bird watcher. That feeling of shyness is perfectly normal, and happens to almost everyone who takes up a new hobby or avocation. I can remember feeling that way for years until I felt confident enough to ask others questions. This book removes a lot of that awkwardness for you. I'm not promising that you won't ever have to ask a bird question again, but I am sure that lots of the questions you have now will be answered by the time you read a few chapters. In the meantime, while I'm heading off to look at some birds, you can take a look at how the parts of this book are broken out.

Part I: Watching Birds: A Natural Habit

To get started in bird watching, you need to know exactly what bird watching is. Next, you need a few tools that help you see and identify the birds, namely a field guide and some binoculars. Knowing how to use these tools is pretty essential, but don't worry, it's easy to do. In this part, I show you all this stuff and more, including chapters on why birds do what they do (bird behavior and how to interpret it), and why birds make the sounds they do (bird songs, and how to recognize birds by their songs). I wish I had had such a good start when I was a young whippersnapper, just discovering birds!

Part II: Backyard Bird Watching

There's no place like home to get your maximum bird watching enjoyment when you're a beginner. But even advanced bird folks can get something out of this part because it covers every aspect of watching, attracting, and providing for birds in your immediate surroundings. Even if you live in a city apartment, you can easily do a number of things to welcome birds into your midst. I show you how to make a bird-friendly yard, how to become an expert bird feeder, how to offer housing for birds, how to make a garden or landscape for birds and wildlife, and how to solve the problems you may encounter. I even include a chapter about specific birds that people love to watch and care for in their backyards and beyond.

Part III: Bird Sighting 101: Using Your Tools

In this part, you get the specifics on how to use your bird watching tools. You also get insider tips on improving your birding skills and on keeping records and lists of the birds that you see. For the beginner wishing to move to the intermediate level, this part is a big help. After reading this, you'll be able to watch birds anywhere in the world (and look like a pro while you're doing it).

Part IV: Beyond the Backyard

Birds are everywhere — but most of them hang out far from your backyard. Eventually, if the bird-watching bug bites hard, you want to go where the birds are — wherever they are. This part tells you how to take a field trip, where to go, and how to equip yourself. It also lists some festivals and other events that bring birders together across the continent. Guidelines for taking a birding tour are also given. And I close with some birding activities done through bird clubs and other organizations to help scientists keep track of the world's bird populations, along with other projects you can get involved in, such as founding bird clubs, teaching kids about birds, and wildlife rehabilitation.

Part V: Once You're Hooked

Lots of people have told me over the years that once they got into bird watching, they quickly became addicted to it. Believe me, many other addictions are far worse than this feather-chasing one. You, too, may find yourself devoting all your waking hours (and many of your sleeping ones) to thoughts about birds. This part offers several outlets for the extremely interested bird watcher, including improving your optics, demystifying advanced bird identification, sketching birds like an artist, and finding birds online. I even offer advice on extending your passion to other flying creatures, such as butterflies and bats.

Part VI: The Part of Tens

In this part I get to make some lists of stuff that are both fun and informative.

Appendix

I really like this part of the book, but then again, I'm the only one I know that still has his own appendix (and tonsils, too). The lists of books, companies, and sources of additional information are pretty complete and help to get you started into the big, bold world of birds that exists outside the pages of this book. Happy trails!

Icons Used in This Book

I guide you along on this birding trip with a series of icons. Think of them as roadside signs along the bird watching highway. They alert you to upcoming tips, valuable advice, pitfalls, and even a few of my own bird watching tales.

Marks things you can do to improve your birding and bird ID skills.

Identifies ways to make your backyard a paradise for birds.

Flags bird-watching terminology so you can chatter along.

Helps you mind your manners with birds and bird watchers when out in the field.

Points out tips to improve your bird watching skills wherever you are.

Highlights real stories about bird watching life.

Watch out, but don't keep your head in the sand — pay attention or your birds may have flown.

Reminds you of important information to keep in mind.

Denotes ecologically sound practices that benefit birds, people, and other wildlife.

Part I
Watching Birds:
A Natural Habit

The 5th Wave By Rich Tennant

"The house itself isn't that great, but the tree gets Evening Grosbeaks, Cedar Waxwings and 16 different species of warblers."

In this part . . .

People have always enjoyed watching birds. This part tells you why, and what you need to get started on your own bird watching hobby — from some basic equipment to the clues you get from the birds themselves as to their identities. You get information on features of birds that distinguish them from each other, how birds behave and why, and bird sounds and songs so you can hear the difference.

Chapter 1

Birds and the People Who Love Them

Do you ever look up, see a bird in flight, and find yourself wondering what kind of bird it is? You stare at it — noting its color, its shape, the spread of its wings. You watch it flit from branch to branch and fly away. And you wonder. Maybe you describe the bird to a family member or friend who may know what it is. Or you go to the library for a book about birds in the area to look up its picture. Or you wait, hoping to see it again just to appreciate the bird's beauty and song. That's bird watching. And you're already a bird watcher. Isn't that easy?

Unk! Ragnar See Bird!

Bird watching is an activity that comes naturally to us humans. Our ancestors watched birds — you can find their sightings painted on cave walls. Birds helped determine the seasons and predict the weather. And they provided meat for the evening feeding frenzy.

Today, bird watching (or birding) is a hobby enjoyed by millions and millions of (somewhat more advanced) people. Why? Because birds are fun to look at, birds are beautiful, many birds sing beautiful songs, and bird behavior is fascinating. Besides, today when folks want meat for their evening feeding frenzies, they can shop at supermarkets and leave the birds alone.

Yet birds still foretell the changing seasons by their northward and southward migrations. And birds sometimes have feeding frenzies of their own just before or after a blast of bad weather. So if you want to throw out your calendar and the local meteorologist, go right ahead. You won't need either in your cave — and you'll still have the birds.

Wings and Feathers and Flight, Oh My!

A number of scientists now believe that birds may be living examples of the dinosaurs that once roamed the earth. One of the earliest-known birds is *Archaeopteryx,* discovered from fossilized remains found in Bavaria in 1851 (see Figure 1-1).

Figure 1-1: Archae-opteryx — a pre-historic bird in flight.

Archaeopteryx existed about 140 million years ago and had skeletal characteristics identical to those of small dinosaurs that lived during that same time. This creature also had a toothed jaw and feathers that allowed Archaeopteryx to glide from place to place (although its main mode of transport was likely running).

Because of these features, some scientists believe that Archaeopteryx is one link between dinosaurs and what today we consider birds. Even though this creature didn't have the specialized bones and flight muscles that true birds have, Archaeopteryx is considered by many to be one branch of the evolutionary tree from which all birds may have descended. The link between Archaeopteryx and birds is a greatly debated subject that gets evolutionary scientists very worked up. I'll leave this one to the folks in the white lab coats. But one thing Archaeopteryx and birds have in common that seems to give them kinship is feathers. Because, at its most basic, a bird is a creature that has feathers (see Figure 1-2) — the only type of creature that has feathers.

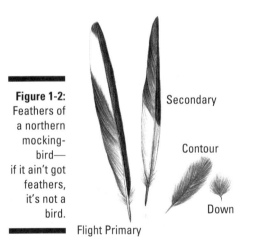

Figure 1-2:
Feathers of a northern mocking-bird— if it ain't got feathers, it's not a bird.

Secondary

Contour

Down

Flight Primary

These feathers — along with lightweight, air-filled bones acquired through evolution — allow most birds to fly. Feathers are really highly evolved scales, like those found on reptiles such as snakes and lizards. (You can see the remnants of their reptilian ancestry on most birds' scaly legs and feet.) Besides promoting flight, feathers (also called plumage) regulate birds' temperature and provide physical protection while giving birds their shape and color.

Here's a bonus obscure fact for you: A small songbird has more than 1,000 feathers on its body. A large swan, plucked by some patient soul, was found to have more than 25,000 feathers. Figure 1-3 shows a mute swan ruffling some of its 25,000 feathers.

Figure 1-3: Feathers help keep birds, such as this mute swan, comfortable, mobile, and beautiful.

Families and species

Without getting too technical, you need to understand two terms that bird watchers use a lot when referring to birds: *family* and *species*. Although I'm sure my ornithology professor will cringe (he always did anyway, which is probably why I got a C!), here are Dummies-approved definitions for the two terms:

- ✔ A *species* of birds is defined as a group of individuals that have similar appearance, similar behavior, similar vocalizations, and that interbreed freely to produce fertile (able to breed successfully) young. When you identify a bird, you determine what species it is.

- ✔ A *family* of birds is made up of species that are very similar, but don't interbreed. You can find a more scientific definition of a bird family, but most bird watchers use this term to mean a group of birds that look, sound, and act in a similar way. For example, there are lots of different sparrow *species,* most of which belong to the sparrow *family.*

Remember both terms handily because you often hear them used when bird watchers try to identify a bird. If you see a small bird zipping through your flower garden, you may know to what family it belongs (hummingbird). Later, when you get a good look at the bird, you can identify its species (ruby-throated hummingbird).

Each species of bird has two types of names: a common name and a Latin name.

- ✔ The common name of a bird is the one that you're most likely to know. Common names, such as American robin, are the currency of bird watching.

- ✔ The Latin or scientific name, *Turdus migratorius* in the case of the American robin, is made up of two parts: the genus (*Turdus*) and the species (*migratorius*). Genus and species are two parts of the scientific classification system used to name all living creatures. Think of them as you would the first and last names of a person. Latin names are used to clarify the classification of birds and to help bird watchers and ornithologists (bird scientists) avoid confusion over regional and international differences in bird names. Just because they're Latin, don't let them scare you off. You won't be getting a pop quiz! And most bird watchers you encounter won't be fluent in the Latin names of birds, so you needn't be, either.

Bird Watching: From Guns to Binoculars

People's fascination with birds naturally made them want to get a closer look. Until late in the last century (that's the 1800s for those of you reading this book in 2025), the only accepted method of identifying a bird was to have it in your hand. And given the fact that very few birds hopped happily onto the palm, the quickest way to get a bird in the hand was to kill it and hold it there. From rocks to spears, and later, arrows, slingshots, and shotguns, once you had the bird in your hand, getting a good look at it was easy (but not very easy on the bird!).

Shotgun bird identification fell into deserved disfavor in 1934 when Roger Tory Peterson, generally considered the father of modern bird watching, published the first modern field guide. Combining black-and-white illustrations of all the birds found in the eastern half of North America with descriptive text for each species, Roger Tory Peterson's easy-to-use system of identifying birds was based upon a concept known as a *field mark* — a distinctive characteristic or visual clue that's a key to identifying

BIRDY WORDS

Taxonomy: From dinosaurs to chickadees

The method used to organize birds — that is, to decide which birds are related, which are closely related, and which are not closely related — is called taxonomy. Taxonomy has nothing to do with the Internal Revenue Service (though it can be a taxing exercise); rather, taxonomy is the method by which birds are placed in the evolutionary tree.

As birds evolved, they did so in many ways, much as a bush grows many branches from the ground, with each branch growing more branches, and so on. The birds that most closely resemble their ancient ancestors are considered the oldest of our birds and are found in the front of bird-watchers' field guides. Those birds that kept evolving (through many more branches, then smaller branches, then twigs) are considered the newest, most recently evolved birds, and they're found near the back of field guides. All perching birds, for example, are considered fairly far advanced, and are found in the back of field guides. The earliest bird taxonomists used Latin to help with their classifications, and their Latin names remain the foundation of bird classification today. See Chapter 13 for more about taxonomy.

The influence of shotgun ornithology

Many bird names today still reflect the influence that shotgun ornithology held in its time. A prime example is the red-bellied woodpecker, one of North America's most common woodland birds. You'd expect a bird by that name to have a red belly. But if you go out looking for a red belly on a wild, free-flying, red-bellied woodpecker, you'll be disappointed.

Because the first bird enthusiast to catalog this species likely shot one and then examined it in the hand, we have a name that doesn't fit the bird. Although the lower belly feathers on most adult red-bellied woodpeckers are, in fact, tipped in red, these feathers are extremely hard to see when the bird's belly is pressed against some tree trunk, in typical woodpecker fashion. Ol' Mr. Trigger Happy should have named this bird the red-naped woodpecker, because that's where the red is most visible!

a bird. Birds thus became identifiable by their most obvious feature (the red crest of a cardinal, the long pointed tail of the pintail duck) with the help of magnifying optics.

No longer are birds identified over the sights of a shotgun — now, the magnified view of the bird as seen through binoculars is all that's needed. Unlike the low-powered opera glasses of 60 years ago, binoculars today are so advanced that you can see the eyelashes on an egret (unless you know already, you'll have to guess whether or not egrets have eyelashes). Once separated from the shotgun, the popularity of bird watching soared, and the birds breathed a collective sigh of relief.

The number-one spectator sport

Today, an estimated 80 million people of all ages and physical abilities point their binoculars toward feathered creatures. Bird watching is second only to gardening as a favorite leisure time activity among North Americans. What's more, bird watching is considered the number-one spectator sport in North America!

Most of these 80 million people are watching the birds that come to their backyard feeders, but an increasing number of bird enthusiasts are venturing beyond their backyards to find more and different birds. And non-bird watchers are noticing. The average active bird watcher is estimated to spend more than $1,000 annually in pursuit of this hobby. I'm no good at math, but $1,000 x 80 million bird watchers is a lot of moolah. We bird watchers pack a significant economic wallop.

Bird watchers of a feather . . .

Bird watchers come in many types, from casual backyard looker to rabid, globe-trotting birder, and everything in between. I'm guessing that you're somewhere in between. Perhaps you already feed birds, and maybe you already own a pair of binoculars, but you don't yet consider yourself a bird watcher. Well, you've come to the right book.

Because you're reading this hypnotic prose of mine, you're already indicating an interest in the subject matter. What's great about bird watching is that you can enjoy it almost anywhere, at any time, and at any level of involvement — always at your own pace.

Most folks who get into bird watching start by seeing birds in their backyard. Or perhaps somebody tugged their arms until they took hold of the binoculars being offered and looked at — oh my gosh! — a beautiful bird! What is it? Next comes getting a bird book, borrowing a pair of binoculars, and going out on their own to see birds. Soon they find a nearby bird club, join, and take some local bird trips. Maybe later they decide to go on a field trip to Florida or Texas with the club. At each point, more birds are seen and more friends made. Bird watchers can evolve much as birds have evolved.

Long gone are the days when the stereotypical bird watcher was a little old lady in tennis shoes or an absent-minded professor in a pith helmet (though these folks still exist). In those happily forgotten times, bird watchers were often the object of ridicule. The nerdy spinster character portrayed in *The Beverly Hillbillies* probably set bird watching back several decades as a socially acceptable activity.

If you find yourself wondering what your neighbors, coworkers, or friends will think, consider this: When you show an interest in birds, chances are, more than one of those folks will say, "I never knew you were a bird watcher! I love watching birds!"

Why watch birds?

Cheep and easy fun. That's how I like to describe bird watching. Once you've got some optics (binoculars) and a field guide to the birds, you're ready to go. Unless you want to get into a private preserve, a state park or national wildlife refuge that has an entrance fee, or go on a guided tour, you've spent all you need to spend to be a bird watcher. (Okay, you do still have to eat, and wear clothes, and of course, pay your mortgage, but you'd be paying for those things anyway.) Perhaps only plant watching is cheaper — you don't need binoculars to identify plants.

BIRD TALES

Gratuitous personal anecdote

I remember my high school basketball coach asking me once why I was late for practice. I'd been taking part in the annual Christmas Bird Count, and I explained this to him. "THE CHRISTMAS BIRD COUNT!??? What the heck is that? Some kinda activity for wimps? Give me 20 sit-ups, Thompson!" Well, Coach, there are now more bird watchers than basketball players in North America, so you should mind your manners. Better yet, go out and identify 20 bird songs, and report back to me, pronto! Revenge is sweet, if not endearing.

Bird Watcher or Birder?

With bird watching's rise in popularity, a minor controversy has simmered about the proper noun or verb used to describe it: Are you birding or bird watching when you use binoculars to look at an avian creature? Do you tell your friend: "I'm a bird watcher" or "I'm a birder"?

The real answer lies within your soul, or at least it's a matter of personal preference. I consider myself a bird watcher because even though I enjoy the occasional Big Day or rarity chase (I explain these later), I love to sit and watch birds do what they do.

When my family started our bird magazine, we chose the name *Bird Watcher's Digest,* though we use the two terms interchangeably in our editorial material, because that's what we are: watchers of birds.

BIRDY WORDS

For those who prefer exact definitions, most bird enthusiasts make these generic distinctions:

- ✔ A *bird watcher* is someone who prefers to watch and enjoy birds. This person may be primarily interested in, but not at all limited to, his or her backyard for involvement with birds. Bird watcher is the preferred term in Great Britain, which has, per capita, the most bird watchers of anyplace on Earth.

- ✔ A *birder* is perhaps more avid and may be less interested in spending time observing birds than in seeing or listing as many as he or she can in a given outing, day, or year.

I know many longtime bird enthusiasts who insist on being called bird watchers. And I know just as many folks who cringe at the very thought of being pasted with the same label.

A third category for a person who studies birds is *ornithologist*. Ornithology is the scientific study of birds, and an ornithologist is a practitioner of ornithology. Much of the knowledge we have about birds has come from the work of ornithologists. But bird watchers make contributions to this science, too. See Chapter 21 for some examples.

But why get hung up on terminology? Use whichever term you prefer, or use all three, or come up with a new term! Here's a better idea: Go watch some birds!

Meeting your spark bird

For every bird watcher and birder, there's one bird that provided the catalyst, set the hook, was a spark (choose your metaphor) to begin that person's interest in birds.

For me, the spark bird was relatively nondescript, the American coot. Here's how it happened: I was sprung from school on a spring Friday and was allowed to accompany the local ladies' bird-watching club, of which my mom was a member. Because I wasn't interested in the birds they sought, I ran down the dirt road in the area where we were birding to see how many rocks I could throw off the bridge into Rainbow Creek. Just as I raised the first projectile into the air, I noticed something moving below. It was some kind of bird — perhaps a duck. I knew the gals up the road had yet to see a duck that day, so I ran to tell them of the sighting. They were incredibly thrilled! Coots in spring were not that common then in southeastern Ohio. I was surprised and a little embarrassed by the profuse shower of praise from the women. Soon they had me drumming up all sorts of birds. I was proud to point out birds to them. The following month, when I got a Friday off for another bird watching trip, I didn't throw a single rock. I was hooked on birds.

A spark bird for you may be the scarlet tanager that your high school science teacher pointed out, or the red-tailed hawk shown to you by a scout leader. Better yet, it may be the singing male warbler you found yourself. Because you're reading this book, you may have found your spark bird already. If not, I envy you because the spark bird is a wonderful experience, and the start of a great adventure.

What makes a good bird watcher?

Two ingredients that a successful bird watcher has are a natural curiosity about the world and a healthy dose of enthusiasm. Both of these are invaluable. Why?

The natural curiosity leads you to do things you'd never do otherwise, such as get up at dawn on a beautiful May morning to hear the birds start singing. And the healthy dose of enthusiasm keeps you going on all those days when you've got more thumbs than there are birds to see. In that case, you make the most of the birds you *can* see.

Both of these admirable traits are great ones to pass along to friends who are beginners. It's the natural legacy and responsibility of all birders to pass the torch to those who come later. Return the favor to a beginner, just as you were guided by someone else.

Where the Birds Are

Birds are found almost everywhere. You'll read this statement repeatedly in this book. And here's another gem that bears repeating: Birds have wings and they tend to use them.

What these statements mean is that anywhere you're likely to be (outdoors, of course) you encounter birds. Going to the Arctic Circle on New Year's Day? Keep an eye out for snowy owls and snow buntings. Going to Antarctica for the 4th of July? You'll be seeing penguins and other seabirds. Better have your binocs handy. Stepping out your backdoor to get some fresh air? No matter where you live, birds will be there, too.

The point is that you can be watching birds anytime and anywhere. Once you get the hang of it, you'll be doing exactly that.

Chapter 2

Tools that Take You Up Close and Personal

. . . .

In This Chapter

▶ Binoc basics

▶ Your guide to the field

▶ What to wear

▶ What to carry along

. . . .

As a bird watcher, you need very little in the way of gear or stuff in order to enjoy bird watching. In fact, I recommend only two primary tools that are essential to getting the most out of this sport: *binoculars* and a *field guide* to the birds.

The only other thing that you need is a place to watch birds, and that can be almost anyplace. Birds are among the planet's most common and widespread creatures (beetles are number one). Walk out your front door, drive to work, and look out the window — you've probably had bird accompaniments the whole trip. It's hard to be someplace where you're not a step or two away from a perky or pesky bird. You see birds almost everywhere.

The Optics Option

Okay. If you see birds everywhere, why do you need binoculars or other optical help?

Well, let me clarify one thing about optics: You *don't* need to have binoculars and other optics to watch birds. If you're satisfied and utterly fulfilled by looking at a bird in a tree 50 yards away and saying to yourself, "Hey, there's a bird!" you don't need optics.

But if you're like most members of our species (upright-walking, thumb-using, living indoors . . .), you'll want to *identify* that bird. Is it a sparrow or a finch? Or just a blurry-yellow-thingie-with-wings? How will you know if you see it again?

Binoculars let you get a closer look. And a closer look lets you see clues to the bird's identity. With these clues (and a field guide!), you can solve the mystery of just about any bird's identity.

I don't want to show disrespect to the millions of people who are perfectly happy to see birds only at their backyard feeders. That's where most of us start out with birds. And the birds you invite for dinner can put on quite a show.

But let's face it, even birds that appear at your feeders have names, and you won't know many of them without a good look at the bird and a corresponding look at a good field guide. And beyond your backyard is a whole world of amazing birds just waiting to introduce themselves when you get them in your sights. I guarantee that if you decide to become a bird watcher, you'll be much happier looking at birds through binoculars.

Bird watchers use many different terms for their binoculars. Two of the most common are *binocs* and *bins*. Generically, binoculars and the telescopes (see Chapter 24) used for birding are called *optics,* which is easier to say than optical equipment. I also have heard bird watchers use some unprintable names for their binoculars, often after they missed seeing a bird because their binocs were fogged or of poor quality.

Beg, borrow, or buy some binocs

If you're just starting out and you're unsure about investing in some optical equipment (after all, you may decide you don't *like* this bird stuff despite its obvious appeal), I suggest you beg or borrow a pair of binoculars (stealing is not really an option) from a friend, relative, scout leader, school, or local bird club. I started out with a pair of old Army binocs that my great aunt had in her attic (no, she wasn't in the Army). These old binocs were awful, but they gave me a better-than-naked-eye view of birds. Once my folks saw my interest in birds, we got a family pair of binocs. These weren't much better, but at least they didn't have 100-year-old mayonnaise on the lenses.

Somebody you know has some binoculars lying around that you can borrow. (Check with that neighbor who has nosebleed seats at the ball game.) Ask to use the binoculars for just a few hours. If you can borrow them for a few days or a weekend, that's better yet. You'll need a bit of time to get used to them. Take the binocs outside, weather permitting, and practice by looking at a distant stationary object. (If you do unearth some old optics, be sure to clean the lenses before using them. See Chapter 12 for more details on how to use and care for your binoculars.)

When buying binoculars, you have two rules to live by:

1. Get the best you can afford.

Quality and cost are very connected in the world of bird watching optics: The more you pay, the better quality you get. All buying decisions should be so easy.

2. Make sure the binoculars you get are very comfortable to use.

They should feel good in your hands, be easy to raise and lower, easy to focus, and they should not leave you with a dizzy feeling or a headache after you lower them from your eyes (this is eye strain caused by out-of-focus or poorly aligned binoculars).

An inexpensive pair of beginner's binoculars can cost from $35 to $100. If you buy in the upper range (near $100), chances are good that you'll have a decent optical start to your bird watching. But I guarantee that if you buy a pair of $35 binoculars (or cheaper ones), one of two things will happen:

- ✔ You'll give up bird watching because you can't see the birds well enough (probably due to the budget optics).
- ✔ You'll love bird watching so much that you'll want to get a better pair of binoculars at the first opportunity. This is what happened to me.

The next level of quality in binoculars is the $100 to $250 range. You can get very nice binoculars in this range, especially at the upper end. If you plan to buy binoculars, check out Chapter 12 where I cover important issues that you need to consider.

Using binoculars

Using binoculars to look at birds is pretty easy once you get the hang of it. The hardest part is finding the bird or other object once you put the lenses up to your eyes.

Remember this: *Keep your eyes on the bird and bring the binoculars up to your eyes.* If you keep your eyes locked on your targeted bird, finding the bird with your binoculars becomes a simple matter of raising the bins to the level of your eyes.

Calibrating your binoculars to your eyes is something you should do every once in a while, so that the binoculars focus properly when that rare bird flits by. Here, in a nutshell, is how you do it:

1. Adjust the two barrels so that the eyepieces are the right distance apart for your eyes.

You should see a single image when using both eyes.

2. **Turn the center focusing knob all the way to the right (clockwise).**

3. **Choose a stationary object in the middle distance on which to focus.**

4. **Close your left eye and, using the right eyepiece, turn the eyepiece until the object is in focus for your right eye.**

   Note: Some binoculars have a second focusing knob or wheel (on my bins it's at center front) that controls the right side focus, rather than using the right eyepiece.

5. **Open your left eye and turn the center focus knob until the object is in focus for both eyes.**

   This may require you to refocus slightly, using the right eyepiece. When you get the focus just right, the image you see "feels" right to you. It almost looks like a three-dimensional image. And your eyes won't be straining to resolve the image, they'll feel relaxed.

6. **Look at the symbols or numbers on the right eyepiece or secondary focus knob; note where your focus point is and remember it.**

   Next time you pick up your binocs (especially after someone else has used them), you can automatically adjust the focus setting to this position.

If your bins are properly calibrated, now all you have to do when you spot a bird is turn the large focusing wheel until you get a sharp image. For more complete information on using binoculars, see Chapter 12.

Take my advice: *Don't try using binoculars without a neckstrap.* If the binocs you have are outfitted with a neckstrap, by all means use it! If not, buy a good neckstrap (see Chapter 12 and Chapter 22 for recommendations). But no matter how old or inexpensive your binoculars are, *never carry your binoculars by the strap.* Hang them around your neck, the way nature intended. Here's why:

In college, I was leading a bird walk for a biology class. I owned three pairs of binoculars at the time, two of which were pretty crummy, and my regular pair, which I was using. The other two I had loaned out to a couple of students to use during the walk. We were having a great spring morning of bird watching, with lots of colorful birds easily seen by all. I had asked one of the students who was using one pair of my "loaner" binocs to quit swinging them by the strap and put the strap around his neck. As we approached a high bluff overlooking a small river, I spotted a belted kingfisher. As we were *oohhing* and *ahhing* over the bird, I heard "*Oh, NO!!*" and caught a glimpse of those same loaner binocs as they plummeted to their watery destiny in the river below. When the fumble-handed scholar climbed back up the bluff, huffing and puffing with the rescued optics, I put them to my eyes — out of habit, I suppose. All I could see were tiny fish swimming in cloudy water. Inside the binoculars.

It's valuable lessons like this one that I remember most clearly from my college days. And I always keep my binoculars around my neck using the neckstrap.

Your Field Guide

The second piece of very useful equipment for bird watching is a field guide to the birds. If you're a beginning bird watcher, the field guide can be a big help as you learn to identify birds.

A field guide is like a family album of birds, but even better. It contains color images of birds, maps showing where the birds can be found during certain seasons of the year, and descriptive text that covers information about the bird that can't be conveyed by either images or maps.

Remember those games you played as a kid where you matched the colors with the shapes? The purple square with the other purple square, and so on? Using a field guide to identify birds is just like that. You see a bird that you don't recognize; you make a mental note about its color, shape, and general appearance; and then you look for a matching bird image in the field guide.

Bird watching is the process of seeing and identifying birds. True, you don't have to identify each bird that you see. You don't even have to identify *any* of the birds that you see. But I think one of the most fun things about bird watching is solving the mini mystery of each bird's identity using the clues that I'm able to gather. Maybe I get a nice long look at a wading waterbird or a perched bird of prey, giving me plenty of time to gather identifying clues, or *field marks*. Or I may get a brief glimpse of a tiny warbler flitting through the tree tops. In both cases, I take the clues and begin my detective work using a field guide.

More information on using, choosing, and understanding a field guide is available in Chapter 13.

A matter of choice

Depending upon where in North America you live (or where on the planet you live), you have several field guides from which to choose:

- Some guides cover all the birds of North America (north of Mexico) in a single book; others divide the continent up into East and West.

  Bird watchers in the eastern third of the continent can get by with just an eastern guide, and those in the western third can get by with a western field guide. But those folks in the middle third of the continent need to have access to information about all the birds, east and west.

- Specialty field guides are also available. Some cover all the birds of a given region, such as the Pacific Northwest, the Great Basin, Texas, Arizona, or Florida. Other guides are focused not upon geography, but upon families of birds, such as guides to the hawks of the world, warblers of the world, or ducks, geese, and swans of the world.

- Major, non-specialty field guides also have much variation. Some use photographs to show you the birds, while others use artwork. Some guides feature the bird image, descriptive text, and species' range maps on the same page.

Some guides are better for beginners; others are preferred by more experienced bird watchers. For help in foraging through the forest of field guides, see Chapter 13.

Don't leave home without it

I know it seems like I'm trying to get you to spend all your money, but trust me: You *will* want more than just one field guide.

I like keeping one in the car, one at the office (okay, I have dozens at the office), and several at home. Even though I've been bird watching for 25 years, I still prefer to have a field guide with me whenever I go out to watch birds. I may not carry it with me, and I may not even need to open it the entire time that I'm in the field; but when I need the guide, I *really* need it. You just never know when something unfamiliar will turn up, or when the field guide will provide the clinching bit of information to solve the day's greatest bird identification mystery. You'll find, however, that as you get more familiar with bird identification, you'll need to refer to the field guide less and less.

Chapter 3

Identifying Birds
("If It Walks Like a Duck . . .")

. . . .

In This Chapter

▶ Parts is parts

▶ First impressions

▶ Field marks

▶ Bird behavior and other clues

▶ Field guide inspection

. . . .

ll birds have an identity, also known as a species name (see Chapter 1). Central to the joy of watching birds is identifying those birds you see.

Bird identification is a matter of sifting through various clues to solve the mystery of a bird's identity. It's a process of elimination in which you eliminate all the birds that aren't the one you're looking for. Most of these clues — behavior, size, shape, color, habitat, and important field marks — are visual. Sound plays a role with some birds — bird song, wing whistle, and so on — but your eyes do most of the clue sifting. (I've yet to see a guide to birding by nose. Perhaps it's just a matter of time.)

The first time you try to identify a strange bird, you may be overwhelmed and confused by the possibilities. What seems like a perfectly obvious small brown bird sitting on your feeder leads to pages and pages of small brown birds to choose from in your field guide. Don't despair. Identifying birds *is* possible, and you don't have to be a genius or devote your life to the study of small brown birds.

Remember, everyone starts out knowing nothing. Millions of bird watchers have mastered the trick of casually throwing a name (sometimes the right one!) on the birds they see. Most of these watchers are no smarter than you. They all started out just like you — appreciating the beauty and wonder of birds and wanting to know more about them. This chapter takes you through the basic steps of identifying a bird.

Before long, that small brown bird at your feeder becomes a female house finch. See, you're learning already!

The Parts of a Bird

Knowing the parts of a bird is very helpful when it comes to bird identification. If you see a strange bird that has some yellow on it, this information is of no use unless you know *where* the yellow is on the bird. If you're new to bird watching, some of the bird parts may also be new to you.

Think chicken

Figure 3-1 shows some of the most common parts used by bird watchers to identify birds. Some parts have more specialized names that are used in bird identification.

If you've ever cooked, eaten, or looked at a chicken, you already know almost all the parts of a bird (see Figure 3-2). You don't need to be a bird watcher to know where the legs, breast, head, bill, wings, tail, and feet are. By the time you eliminate all the words and parts you already know, you're

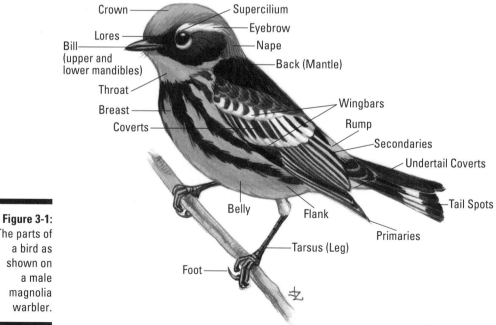

Figure 3-1:
The parts of a bird as shown on a male magnolia warbler.

left with about half a dozen words that are unique to bird watching. Yes, these words may be unfamiliar, but everyone can remember at least six words. For most people, it takes about 15 minutes, the time you take to have that morning cup of coffee.

Figure 3-2: A chicken and a robin: kin under the skin.

BIRDY WORDS

Non-chicken bird parts defined

Eyeline: A line of contrasting color (usually black or white) that goes through or above the eye.

Eyering: A ring of color (usually white) that encircles the eye. A broken eyering is one that isn't continuous.

Wingbar: Contrasting stripes of color on the bird's wing in the shoulder area.

Rump patch: A patch of color above where the tail connects to the body.

Breast: Okay, chickens do have these. The area from below the bird's throat to the midway point on its lower body. The area below the breast is the belly.

Lore: Zone between the bird's eye and bill.

Supercilium: The area above the bird's eye, also called the eyebrow.

Flank: The area between the bird's side and tail.

Nape: The back of the bird's neck.

Mantle: Between the bird's wings, below the nape.

Mandible: The bird's bill comprises two parts, the upper mandible and the lower mandible.

Primary feathers: The longest of the wing feathers; the ones that form the pointed edge when the wing is folded.

Secondary feathers: The feathers that form the trailing edge along the middle of a bird's wing. The secondaries are located on a wing, between the bird's body and its primary feathers.

Take a few minutes to study the parts of a bird. Once you know what a *flank* and a *supercilium* (the area above the bird's eye) and a *wingbar* are, and say the words aloud, the terms lose their mystique and their ability to cloud your mind. Not only does the descriptive text in the field guide now make sense, but you can now toss these words casually into bird watching conversations with others so that you sound like an expert, even if you still have trouble telling a bald eagle from an oven-ready roaster.

Pay attention to field marks

Field marks are unique characteristics that separate one bird from another. Almost all birds have a distinctive set of field marks that make it possible to tell one species from another. Finding out how to identify a bird is understanding what its field marks are. In very few cases, the field marks are so subtle, they can't be seen in the field. Consider those birds a challenge to be tackled at a later date. A good pair of binoculars is indispensable in picking up the broadest range of field marks. (See Chapter 12 for tips on your binoculars.)

As you progress, you find yourself automatically noticing the field marks of each bird you encounter, much as you would recognize a friend after a while. Here's something to get you started on the road to bird identification enlightenment.

Before you grab (or run out and buy) a field guide to the birds, take this simple test of your observation skills. This exercise calibrates your visual settings and helps you to look at each bird in an analytical way. You can do this exercise even if you don't have a field guide.

✔ Pick a common bird, one you can easily see in your area or yard, such as a cardinal, robin, or chickadee. Already knowing the species of the bird helps. For this example, I use the male cardinal (forgive me if you aren't familiar with this species). Every time I write, cardinal, you just mentally fill in the blank with your choice of a familiar bird, okay?

✔ Look at the familiar bird and make written notes about its appearance. Note anything you feel may be a clue to its identity.

What you write probably looks something like this:

A bright red bird with a red point of feathers on its head. A black face. Average size, not small, but not huge. Hopping around beneath the bird feeder eating sunflower seeds. Chips loudly every so often.

Here's what a field guide may say about the cardinal:

The only all-red bird found in North America. Adult males are bright crimson all over with a prominent red crest. Females are also crested, but are dull rosy brown, lacking the males' bright red coloring. Common in woodland edges, along roadsides, and in backyards in the eastern two-thirds of North America. Frequents bird feeders where it eats sunflower seed. Both sexes emit a loud ringing chip! . . .

See how similar the two descriptions are? As you get more experience, you remember more things about the birds you know, and automatically look for more things on the birds you don't. Such observation skills are what identifying birds is all about. (See the section "Field marks: Front to back," later in this chapter for more about using field marks to help identify birds.)

Look at the Bird, Not the Book

Sooner or later all bird watchers get a field guide. It's part of the trio of things that make up the activity called bird watching: **bird, binoculars, field guide,** oh, and **you,** I guess that's four things — a quartet!

Unless you're some kind of birding *savant*, born with encyclopedic bird knowledge, the steps you take to identify a bird go like this:

1. **See a bird.**

2. **Watch the bird for as long as you can, making notes on its appearance and behavior.**

   A good pair of binoculars helps immensely.

3. **Consult a field guide to confirm or find an identity for the bird.**

One of the pitfalls in using a field guide is the tendency of the beginning bird watcher to rely too heavily on the guide. Resist the temptation! Look at the bird for as long as you can. The picture of the bird in the book will always be there, but the actual living bird may only linger for a moment. Catch it while you can! The following sections help you remember what you see.

A mental checklist

Experienced bird watchers go through a mental checklist when looking at an unidentified bird: What is it doing? What size is it? What shape is it? What color? What are its main field marks? Does it have wingbars, an eyeline, a long tail?

You can do the same thing. Take a logical approach to looking at a bird. The first 10 or 20 times you have to make a conscious effort to remember all the things to look for, but after that, the checklist becomes automatic.

The following sections are designed to help make sure you see all the important bird features.

Talk to yourself

Ask yourself this question first: *What is most noticeable, most obvious about this bird?* Go ahead and talk to yourself. Memory is a leaky cup. When you're looking at the bird, you naturally believe you'll remember all the key points. It ain't so. By the time you get to the book, you may not remember whether the bird had wingbars or an eyering.

A useful trick is to say the bird's features (often called *field marks*) out loud while you mentally tick them off. This process works best if no one else is around, of course, although it can be helpful if you're sharing the moment with another observer who is as new to the game as you. By repeating the field marks out loud, you simplify later access to your memory bank, which, like all banks, is often closed when you need it most.

After you discover the *most* obvious clue to the bird's identity, look at the next most obvious clue, and then the next, and so on. As you gain experience, you mumble to yourself less and less. Experience makes much of the process so fast and automatic that vocal reminders aren't necessary. Until you reach that point, the social downside of being seen as a mutterer is offset by the advantage of being able to identify more birds.

Now your problem is how to remember all these clues.

Make notes, sketches, recordings . . .

Being a quick sketch artist is one way to help your brain remember the field marks of a mystery bird. This sketch requires no artistic skill whatsoever. Simply carry a small notepad and a pencil (with an eraser). Use these tools to jot down as much information as you can while the bird is still in front of you. Better yet, draw the outline of the bird, labeling the pertinent field marks as you go (see Chapter 24 for more on field sketching).

The high-tech version of this method is to carry a microcassette recorder with you. When you encounter an unfamiliar bird, you can whisper your observations into the microphone. Later, with a field guide in hand, you can play back the recording, listening to your notes (and reliving the moment).

First Impressions

First impressions are important. A small yellow bird is not a big gray bird and isn't even a small gray bird. The first impression is the outline that you use to organize the specifics. Sometimes the impression is enough by itself, but most often it serves to get you to the right three or four pages in the field guide (at which point you can start to nail down the bird's ID).

The first impression is made up of several fairly obvious steps. Look at the bird and record your impressions of the following features:

- The bird's most obvious characteristic (or two)
- The bird's behavior (what is the bird doing?)
- The bird's size, shape, color
- Whether landbird or waterbird

Pay attention to *where* you see the bird. The where is often a good clue to *what* the bird actually is. These things take a lot of time to explain (but less than a few seconds to do when you're actually looking at a bird).

The most obvious characteristic, simply stated, is what stands out about the bird. What made you notice it? The following sections cover bird characteristics that provide clues to a bird's identity.

Size — bigger than a breadbox?

Size matters. In birding lingo, *size* refers to the measurement of the bird from bill-tip to the end of the tail. Make a quick judgment, using whatever standard is familiar and comfortable.

- Is it bigger than a breadbox (or in this day and age, a cellular phone)?
- Is it about six inches, or is it more than a foot long?
- Is it shorter than your binoculars, or bigger than a small child?

Which method you use doesn't matter, as long as you have a reasonable idea of how big the bird is. Figure 3-3 compares relative sizes of birds.

You don't need to be precise. The difference between a six-inch bird and a five-and-a-half-inch bird in the field is beyond most observers. Just get in the ballpark. Field guides aren't usually organized by size, but knowing how big or small the bird is helps to eliminate a lot of choices.

Figure 3-3: How big is big? From left to top right, comparing the sizes of a wild turkey, American crow, American robin, house finch, and ruby-throated hummingbird.

POINTER

Pick a common bird — one you're very familiar with — as a size reference point: rock dove, starling, robin, and so forth. Then you can discern if a mystery bird is "smaller than a robin." Size is an excellent clue to identification.

Shape

By looking at a bird, even one silhouetted in poor light, you can make out its general shape. Shape is an important ID clue. You can use the same descriptive terms you use for humans: tall, lanky, thin, leggy, fat, squat, chunky, round, big-headed, small-headed, pointy-headed, and egotistical (oops, not that one!). You get the picture.

With a good idea of the bird's shape, you can narrow the possibilities, throwing out those species that the bird cannot possibly be.

CAREFUL

Be aware that birds can and do change their shape. In cold weather, birds may puff out their feathers to increase heat retention. This puffing out process makes them appear larger than they actually are. Herons can fold their necks up until they appear to have no neck at all. A careful look at the bird helps you avoid being fooled.

Color

Color is one of the most easily grasped clues to a bird's identity. But color is not a foolproof, one-step ID tool. Why not? Because not all individual birds of a given species are the same color.

Variation exists among young (juvenile) and adult birds, among some males and females (called sexual dimorphism), and even among same-age, same-sex individuals. Further clouding the issue is the seasonal changing of plumage (feathers) that most birds go through.

An adult male American goldfinch in June looks like a brilliant golden and black jewel. The same bird in January wears colors of dull brownish yellow like a faded color photograph of the summer version.

 Even with the confusing variables, you can use color to your advantage. When you see an unfamiliar bird, describe the color to yourself. Don't be afraid to mix the colors together. If the bird looks yellowish-greenish-brown to you, that's great! Better yet, try to remember what parts of the bird are a distinctive color. Does the bird have a dark cap? A rusty belly? White wing patches?

Remembering colors and where they appear on the bird is a great start to knowing more about field marks.

Wet or dry?

Birds are commonly separated into groups.

The easiest distinction is between landbirds and waterbirds. If the bird is swimming around in the middle of the lake, it probably isn't a sparrow. If the bird is sitting in a bush or hanging on your feeder, it probably isn't a duck.

Waterbirds include: loons, grebes, seabirds, pelicans, cormorants, shorebirds (such as plovers and sandpipers), ducks, geese, swans, herons, egrets, ibises, cranes, rails, gulls, and terns, among others. Most of the waterbirds are located in front of any field guide.

Landbirds include: all the other birds you can think of.

In a very few instances this process of elimination won't work, but this method is always worth a try.

Field marks: Front to back

Start at the front end of the bird, the one with the bill, and work your way over the bird to the back end (the one without the bill). On many birds, the key field marks are found on the head. At the very least, the marks found on the head eliminate a lot of similar looking birds. Starting at the front/top end and working toward the tail is logical and helps you keep the information organized.

Pay (attention to) the bill

The bill is important. Birds are adapted to a specific way of life, and one of the most obvious adaptations is the bill. Bird bills come in a remarkable variety of shapes and sizes, each designed to a specific lifestyle. Is the bill long or short? Thick or thin? Hooked? Flattened? Broad? For example, sparrows have short, thick bills used for cracking seeds. Hawks have strong, hooked bills for tearing flesh. Herons have long, dagger-like bills for spearing fish. Figure 3-4 shows how different bills can be.

Figure 3-4: Bird bills with their different shapes resemble the tools named in parentheses. Use the tool names to help you identify the shape of a bill.

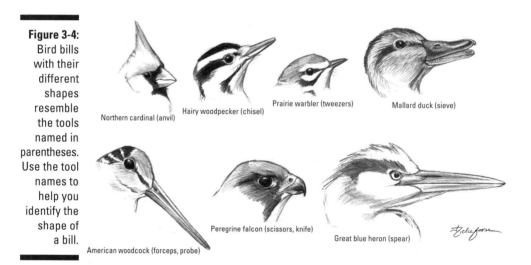

Northern cardinal (anvil)

Hairy woodpecker (chisel)

Prairie warbler (tweezers)

Mallard duck (sieve)

American woodcock (forceps, probe)

Peregrine falcon (scissors, knife)

Great blue heron (spear)

The bill usually tells you to which family or group your bird belongs. With a little practice, you can look at a bird's bill and say, automatically: "That's a chickadee." On some birds, such as pelicans and spoonbills, seeing the bill is virtually all you need. On others, the bill gets you to the right family of birds.

The head

More field marks appear on the heads of most birds than on any other part. Birds' heads can have eyerings, eyestripes, supercilia (don't worry, that's the plural of supercilium), and ear patches (on the side of the bird's head — birds' ears are usually concealed by feathers). In most cases, the field marks that matter on the head are stripes on the top (crown), eyerings, and a supercilium.

Look for obvious patterns, such as the crown stripes of a *white-crowned sparrow,* or the dark cap of a *black-capped chickadee*. Later, if the bird is still around, you can go back and look for subtleties.

Dozens of other field marks are associated with the head. Birds can be bald, bar-headed, beardless, bridled, browed, crested, crowned, capped, cheeked, chinned, collared, eared, eyed, faced, hooded, horned, masked, naped, necked (even red-necked!), nosed, plumed, polled, ringed, spectacled, striped, throated, tufted, and whiskered. And that's just the head.

Some body

Any reasonable person would conclude that a bird's body is one solid object. From the point of view of bird identification, however, a bird's body comes in two connected sections: the upperparts and the underparts. Many birds are named for their most noticeable body part, such as the *yellow-throated* warbler, or the *black-headed* grosbeak. Some birds are (stupidly) named for a marking that can only be seen on a bird held in the hand: *red-bellied* woodpecker and *ring-necked* duck are two examples. You never see either field mark unless you happen to be bird watching with the Hubbell telescope.

Upperparts

The upperparts are the *back* and top surface of the *wings,* sometimes called the *mantle,* plus the area extending down to the base of the tail. The key field marks, if any exist on the upperparts, are usually found on the wings.

Many groups of birds (vireos and warblers, for instance) are divided into those that have wingbars and those that don't. Wingbars are pale stripes across the *shoulder* of the wing. On some birds, subtle distinctions exist in the size, width, and color of the wingbars, but you can be content simply to notice whether or not the wing has bars.

The back isn't vitally important to determining a bird's identity, but whether the back is streaked or plain is worth noting. If you can see the rump — the patch of feathers on the lower back, just above the tail — try to notice its color, too. You're in for a surprise the first time you see a yellow-rumped warbler!

Underparts

The underparts are the *breast, belly,* and *vent* (also called *undertail coverts*). In many birds, such as sparrows, noticing whether the breast is plain or streaked is important. In some hawks, the breast is *barred* (the streaks go sideways). Some birds have a breast that's one color and the belly another.

The underparts are unimportant for identification purposes on a number of birds, however. Ducks are a good example — ducks are usually seen swimming on a body of water and the underparts can only be described as, well, wet.

The tail

The tail can be a very helpful clue to a bird's identity. You most often note the tail on flying birds, but you can sometimes see the tail clearly when a bird is perched in a tree or hopping on the ground. For some species a wagging or flicking movement of the tail is a diagnostic field mark. Tails can be relatively long or short, forked or square. On some birds, such as the *scissor-tailed* flycatcher, the tail is THE field mark. Look up the scissor-tailed flycatcher pictured in the color section of this book. It's a beaut!

The legs

The legs are often overlooked, but sometimes are important for identification purposes. Bird feet aren't as helpful as ID tools, but they do tell you something about how the bird makes its living (see Figure 3-5). For example, hawks and owls have sharp, taloned feet used for grabbing and killing their prey. Ducks have short legs and webbed feet for swimming.

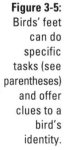

Figure 3-5: Birds' feet can do specific tasks (see parentheses) and offer clues to a bird's identity.

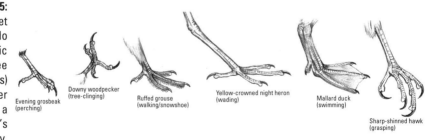

Evening grosbeak (perching)

Downy woodpecker (tree-clinging)

Ruffed grouse (walking/snowshoe)

Yellow-crowned night heron (wading)

Mallard duck (swimming)

Sharp-shinned hawk (grasping)

Look for length and color of the legs. Herons have proportionately long legs for wading in deep water and long toes for support and balance; most land-birds have short legs. Color is often more important than length when looking at bird legs. Some birds, like lesser yellowlegs, are named for their leg color.

The lesser yellowleg is a medium-sized shorebird. This bird is one of a half dozen medium-sized shorebirds with yellow legs (including the confusingly similar greater yellowlegs), but then, the naming of birds isn't always logical.

Be careful with leg color. Birds that have been walking around in mud have black or brown legs. Birds that have been wading in oily water often appear to have red legs.

Plumage

Birds' feathers, called *plumage,* are what make birds different from all other animals on earth. And it's their feathers, or rather the color of their feathers, that make birds so compelling and so beautiful.

Because birds replace feathers as they wear out, you may see the same birds with slightly different plumage at different times during the year, just as you change from a suit and tie when you get home from the office, put on jeans and a sweatshirt to clean out the garage, and then don a tux to go to the ball.

Because worn-out out feathers provide very little protection from cold and don't help much when a bird needs to fly, birds replace most of the feathers on their body every year. They do this by a process called *molt.* When birds molt, the old feathers fall out and a new set of unworn, unbroken feathers grows in. Most birds molt all of their feathers in the fall and a few feathers in the spring.

Sometimes, after molting, the bird's appearance changes. Greenish male scarlet tanagers change their drab feathers by growing in a set of brilliant red ones, offset by black wings. In late summer, many adult warblers begin a molt that makes them less boldly colored than they were just a few months prior. Bird molts provide another opportunity for bird watchers to study, or be frustrated by, birds.

Some birds, such as many male ducks, look different in the winter than they do in the summer. In some birds, such as many orioles, males look different than females. This isn't so that the males and females can tell each other apart. Birds never seem to have that problem. Rather, it reflects the different roles male and female birds have in the wild (sexism, I know, but the birds don't seem to mind).

In almost all birds, immature birds (young) look different from adults. Usually their plumage is duller and streakier. Although this difference typically lasts less than a year, in some cases (such as gulls and bald eagles), young birds can look different from adult birds for several years. The following plumage stages are typical of most birds:

- ✔ **Downy:** The fluffy white feathers most baby birds have while they're still in the nest. Adult birds retain some down feathers beneath their main contour feathers. This down helps insulate the birds, just like a down coat.

- ✔ **Juvenal:** The first real feathers a bird has after leaving the nest. Usually these feathers last about a month. Juvenile birds wear juvenal plumage.

- ✔ **Immature:** The feathers a bird wears for much of the first year of its life.

- ✔ **Adult:** The feathers the bird has after its first full year. This is the plumage commonly shown in field guides. Adult plumage often coincides with a bird's first breeding season. Reaching can take as little as nine months, or in the case of bald and golden eagles and many gull species, several years adult plumage.

Here are some seasonal plumages that adult birds have:

- ✔ **Breeding:** Breeding plumage is the equivalent of courting clothes. This plumage is often the bird's most colorful, especially in birds such as tanagers, many warblers, and ducks. Breeding plumage is commonly associated with adult males, whose bright feathers and loud song serve as an advertisement for a mate during the spring breeding season. Adult female birds, by and large, get the short end of the stick when it comes to flashy spring plumage. Female birds *do* get a new set of feathers each spring, but not eye-catchingly brilliant ones. A brightly colored female bird sitting on a nest would be easier for a predator to spot. So evolution has pushed female birds away from fashionably bright avian attire.

- ✔ **Non-breeding:** Generically speaking, this is the bird's everyday dress — the plumage that birds are in when not in breeding season. It's also known as fall plumage, alternate plumage, and winter plumage.

These plumage terms are not something you need to memorize. They help you when you're using a field guide to identify a bird. Field guides show many different plumages for each bird species, so knowing some of the basic terminology is a bonus.

Most songbirds, such as cardinals, California quail, and house finches, are *sexually dimorphic,* that is, the males and females look different from each other. Most hawks, gulls, shorebirds, and sparrows, however — which are not songbirds — aren't sexually dimorphic, meaning that males and females resemble each other more closely. Although exceptions to these groupings do occur, of course, knowing about sexual dimorphism is helpful when watching birds. Although the female cardinal doesn't look like the bright red male, other important clues tell you it's a cardinal. And as long as birds can tell the difference (and they can), identifying the male or female of a species adds to the challenge that bird watchers embrace.

Behavior watching

Behavior (the bird's, not yours) can often lead you to the correct identification when all else fails. Chances are, the reason you're looking at a bird is because some aspect of its behavior attracted your attention. The bird flew past you, or you heard it sing, or saw it move high up on a branch. Because bird behavior is so easily observed, it's an excellent first-impression clue to a bird's identity.

The world of bird behavior encompasses a lot of interesting information. For identification purposes, here's a taste (an appetizer, if you will) of how behavior can be useful. (For a full course on bird behavior, see Chapter 4.)

Bird behavior clues

Some birds constantly wag their tails (like palm warblers and phoebes); some (such as ruby-crowned kinglets) constantly flick their wings. Some birds hop, some walk, some creep, and some flutter. Some ducks dive while others feed by tipping over and sticking their backsides straight up in the air. Woodpeckers and nuthatches hop and scoot along tree trunks and branches searching for food. Hummingbirds hover over flowers to drink nectar. All are examples of bird behavior.

When gathering your first impression, ask yourself: What is this bird doing?

Bird sounds

Bird noises are an entirely separate area of endeavor (see Chapter 5 for more about bird sounds). Birds have a wonderful and bewildering variety of sounds — from songs to calls to alarm notes. Some warblers have as many as eight or ten different types of vocalizations, depending on to whom they're talking and what mood they're in.

Pleased to meetcha, Miss Beecher!

Growing up in southeastern Ohio, I looked forward to spring each year and the return of the colorful warblers, orioles, tanagers, and other migrants. Because this part of Ohio is thickly wooded, making even these brightly colored birds hard to find, most area bird watchers are forced to discover bird songs as a means of finding and identifying these birds. To this day I still use lots of the clues I was taught as a kid for remembering bird songs. For example: the chestnut-sided warbler sings *Pleased to meetcha, Miss Beecher!* The black-throated blue warbler sings *I am so lay zeee!* These tricks have stuck with me for 25 years and they've never let me down. You can come up with your own devices for remembering bird songs — just remember to remember!

It's worth noting any distinctive noises the bird is making. Is the bird cawing like a crow? Croaking like a raven? Screaming like a jay? Mewing like a catbird?

Field Guide Time, at Last!

Okay, you've stared at the bird until you're glassy-eyed; you've catalogued (out loud) important field marks; you've watched the bird stretch, hop, and wiggle; and you've listened to the bird chip, warble, and sing. You've got enough evidence to solve this identification mystery. It's time to open the field guide and put a name on this thing.

When going to the field guide with a bird in mind that you hope to identify, you have two choices:

- ✔ If you have a general idea of the *kind* of bird you're looking for, you turn to the part of the guide that deals with that kind of bird.
- ✔ If you have *no clue* of what you're looking for, you have to flip through the whole guide page by page.

Option one — figuring out the kind of bird and looking for that type of bird in the guide — is the way to do it!

Option two is time consuming, and your memory slowly goes south on you with every page that passes. Before long, you have trouble distinguishing between what you actually saw in the field and what you're seeing in the book. For help with using and understanding your field guide, see Chapter 13.

Because waterbirds are in the first half of the field guide and landbirds are mostly in the second half, start by cutting the problem down.

Suppose that you've found the right section, and three or four pages of birds look pretty much alike. Glance quickly at each set of pictures to see if one of them jumps (or hops) off the page screaming, "It's me. It's me!" You've completed the journey, accomplishing the task at the heart of the bird watching experience. You've put a name on the bird. Now you're ready to move on to the next challenge, and the next bird.

Not so fast!

A lot of people, including experts, make the mistake of stopping here. You need to take a few back-up steps:

1. **Keep looking!**

   A lot of people find a bird in the book that looks like the one in the bush and quit on the spot. They don't realize until much later that there's another bird, two pages later in the guide, that looks even *more* like the one they saw. Make sure you consider all the possibilities.

2. **Don't cram the bird into the picture!**

   Well, the bird you saw looks a lot like the one on page 235 of the field guide, except you didn't see the big white patch on the wings. Oh well, you may think, you probably just overlooked it. Sorry, that won't hold up in court. It's likely that you're looking at the wrong bird in the field guide.

   If you find yourself working too hard to explain field marks that don't quite fit, you probably have made a mistake.

3. **Look at the map!**

   You may not know which birds are supposed to be in your backyard and which ones are only found on the other side of the continent (or which ones only visit your area during a certain season of the year). That's why field guides have range maps. Isn't that brilliant? What's not clear is why so many people never look at them. Maybe it's the same unexplained phenomenon as why men never want to stop the car to ask directions.

Home on the range

Range can solve a lot of identification problems. If you have a chickadee coming to your feeder, and you live in California, you can take one glance at the map and eliminate Carolina chickadee. If you confidently have identified the small brown bird in your Virginia backyard as a wrentit (a western bird), you may have made a mistake. So, after you think you know what you're looking at, check the map and make sure the bird can be seen in your area. If the bird doesn't occur in your area, go back to the pictures and try again.

Birds have wings and tend to use them. They are very mobile creatures.

Just because your field guide's map says the bird you've identified shouldn't occur where you're seeing it, that doesn't mean that it can't happen. Either you've misidentified the bird or the bird misread the map in the field guide. A bird far from its normal range is called a *vagrant* or an *accidental*. If you think your bird is one of these, ask another bird watcher to help you confirm the identification. Finding a vagrant bird is an exciting experience.

Don't ever be afraid to ask questions of other bird watchers, particularly if they're more experienced than you. Ask for help with a tricky bird ID, or ask "How did you know that was a . . . ?" You pick up lots of great ID tips this way. And you'll probably make a few friends, too.

If All Else Fails . . .

If all else fails, start over. You may find it frustrating, but go back and look at the bird again, assuming it's still around. If it isn't, go on to the next bird. You don't have to identify every bird you see. No one does, and no one is keeping score. This process is supposed to be fun! Smile! Do what every other bird watcher does — grade yourself on a very generous curve.

Mistakes happen. . . . Big deal!

Three outcomes are possible when you attempt to identify a bird:

✔ **You get it right — you correctly identify the bird.**

It may take a while before you're absolutely sure, but you *will* get it right.

✔ **You don't figure it out, and the bird takes off before you can solve the mystery.**

You don't forget the one that gets away. When you see it again, you'll be ready.

✔ **You get it wrong — you (gasp!) misidentify the bird.**

You may not realize it at first, but as you see more birds and become more confident in your identification, you know that you got it wrong.

The newer you are to bird watching, the more likely the result will be #2 or #3. Because we all hate to admit failure, #3 will be more common than #2, whether you know it or not. You will — and this is an absolute certainty — misidentify birds when you first start out. In fact, you'll do it for the rest of your bird watching life. I misidentified a rock dove yesterday as a Cooper's hawk. My wife rubbed it in, but she didn't leave me. (She did point at me and whisper something in our daughter's ear, however.)

Don't worry about it if you misidentify a bird. The Fate of the Free World doesn't hang in the balance. Misidentifying birds isn't a social crime equivalent to dipping into the collection plate or secretly dumping your leaves into your neighbor's yard. Misidentifying birds is part of the process of becoming a bird watcher. Eventually, you'll correctly identify almost all the birds that you see.

Chapter 4
Watching Bird Behavior

- -

In This Chapter

▶ Bird behavior: anything goes

▶ Catch the action in your own backyard

▶ Foraging, preening, courting, and what comes after

- -

*A*nything that a bird does can be considered part of its behavior, and when you think about it, birds do a lot. They fly, sing, forage for food, perform mating displays, select mates, breed, fight, build nests, lay eggs, preen, bathe, and do lots of other stuff.

Bird behavior provides you, the bird watcher, with two primary things: entertainment and information. The entertainment is easy to understand: It's neat to watch birds do their thing. The information aspect of bird behavior provides clues to a bird's identity and gives us insight into the lives of birds. Of course, birds get lots more out of their behavior than we, the watchers, do.

What Is Bird Behavior?

Bird behavior, at its most basic, is simply a bird being a bird. Anything and everything a bird does is bird behavior. Even a bird, say a song sparrow, sitting still for a moment on a sun-drenched perch on a chilly spring morning — apparently doing nothing — provides an example of bird behavior. The bird is sun-bathing, catching some solar warmth, just as we humans do on a sunny day.

Birds behave more like humans than you may think. They form reasonably loyal pairs between males and females (though studies show there is some avian hanky-panky), raise mostly helpless young (babies that cannot immediately feed and fend for themselves), defend their home territories, have food preferences, and so on. Some ornithologists speculate that it's because birds form loyal pair bonds that we humans are so fascinated with their lives. If you've ever watched a pair of birds nest in your backyard, you'll know what I mean. You get pretty attached to those birds. They become *your* birds!

Some common (and easily observed) examples of bird behavior include foraging, bathing and preening, singing, territoriality, courtship, nest building, roosting, flocking behavior, and migration. Of course, you can observe many, many other aspects of bird behavior. For more in-depth information on bird behavior, check out some of the books listed in the Appendix at the end of this book.

Why do birds do that?

Bird behavior is easy to see, if you're aware of the opportunities you have to see it. When you see a bird's activity that attracts you, try to figure out what the behavior is. A friend of mine once said, "Birds are not aimless creatures. Everything they do has a reason behind it. The fun is in trying to figure out *why* a bird is doing what it's doing."

A bird's behavior is what allows it to survive life in a harsh environment. Don't you wonder how birds survive in extreme weather? How would *you* like to spend all day in the freezing rain and then have to keep warm all night when the moisture freezes into ice? Under such conditions, birds change their behavior to improve their chances of survival:

- ✔ They move around less to save energy.
- ✔ They may spend more time at a reliable food source, whether natural or artificial (such as a bird feeder).
- ✔ They puff up their feathers to trap and retain body heat.
- ✔ They seek shelter.

These changes in behavior are not decisions they make; these behavior changes are instinctual. They're a response to the stimulus of the weather.

Are birds smart?

You've no doubt heard the phrase *bird-brained* used to describe someone or something that's not very smart, or that's even pretty stupid. Well, if it means having a brain the size of a mourning dove, it's a pretty accurate phrase. Mourning doves have tiny heads and tiny brains. But if the phrase is referring to a raven's large, complex brain, then I must protest! Although not all birds receive an equal share in the smarts department, saying that birds are smart or stupid is not really accurate. What's most impressive about birds is their ability to learn, retain information, and alter their behavior accordingly. In other words, a bird is exactly as smart as it needs to be.

Mourning doves may seem stupid when they build a flimsy stick nest on a slender branch high in a tree. The wind blows, the eggs fall through the bottom of the nest, and the female dove sits there with a blank expression. Because these doves are so prolific (in some areas they nest year-round), they really have no reason to alter their behavior. The female dove will just build another flimsy nest and lay more eggs. It may seem like a stupid way of coping, but it's the method the mourning doves have been blessed with by evolution, along with a small head and tiny brain. And they seem to be doing fine.

Ravens, on the other hand, are great learners. Consequently, they've been studied by ornithologists and behaviorists for a long time. One particular study was conducted to see if ravens could solve a problem:

A hunk of suet was suspended by a string from a horizontal branch. Ravens attempted to get at the suet, which was suspended far enough below the perch to prevent the ravens' reaching it by simply leaning down. Because ravens are large and heavy birds, hovering to get the food isn't possible. Before long, several ravens discovered how to pull the string up in stages, by holding the slack string under their feet. Once a raven solved this problem, it had no trouble repeating the process when faced with the situation again. Dummy strings that had no suet attached were largely ignored.

Such trial-and-error learning is extremely valuable to birds in the wild. This process is how birds come to know about predators, prey and food, and other skills necessary for survival.

Some birds can count, which helps them keep track of the many eggs in their nests. Other birds that hide food in secret places, such as jays and crows, can remember the location of these caches months later, when they return to consume the food.

Rather than saying that birds are smart, you can say that birds are incredibly adaptable creatures who can change their behavior to suit a situation and thus enhance their chances of survival.

Bird behavior doesn't just occur on nature shows filmed in the tropics. It's happening right now, outside your windows, in your own backyard. The following sections describe some of the most easily observed, everyday examples of bird behavior.

Foraging

Foraging is the act of finding food. All birds have a distinct means of getting food. Robins scamper along on the lawn looking for earthworms (I have yet to see a robin standing in line at the bait shop), swallows swoop through the air catching flying insects, and woodpeckers hitch up tree trunks and branches looking for insects to excavate from the bark.

Birds can be generalists in their foraging, looking anywhere and everywhere for food. Good examples of generalists are European starlings and ring-billed gulls, both of which can be found seeking food in a variety of places, from shoreline to city park to fast-food-restaurant dumpster.

Birds can also be very specific in their foraging techniques. Members of the sapsucker family have an interesting foraging method. These birds drill a series of holes in tree trunks or branches. These holes cause the tree to produce protective sap, which oozes out of the holes in small amounts. It's the same concept that humans use to tap maple trees to make maple syrup. Later, the sapsuckers return to consume the sap. Other birds have learned about sapsucker holes, too. Many warblers, hummingbirds, and other small songbirds visit the holes for sap and to dine upon the insects that the sweet, sticky sap attracts.

Even closely related bird species can have very different foraging behavior. Take the pelicans, for example. White pelicans forage cooperatively in groups, floating along the water's surface, herding fish in front of them and scooping them up in their pouched bills. Brown pelicans, on the other hand, forage by diving into the water from a height. They may dive in loosely grouped flocks, but each individual is seeking its own targeted fish. If you've been to the beach in the southern portion of North America, you've probably seen brown pelicans flying above the water looking for fish. When a fish is spotted, a brown pelican wheels and dives headlong into the water.

Singing and Sound-Making

Bird song plays an important role in courtship and territoriality among birds (which I discuss later in this chapter). Although the males do the singing in most, but not all, bird species (to attract a female for mating), all birds make other sounds, too, such as chip notes, alarm notes, scolding notes, and even non-vocal sounds such as wing whistling (a sound made by air passing through a flying bird's wing feathers). If you've ever heard a mourning dove launch suddenly into flight (as when scared), you've probably heard the whistling sound the dove's wings make.

Some wren species keep the sexes equal when it comes to vocalizations by performing duet singing. These songs, performed in tandem from separate locations, are thought to help maintain the pair's bond with each other. Wrens also have many contact calls — short whistles or peeps that serve to say: "I'm fine, dear, and I'm over here eating spider eggs in the wood pile." Sort of like calling home just to check in.

 Vocal mimicry among birds is a fascinating thing. One of North America's best mimics is the northern mockingbird, which has been recorded imitating the songs and calls of more than 30 other bird species within a ten-minute span. If you have mockingbirds near you, you may have been lucky enough to hear the male sing his full repertoire all night long during a full moon. If you're a light sleeper, this can be pretty annoying. Mockers are thought to imitate the songs of other birds as a means of fueling their need for continuous song, which is part of their intensely territorial behavior. They borrow bits and snippets of other birds' songs and blab day and night. If you watch a singing mocker long enough, you may see him catapult vertically from his perch, fluttering back down on flashing black-and-white wings, never missing a beat in the music.

Another neat example of birds using vocalizations is the blue jay's crafty method of clearing off the bird feeder. I didn't believe this until I saw it myself at our feeders. A jay (or several jays) sees a feeding station crowded with birds. Instead of flying in and muscling its way to the seed (which could result in an injury), one of the jays gives an alarm call. Some jays even imitate the scream of a hawk. The effect this has on the smaller feeder visitors is akin to that of a person yelling "Fire!" in a packed movie theater. The little birds scram, and the jays take over the feeder. How's that for bird brains?

For more information on bird sounds, see Chapter 5.

Bathing/Preening

If you were to go without a bath for a few days — make that a *phew* — or few weeks, your family and friends would start making comments about it, such as "Plumbing not working at your house?" If a bird were to avoid bathing for the same amount of time, it may not survive. The personal hygiene of birds is a matter of life and death. Feathers that aren't clean don't function efficiently, either in flight or in protecting the body from weather and wear and tear. And let's not forget looks. Gaudy-plumaged males need to look good if they hope to attract a mate.

Several kinds of bathing behavior exist among birds, but the most common are water bathing, dust bathing, and sunbathing.

Water bathing

Water bathing is the most common behavior, and it can be easily observed if you offer water to birds in your yard (see Figure 4-1). For additional information on bird baths, see Chapter 6.

Birds don't bathe like humans do. Most birds that bathe in water prefer to wade into water that's a few inches deep and then splash the water onto their bodies. After bathing for a few minutes and getting thoroughly soaked, a bird flies to a safe perch to preen.

Preening is just like a bird combing its hair, but instead of using a comb or brush, birds use their bills. Preening smoothes down the feathers and feather edges and removes dirt and parasites from the feathers. Preening also allows the bird to distribute natural oil over its feathers. This oil, which comes from the bird's oil gland located at the base of the tail, helps give feathers durability and a certain amount of water resistance.

Birds don't rely exclusively on our bird baths for bathing. They use any shallow or splashing source of water, including puddles, ponds, sprinklers, and even the water caught in leaves after a rainstorm. In fact, many bird species use a rainstorm as an opportunity to take a shower.

Dust bathing

Certain species of birds, such as quail, pheasants, grouse, and turkeys, prefer to dust bathe, using fine dust or loose dirt to help keep their feathers clean.

Figure 4-1:
An American robin, luxuriating in the bath.

"But how can they get clean in the dirt?" I hear you ask. Ornithological studies have shown that dust bathing improves feather fluffiness and also discourages or dislodges parasites, along with reducing excess moisture and oil.

On our farm, I love to walk along the dirt road to the well during hot summer afternoons. If I'm lucky, I'll see dust-bathing birds in action. The road is dried red clay, which is very fine-grained — excellent for dust bathing. Our ruffed grouse and wild turkeys love to scratch out a small, football-sized area in the roadbed. The clay cooperates by breaking down into a fine dusty powder quite easily. The birds then fluff their feathers until the dust thoroughly covers them. We find dozens of molted feathers near these dust wallows every few days. Other birds take advantage of these wallows to dust bathe, too, including brown thrashers, house wrens, and house sparrows.

Sunbathing

Birds also enjoy bathing in bright, hot sunlight (just as humans do). If you watch some of your familiar backyard birds during warm, sunny weather, particularly following a cloudy, rainy, or cool spell, you may see this behavior.

A sunbathing bird doesn't get out the shades and suntan lotion. Instead, it spreads out its wings and tail and raises its feathers so that the sunlight strikes its bare skin in several places. Sunbathing birds often sprawl on the ground or on rooftops, looking dazed, their bills agape. Many theories exist to explain what birds get from this; these theories include increased vitamin production from the sunlight, increased warmth, and a benefit in driving parasites from the bird's back to its breast, where these pests can be preened away.

Anting

One fascinating feather-cleaning method employed by some birds is called anting. There are two types of anting: active anting and passive anting. In active anting, birds crush ants with their bills and wipe the crushed ants through their feathers. Ornithologists believe that the acidic juices of the crushed ants help the birds ward off feather mites, lice, and other parasites. In passive anting, a bird lies down on the ground on or near an anthill, with wings and feathers spread apart, and lets the ants crawl all over it. It's believed that the ants seek out and remove parasites from the bird's plumage. Worldwide, more than 200 bird species have been recorded as engaging in anting behavior. Among the North American species that use anting are American robin, American crow, blue jay, Northern cardinal, evening grosbeak, and purple finch.

Dating and Mating: Courtship

Remember your first date? Remember that head-over-heels, dizzy feeling you got? You planned out the whole thing, right down to the wedding attendants. Okay. You can stop now. Let's talk about birds. Sorry to distract you. . . .

Bird courtship is a spring phenomenon across most of North America, except for the southernmost reaches where the climate is warm year-round. Most of what birds do in the spring involves courtship, either directly or indirectly, including setting up territories, singing, performing visual displays, and taking off in hot pursuit.

Male ruby-throated hummingbirds perform an interesting courtship display flight (see Figure 4-2). When they locate a female hummer perched nearby, the males zoom above her in a swooping, U-shaped arc. This is called the *pendulum display* because the pattern resembles the path of a ticking clock's pendulum. During the display, the male chatters, his beating wings buzz, and he tries to maneuver himself so the tiny feathers on his gorget (throat) catch the sunlight and show off his ruby-colored throat to the watching female.

Have you ever noticed how, on warm days during the late winter and early spring, the birds seem to get much more active? This activity is caused by the birds' raised hormonal levels, which are affected by warmer temperatures and increased sunlight. It's a kind of avian spring fever.

Figure 4-2:
The swooping courtship display flight of a ruby-throated humming-bird.

Signs of spring on our farm are first apparent in early February when the red-shouldered hawks begin forming pairs. Soon after, our bluebirds begin peeking into their nest boxes, singing and waving their wings in courtship display.

The first thing a neotropical migrant, such as a male yellow warbler, does upon returning to its nesting grounds is select a territory and begin singing. Singing serves to attract a mate and to repel potential challengers for both mate and territory.

Bird courtship displays are designed to show off the male's color and markings to his best advantage: the male American redstart fans its wings and tail to show off the bright orange patches that would otherwise be concealed. Male meadowlarks puff out their bright yellow breast feathers and sing from an exposed perch. Even male city pigeons put on a show, bowing and cooing while fanning their tails and inflating their necks to show off iridescent feathers.

At your backyard feeder, you may observe another type of courtship behavior, especially if you have cardinals. The male cardinal selects a seed (it has to be just right, I'm sure) and feeds it to his mate in what is sometimes called a *courtship kiss*. When receiving the seed, the female cardinal quivers her wings in excitement, just like a fledgling bird begging for food. The male cardinal continues to feed his mate while she incubates eggs on the nest, as do many songbirds.

Nest Building

Birds can be classified by their nest types as follows:

- ✔ **Ground nesters** make their nests on the ground; some create a nest, some use just a shallow scrape, and some don't improve the nest site at all. Examples of ground-nesting birds are turkeys, some ducks, larks, towhees, and most shorebirds.

- ✔ **Cup nesters** create the stereotypical bird's nest woven out of plant materials. Most North American bird species construct open-cup nests. Examples of cup nesters are robins, most warblers, tanagers, most flycatchers, most hawks, and hummingbirds.

- ✔ **Cavity nesters** use hollow, enclosed areas, such as a hollow tree, for nesting. Woodpeckers create their own cavities by excavating holes in trees. The excavation of a nest hole is an important part of woodpecker courtship, so woodpeckers create new cavities each spring for nesting. Old woodpecker nests are used in subsequent years by many other cavity nesting species, such as titmice, chickadees, bluebirds, great crested flycatchers, some ducks, and owls.

FIELD TIP

Courtship of the Timberdoodle

If you know the time and place in spring to look, the courtship display of the male American woodcock is one of the most spectacular displays of all North American birds. Beginning as early as February, these comical-looking birds (which are also known as timberdoodles and bogsuckers) seek out brushy meadows and old fields from which to launch their nightly display flights, as shown in the figure.

Just as dusk turns to darkness, these portly woodland shorebirds begin to call, a short, nasal *peent!* After several minutes of peenting, the male woodcock begins a circular, ascending flight over his chosen display area. As he flies, his wings whistle with each flap, a sound caused by specially evolved, narrow primary feathers on the front edge of each wing. At the top of his ascent, the woodcock begins a freefall toward the ground, all the while singing a whistling twitter. Near the ground, the male swoops to a soft landing and begins the peenting process all over again.

This entire display is done to attract the attention of any female woodcock that happens to be listening. The male mates with as many females as will visit him during his spring displaying time.

With a few exceptions, almost all birds build structures for nesting, often using specific materials. Robins use mud in their nests, chickadees use moss, tree swallows use white feathers, gnatcatchers and hummingbirds use lichens and spiderwebs, while chipping sparrows line their nests with hair.

If you visit Florida in late winter, especially in the Everglades or another very birdy area, you'll see herons and egrets, and even ospreys flying through the air carrying sticks and branches in their beaks or feet. They're not spring cleaning! They're nest-building, a behavior that's a big part of the courtship and bonding of these species.

Nest-building behavior can include many activities. Gathering of materials, such as grass or sticks, site selection by mated pairs, and the actual building of the nest are all readily observable examples of this behavior. Find a bird that you know nests in your part of the continent and watch its activity during the spring months (see Figure 4-3). See if you can pick up clues that tell you if it's nesting in your immediate area.

The wooded hillsides on our farm are home to several pairs of ovenbirds, a ground-nesting warbler that's named for the way its nest is constructed. Ovenbird nests resemble tiny Dutch ovens — a domed cup with a small

Figure 4-3: An ovenbird at its Dutch-oven shaped nest.

entrance on one side. Ovenbirds build these nests on the ground, often near a woodland path or road. The materials include moss, twigs, dead grasses, rootlets, and animal hair. A roof of dead leaves helps both to conceal the nest on the forest floor, and to keep out the rain.

You can watch birds in your yard collect nesting material by offering them short pieces of soft string, yarn, human and pet hair, and even dryer lint. Scatter it about your yard in obvious places, or offer it in an unused, wire-basket suet feeder and watch the birds investigate. When my beloved wife goes to the beauty salon (and I'm at the beauty saloon) for her annual big haircut, she asks for the clippings of her own hair. I know this seems weird, but that's my wife (hey, she married *me!*). She brings the hair home in a plastic bag and scatters it around the lawn and garden. In the fall, we find several different chipping sparrow nests lined with her hair. She gets a kick out of that.

Female birds are the nest builders in most species with little or no help from the male. In some species, such as chickadees, titmice, hawks, and eagles, the males help out with the building. House wrens and marsh wrens are different in that the males construct several different nests from which the females select their favorite for actual use.

Some ground-nesting birds, such as nighthawks, killdeer, and terns, build no nests at all; rather, they rely on the natural camouflage of their speckled eggs to protect the nest, which may be no more than a shallow scrape in rocky or sandy soil.

For more information on providing nest sites for birds, see Chapter 9.

Defending My Space: Territoriality

Much of the same behavior that birds use in courtship is also associated with territoriality. Only this behavior is redirected at interlopers, rivals, and even potential predators rather than at potential mates.

A bird's *territory* is that physical area that a bird defends against other members of its own species. Bird territories can be defended year-round by nonmigratory birds, such as mockingbirds, or as temporarily as the small spot of ground that a sanderling defends while feeding along the ocean beach. Territories can range from vast amounts of land to small zones a few feet square.

During the spring and summer breeding season, you notice most territorial behavior among birds. This is when males compete for mates, for prime territories, and for dominance over rivals with nearby territories.

Examples of territorial behavior include the males' singing from prominent song perches, such as the top of a tree; fighting among rivals along territorial boundaries; chasing interlopers from a territory; and scolding, which is a harsher, less musical vocalization than singing.

Tips for Watching Bird Behavior

If the definition of bird behavior is anything that a bird does, then behavior watching is defined as *watching* anything that a bird does. It doesn't get much simpler than that.

Behavior watching gains popularity with bird watchers as they become more familiar with certain common bird species. Backyard watchers especially enjoy observing the behavior of those species that regularly appear in their yards and at their feeders.

You can easily give behavior watching a try with the next bird you see. Focus your attention on observing what the bird does, and see if you can guess why it's doing what it's doing.

Birds aren't little people. Although it's both fun and tempting to *anthropomorphize* — attribute human traits, such as feelings of love, joy, hate, and so on, to birds and other non-human creatures — it's not realistic or accurate. Bird behavior is almost always a reaction to a stimulus. A bird is hungry, so it looks for food. When it finds food, it doesn't stop to think, "Boy, am I feeling full. I ate too much. I need to watch my weight!" Birds just act and react, despite how much we'd like to think they're really rational and feeling, like us humans. By the way, you should do as I say, not as I do.

Weird nest materials

Here are some examples of unusual nest construction and unusual materials used by birds in their nests.

Great crested flycatchers, which are cavity-nesters, often place shed snake skins trailing out of the nest hole. Scientists theorize that this may ward off potential avian predators or nest hole competitors. Great crests may use cellophane if snakeskins are scarce.

Rock dove: One nest near a metal factory was composed entirely of metal shavings. Another dove nest was found to be made of multicolored electrical wire.

Chimney swifts use their own saliva to bind their stick nests to the inside walls of chimneys.

Baltimore orioles make a baglike nest suspended from a branch, often over water.

Belted kingfishers excavate a hole in a riverbank or muddy hillside.

Sound-out at Bill's bluebird corral

At our farm, we have bluebird boxes on either side of the house. In late February, especially on warm days, our bluebirds really get fired up. The males begin each dawn singing from their favorite song perches, proclaiming to all other male bluebirds within earshot: "Yo! This is MY turf over here. I'm the king of this section. Don't mess with me or my mate. And stay away from this wonderful house over here. We're already in it, and we're not moving. I DARE you to fly across my territory." Sure enough, a male from the other side can't resist a challenge, so he flies across one tiny corner of male #1's territory, singing "There ain't enough room in this here yard for both of us! Bring it on, if you think you're so tough. I may just fly over and flirt with your mate!"

A fight ensues, and one male wins, which puts the other one in his place until later in the summer, when both pairs breed a second time. By then, a truce has been worked out, and the pairs take turns at the birdbath with nary a turned feather.

When and where to look

Birds are most active during the early morning hours and in the late afternoon, so naturally these are the times when behavior is most evident. But behavior can happen anytime and anywhere. Nearly all owls are most active at night. Their daytime behavior consists of sleeping. In the summer months, male songbirds sing most of the day, making this behavior pretty easy to observe and to hear.

I suggest that you start by looking for bird behavior among your backyard birds. Or look at a nearby park, where ducks may be on a pond or herons stalking fish along the edges. Even pigeons (rock doves) in the city have amazing and easy-to-observe behaviors, such as courtship, fancy mate-impressing display flights, territorial fights, and a variety of vocalizations. Bird behavior, like birds, is everywhere.

What to look for

Because almost anything that a bird does can be classified as behavior, choose an easy-to-observe bird and watch it for signs of interesting behavior. For example:

> ✔ Birds at rest may engage in preening, or they may hunker down and tuck their heads into the scapular or shallow feathers.
>
> ✔ Foraging birds use many methods to get food, including gleaning from tree trunks and branches, flycatching, probing in the ground, excavating in wood, diving into water, hovering, scraping, prying, and even scaring prey into the open by flashing their tail and wing feathers.
>
> ✔ Birds in flight can exhibit behaviors such as predator evasion, elaborate courtship displays, migration, and territoriality.

When you see birds in action, ask yourself what it means. Why is the bird doing that? Lots of bird behavior is repetitive, so you may have more than one chance to catch a certain behavior and figure it out for yourself.

My favorite time of the year for watching bird behavior is the springtime. This is when the migrants return from the tropics, and all the birds, even our resident species, get sort of crazy with the onset of the breeding season. The morning is full of bird song, and the trees and fields around our farm are alive with all kinds of foraging, preening, singing, and chasing behavior. I love to pick out one bird and try to watch it for as long as possible. I get to see into this one individual bird's world — watch it live its life — while the bird is totally oblivious to me and my world. Time spent in this way is incredibly interesting, and wonderfully peaceful.

I wish I could be out there right now. But it's February and snowing. And I'm sitting in front of the computer, writing this book. Do me a favor. Go out and see a few birds for me, will you?

Do birds just wanna have fun?

I've often been asked by interested behavior watchers if birds ever like to have fun. The answer is both yes and no.

Birds do things for a reason. Even when birds are playing — such as when tree swallows seem to play catch with a light, floating feather — this playing has a purpose. Play among birds is probably driven more by instinct than by a desire to have fun. Swallows swooping to catch a falling feather, and then flying higher, only to drop it again, probably are developing their flycatching skills. This feather play may also be important for courtship, because the nests of tree swallows invariably are lined with white feathers. But when you see this feather-playing behavior, it certainly *appears* that the swallows are having a great time. (I saw a young peregrine falcon playing the same game with an unfortunate monarch butterfly in the strong updrafts over cliffs at Martha's Vineyard. It caught, dropped, and recaptured the butterfly a dozen times. I felt sorry for the butterfly, but was equally impressed with the behavior of the falcon. It was practicing its hunting technique.)

All bird behavior can be explained as a reaction or response to a stimulus (something that prompts a bird to action). And although we humans have been studying bird behavior for centuries, we probably don't know as much about it as we *think* we know.

Several years ago, I got a letter at *Bird Watcher's Digest* from a reader in Texas. She explained that she and her husband had seen a dark-eyed junco with two heads at their feeders! Somewhat dubious, I wrote back asking if she had any photographs. Well, yes, she did, along with several pages of notes on the bird's behavior and general appearance. We published her observations in the magazine. Afterward, I received calls and letters from several ornithologists asking about this bird. No photographs had ever before been published of a living, apparently healthy, two-headed bird. She had made ornithological history by closely watching the birds at her backyard feeder!

And that's what makes bird watching great: Anyone can contribute to our growing knowledge about birds, simply by being observant.

Keeping notes

An interesting part of behavior watching is keeping notes on what you observe. For many years, we've featured a column in *Bird Watcher's Digest* on bird behavior, and it's always among the most avidly read parts of our magazine. Of special interest is the feature at the end of the column in which reader questions and observations are shared and, when possible, explanations of bird behavior are given. Over the years, we've gotten some incredible observations, mostly from careful observers who took notes on what they were seeing.

Keeping notes is very simple. Carry a small notebook with you when you plan to watch birds. When something unusual occurs, you're ready to record your observations while they're still fresh in your mind. Here are some things to consider when recording your observations:

- What species is the bird?
- What sex is the bird or birds?
- What is the season (spring, summer, fall, or winter)?
- What is the time of day or night?
- How would you describe the bird's behavior?
- What do you think was the cause or purpose of the behavior (mating, courtship, foraging, and so on)?

✔ Describe the habitat or location in which the behavior was occurring (berry-filled tree, deep woods, at the bird feeders, and so on).

✔ Make notes about any other factors which may have affected the behavior (weather, contested food source, presence of predators, and so on).

For more information on keeping records of the birds and behavior you see, see Chapter 15. If you enjoy keeping notes on behavior, you'll really enjoy referring to these notes in the future, long after the actual incident has faded from memory. Your behavior notes provide a wealth of information.

Behavior as an ID Tool

The behavior of birds is very useful in determining a bird's identity. Many bird species have distinctive behavior, such as tail wagging or flicking; certain styles or patterns of flight; feeding styles, such as probing in the mud or flycatching in midair; and, of course, all types of vocalizations can be used as tools for bird identification.

Suppose that you see a bird that you can't identify right away — perhaps it's a life bird for you (one you've never seen before in your life). You can tell it's a small yellowish warbler. It's spring, so you know that warblers are present as they migrate through your area. This warblerlike bird is flitting from low branches to the grassy ground. All the while it's pumping its tail up and down as it forages. You catch a glimpse of a rusty patch on the bird's head just before the bird flies away. You make a mental note about the bird, particularly about the wagging tail. Later on, when you look at your field guide, you find several yellowish warblers that can be found in your area in spring, but only one with a rusty cap and a constantly moving tail: a palm warbler. Bird behavior was the clinching clue in that bird's identification.

When you see a strange bird, one that's not immediately recognizable to you, look for signs of unusual behavior, along with the bird's physical field marks. Behavior is a great ID tool, and one many bird watchers forget to use.

Bird behavior keeps veteran bird watchers interested long after they've exhausted the possibilities for seeing new birds every time out. If you're interested in finding out more about bird behavior, I have two suggestions:

✔ Watch as many birds as you can at every opportunity. Careful watchers see lots of amazing behavior.

✔ Consult the list of publications in the appendix. Most of these are excellent sources for insight into the behavior of birds.

I have to stop writing now. The red-bellied woodpecker is hammering on the side of my house, near the kitchen window. He knows that when he does this, I'll come outside to refill the peanut feeder and the suet feeder. It's his way of getting me to respond to his behavior. I think he has me pretty well trained. Don't you?

Chapter 5

Bird Sounds: News and Entertainment

*B*irds are very noisy creatures when they want to be. This fact is both good and bad news for you, the bird watcher. The news is good because when a bird is making noise, you can more easily locate it and perhaps identify the bird without needing to see it.

The bad part about bird sounds is that — to the beginner — the vast array of songs and calls made by birds on a spring morning can be unbelievably daunting. Experiencing bird sounds can seem like you may never figure out who's singing what. But take heart, I share some tricks of the trade to help you sort things out.

A bird uses two primary senses, sight and sound, to communicate with other birds. *Sight communication* involves colorful plumage and plumage patterns (see Chapter 3), as well as physical movement such as flight displays. *Sound communication* includes the vast array of sounds that birds can make. Most (but not all) of these sounds are vocalizations, which are generically called *bird song.*

In this chapter I discuss the basic types of bird sounds and how birds use these to communicate. And I tell you how to begin understanding bird songs and calls, especially as they pertain to bird identification.

Types of Bird Sounds

Birds make these basic kinds of sounds: songs, calls, and non-vocal sounds. All three types of sound have a purpose, but not all birds make all three sounds. Most bird species, however, rely on songs and calls. Some species — such as woodpeckers and some gamebirds, such as the ruffed grouse — lack the vocal skills of, say, the warblers, and rely on other means to make noise and attract attention. And bird sounds are all about getting noticed.

Bird songs

Strictly defined, *bird song* is a repetitive pattern of musical notes or vocalizations. Birds produce their songs using a complex muscular organ called the syrinx, which is roughly analogous to our larynx. The syrinx allows birds to produce beautiful vocal sounds. The syrinx also allows birds to produce several tones at one time, unlike most humans who can only produce a single tone at a time. When recorded and played back at a slow rate, the simple *chickadee-dee-dee* call of the black-capped chickadee is found to be composed of several harmonic tones, all sung at once.

Among North American birds, true song (that is, a complex vocalization designed to attract a mate) is almost exclusively performed by adult male birds on, or en route to, their established territories during the spring and summer months, which is the breeding or nesting season. The bird species that perform elaborate vocalizations are known as songbirds (see Figure 5-1), but this label can be a little misleading. A northern bobwhite is not considered a songbird, but I love listening to this bird's cheery whistle.

It pays to advertise

The primary purpose of bird song is, believe it or not, *advertising*. But a bird's vocal advertisements have nothing to do with Madison Avenue (thankfully). The songs of male birds (remember, most females don't sing) advertise two things:

"Here I am, females of my species! Check me out! I'm ready for action! All I need is the right female to choose me, and I'm ready to settle down!"

and

"Attention! All other males of my species! This is my territory here! Don't mess with me. Trespass at your own risk!"

Does this remind you of some chapter in your own life? Are you sorry I mentioned it?

Figure 5-1:
A male
indigo
bunting in
full song.

These musical messages are how birds sort themselves into pairs for breeding and into territories divided among rival males and rival pairs.

Bird song does have a seasonal nature. Although some species (such as mockingbirds, Carolina wrens, and wrentits) perform songs at all times of year, most song begins with the longer days and increasingly warm temperatures of early spring. The increased daylight causes changes in the hormonal levels in birds, which in turn affects their behavior. On a cloudy, cold, late-January day in your backyard, the birds may be actively visiting your feeders, uttering chips and scolds at each other. But if the next day dawns clear, sunny, and warmer, some of your backyard visitors begin to sing their spring songs in anticipation of the changing season.

A song of spring

Spring song starts earlier in the southern parts of the continent than it does in the northern parts. Spring song in southern Florida may begin in earnest in late January, while folks in the Rocky Mountain regions of Colorado, or those in New Hampshire, may wait until early April for the birds to get going vocally. In other parts of the West, where the seasonal differences in temperature and weather are not as great, the advent of spring song is strung out over many months.

Bird song reaches its crescendo across much of the continent during spring migration when birds that are already on territories (early-arriving migrants and resident or nonmigratory species) are joined by passing migrants. These migrants — thrushes, vireos, warblers, orioles, and tanagers — are singing their way northward to establish territories of their own.

Watch the birds in your backyard in early spring. As they sort out their turf boundaries, the males begin to perform most of their singing from favorite spots within their territories. These prominent locations are called *song perches.* Males use song perches to display themselves to the best advantage, both to potential mates and to nearby rivals. You can find the song perches in your backyard at the tops of trees, at the peak of a roof, or perhaps from the top of a brushpile. Song perches offer a reliable place to look for territorial male birds during the breeding season.

The drive to sing

Young birds can learn their songs by hearing them sung by adult birds, but it's believed that most songbirds are born with a preprogrammed song embedded in the behavioral portions of their brain. The song and the instinctual drive to perform it are inherited traits passed on from parents to offspring. Hearing a parent sing the song triggers its release in a young bird.

Imagine sitting in a chair all day listening to the same bird singing the same song over and over again. Could you do it? Some patient souls have done it, and among the things they discovered were:

- ✔ A male red-eyed vireo sang his song 22,197 times in one day between sunrise and sunset.
- ✔ The average songbird sings its song between 1,500 to 3,000 times daily during the breeding season.
- ✔ Songbirds sing most actively from pre-dawn to near mid-day, and again from late afternoon to before sundown.

Bird songs are amazingly varied. They range from low-impact squawks and whistles to the long, sweet tilling melody of the winter wren — a song that lasts for several seconds and includes more than 100 notes. Hearing a bird song is, to me, as pleasing as seeing the visual beauty of birds.

Bird calls

Not every vocal sound that a bird makes is a song. Many short chips, whistles, trills, twitters, and chirps are uttered by birds. All of these sounds, referred to as *bird calls,* have a communication role among birds.

Calls are used by birds in a variety of ways. Among the uses of calls are

- ✔ To keep contact among the members of a flock, family, or pair of birds.
- ✔ To warn off predators.
- ✔ To signal food.

The primary difference between bird songs and bird calls is that calls are much shorter in duration and may be less musical. Some birds, such as the American crow, don't have very musical songs, but they do possess an array of calls. I think of bird calls as being strictly functional, like a tool, whereas true bird song sounds more artistic, more musical.

All birds, including very young birds (nestlings), use call notes for communication. If you listen to the bird sounds in your yard, you can pick out the sounds that are obvious call notes, and those that are actual, full-fledged song.

Some of the calls you may encounter among the common birds in your area are the *pit-pit-pit!* alarm call of the American robin; the *pickk!* call of the downy woodpecker; and the *chicka-dee-dee-dee* call of the black-capped chickadee, or of the very similar Carolina chickadee, found in the southeastern portions of the United States.

Non-vocal sounds

Can you sing? Not everybody can. And if you've been to Karaoke Night lately, you've had a painful reminder of this fact. Not all birds can sing, either. Some birds have evolved, over the eons, to make their courtship and territorial points using non-vocal sounds. These sounds may be produced by specialized feather shafts that whistle in flight (woodcocks and some duck species have these feather shafts), or by specialized displays that involve a booming sound produced by flapping wings (the male ruffed grouse's drumming), or by some other specialized behavior, such as a woodpecker's drumming on hollow trees to make noise.

Non-vocal bird sounds serve the same purpose as the most beautiful phrase ever sung by a winter wren. These sounds proclaim: "Available male seeks seasonal female companion!" and "Macho guy lives here. Keep out!"

Mimics

Birds are the only living creatures, other than humans, capable of imitating sounds that they weren't born to produce. This ability to learn and imitate strange sounds is called *vocal mimicry,* and the birds that can do it are called *mimics.*

The almost-indisputable champion of vocal mimicry among North American birds is the northern mockingbird. The mockingbird, a gray bird with a long dark gray-and-white tail, is a year-round resident and a year-round singer wherever it's found. Because mockers must eke out a living on the same territory throughout the year, they defend winter feeding territories against intruders, and their song is one weapon in this defense.

How good are mockingbirds at singing and mimicry? One mocker was heard to perform the songs of more than 50 different species in one hour. Most mockingbirds have a repertoire that includes two dozen or more songs and calls. Some have learned to imitate doorbells, ringing telephones, whistles, and even the notes of a piano.

What is the purpose of such vocal mastery? The original theory was that mockingbirds, by imitating the songs of many other territorial male birds, would discourage other birds from choosing that area for their own territories and thus reduce competition for food. Newer studies have indicated that the bigger a male mocker's song repertoire, the more appealing he is to potential female mates and the more dominating he is to other male mockers. I find it interesting that mockingbirds seem to learn their songs from other birds singing in their vicinity, so a mocker in southern California learns the songs of birds in that area, while one in New England draws on that area's vocalizers for material.

Other excellent mimics in our midst include the gray catbird, brown thrasher (some bird people believe the thrasher, which can have as many as 1,000 song bits in its repertoire, is the king of the mimics), blue jay, yellow-breasted chat, and the European starling. The mockingbird, thrashers, and catbird are all members of the genus *Mimidae,* which is Latin for *mimic.*

Song as an Identifier

Bird song is a very useful identification tool for bird watchers. I can't count the number of times that bird song has been the clinching clue to a bird's identity, especially when I've had a less-than-perfect look at the bird. I remember the song or call, and later consult a field guide for a description of the song, or better yet, listen to an actual recording of the bird's song.

In fact, some birds are most readily identified by their vocalizations. One example is the group of drab gray-green birds known as the *Empidonax* flycatchers. *Empidonax* is Latin (the literal translation is "mosquito king") for the group of small, indistinctly marked flycatchers. The Acadian, willow, alder, least, and yellow-bellied flycatchers live in the eastern portions of North America. Western bird watchers get to thrill to the calls of the least and willow flycatchers, as well as the Hammond's, dusky, western, buff-breasted, and gray flycatchers.

These flycatchers are so similar in appearance that most bird watchers rely on the calls of each for positive identification. When faced with a non-vocal Empid, as these birds are generically known, birders everywhere do one of three things: make an educated guess, shrug and list the bird only as Empid species, or sit and wait patiently for the bird to make a peep.

Each bird you encounter is an individual, so don't be surprised if you encounter differences in the songs you hear from two members of the same species — just as each person has a distinctive voice and even an accent. Bird watchers listening to recordings of bird songs often remark, "That doesn't sound like our (wren/warbler/whatever) at all!" That's because birds from different parts of the continent have different dialects, sometimes even different songs. Listen for common characteristics that give you a composite aural picture of the species' song: pitch, tone, pattern. Is the song ringing? Sibilant? Syncopated? Thin and wiry or rich and chortling?

You'll have lots of situations in which you, my fellow bird watcher, will hear but not see birds. At night, owls and nightjars (whip-poor-wills, nighthawks, and their kin) will be calling, but offer you little to look at. There will be thick vegetation, fog, poor light. There will be treetop-singing warblers. There will be annoyingly persistent singers that you *just can't seem to locate!* The picture I'm painting here is that you will greatly benefit from opening your ears to the wonders (and usefulness!) of bird songs. All you have to do is listen!

An ear for birds

Growing up in heavily wooded southeastern Ohio, I was forced to identify birds by their songs. By mid-May each year, the tree-covered hills and hollows of this region are thick with new green growth, mostly leaves on trees. All this leafiness served to obscure any birds that were present in the trees, but the sounds were not blocked out. In order to locate and identify birds, I discovered bird songs, a slow and difficult process. But I knew I had made it as an *ear-birder* when I later moved to a less-forested area of the East Coast. My fellow bird watchers there remarked often on my "good ears." I realized then that knowing bird songs was a real advantage to the bird watcher. Years later, when I first visited the tropical rainforest in Costa Rica, I laughed because I had to start all over again. But this time the bird songs and calls were *really* weird, and the jungle was far thicker and more impenetrable than anything in North America. ¡Así es la vida!

Start with a Reference Bird

To begin deciphering and recognizing bird songs, I suggest you pick a *reference bird.* Choose a common species, preferably one that sings regularly in your area. Perhaps this bird is a cardinal if you live in the East, or a white-crowned sparrow if you live in the West. The American robin is reasonably common all across the continent, so maybe the robin works as a reference bird for you.

Listen to your reference bird's call and songs as often as you can. Soon, you become familiar with this species' vocalizations, and you're able to pick them out if they're singing, no matter where you are. This practice establishes a good reference point for your future bird song adventures.

When you next hear a bird song that you can't identify, use the song of your reference bird as a comparison. If your reference bird is a robin, which has a rich, throaty, warbling song, compare the mystery bird's song to that of the robin. Is it thinner-sounding? Is it harsher? More musical? While you're making the comparison, try to make visual contact with the mystery bird.

If you're just beginning with bird songs, I suggest you start by trying to sort out the early spring songs of common birds in and around your backyard. Get outside and listen before all the spring migrants come through, and before all the summer nesters begin to set up territories. Believe me, you have fewer songs to sort out in the early spring than at the height of migration in your area. The peak period of bird migration varies greatly from north to south and east to west. For much of North America, spring migration starts early in the year — as early as late January — and ends in mid-to-late June. Knowing the songs of your locally common and resident (nonmigratory) birds gives you a great head start later when these songs are mixed with dozens of others. Knowing these few songs, you can put them aside and concentrate on the new ones you're hearing.

A phrase to remember

Pleased to meetcha, Miss Beecher! is one of my all-time favorite phrases used to describe a bird song — in this case, a chestnut-sided warbler. The genius of this phrase is that it not only *sounds* like what the bird sings, it's weird enough that you're not going to forget it immediately.

Field guides to the birds invariably include a description of the vocalizations of each species. These descriptions may be straightforward ("a buzzy trill ending on an upward phrase") or poetic ("a melodic series of ethereal, flutelike notes"). But my favorites are the old-fashioned "sounds like the bird is saying" descriptions, such as *Quick! Three beers!* (olive-sided flycatcher), *Drink your tea!* (eastern towhee — formerly called the rufous-sided towhee), and *Spring of the year!* (eastern meadowlark).

Table 5-1 lists some phrases that may help you remember a bird by its song.

Table 5-1	Bird Songs to Remember
Name of Bird	*Sounds Like*
Red-eyed vireo	Here I am. Look at me. I'm up here!
Yellow-throated vireo	Helen, Helen! Come here!
White-throated sparrow	Old Sam Peabody, Peabody, Peabody! (or) Oh Sweet Canada, Canada, Canada!
Carolina wren	Teakettle, teakettle, teakettle!
Barred owl	Who cooks for you? Who cooks for you-all?
California quail	Chi-ca-go!
Olive-sided flycatcher	Quick! Three beers!
Black-throated blue warbler	I am so lay-zee!
Yellow warbler	Sweet, sweet, I'm so sweet!
Indigo bunting	Fire! Fire! Where? Where? There! There! Put it out! Put it out!
Eastern (rufous-sided) towhee	Drink your tea!
Golden-crowned sparrow	Oh dear me!
Eastern meadowlark	Spring of the year!

Squeaky wheel: An image of sound

Not all bird songs are translatable into the language of humans. But many that aren't fit for descriptive sentences can be remembered using descriptive *imagery*. A good example is the song of the black-and-white warbler, which is often described as sounding like a squeaky wheel. The ring-necked pheasant's call sounds like a very rusty gate being opened quickly. The notes of the red-breasted nuthatch's call sound as though they're being played on a tiny tin trumpet.

As you become more familiar with the songs of the birds you hear, feel free to come up with your own descriptions. How goofy they are doesn't matter, as long as they help you to remember.

Is there a pattern here?

Another method for remembering a bird's song is to tie the rhythm or cadence of the song to a pattern. A good example of this is the description used for the song of the American goldfinch, one often sung in flight: *Po-ta-to chip! Po-ta-to chip!* For my money, what the goldfinch is singing does *not* sound like the actual phrase "potato chip" but the rhythmic pattern of that phrase and the bird's song are unmistakably similar. "Potato chip" is an excellent reminder of the song's pattern. And since potato chips are a bird watcher's staple when out in the field, the phrase is never far from your mind.

Birding by Ear

With experience you'll become more comfortable with your ability to identify birds by their songs, calls, and sounds. Getting experience is the same as getting directions on how to get to Carnegie Hall: *practice, practice, practice.*

I know that getting experience sounds boring, but it's not. All you have to do is go out bird watching and remember to take your ears with you. Unless you're Vincent VanGogh, this should be easy to do.

- ✔ While in the field (or in your backyard), listen for bird sounds that you don't recognize.
- ✔ Choose a sound and try to locate its source.
- ✔ Once you find the singer, listen to its song a few times and make mental notes about the song's pattern and quality.

While you're listening, watch the bird carefully; it may do something that cements the moment (and the bird's song) in your mind forever.

As you gain experience in birding by ear, you'll find yourself stopping whenever a strange call or song catches your attention. That's how it's supposed to happen! You'll find many interesting — even unexpected — birds if you use your ears in conjunction with your eyes.

Looking for singers

You hear a strange bird song, but you can't find the bird. What do you do?

Stop. Listen. Look.

That's the best way to find a singing bird. Each time the bird sings, try to figure out the direction from which the sound is coming. As you narrow the possibilities, try this trick:

BIRD TALES

Song on the mountain

The first blackburnian warbler I ever heard was also the first one I ever saw. In early June I was hiking to the top of a ski run at a West Virginia ski resort. You know, it's amazing the things that fall out of people's pockets when they're skiing. All that stuff ends up on the ground after the snow is gone. I was richer by about $6.25 in coins, a few combs, a moneyless money clip, and a pair of barely broken sunglasses when I heard an extremely high-pitched bird song coming from the pines at the very top of the mountain. I scrambled to the summit and found myself looking up 10 feet into the fiery gaze of a male blackburnian warbler. He sang again. My heart pounded. I felt light-headed. He sang once more and then flew off down the mountain. The high altitude, the high-pitched song, and the Bengal-tiger-like face of the male warbler were the highlight of that entire summer. I'll never forget that moment or that song. Each time I hear it in the spring, when the blackburnians pass through our farm on their way north, I am transported. And I find myself scanning the ground beneath me for loose change.

Turn your head slightly from side to side, as if you're telling someone "no" in slow motion. Your ears will narrow down the directional possibilities as your head turns and the sound hits your eardrums from different angles.

If you have a good idea of the bird's direction, move slowly toward it, stopping to listen each time the bird sings. If you think you have the general location, scan it carefully for signs of movement. Once you find the bird, watch to see if it really is the one making the noise that you're following. Birds can put most human ventriloquists to shame.

If you're having trouble locating a singing bird, try cupping your hands behind your ears. This cupping helps to scoop the sounds into your ears more efficiently. It's a poor man's sound amplifier.

Helping your hearing

If you're even a little hard-of-hearing, you may have difficulty hearing high-pitched bird songs, such as warbler songs. Many bird watchers, especially men over the age of 50, naturally lose the high-end register of their hearing. This fact can be depressing to longtime birders who can *see* a male warbler singing but can't *hear* the song.

Some help is available for lost hearing, however. The help comes in the form of hearing aids adapted for use outdoors. These products were initially designed for use by hunters, but work equally well for bird watchers. In some cases, such as with a large group of birders, these hearing devices can amplify normal human conversation to painful volumes, but the fact remains that many a warbler song has been re-found with the help of modern hearing technology.

Consult a hearing specialist or an outdoor outfitter for brand names and ordering information.

Using Recordings

I'm one of those people who really suffers from acute spring fever. The champagne from New Year's Eve has barely gone flat before I'm scanning the southern horizon for migratory geese and turkey vultures, signs of spring in my neck of the woods. By the time the woodcock males start displaying in late February, I'm getting mighty itchy for warblers and tanagers — birds that are still flitting about on their wintering grounds in Central America!

To comfort myself, I listen to recordings of bird songs. It doesn't matter if the recording is just a series of songs with the species name intoned before each singer (I think the narrator's name is Lurch). It doesn't matter if the birds aren't identified at all — if it's just a recording done by sticking a microphone in the middle of a freshwater marsh for the dawn chorus. I still love listening to the sounds of spring. Listening to the sounds gives me a vicarious thrill that I'd otherwise have to wait months (or fly to the tropics) for.

I also have another motive for this behavior: fighting the rust. Because *months* have passed since the birds were here and singing, I've forgotten many of the subtleties, the nuances, the silly phrases that help me to identify birds by their songs. Plus, I want to be quicker on the draw than my (very competitive) wife with an ID of the spring's singing migrants. The recordings help me to polish up my rusty ears and to blow the cobwebs off the lobe of my brain where this type of knowledge is stored.

Try listening to a tape of bird song. The Appendix has a list of recordings that are popular among bird watchers. If nothing else, you can close your eyes and pretend the birds are really there singing all around you.

Part II
Backyard Bird Watching

The 5th Wave
By Rich Tennant

"Oh great! It's not bad enough we get rats and squirrels robbing our feeder — now we're getting personal injury attorneys."

In this part . . .

Your backyard is a good space to begin your bird watching adventure. This part covers every aspect of watching, attracting, and providing for birds in your immediate surroundings. Even if you live in a city apartment, you can do many things to welcome birds into your midst. I show you how to create a bird-friendly yard, how to attract birds with food and flowers, how to maintain nest boxes and be a good bird landlord, and even how to solve the problems you may encounter. As an added incentive, I include a bonus chapter about some specific birds that people love to watch and care for in their backyards and beyond.

Chapter 6

Making a Bird-Friendly Yard

The best place to start watching birds is close to home. Birds are present in most yards and gardens, no matter how small or urban the space may be. But why settle for the random robin? If you provide birds with a few perks and pleasures, they'll hang around your yard because it's a nice place to be. (I know, you probably believe that it's you they love.)

Think of it this way: Suppose you're faced with choosing between two parties given by the neighbors. One party is held in a large room with no furniture, a few stale crackers, some Cheez-whiz, flat cola (no glasses), and an AM radio. The other party (in an equally large room) has big, soft sofas, lots of comfy chairs, a huge table of food, a vast selection of beverages in an open bar, and a live band playing Calypso music. Which one would you choose? Hint: If most of your neighbors choose the first one, I would consider moving.

Attracting birds to your yard works the same way. Provide the things birds need and want, and they will come. (Birds don't want Cheez-whiz or cola, but the crackers are probably okay.) This chapter gives you tips for turning out a truly hospitable bird environment in your own backyard.

The Four Basics

Birds need four basic things to survive: Food, water, shelter, and a place to nest. You can attract birds with these four offerings, no matter where you live, even in the urban heart of a large city. The first three — food, water, and shelter — are fairly simple to offer. The last, a place to nest, requires a bit more effort, but offers far greater rewards to you and the birds.

Start by briefly looking at ways to attract birds with food. You can nibble and sip lightly at all four topics in this chapter. I revisit them all in greater detail later on in the book. For now, let's all chow!

Eating like a bird

Consider your bird feeding to be an ongoing experiment. Use trial and error to determine what foods your birds like. Also experiment with how you offer the foods to birds, because not all birds like to eat in the same way. Not all people like lasagna, or drumsticks (yes, I'm getting hungry), or drive-through windows, or fancy restaurants, and not all birds like all bird foods or all bird feeders.

Where you live in North America has a bearing on what birds you can attract to your yard. The birds at the feeders in my rural Ohio farmyard are very unlike those in my friend Hugh's yard in central California. He gets California quail and yellow-billed magpies. I get cardinals and blue jays. I'm sure we'd be happy to trade a few, but that's not legal.

Seeds

In the most general terms, bird feeding involves seeds. Black-oil sunflower seed is the most universally used seed for bird feeding because it's eaten by many feeder visitors, including chickadees, titmice, finches, grosbeaks, cardinals, jays, nuthatches, and woodpeckers, among others. Bird feeding's other popular seeds include: striped sunflower seeds, sunflower hearts, millet, safflower, cracked corn, peanuts and peanut bits, niger or thistle seed, and mixed seed containing milo, wheat, millet, and cracked corn.

The bottom line on bird seed can be found in Chapter 7 and in the bird seed preference chart in the Appendix.

Feeders

Today, as many feeder types and styles are available as there are sunflower kernels in a 50-pound bag of seed. I keep the subject of feeders simple for starters.

The ideal feeding station has

 ✔ A large platform feeder a few feet off the ground with sunflower seed and mixed seed on it

 ✔ A tube feeder or two offering sunflower seed, sunflower hearts, or thistle seed

 ✔ A hopper feeder dispensing sunflower seed

✔ A satellite feeder with sunflower seed, hearts, or peanut bits

✔ An area of open ground for scattering mixed seed, with a nearby shelter or brushpile

BACKYARD TIP

Start simply with one or two of the feeders shown in the illustration of a feeding station in the color section. Expand the feeding operation at your own pace. Once you've got the basics down, you and your birds can move on to other areas of bird feeding, including offering fruits, nuts, suet, and specialized foods and feeders to cater to (or discourage) certain feeder visitors.

Check out Chapter 7 for specifics on feeder types and for more Dummies-approved tips to great dining for birds. See the illustration in the color section for an ideal feeding station.

Getting water

Few creatures on the planet can survive without water. (Rocks don't count.) Birds are no different in their need for water. Birds need water for drinking, to help with digestion, and for bathing (see Figure 6-1). There's nothing worse for a bird than a bunch of dirty, matted, haven't-been-washed-in-days feathers. Dirty feathers don't insulate well, they don't offer optimal flight, and, let's face it, dirty feathers don't look good.

Figure 6-1: An American goldfinch and a brown thrasher enjoy a birdbath with a dripper. Fine tubing connects to an adapter at the hose spigot; a stopcock adjusts the rate of drip.

You can do your part for avian hygiene by offering water to the birds in your yard. If you don't have a naturally occurring stream or pond on or near your property (and you probably don't), consider putting out a bird bath.

Bird bath basics

Remember the following for an ideal bird bath set-up:

- ✔ The bath should have a large, shallow, cement stone, or composite bowl elevated slightly above ground. By shallow, I mean less than 3 inches deep. The shallower the better. (Most birds don't like the deep end.)

- ✔ The surface of the bath shouldn't be so smooth that birds can't get a secure footing. If it feels slippery to you, consider roughing up the surface of the bath a bit. Or consider adding a few handfuls of small, coarse gravel to the bottom of the bath. This makes for better bird footing.

- ✔ Flat rocks should be placed in the water to provide shallow areas and secure footing. Not all birds like total-immersion bathing.

If you can't put your bird bath in the shade of a tree, place it near some type of cover. Birds get nervous when they're all wet (wet birds can't fly well). Shelter makes them feel better and, if shelter is near, they're more likely to stop and bathe than to sip and fly, or not stop at all.

If your bath is in the open, erect a dead tree branch in the ground next to it. (Find a large branch, dig a hole next to the bath, put the thick end of the branch in the hole, and refill the hole around the branch with dirt. Wash your hands before sitting down to dinner.) Don't let branches hang directly over the water — birds have an uncanny ability to relieve themselves where it is least appreciated. This branch provides a perch for birds drawn in by the water and for those waiting their turn to bathe or drink.

Locate your bath where you can see and enjoy it from a convenient vantage point — say, your living room window. Here's another tip: Locate your bird bath where you can reach it easily with a garden hose for regular cleaning and refilling.

Regularly clean your bird bath, at least once a week. Birds drink this water. If you had to drink out of your tub, wouldn't you rather it had just been cleaned?

I keep an old scrub brush handy at the base of the bath, so that I can loosen the gunk that inevitably appears and then blast the bath clean with the garden hose. For tough algae and scum, grab a handful of gritty soil or a lump of soil with roots attached and rub it around on the inside of the bath. The soil acts as an abrasive to remove scum.

Although nearby shelter or cover is important for birds at both feeders and bird baths, you don't want to give the neighbor's cat a hiding place from where it can ambush birds. Keep feeders and baths a cat's-leap or two away from dense cover, and slightly elevated.

Driving birds crazy

Want to really make your bird bath irresistible? Make the water move. Everyone I know who has added a feature to their bird bath that makes the water move has raved over the bath's new-found popularity. Water movers drip, sprinkle, spray, or otherwise create motion in your bird bath. This motion catches the eye of a passing bird. That bird tells two friends, and they tell two friends . . . well, you know how it goes.

A simple dripper: Got a milk jug?

Is there an empty plastic milk jug sitting in your recycling bin? No? Well, then please drink the rest of your milk and rinse out the jug. Good. (Wipe off that milk mustache, please.)

Grab some rope or heavy string, a small nail, and that empty jug. Fill the jug with water and replace the lid. Place your bird bath under a convenient tree branch or other object from which you can suspend the filled jug. Using the rope or string, suspend the jug over your bird bath. Punch a tiny hole in the bottom of the filled jug so that the water drips out of the hole and plops into the bath. If the water doesn't come out, unscrew the jug lid slightly. Still no water? Poke a tiny hole in the top of the jug, above the waterline.

Now you have a cheap, socially responsible, if not beautiful, bird bath dripper. The birds will love it. Remember, you have to refill the jug occasionally.

Gimme shelter

Suppose you're a white-throated sparrow absent-mindedly kicking through the seeds scattered on the ground below a feeding station. Suddenly, one of those annoyingly perky black-capped chickadees sitting on the tube feeder above you gives an alarm call that means a hawk is nearby.

Swooooooosh!

A sharp-shinned hawk (sharpie) makes a quick pass at the feeder, looking for a victim. "Oh man," you the sparrow say to yourself, "this is a serious sparrow-eater and he's just waiting for me to bolt to the woods in a panic."

Lucky for you, the kind human owner of this backyard has placed the feeders near several evergreen trees and a humongous brushpile (see Figure 6-2). Good shelter. That's why you liked this yard and decided to stop here for a bite to eat. Being a denizen of the brushy field edges, you calmly hop into the center of the brushpile and wait for the sharpie to get bored (or lucky) and leave.

Figure 6-2:
This brushpile provides welcome respite for a tree sparrow and an eastern towhee.

A backyard can have all the perfect feeders and best bird foods, but the birds will ignore it if no decent shelter, or cover, is available nearby. They're not stupid. Like people, birds need shelter from bad weather. And birds and people want a cozy place to sleep, roost, and hide from predators. If the shelter is nice enough, some birds may even decide to nest in your yard as shown in Figure 6-3. (See Chapter 9 for more on nesting.)

Figure 6-3:
Tufted
titmice
nesting in
an old
woodpecker
hole.

Shelter can come in many forms: weedy areas, shrubs and brush, trees, brushpiles, woods, and even buildings (barn owls and barn swallows got their names in this way).

When you look at the setup of your feeding station, try thinking like a bird. If you're a bird at the feeder, think about:

- ✔ Where is the nearest place you can go to hide from danger?
- ✔ What about in bad weather? Are the feeders exposed to direct wind, snow, or rain?

If no shelter is convenient to the area of the feeders, create some shelter, such as an instant brushpile.

Nest boxes for birds: Making a house a home

All birds that venture into your yard benefit from a varied habitat. Some species take advantage of human-made shelter — commonly called bird houses or nest boxes. Bird houses come in hundreds of shapes and sizes, designs, and colors.

As you get to know the birds in your yard, you can target the housing you provide to maximize the birds' benefit. Among the species that use housing are bluebirds, chickadees, titmice, woodpeckers, nuthatches, swallows, some flycatchers, and even a few warblers, ducks, hawks, and owls. But remember, not all birds use bird houses, just as not all birds visit bird feeders.

Replacing lost habitats

The presence of several bird houses in a yard can compensate somewhat for the loss of natural nest sites. As cities and towns grow, consuming the surrounding countryside, a great deal of nesting habitat is lost. Things such as dead or hollow trees, scrubby woodlots, and brushy road and field edges may look messy and unkempt to people, but such places are prime habitats for nesting birds. You won't replace all lost habitats by putting up bird houses, but you may be helping a few cavity-nesting species (birds that like to nest in holes) to produce the next generation of birds.

Varied habitats are very nice

For those birds that don't use nest boxes, the best thing you can do is create a variety of habitats in your yard. An easy way to plan this is to think about providing habitats (landscaping, plants, trees, and other types of shelter) in a mixture of differing heights and textures. Start with the short stuff like grasses and ground cover, and then move up to flowering plants and a garden area. Next come shrubs, hedges, and small bushes, followed by trees, and even woodlands.

An excellent selection of backyard plans is available in *Gardening For Dummies*, written by Michael MacCaskey and editors at the National Gardening Association and published by IDG Books Worldwide, Inc.

Any experienced bird watcher will tell you that you find the most birds in the "edge habitat." *Edge habitat* is the area where two or more habitat types meet, such as where a meadow habitat meets the edge of a woodland habitat. Or where a thick, overgrown brushy area abuts a roadway. The greatest variety of habitat occurs where habitat types meet, so it's not just a coincidence that edge habitat is where the birds are. Birds preferring each individual type of habitat can potentially be in the place where these habitats meet. And with some creative thinking, that place could be in your backyard.

If you can leave an old dead tree safely standing on your property, you'll be doing the local birds a big favor. This year's woodpecker nest hole may be home to bluebirds next year and chickadees the following year. Because woodpeckers tend to drill new nest holes every spring, a tree full of old woodpecker holes is a tree full of nest sites for other birds.

For the motherlode of information on providing housing for birds, see Chapter 9.

Bird-Friendly Plants

If you're a gardener, or plan to landscape your yard anyway, consider planting species (*sp.*) that provide both food and shelter to birds. Think of these species as bed and breakfast (B+B) plantings for birds.

Some of the most popular B&B plants include:

- ✔ Annuals: amaranthus (*Amaranthus sp.*), coreopsis (*Coreopsis sp.*), cosmos (*Cosmos sp.*), marigold (*Tagetes sp.*), sunflower (*Helianthus sp.*), and zinnia (*Zinnia sp.*)

- ✔ Perennials: aster (*Aster sp.*), black-eyed Susan (*Rudbeckia sp.*), golden-rod (*Solidago sp.*), purple coneflower (*Echinacea purpurea*), and many grasses such as little bluestem (*Andropogon*)

- ✔ Shrubs: sumac (*Rhus sp.*), elderberry (*Sambucus sp.*), viburnum (*Viburnum sp.*), and boxwood (*Buxus sp.*)

- ✔ Small trees: holly (*Ilex sp.*), serviceberry (*Amelanchier sp.*), and dogwood (*Cornus sp.*)

- ✔ Fruiting trees and shrubs: blueberry (*Vaccinium sp.*), cherry (*Prunus sp.*), crab apple (*Malus sp.*), hawthorn (*Crataegus sp.*), mountain ash (*Sorbus sp.*), spicebush (*Lindera*), sassafras (*Sassafras*), and black gum (*Nyssa sylvatica*)

Any fruiting tree is of interest to some bird species, but you have to be willing to share the crop with the birds. On our farm, an old orchard exists from which we never get any cherries or crabapples. We do get lots of waxwings, robins, thrushes, and bluebirds, however.

A more comprehensive chart of plants for birds is in Chapter 10. Ask someone at a local garden center or your state agricultural agency about plants appropriate for your hardiness zone or growing region. These same sources may even have plans for making a wildlife-friendly backyard.

Avoid certain plants

Every part of North America has a list of non-native plants that have invaded from some foreign habitat and taken over. Often these invaders thrive at the expense of native plant species, and the birds and animals that rely on native plants for food and shelter may not get the same benefits from the invaders. In our area, species such as Japanese honeysuckle, crown vetch, and multiflora rose have taken over huge portions of the habitats. While these species do provide some value as food plants and as shelter, they are hard for landowners to keep under control. Before you begin planting new species in your backyard or garden, consult your local conservation authorities, garden centers, and garden clubs for tips on what plant species you should avoid. You'll be glad you did your homework!

Backyard Bird Conservation

Providing the four basics to birds (food, water, shelter, and a place to nest) in your backyard is a good start to backyard bird conservation. You're thinking globally and acting locally. Of course, not all birds will visit your feeders or bath, nor will all the birds stay around to nest in your yard. But all birds that pass through your yard will take advantage of whatever the habitat has to offer.

Chemical-free is the way to be

The most responsible thing you can do for birds in your yard is to keep their environment free of harmful, unnatural things such as chemical pesticides and herbicides, human-made trash, and potentially unhealthy bird feeders.

Environmental impact studies done on the effects of chemicals on birds have shown that surprisingly low amounts of herbicides and pesticides, such as those used to make beautiful lawns, can be toxic to birds such as robins and bluebirds. The full impact of the chemical DDT on the environment took years to discover. Today, bald eagles and ospreys — two of the bird species nearly wiped out by the cumulative effects of DDT — are doing better because this harmful chemical is banned in North America. But DDT is still widely used in Central and South America, so migrant birds are still exposed to it.

Will the popular lawn and garden chemicals of today be tomorrow's banned substances? Only time will tell. In the meantime — if you can manage it — keep your yard as chemical-free as possible.

Putting out the welcome mat

Nobody wants to have a silent spring when no birds sing because there *are* no birds. Almost all migratory birds are experiencing population decreases due to loss of habitats and environmental contamination. Nonmigratory resident birds, too, are feeling the effects of the growing human population. This is not a call to rally on the White House lawn. You can do your part in your own backyard. Here are some suggestions:

- ✔ Keep your yard as chemical-free as possible.

- ✔ If you must quest for the perfect lawn, keep one area untreated and let it grow nice and weedy. The birds (and other creatures) will love it.

- ✔ Clean your bird feeders and bird bath regularly to prevent the spread of disease (see Chapter 7 for cleaning tips).

- ✔ Offer only as much food on platform feeders (or on the ground) as can be eaten in one day. Old food can get wet, spoiled, and can carry disease.

- ✔ Provide housing for cavity-nesting birds.

- ✔ Plant and maintain your property for other creatures like bats, butterflies, reptiles, and mammals.

- ✔ Keep cats indoors or take them out on a leash. Domestic cats kill millions of songbirds annually. This tragic toll can be easily reduced. Bells on collars don't work. Stealthy cats can hunt without making them jingle.

- ✔ Prevent window strikes (birds flying into large windows) by placing screening over problem windows. Flying birds cannot discern reflection from reality. Large glass windows reflect the surrounding habitat. Anything placed over the window breaks up the reflection and birds aren't fooled by the illusion.

- ✔ Pick up trash, such as rusty cans, plastic bags, fishing line, six-pack rings, and so on. Birds can become entangled or even be choked by these unnatural items.

If you realize that you're already doing all these things for birds in your backyard, you should be enjoying plenty of birds already. In that case, you may want to branch out beyond your backyard to find and care for a greater variety of birds. You can definitely go to the head of the class (or skip to a later chapter of this book).

On the other hand, if some or all of these ideas and suggestions are new to you, get ready for some real fun. Your yard is about to become as busy as a shopping mall on December 24.

Chapter 7

Bird Feeding: The Start of It All

● ●

In This Chapter

▶ Where to feed

▶ Free feeding stuff

▶ Problems to avoid

▶ Keeping it clean

▶ What makes a good bird feeder?

▶ From suet to nuts

● ●

Do you want to watch birds? Which birds are you going to watch? Are there any outside your window? No? Well, I have a suggestion: Why don't you try to attract some birds? It's as easy as rolling off a log, or pinching your finger in the car door. Just get some bird seed and place it in an easy-to-see spot outside your window. You can put the seed inside your window, but trust me, you'll get more birds (and fewer mice) if you put the seed outside.

There's No Place Like Home

The story is the same for feeding birds as it is for bird watching in general: start at home. Unless you live on the 999th floor of the Sears Tower in Chicago (or some similarly tall, hermetically sealed building), you, too, can enjoy luring unsuspecting birds in close, where you can ogle them to your heart's content. I start off with the Dummies-approved, totally basic and fool-proof method of feeding birds: throw seed on the ground.

From the ground up

Believe it or not, starting a bird feeding station can be as simple as flinging a few handfuls of seed on the ground. I knew a dear old Connecticut Yankee who for 50 years did nothing more than this and had a devoted following of birds including fox sparrows, towhees, cardinals, chickadees, and a couple of titmice who learned her daily routine. They would peek into her bedroom, bathroom, or kitchen windows and tap on the glass if she was a little late in rising to throw a coffee can full of sunflower seed and table scraps out the back door!

There are a couple of messages in this little story. First, you really don't have to have expensive bird feeders to feed birds. Second, unexpected joys and surprises await you when you start feeding birds.

No takers

Sometimes people tell me, "I put up a bird feeder, but no birds will come to it." I never really understood why this would be so, until we moved to a rural area with heavy agriculture and very little tradition of bird feeding. I put up a bird feeder and nobody came! For weeks!

So I took a fresh look at bird feeders, from the point of view of a wild bird. Your typical tube feeder — all slippery Lucite and shiny metal — is really a pretty scary thing to a naive wild bird. There's nothing natural about it, and even though you can see the seed inside it, a skittish bird may not want to land on it to figure out how to get at the seed.

So I dragged a hollow log out of the woods, sprinkled seed over it, and built a low, rough plywood and block table — nothing fancy — then stuck a bunch of dead branches into the ground around the whole setup. This gave birds some natural surfaces to land on and investigate. They came, they ate, they stayed — and they completely ignored the hanging tube feeder until the day a bold chickadee landed on it, scolding, and took the first sunflower seed. The other birds watched and learned, and I was on my way to having a great feeding station.

Feeder freebies

Bird watchers are used to free entertainment. If you don't think so, watch how many of them brown-bag it in favor of eating out while birding, or listen to them hem and haw over purchases of any bird-watching accouterment (except seed, and this book, I hope).

A lot of free materials are available out there that you can use to improve your bird feeding station. I already mentioned hollow logs, which make a natural and attractive stage for ground-feeding birds, and which help keep the seed up off the wet ground. Branches, or dead snags (still-standing, broken off tree trunks or branches — birds like to use them as perches), can immediately enhance the attractiveness of your yard to everyone except your meticulous neighbor. Just take a post-hole digger and stick a few big dead vertical branches in the ground. Voila! You've made a perch where there was none, and given woodpeckers and hawks and songbirds a reason to pause in your yard.

Snags are a potent attractant; they can serve as song perches for territorial birds, lookouts for still-hunting insect-eaters like bluebirds and flycatchers, prey-spotting perches for hawks, or drumming boards for woodpeckers. Try a few. They're free, and when they eventually rot and fall down, plenty more are out there in the woods to choose from.

Think natural!

Sticks and stones. Think natural, and you'll be thinking like a bird.

Imagine yourself, a timorous little sparrow, skulking around the edge of the woods, scratching in the leaf litter for food. Would you fly across a big open green lawn, even if seed was on the ground? Wouldn't you be afraid of hawks and cats, dogs and people? Now, imagine a big, sheltering brushpile with lots of nooks and crannies to hide in smack dab in the middle of that feeding area. Sparrow heaven.

Lots of other birds will thank you by coming to your feeders if you build them a brushpile. We're not talking about something huge here, just a modest pile of sticks and brush, the kind of stuff you trim off your trees and shrubs on a Saturday afternoon, and then wonder what to do with. Toss it off to the side of your feeding station and watch the cardinals, sparrows, towhees, juncos, and chickadees pop in and out of it. You've given them a place to go when a hawk zooms by or the back door suddenly opens. It provides an out for the more skittish birds; they'll feel much freer to visit, knowing there's a place to hide nearby.

High or Low: Where Birds Feed

Feeding birds can take place in many ways. The two most basic methods are: on the ground and from a suspended feeder. Most feeder operators do both to cater to the widest variety of birds, while some do only one or the

Where to dump your Christmas tree

Got a Christmas tree, just de-tinseled, to dispose of? Prop it up in the middle of your brushpile. Instant tree. I've always thought Christmas trees looked best outside, with a cardinal or two in them. Your tree will serve you and the birds well, as shelter from cold, snow, and predators. Come warm weather, when it's looking a little crispy, we have a May Day ritual on our farm, where the burning laws are lax at best — we set the whole brushpile and Christmas tree ablaze and dance around it, howling. Gets the farm dogs going for miles around. Not to mention the neighbors within earshot.

If you can think a month or two in advance about disposing of your holiday tree, find a good spot in your yard and drive a four-foot-tall stake into the ground. Do this before the ground freezes, it's easier (that's the thinking ahead part). When you're done with your tree, you have a sturdy support to which you can tie it. This keeps the tree upright in all manner of high winds and heavy snow.

other to discourage unwanted feeder visitors. Yes, some birds (and other critters) can become unwelcome at your feeding station. If you already feed birds, you probably know what I mean.

Beyond the basic ways to feed birds is the vast ocean of what to feed them.

Ground feeding

Ground feeding is great. Most of the bird species that come to feeders take all or part of their natural food from the ground anyway. In winter, though, there's snow and rain. That can spoil seed that's scattered on the ground, and spoiled seed can lead to sick birds. To avoid this, clever humans have come up with a variety of feeders that either keep the seed up off the ground, keep it dry by dispensing a little at a time, or both. The most basic bird feeder is a low table, called a platform feeder (see Figure 7-1).

These feeders are easy to make with a couple of cinder blocks and a sheet of plywood. If you want to get fancy, you can tack some quarter-round around the edges to help contain the seed, and drill $1/2$-inch drain holes in the plywood. Bird tables are a nice, non-threatening way to keep seed up off the ground but are still accessible to ground-feeding birds like juncos, sparrows, towhees, doves, and cardinals. Big flocks of birds can feed without the jostling and bickering engendered by tube or hanging feeders. Make sure to clean your platform feeder frequently.

Figure 7-1:
A pair of California quail, a green-tailed towhee, and a tufted titmouse visit a platform feeder.

A slightly different version of this simple bird table replaces the plywood bottom with screen. It's best to go for stainless steel screen, with a fairly coarse mesh. This lets water drain right through the seed, and lets air get to it to dry it out. It still gets clogged up, of course, but a knock on the ground or blast with the hose will clear it right out. Several commercial screen-bottomed feeding platforms are out there, or you can make your own.

The drawback to ground feeding is that the seed is exposed to the weather so it gets soaked by rain and covered up by snow and ice, and so on. There's the additional problem of hygiene: Birds feeding on the ground don't politely fly away when they need to relieve themselves, so the food can get contaminated. The answer is to offer food in raised or hanging feeders.

Suspended or raised feeders

Birds that find their food in bushes, trees, and in other off-the-ground places prefer to feed at bird feeders that are elevated. These are the stereotypical bird feeders that hang from a tree branch, deck railing, or window frame. You can find many variations on the design of hanging feeders.

Hundreds of types and styles of bird feeders exist. If you're just starting out in bird feeding, I recommend that you keep things simple. Get one or two simple feeders and feed one or two seed types, until you get a feel for whether you and the birds are enjoying this new adventure. Don't make the mistake of going whole hog with 12 new feeders and a half-ton of seed. You'll be worn out from just filling the feeders!

Buying Feeders

Let's talk about commercially available feeders. These shiny, clanky things have a lot going for them. First and foremost, they keep the seed fresh and dry. It can be snowing like mad, covering up your bird table and ground feeding area in seconds, and a good hanging feeder will still be calmly dispensing seed to the hungry.

Feeder types

Commercial feeders come in three basic types: hopper, tube, and satellite.

Hoppers (not Dennis)

Hopper feeders have a lot of different styles, but the old favorite looks like a little barn or covered bridge, minus the young lovers and graffiti. The sides are usually panels of Plexiglas that allow you to see how much seed remains, and access is usually through the top (see Figure 7-2).

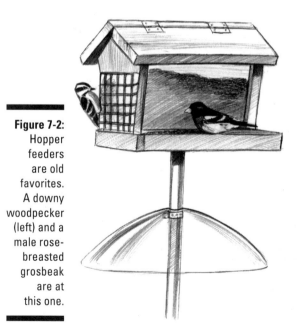

Figure 7-2: Hopper feeders are old favorites. A downy woodpecker (left) and a male rose-breasted grosbeak are at this one.

A good hopper feeder can be completely disassembled to be cleaned (more on this later). Hoppers can be pole-mounted, often with a threaded sleeve that screws onto the threaded top of a plumber's galvanized pipe. They can be suspended, too.

The two best features of hoppers are

✔ They hold a lot of seed, so that you don't have to go out every day to refill them.

✔ They're big and bird-friendly. Shy birds, or big birds like doves and jays and woodpeckers, are able to land and feed from them comfortably.

When I've had unusual species such as rose-breasted grosbeaks at my feeder, they've come to hopper feeders. Birds that are reluctant to perch on tube feeders or cling to satellite feeders will happily come to a hopper feeder.

You can feed any kind of seed in a hopper feeder because the seed usually comes out of slots at the bottom of the Plexiglas panels. Sunflower seed is a favorite of many hopper feeder visitors, but seed mixes containing millet, corn, and peanut hearts can be fed in these feeders, too.

Totally tubular

Tube feeders — long cylinders with perches at the feeding ports — are the classic feeders for woodland birds like chickadees, titmice, woodpeckers, and nuthatches, as well as for finches like goldfinches, siskins, and house finches. All these birds are small, and they can perch comfortably on the usually short metal perches most tube feeders have (see Figure 7-3).

Tube feeders are great for screening out big birds like blue jays, grackles, blackbirds, and doves, if you're into avian discrimination. But they also keep grosbeaks and cardinals away, too, because these birds aren't so good at clinging, and they're just too big for the perches. They'll go to the hopper or platform feeders, or onto the ground. When you're looking at tube feeders, make sure the seed you're planning to put in them will fit through the holes at the feeding ports. Most have big holes that let sunflower seed through, but others are made especially for the tiny thistle or niger seed.

Satellites (going global)

Speaking of tiny, if you want to cater only to little birds like chickadees, titmice, nuthatches, goldfinches, and siskins — note that I didn't mention house finches — pick a globe feeder. These look like flying saucers, or satellites, and they're suspended from a wire so that they spin when a bird lands on them (see Figure 7-4). Dizzying, but no problem for all these little clinging birds.

Figure 7-3:
Small,
seed-eating
birds
such as
finches and
chickadees
like tube
feeders.

Figure 7-4:
Clinging
birds
can hang
from a
globe
feeder.

If you're sick of shoveling feed into the maws of packs of house finches, try a satellite feeder. Birds must approach them from the bottom and cling upside-down to feed from them. But you fill them with seed from a small capped opening in the top. Some satellite feeders have a domed baffle on top to keep squirrels out, too. House finches just can't do the cling thing; their legs aren't strong enough. So if you see your chickadees politely trying to fit in edgewise among the house finches at the tube feeder, hang a satellite feeder just for them.

What to look for when buying

Many feeder styles are on the market, but any feeder you buy should be easily filled, emptied, and cleaned.

- Beware of feeders that require you to use a funnel to fill them because you'll quickly tire of lugging a funnel out every time you have to replenish the seed.

- Wooden parts of hopper feeders should be made of weather-resistant cedar, or stained or painted to protect against moisture. Plastic feeders should be reinforced with metal around the feeding ports to ward off chewing squirrels. Perches should be metal or replaceable dowel, for the same squirrelly reasons. Because you may be looking at a feeder for a decade or more, it pays to buy the sturdiest and most easily maintained one you can.

- With tube feeders, look at the bottom port. Is there dead space beneath it where seed can collect because the birds can't reach it? This seed gets all icky and moldy — a waste of food, and dangerous for the birds.

- Can you take the feeder apart to scrub and clean it? If it looks like you'll need fancy bottle brushes or an act of Congress to get it clean, pick one of simpler design.

- Beware of super-cheap feeders. Not all of the $5 to $10 feeders available for sale are going to last you for more than one season of feeding. Remember, these things are going to be filled with seed and hung out in the weather. Look for durable construction if you want to get your money's worth.

The ideal feeding station

By now, a picture should be emerging of an ideal feeding station — one with a variety of different feeder styles, at different heights, where the greatest diversity of birds can find food. It should provide shelter from wind, rain, and predators in the form of shrubbery or the instant habitat of brushpiles and found materials. It should have a wide variety of foods, and some water should be available year-round. The color section later in this book shows what an ideal feeding station can look like.

Feeding Times: When to Start, When to Stop

The vast majority of people feed birds only in winter, when it's truly tough out there and the birds look so pitiful all puffed up against the cold. As you see in the "Summer Feeding" section, feeding birds year-round has lots of benefits. It's up to you.

If you do want to keep feeding to winter, start feeding in autumn before the weather turns really nasty. This way, you'll entice birds into including your feeder in their winter feeding routes. Think of the flocks using your feeder as an ever-changing river of birds and you'll have a good idea how it works. You may think you have the same five chickadees all day long, but it's more likely that you have 30 or 40 chickadees who stop in for a few minutes every day, and then go on their merry way looking for caterpillar cocoons, scale insects, and spiders hiding under tree bark. So the sooner in autumn you have the station going, the more birds you're likely to snag.

The birds give you clues

The birds tell you when you can stop feeding in the spring. Long after the grass has greened up, you'll still have lots of birds at your feeder. Even after the weather has warmed up, nights can still drop below freezing, which keeps the insects inactive. But one fine April or May day, as the leaves are unfurling, it occurs to you that the feeders just aren't emptying as fast as usual, and you aren't going out quite as often to fill them. In our yard, this is quite dramatic, because we have a flock of about 250 American goldfinches who pig-out at the feeders all winter. By late April, the males have shed their dull winter plumage for brilliant yellow, trimmed with black wings, cap and tail. They're singing like crazy in every treetop; it can be deafening. And all of a sudden, they leave, dispersing to the surrounding countryside to pair up and eventually breed. It's quiet. And by then, I really don't miss them at all!

Migratory birds follow their instincts

Birds are happy to desert your feeders when it's time to migrate, or when protein-rich insects become available. You don't need to worry about getting them addicted to seed, or keeping them from their normal migratory behavior. But this leads to another question.

Suppose that Aunt Reba just called. The condo in Florida is free for ten days. You take a look at the 20-pound icicles hanging from the eaves and say, yes. Only as you're locking the door behind you does it occur to you — who's going to feed the birds? Will they die without the handouts they've grown accustomed to?

There's no really clear-cut answer to this because a lot depends on whether other feeding stations are nearby. Here's a story:

When I lived on a nature preserve in New England, I had an annoyingly huge flock of perhaps 70 house finches who camped on my feeders all day long, mowing through 50-pound bags of sunflower hearts (seeds with the shells removed) at a pocket-emptying pace. A friend who lived, as the finch flies, two miles away often gloated to me that the house finches that once plagued her feeders had disappeared once I moved in. I was feeding better stuff, I guess; they didn't even have to crack the shells at my place. Well, one day I was called away on business, and my feeders went empty for two days. Guess where the flock went? Back to Barbara's house. After that, I sometimes waited to refill my feeders until mid-day, and could barely suppress a cackle when Barbara would call to scold me for foisting the flock off on her.

Color-banding lets researchers identify individual birds by placing colored plastic markers on the legs. Such studies have shown that chickadees take, on average, only one-quarter of their daily food from feeders. Flocking species, like goldfinches, siskins, and house finches, though, seem more inclined to camp out at feeders, relying more heavily on them for their daily meals. As my house finch experience shows, though, birds are intelligent and resourceful enough to move elsewhere when a food source is exhausted.

Resident birds need continuity

Some bird species keep winter territories from which they don't wander. Cardinals and white-throated sparrows are two examples. For them, a stop-and-start feeding program can be worse than none at all.

When you have a successful feeding station, populations of birds can explode. And even though the birds may be taking most of their food from your feeders, the natural food supply in the immediate vicinity of the feeders is bound to be exhausted soon. There's not much for the birds to fall back on should the feeding stop. Pulling the rug out from under territorial species who live right around your yard is unfair, at best.

If you're going away for only a couple of days, fill all your feeders, and scatter a lot of seed on the ground and under shrubbery. For longer vacations, we pay a neighbor to fill our feeders while watering our plants and feeding our indoor pets. We look at it as having a few hundred outdoor pets.

Is feeding good or bad for birds?

Let's face it: Bird feeding is really more for people than birds. Birds have been getting by for eons without the artificial supplementation of millions of tons of sunflower, millet, corn, and other things we throw at them all winter. Time was when people just threw a few crusts of stale bread out on a particularly nasty day and called it feeding.

The craze we're part of really only got a foothold in the 1960s and has been growing ever since, along with the populations of birds that use feeders. The fact is, we know comparatively little about the relative benefits and drawbacks of bird feeding, but it makes for some interesting discussion among bird feeding proponents and opponents, complete with fist shaking and yelling.

Wisconsin researchers Margaret Brittingham and Stanley Temple studied black-capped chickadees that had access to feeders and compared them to chickadee flocks that did not. Although chickadees take, on average, only 20 to 25 percent of their daily food from feeders, the researchers found that feeder-using birds had a higher winter survival rate than their wilder counterparts. Chickadees using feeders had a month-to-month survival rate of 95 percent, compared to 87 percent for birds in the wild with no access to feeders. And get this: 69 percent of feeder-using chickadees survived the winter, while a paltry 37 percent of the feeder-shunning birds made it through.

Maintaining Your Feeder Station

Okay now, let me talk about hygiene. It makes me feel better.

When you feed several hundred individual birds, as we do at our rural feeding station, things can get whitewashed in a hurry, and it's not nice — for the birds or for their poor human servants who have to refill the feeders.

Keep cleaning stuff handy

I keep a pair of rubber boots by the front door that I wear only to fill the feeders, so that I don't track all that stuff through the house. At the feeding station, I keep an old spatula, a couple of chopsticks, and a scrub brush. The spatula is great for clearing away seed hulls on table and hopper feeders. The chopsticks can quickly ream out drainage holes or get at gunk stuck below feeding ports in tube feeders. The scrub brush, with a bucket of hot water, takes care of that sickly sweet-smelling sunflower guck that accumulates in wet weather. It's made up of bits of uneaten sunflower meats, hulls, and goodness knows what else. Phew.

When I'm truly in a Teutonic frenzy, I get out the Clorox and make a solution of one part bleach to nine parts hot water. I soak the feeders in this, scrub them out, douse the platforms and scrub them . . . just do a good number on the whole feeding station.

Clean up for healthy birds

There are good reasons other than one's personal hygienic orientation to keep your feeders well-cleaned. Disease. Yup. You can do a whole lot of good by feeding birds. But you can also do harm by inviting so many guests to one table because, unlike most human dinner guests over two years of age, birds poop while they eat. Being birds, they don't pay a whole lot of attention to where, either. It's not something birds have to deal with when they're flying around free, but when you get a couple hundred birds in maybe 20 square feet, you have a poopfest. And along with this goes the potential for spreading disease in your feeder flock.

Watch where the food falls

To get around this problem, you can start by keeping your ground feeding out from under the hanging feeders and perches. I usually throw the seed in a wide circle outside the immediate feeder area, and I keep changing the place I throw it. Enough seed will fall out of the feeders that you'll always have birds directly under the feeders, too. Remember that brushpile? Not only do we burn it in May, but we also change the brush a few times each winter. If the feeding area gets really disgusting, we move it, lock, stock, and barrel, to a different part of the yard.

When we first started feeding, we hung the feeders right off our deck. Hoo, boy. The flocks sat up on our television antenna in between meals and made a real mess of our deck. If you're into hosing and scrubbing a lot, feeding birds over your deck may be an option, but it's better to hang the feeders over grass, where you won't be walking.

Here's an idea that may work for you. Because the grass under heavily used feeders takes a beating, try spreading bark mulch under your feeders. When it gets full of hulls and droppings, rake it up, compost it, and spread a fresh layer of mulch.

Bird Seed Types

Just like people, birds eat just about anything they can digest. And just like people, all birds have certain food types that they prefer enormously over others. The good news for you is that people have been feeding birds for many decades, so that you get the benefit of all that trial-and-error experimentation. These days, we, the bird-feeding public, already know what foods birds prefer. At the feeders this means seeds.

But which seeds are the best?

Table 7-1 provides the general food preferences for the most common feeder birds of North America. Foods are listed in approximate order of preference. Check out the color section in this book to see what the seeds look like.

Table 7-1	Bird Food Preference Chart
Species	**Preferred Foods**
Quail, pheasants	Cracked corn, millet, wheat, milo
Pigeons, doves	Millet, cracked corn, wheat, milo, niger, buckwheat, sunflower, baked goods
Roadrunner	Meat scraps, hamburger, suet
Hummingbirds	Plant nectar, small insects, sugar solution
Woodpeckers	Suet, meat scraps, sunflower hearts/seed, cracked corn, peanuts, fruits, sugar solution
Jays	Peanuts, sunflower, suet, meat scraps, cracked corn, baked goods
Crows, magpies, and nutcracker	Meat scraps, suet, cracked corn, peanuts, baked goods, leftovers, dog food
Titmice, chickadees	Peanut kernels, sunflower, suet, peanut butter
Nuthatches	Suet, suet mixes, sunflower hearts and seed, peanut kernels, peanut butter
Wrens, creepers	Suet, suet mixes, peanut butter, peanut kernels, bread, fruit, millet (wrens)
Mockingbirds, thrashers, catbirds	Halved apple, chopped fruits, baked goods, suet, nutmeats, millet (thrashers), soaked raisins, currants, sunflower hearts

(continued)

Species	Preferred Foods
Robins, bluebirds, other thrushes	Suet, suet mixes, mealworms, berries, baked goods, chopped fruits, soaked raisins, currants, nutmeats, sunflower hearts
Kinglets	Suet, suet mixes, baked goods
Waxwings	Berries, chopped fruits, canned peas, currants, raisins
Warblers	Suet, suet mixes, fruit, baked goods, sugar solution, chopped nutmeats
Tanagers	Suet, fruits, sugar solution, mealworms, baked goods
Cardinals, grosbeaks, pyrrhuloxias (a type of cardinal)	Sunflower, safflower, cracked corn, millet, fruit
Towhees, juncos	Millet, sunflower, cracked corn, peanuts, baked goods, nutmeats
Sparrows, buntings	Millet, sunflower hearts, black-oil sunflower, cracked corn, baked goods
Blackbirds, starlings	Cracked corn, milo, wheat, table scraps, baked goods, suet
Orioles	Halved oranges, apples, berries, sugar solution, grape jelly, suet, suet mixes, soaked raisins, and currants
Finches, siskins	Thistle (niger), sunflower hearts, black-oil sunflower seed, millet, canary seed, fruits, peanut kernels, suet mixes

In a nutshell, sunflower seed is the best. So if you're just starting out in feeding, I suggest you buy some black-oil sunflower seed at a local hardware store, feed store, specialty bird store, or even at a major retail chain store. But you need to watch out for certain things when buying seed. The following sections describe the best kinds of seed, in descending order of popularity.

Black-oil sunflower

Driving across northern Wisconsin, I was delighted by mile after mile of golden sunflowers nodding in the breeze, heralds of a quiet revolution in bird feeding. First, there was bread for feed. Then, there was sunflower seed, the gray-striped or white-striped kind, with thick, woody shells accessible only to heavy-billed cardinals and grosbeaks as well as birds like jays, chickadees, and titmice, which can hammer the thick shell open with their bill as they hold the seed in their toes. Since then, black-oil sunflower seed, such as I saw growing in Wisconsin, has almost completely overtaken gray-striped seed in sales.

Smaller than gray-striped sunflower seed, with a thin, all-black, papery shell, black-oil sunflower seed can be cracked by sparrows, juncos, and even small-billed goldfinches. It's a better buy, too, because 70 percent of each seed is meat, compared to only 57 percent for striped sunflower. Its high oil and fat content helps birds get through cold winter nights. Black-oil sunflower seed is the heart of any feeding program because it's the seed accepted by the greatest variety of birds. You can feed it out of hanging feeders, put it in hoppers or on tables, or scatter it on the ground — preferably all of the above.

Have a sunflower heart

If I were to pick only one food to offer at my feeding station, it would be sunflower hearts. Yes, they're expensive, but a bag of sunflower hearts (no shells, just the meat of the seed) lasts more than three times as long as a bag of seeds with shells. Not only this, but every species that comes to my feeding station eats them. Being hull-less, hearts are accessible to weaker billed birds like siskins, redpolls, and Carolina wrens. Goldfinches love them.

Keep dry

Compared to seeds with hulls, hearts are relatively free of waste and of the messy shells that pile up to smother grass and rot decks. The only drawback is that the hearts shouldn't be exposed to wet weather; thus, they should be fed only from feeders. They rot quickly when damp. On dry days, it's fine to spread a handful on the bird table, but otherwise, stick to weatherproof feeders. You'll be surprised how little it takes to feed a lot of birds.

Getting a good mix

Mixed seed, often generically referred to as "wild bird seed," is a vital addition to any feeding program. Not all mixes are created equal, however, and what is eagerly eaten in Arizona can go to waste in New York. A prime example is milo, a round, reddish seed that looks like a BB. You'll see it, along with wheat, oats, and even barley, in the grocery-store mixes mentioned next in this chapter. In the East, milo and wheat are spurned by most birds except blackbirds and doves. In the West, however, quail, doves, towhees, and sparrows eagerly eat milo.

CAREFUL

Don't look for it at the grocery store!

Grocery stores may have lots to offer people, but they're mostly in the Dark Ages where birds are concerned. The wild bird feed offered at the supermarket is usually of the lowest quality available, for the highest price! Packed in small, five- or ten-pound bags, grocery store mixes are usually full of wheat, barley, and milo, seeds that most birds, at least in the eastern half of the country, ignore.

To find bird seed, go to a feed store, or hardware store, or speciality bird store that carries bird feed and feeders — and buy it in bulk. It pays to know what you're after. If your local grocery store has good mixtures of readily eaten seed types, that's great! You're lucky.

Millet

Despite certain regional preferences, birds everywhere will eat some foods. Go for a mix that consists primarily of white proso millet, a little, round, shiny, cream-colored seed. It's a staple for most sparrows and juncos, and birds as diverse as doves, Carolina wrens, thrashers, and cardinals will eat it, too.

The malarkey about milo

In 1987, *Bird Watcher's Digest* (which I humbly edit) published an article about bird feeding that really illustrates how vastly different bird food preferences can be from region to region. The author of the article pointed out how the birds at his feeders never touched the milo seeds, making them a waste as a bird food. Alongside the article, we ran a cartoon that showed one bird saying to another "Real birds don't eat milo."

As soon as the article and cartoon appeared, *BWD* received several letters from readers in Arizona, New Mexico, and California singing the praises of milo. Doves, quail, towhees, and other ground-feeding birds of the Southwest

loved milo. These folks wouldn't part with their milo for a second. And just who did we think we were?

As astute journalists, we investigated further and discovered that, indeed, milo was readily eaten by many western species while eastern birds largely ignored it. Western birds that ate the milo seemed to be better able to crack or digest these hard little seeds. Their wimpier eastern cousins hadn't figured it out yet. (Maybe they were afraid of breaking their beaks?) Why the difference? Who knows? Suffice it to say that bird tastes and preferences (like those of people) vary widely from place to place.

Cracked corn

The second foolproof ingredient of a mix is cracked corn, which is accepted by most birds after the sunflower and millet is gone. Cracked corn is the cheapest and best offering for quail, pheasants, and doves, but it's irresistible to blackbirds, cowbirds, grackles, and house sparrows. If you're inundated by these less-desirable birds, you may want to pull in your corn horns.

Sunflower seed and other ingredients

The third ingredient of a good mix is our old buddy, black-oil sunflower seed. Peanut hearts, which are small, rather bitter byproducts of peanut processing, make bird seed mixes smell good (which is nice for us), boost the price (which is nice for retailers), and may appeal to chickadees, titmice, jays, and wrens. Peanut hearts are not vital and, in my experience, the sunflower always goes first anyway. This isn't to devalue whole peanuts as a food — they can be great if offered in the right feeder.

Other options: thistle and safflower

A couple of the more obscure seeds have their adherents.

Niger, or **thistle seed,** is imported from Africa and Asia. The seed is sterilized, so it won't germinate and take over backyards all over North America. Lots of people are under the misapprehension that thistle seed is the only thing American goldfinches eat. I have a couple of hundred goldfinches here who would faint if I served them this expensive little treat; they do just fine on black-oil sunflower.

In addition to being expensive, niger is subject to mold, especially in hot, damp weather, and you have to shake your feeders every time you fill them to be sure the seed is coming out of the ports properly. If the seed clumps, you may have to dump it out where the birds won't find it, and wash and dry your feeder before refilling it. Fine mesh "thistle socks" are a cheap way to feed niger, and they let air circulate around the seed. I hear from a lot of people about batches of niger that the birds just won't eat; it looks fine, smells fine, but probably tastes bad. All in all, sunflower is a better all-around choice.

Safflower is a white, shiny, conical seed that's gaining popularity among people who find that cardinals like it, and some squirrels and grackles don't. The operative word in that statement is some. Lots of squirrels love safflower seed. You may want to try it and see. Safflower seed is usually found in bulk at better feed stores. You can offer it in any feeder that dispenses sunflower seed, or scatter it on the ground to attract cardinals (who aren't much for perching on tube feeders). Once again, safflower seed is nice to offer, but not vital; any bird that eats safflower will also take sunflower seed.

Other Bird Foods

You can offer birds a vast array of other foods besides bird seed. Here are a few of the most commonly offered parts of the birds' smorgasbord.

Bready or not

Birds and bread just seem to go together in most people's minds. As a child, the first food I ever offered birds was stale white bread. The common backyard birds — house sparrows, starlings, grackles, robins, and mocking-birds — were attracted to it. Bread is fine, but there's so much more!

Baked goods are a valuable side component of any feeding program. Crumble old muffins, doughnuts, cornbread, or cake in along with the seed on your platform feeder. It's a pleasant surprise to the birds that are, unbeknownst to you, always checking out your feeders. Insect-eaters like wrens, mockingbirds, thrashers, and woodpeckers often welcome baked goods, and will quickly spirit chunks away to hide in private stashes in the woods. Don't feed visibly moldy bread or baked goods that have gone rock-hard, though — the birds just ignore it.

Peanuts

Peanuts are a vital part of my feeding program. Offered in the shell, only crows, jays, and the occasional clever titmouse can really exploit them, because peanuts are just too big and cumbersome for most birds to crack open. Better feed and bird-seed stores, though, sell raw, shelled peanuts in bulk. Because I can't always find these in my area, I buy the cheapest, unsalted, roasted cocktail peanuts (sold in jars).

Offer these peanuts in a feeder that keeps larger birds from carrying them away whole. You can use a sturdy nylon mesh onion bag to hold them and hang it from a wire, or you can easily make your own peanut feeder out of $1/4$-inch mesh hardware cloth (see Figure 7-5). Roll the mesh hardware cloth into a cylinder, crimp the bottom shut, cut and fold over a flap for the top, secure it with a piece of wire, and hang it where squirrels can't reach it. And make sure that you don't leave any sharp wires protruding that may injure a bird.

The idea is to allow birds to peck small bits out of the peanuts, not carry whole nuts off. Peanuts offer a great, high-protein boost to winter-weary birds, and help insect-eaters like wrens, woodpeckers, and sometimes even sapsuckers make it through.

Figure 7-5:
A white-breasted nuthatch at a peanut feeder.

Peanuts can be subject to mold in hot, wet weather. Check them often for signs of black mold or the darkening in color that can mean they've gone rancid. Offer only as many as the birds will eat in a few days in warmer weather conditions, doling them out like the gold they are.

Peanut butter: the universal bait

When I was in college, my biology instructor, while showing us how to set live traps for small mammals, referred to peanut butter as "The Universal Bait." "You can catch anything from an elephant to a shrew with peanut butter," he stated.

I started keeping a jar in my dorm room for those late-night munchies. I kept a parakeet named Amaretta, too, and one particularly desperate night I found my hunger unbearable. I remember sticking my finger in the peanut butter jar, and then dipping it in her millet seed. For me. Crunchy and delicious! Universal bait, indeed. (Don't try this at home.)

You probably won't have too many elephants, shrews, or college sopho-mores in your yard if you offer peanut butter, but the woodpeckers, chicka-dees, and titmice will love you for it. You can make a simple peanut butter feeder by drilling shallow one-inch holes in a piece of scrap wood, filling them with peanut butter, and hanging it up near your feeders.

Gouge out a few toeholds underneath each hole to help the birds cling. If the food goes unrecognized, try sticking a few sunflower seeds in the peanut butter — the birds soon get the idea and be back for more. Now you know what to do with those jars of PB in the back of the cabinet, the ones that are just a little too old to devote to toast, or late-night snacking. Soon, you may be buying the cheapest store brands you can find to keep up with the feathered fans.

Suet is fat city

Suet is the dense, white fat that collects around beef kidneys and loins. You'll find it in most grocery store meat counters, sometimes rolled into balls with mixed birdseed on the outside. Avoid this, and just buy it by the chunk; it's cheaper.

You'll be surprised at how many different species eat suet, including some you may need to look up in the field guide. All the regular seed-eaters — chickadees, titmice, nuthatches, woodpeckers — eat suet, as well as wrens, sapsuckers, warblers, orioles, catbirds, creepers, and other birds. A little suet goes a long way.

Keep a couple of things in mind about suet, though. Be sure not to mistake the inedible white "rind" left when all the fat is pecked away for edible suet. And in warm weather, put very small pieces out, as it liquefies and turns rancid after a few days in the hot sun.

Build a suet feeder

Suet is best offered in hardware cloth cages (see Figure 7-6) that are hung by wires, or wired to posts or the trunks of trees (change the location if you notice any bark splitting, disease, or other ill effects on the tree). A natural suet feeder that attracts woodpeckers can be made by drilling one-inch holes in a small log and then suspending it from a wire. You can use a ball-peen hammer to pound fresh suet into the holes.

If you have trouble with jays, crows, and squirrels stealing the suet, you may want to go back to the hardware cloth standby, which keeps whole chunks of suet from disappearing. If starlings plague you, hang your suet log by wires from both ends so that all the holes are upside-down. Doing this poses no problem to small, acrobatic chickadees and woodpeckers, but discourages the less-agile starlings.

Avoid suet spoilage

Suet left out in the hot sun turns into rancid suet. If you smell it once, you'll never let it get that gross again. And think about the poor birds! With little or no sense of smell to warn them away! There oughta be a law! Rancid suet is no good for birds, and may make them sick.

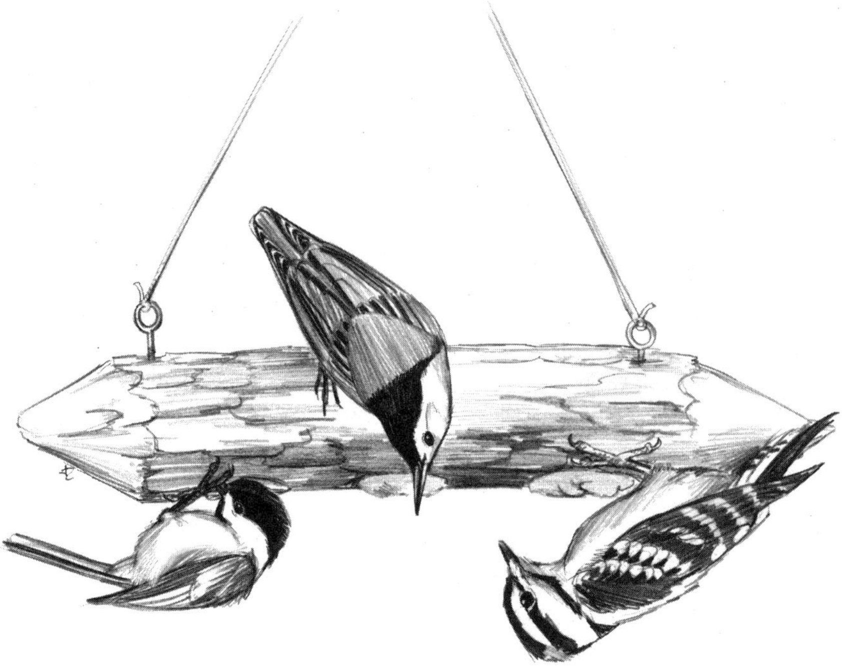

Figure 7-6:
A black capped chickadee, a white-breasted nuthatch (on top), and a downy woodpecker (on right) at a suet feeder.

If you feel you must offer suet all summer, consider doing one of these things:

- ✔ Offer suet in a cool, shaded location. Monitor the suet so if it does go bad, you can remove it.
- ✔ Bring your suet inside during the hot part of the day.
- ✔ Offer one of the commercially available, rendered-suet cakes. Rendered suet doesn't melt so readily.

Render or not

Lots of people like to render suet. They say rendered suet keeps better and is easier to handle because the suet is harder, once it sets up. They melt the suet in the microwave. Then, while the suet is still liquid, they add special ingredients like peanut butter, cornmeal, flour, or chopped peanuts and sunflower hearts. Then they refrigerate or freeze the suet in blocks that fit easily into the commercial suet feeders.

Render the suet outside, if render you must! I tried rendering suet inside in an electric frypan once. Before we moved it outside on the deck, it made the house smell like a cheap diner, it took a long time to make, and then I had a greasy skillet to wash. I went back to offering the raw, unrendered fat, and the birds didn't miss a beat.

Buy suet blocks

Lots of people take convenience a step further and buy commercial suet blocks. Some of these blocks are great; some aren't so great.

Avoid commercial blocks that have whole seed, like sunflower and millet seed, melted into them. These blocks are difficult for birds to use because they can't crack the fat-soaked shells, and they wind up just picking the seeds out of the suet and discarding them.

If you buy blocks, buy those with 100-percent-edible ingredients like peanut hearts, sunflower hearts, chopped raisins, or cornmeal.

In my experience, the fuss of rendering suet, or the expense of buying blocks, isn't justified by any greater enthusiasm on the part of the birds who eat it. They're just as happy with the meat-counter lumps. But do offer suet as part of your feeding program, and you'll be rewarded by lots of interesting woodpecker behavior. Woodpeckers will gladly visit suet feeders year-round. We have whole families of downy, red-bellied, and even hairy woodpeckers all summer and winter. They're just as glad not to have to peck out a living all the time. Think about it: If you had a choice between having chili served in a bowl or having to open the can with your teeth, wouldn't you pick the bowl?

Fruit-full results

When I noticed yellow-bellied sapsuckers, robins, and pileated woodpeckers eating the last shriveled apples and pears in our orchard, I began offering halved apples, impaled on short twigs of the dead branches we put up all around our feeder. Red apples were eaten by red-bellied woodpeckers, sapsuckers, house finches, robins, and starlings, while green ones went untouched. I'm not sure why the birds had this preference. Where's Dr. Know-It-All when you really need him? Or her?

Other fruits you can offer in winter include raisins and currants. These fruits need to be chopped up and soaked in hot water to soften them. Mockingbirds, catbirds, wrens, and thrashers appreciate these most, although bluebirds and other thrushes sometimes take them, too.

Save halved oranges and fruits such as cherries, peaches, bananas, and berries for spring and summer, when the orioles and tanagers that prefer them are back from the tropics.

Summer Feeding

The joy of bird feeding doesn't have to stop when the weather turns warmer and many of your winter feeder visitors vamoose. Summer is the time of year to switch feeding gears, to tailor your offerings to suit the tastes and preferences of a new set of visitors.

Even most of the resident or year-round birds that are feeder regulars change their dining habits in the warmer months. Why? Because they have an abundance of natural food available: insects, fruits, and new plant growth such as buds, nuts, and seeds. Cardinals, for example, switch over to a more insect-oriented diet. They don't shun the sunflower seed at your feeder, but they may not hang out at the feeder all day long chowing down like they did in January. It's still a good idea to keep the feeders going, and to offer many of the old standby foods. Ah, but there's more you can do. . . .

Hummingbirds

If you're lucky enough to live along the Gulf of Mexico, in southern Florida, in South Texas, Arizona, southern California, or along the temperate Pacific Coast, you get to see hummingbirds all year long.

For the rest of us, the poor hummerless masses, it's a long wait from each fall to early spring when the hummingbirds return to our midst. And for those of us east of the Rocky Mountains, we're only waiting for one species (the ruby-throated hummingbird) to return! It's kind of pitiful when you think about it, so I'm not going to (especially since it's 10 degrees outside and snowing right now).

Hummingbirds are named for the sound their wings make as they fly. These tiny birds are so small that they're sometimes confused with insects. Hummingbirds are perfectly built flying machines, capable of hovering in place and flying backwards, upside down, and any way you can imagine.

The method of feeding for hummingbirds is to hover in front of flowers, probing deep inside the blossoms for sweet nectar that the plants produce. This type of flying is very energy intensive. To keep up with their own energy demands, hummingbirds eat an energy-packed diet of plant nectar and small insects.

Any yard in North America can attract hummingbirds during the warmer months of the year. And, most of the hummingbirds native to this continent are reliable visitors to hummer feeders in some part of their range. What attracts a hummer's attention better than anything are bright flowers.

For a complete rundown on flowers and feeders for happy hummingbirds, see Chapter 11.

Other summer visitors

Hummingbirds aren't the only birds around to feed in the summer. Resident birds take advantage of a feeding station that's still in operation, even though most of their diet may have shifted to insects and natural fruits. And migrant songbirds sometimes take advantage of feeders during the warmer months. This section doesn't cover all of the summer feeder visitors that may come to your feeding station, but it does hit the highlights.

Orioles and tanagers

Among the most colorful of all the North American birds are the orioles and tanagers. These birds spend the winter months in Central and South America, where they feed on fruit and insects. When they return to our midst in the spring, crafty feeder operators have orange halves hanging out in the open where curious birds can spot them. These exotic fruits may be strange to resident robins, but tropical migrants recognize them as food. Refer to your field guide for the oriole and tanager species in your part of the continent.

If you live in the southernmost tier of states, you've got an excellent chance of attracting fruit-eaters because citrus fruit grows in your area.

Because these species are not regulars at feeders, you need to put the fruit where it appears to be naturally occurring, such as in a tree. Sections or halves of orange, grapefruit, melon, grapes, pomegranate, and any other tropical fruit will appeal to these fruit-eaters.

Orioles are nectar-lovers, too, though most hummingbird feeders aren't suited to the orioles' large size and lack of hovering skills. Offer nectar for orioles in small, wide-mouthed jars, hung by a wire looped around the neck of the jar. Tie a bright orange ribbon or silk flower to the top of the jar and hang the jar from a sturdy branch in the outer canopy of a small tree, where an oriole is sure to spot it. Don't add artificial color to the nectar; just make it up with 4 parts water to 1 part sugar. Lots of people swear by grape jelly, offered in the same type of jar, for wooing orioles.

I had a pair of orioles come faithfully to my feeders all one summer. The male took nectar from a jar, while the female turned up her beak at that and went for the protein-rich suet. She had a nest to build, eggs to lay, and babies to feed, and needed all the energy she could get.

Young birds

The best thing about summer feeding is the glimpse it offers into the family lives of familiar birds. We're accustomed to having our feeders mobbed with adult birds all winter, but it can be really fun to watch a few resident breeding pairs exploit our feeder, and then bring their peeping, begging young to teach them how to freeload, too.

Two feeder offerings that are really good for young birds are suet and unsalted cocktail peanuts. They're high in protein, and lack troublesome hulls that can thwart tender young beaks. Offer these foods in hardware-cloth cages that keep the birds from absconding with big chunks of food. You'll have to keep a sharp eye on such rich foods in hot weather; put out only as much as will be cleaned up in a few days. If suet starts to melt or smell rancid — or if peanuts turn dark, smell rancid, or get moldy — toss out the stinky stuff, wash the feeders, and replace the offerings. Usually, birds clean you out before this happens. We had two families of downy woodpeckers, one family of red-bellied woodpeckers, and a family of the uncommon hairy woodpeckers all using our suet and peanut feeders last summer.

EEK! A worm!

If you don't mind handling squirmy creatures, put out a dish of mealworms. These protein-rich beetle larvae are odorless, non-slimy, easy to handle, and can be obtained from a bait store or by mail-order (see the Appendix). Mealworms are a potent bait for breeding and migrant songbirds, being 30 percent protein by dry weight. Catbirds, mockingbirds, orioles, and especially bluebirds quickly become common visitors to your mealworm feeding station. To keep the worms from crawling away, you can contain them in a low glass dish. Put the dish wherever such birds frequently perch, as on a deck railing or near a birdbath.

Remember to be patient! It may take a while for the birds to notice, but once you have their attention, you can keep it by keeping up the offerings. Some birds become so hooked on mealworms that they'll take them from your hand over time. By then, you'll have become accustomed to ordering mealworms in bulk, by the thousand. No, I'm not kidding.

As you make your morning omelet, rinse and save the eggshells. Put them on a cookie sheet and bake them in a 250-degree oven until they're just beginning to brown. This disinfects them and makes them easier to digest. Crumble them into small bits and scatter them on table feeders, deck railings, flat rocks, sidewalks, or bare ground. You'll be amazed at the array of birds who come to eat them! Female birds need calcium to replace that lost in egg-laying, and you'll get rare looks at secretive woodland species attracted by the bright white shells. Soon, you may be asking your friends to save their eggshells or haunting area fast-food restaurants for the shells from their breakfast offerings.

Chapter 8

Tackling Pests and Other Feeder Problems

. . . .

In This Chapter

▶ When trouble comes knocking

▶ Problems to avoid

▶ Squirrelly pests and raccoon bandits

▶ Sick and injured birds

. . . .

*B*ird feeding isn't all sunshine and daisies. After you get your feeding station going, you're bound to run into some challenges, frustrations, and downright infuriating problems. The problems that seem to be almost universal are: pest species (birds that you don't want around), squirrels, and sick and injured birds.

Pest Species

A *pest species* is any bird you don't want at your feeders. For some feeder operators, this means starlings and other blackbirds. For others it may be rock doves (pigeons) or even blue jays. For us, at our feeders, it's house sparrows. We dislike these fat, chattering little annoyances because they're non-native to this continent (they're an import from Europe that's made a good living here) and because they're known to kill bluebirds when competing for a nest box (see Chapter 11).

Discouraging blackbirds, doves, and sparrows

The best way to rid yourself of an annoying species is to observe what seed type or food it's eating and then stop offering that food. It seems simple, but it works better than asking the birds to leave in a kind tone of voice.

✔ To get rid of blackbirds, stop offering cracked corn.

✔ To get rid of doves, quit with the mixed seed already.

✔ Stop both of these seed types to discourage house sparrows.

Jays? Well, definitely stop offering peanuts. The jays will switch to sunflower seeds, but hey, you should appreciate jays for being the obnoxious feeder pigs they are. Live and let live.

Getting rid of house finches

What can you do if you're inundated with house finches, and you'd rather not be? Try removing the perches from your tube feeders. House finches are lousy clingers, and this should throw them. There's also a thistle seed feeder on the market that has perches set above the feed ports, which forces birds to hang upside down to access the seed. This is no trick for goldfinches, but house finches find it beyond them. Globe feeders, as mentioned in Chapter 7, can also give them pause, at least for a while.

I can attest that flinging yourself at the window yelling "Booger! Booger!" is successful only in the short term. It's hard to smirk with a hard little beak, but house finches can, and do. If you've got 'em, you may as well learn to enjoy 'em. And remember that bird populations fluctuate naturally. You can always hope that some year the house finch hordes will just fluctuate on out of here.

Squirrels

He was the Flying Wallenda of squirrels. He scaled a thin electrical cable three stories up a sheer brick wall to the Valhalla of my windowsill feeder, and appeared one morning, and every morning thereafter, sitting fat and sassy in a pile of sunflower hulls. Challenged, he'd hurriedly retreat down the cable. As time went on and he devoured more and more seed, keeping the birds hungry, I got less and less considerate about how I routed him. I took to rushing into the room, throwing the window open, and grabbing for him. This would send him on a wild leap out into space, legs splayed, tail spinning for balance, to land with a thud on the lawn three stories below. Unhurt, but mad as you-know-what, he'd start plotting his next ascent as soon as he caught his breath. I hated that squirrel, but I had to admire his resilience.

Eavesdrop at any wild bird store, any feed store counter, and you'll hear talk about squirrels; endless talk about the machinations people go through to thwart them, and the astonishingly fast end-runs the squirrels make around these plans. The darn things may as well have wings for what they're capable of. A gray squirrel can jump $3^1/_2$ feet high from a standing start, broad-jump with a running start 10 feet or more to reach a hanging feeder from an overhanging tree or roof, and it can dangle by its toes from incredibly fine twigs and drop down onto your feeder. Spiderman would hang his head.

Squirrel-proof feeders

Naturally, bird feeder designers have been addressing the squirrel problem since the first sunflower sprouted from the primordial ooze. And the results have shown that there's really no such thing as squirrel-proof. What follows are some examples of what bird-feeder designers have tried:

- ✔ The simplest squirrel-proof feeders are enclosed in a wire cage whose mesh allows small birds inside, while blocking the squirrels.

- ✔ More complex and touchy feeders are precisely counter-weighted to close the feed ports when a heavy bird or squirrel steps on the feeding platform. (In my experience, the squirrels then learn how to open the top of the feeder, or hang by their toes from the top to avoid tripping the lever.)

- ✔ A relatively recent, battery-driven design delivers a mild shock to marauding squirrels, who must stand on a metal tray to access metal feed ports, and thereby complete a circuit — yow! Birds sit either on the metal tray or on the perches, but can't touch both at once.

Baffling squirrels

The best squirrel-proof feeders employ one simple principle: slipperiness.

- ✔ Plexiglas witch hats or domes covering the top of hanging feeders — the bigger the better — can effectively prevent drop-ins. Hang such feeders four feet or more off the ground and far away from any limbs from which squirrels could mount a lateral assault.

- ✔ I've had the most success at foiling squirrels by suspending a thin, taut wire from two eaves of my house, from which I then suspend my feeders. Using clothespins or knots of wire as stops (to keep the feeders from sliding together in the middle), I hang an array of feeders in a relatively squirrel-proof arrangement.

- ✔ When the occasional furry brainiac learns to walk the wire, I break out the 35-mm film canisters and string them like beads in a row on the wire. The little plastic cylinders spin, making footing treacherous. On the same principle, you can use one-foot lengths of garden hose, two or three placed end-to-end on the wire.

✔ Other people have had success with a couple of plastic soda bottles, skewered lengthwise on the wire, and acting as spinning baffles on either end.

The idea behind all of the preceding methods is to create a wide enough obstacle that the squirrel is unable to walk or jump over it without falling off the wire — creating an effective baffle.

Hot and spicy deterrents

Food additives containing hot pepper receive mixed reviews. They work for some people. Others report that squirrels initially refuse the hot seed, then grow accustomed to it, even learning to love it. It's easy to get the hot pepper in your eyes when filling feeders at or above eye level, and hard to forget that special feeling. No one really knows if birds are affected by the scorching capsaicin, an extract of chile peppers. I can attest that parrots, at least, can detect it, and actually like it, but I'm not so sure that juncos and grosbeaks, cold-blooded Northerners that they are, feel the same. *Arriba!*

Let them eat corn

Advocates of the *laissez*-eat school of squirrel management simply spread enough food, particularly whole corn, on the ground to keep the squirrels satisfied.

Some of these advocates are glassy-eyed veterans of lengthy and intensive live-trapping-and-transporting programs. In suburban areas, trapping and transporting animals is an exercise in futility because legions, troops, and masses of subordinate and immature animals are waiting in the wings to occupy prime territory in a yard with feeders.

My wife's father once lamented, "I keep taking squirrels out, and the ones that come in get scrawnier and scrawnier, and there are more and more of them! I miss the ones I started with!"

There's something to be said for humoring the squirrels you've got. They're dominant animals who may aggressively keep great numbers of subordinate animals out of your yard.

Rocky Raccoon

In talking about furry perils, none is more powerful or wily than the raccoon. If a squirrel is a bicycle, a raccoon is a monster truck. If a squirrel is Tori Spelling, a raccoon is Meryl Streep. Almost everything a squirrel can do (except maybe jump), a raccoon can do bigger — and better. Raccoons have the added bonus of being able to totally destroy any feeder on the market, dragging it off into the woods to have their way with it. Raccoons are an increasing problem in both rural and suburban areas as they exploit garbage cans, outdoor pet food, and bird-feeding stations.

You can use the same principles of slipperiness and obstacle-placing to stop raccoons that you use for squirrels, but the baffles need to be bigger and stronger:

- Conical baffles should be 30 inches across, and stovepipe baffles at least two-feet long.
- Suspending feeders from wires works well because raccoons can't walk wires or jump very far at all.

Raccoons are smart — smarter than a lot of people. What keeps them at bay for a week or a month may, one fine night, not work anymore. A raccoon chewed the lid off my extra-tough seed-storage can that probably would have stopped a Ginsu knife. I've had raccoons take down and destroy hummingbird feeders, rip down suet feeders, dismantle tube feeders, and scale ridiculously thin and slick metal poles of platform feeders.

A warning about raccoons — don't, whatever you do, try to keep them satisfied by feeding them elsewhere in your yard. You'll soon be hosting 20 or 30 raccoons every night and giving every other neighbor in your area big headaches. With the potential for raccoon rabies present and growing, especially in the Northeast, feeding raccoons at all is ill-advised.

Sick Birds

Sooner or later, you're going to look out at your feeder and see a bird all puffed up, huddling miserably in the cold. It's sick, and it's come to your yard to die. What to do?

It sounds kind of mean, but doing nothing is your best course. Chances are small that the bird has a disease communicable to humans, but it's really best not to handle a sick bird. By the time a bird is debilitated enough to allow you to catch it by hand, its chances of recovery are pretty small. Leave it alone, and a hawk, owl, crow, jay, or other natural predator will end its suffering soon.

The cold, hard fact is that bird feeding, with its crowding and concentration of birds, can promote disease in wild populations.

Common diseases

Several diseases are common to feeder birds. One of the most prevalent in recent years is blindness, caused by an organism called *Mycoplasma gallisepticum*. It's carried mainly by house finches, but can infect other feeder species such as goldfinches. Affected birds show swelling of the eyes, with loss of sight. This disease has spread very rapidly across the country, and may serve to limit the overpopulation of house finches at feeders. Every population has its checks and balances, and population explosions invite disease.

Look at a large flock of grackles and blackbirds at a feeder, and you're bound to see one with a deformed foot or lesions around the eyes. That's likely to be *avian pox,* a viral disease. Blue jays get *gapeworms* that multiply in their throats and make it hard for them to swallow. Although you almost never see sickly birds out in the wild, around feeders you see more disease because the sick birds are attracted to easy food resources as their strength dwindles.

Although licensed to rehabilitate sick and injured songbirds, most rehabilitators don't want to endanger their other animal patients by bringing in a moribund feeder bird. It's best not to handle them, especially if you don't know what disease you're dealing with.

Who you gonna call?

If you're determined to help, you can start by calling your state or provincial department of natural resources, which should keep a listing of wildlife rehabilitators in your area. You can call and describe the bird's symptoms to the rehabilitator, and allow him or her to decide whether intervention is called for. Be aware that most small animal veterinarians don't treat or handle wild birds. Save yourself some time, trouble, and heartache and call first, before attempting to bring a sick bird in.

If you're seeing several sick birds around your feeder, you should consider stopping your feeding program, at least for a while. You can take the feeders in, soak them in a solution of one part bleach to nine parts water, allow them to dry, and re-hang them in a different part of the yard. Serious disease

BACKYARD TIP

Tips for a clean and healthy feeding station

Follow these tips to keep your feeding station bird-friendly:

- To make sure that seed is feeding properly, give hanging feeders a good shake before refilling. Shake out or pry out with a stick any compacted seed in the bottom. A spoon or spatula is handy for removing old seed from platform and hopper feeders before refilling. You can keep these outside, at the feeding station, for convenience.

- To clean feeders, remove all the old seed residue. Soak feeders in a light water/bleach solution (9 parts water to 1 part bleach) and scrub well. A bottle brush helps to clean tube feeders. Rinse and air-dry before refilling.

- To avoid contamination, limit ground feeding directly below hanging feeders. Rotate ground-feeding areas frequently.

- Rake up and remove accumulated hulls and droppings. Spread mulch (bark or wood chips) below feeders, raking it up when soiled and replacing it with new.

- In humid or wet conditions, feed only from weatherproof feeders. Check frequently for mold. Put out only as much seed as will be eaten in one day.

Be sure to thoroughly wash your hands after filling, handling, and cleaning your feeders.

---

problems may merit stopping altogether until the afflicted birds disperse and/or die. You could be offsetting the nice food subsidy you offer by exposing large numbers of birds to disease. A call to your department of natural resources may help you decide which course to take.

Window Strikes

If you've fed birds for any length of time, you know the sound — that sickening THUNK of a bird meeting plate glass. Birds hit windows not because they're stupid, but because they evolved in a world without glass. Usually, they see the sky and trees reflected and unwittingly fly toward the mirage, especially when startled. The problem may be exacerbated by overcast skies. Most solutions to this problem involve breaking up the reflections on the glass.

Many people report success with hawk-shaped window stickers, or strips of foil hanging from the eaves. A few long, one-inch-wide strips cut from plastic garbage bags and hanging in front of the offending window may help, as can a thin coat of artificial snow sprayed on the inside of the window. I tacked some fine branches to the sill of a small but deadly window, which formed a barrier to the birds but hardly impeded the view.

Itty-bitty birdy feet

"Won't birds freeze their little feet off on the metal perches of my feeders? It's 20° below zero, and there they are, sitting on freezing metal perches! How do they do it?"

I have to confess, I'm in awe of a creature weighing little more than a first-class letter, surviving in winter's howling blizzards. First, they keep their furnaces stoked. That's where you come in. Tote those bags, stoke those feeders. Second, bird feet aren't like yours and mine. They're little more than bone and sinew and scale, not very richly supplied with nerves, so they don't feel the cold quite as much. But nature has a clever way of keeping them warm and functional, when you'd think they'd freeze off. It's called the *rete mirabile*, or miraculous net. Warm blood flowing from the heart comes in the arteries, which are interwoven in a fine netlike pattern with the veins, carrying cold blood from the toes. This system warms the cold blood from the extremities before it gets to the heart, and keeps bird feet warm without batteries or mukluks. Because bird feet lack sweat glands, they stay dry, and they won't freeze to the perches, I promise.

Large expanses of plate glass can be the worst. During spring and fall migration, several birds may be killed each day. Look at the feather imprints to determine where most of the collisions occur, and then purchase a length of very sheer nylon netting at a fabric store. Tack it with thin strips of wood to the window frame, stretching it over the worst collision zones. You may also use the black square-mesh crop netting sold at garden stores. Neither obstruct your view, and both help prevent collisions.

If you find a bird lying stunned beneath your window, leave it alone unless predators are near or the weather outside is wet or cold. Put the bird in a small cardboard box in a warm, quiet place until you hear it hopping around; then release the bird near dense cover to give it more time to gather its strength. If the bird is badly injured, call your state department of natural resources, local nature center, or veterinarian for the name of a wildlife rehabilitator who can care for it until it is releasable.

Place an injured bird in a paper grocery bag, lined with a clean rag. The bag keeps the bird hidden from cats and other predators while it is recovering. Once revived the bird can fly out the partially open top of the bag.

Chapter 9
Nest Boxes and Box Monitoring

- -

In This Chapter

▶ Birds that use bird houses

▶ Troubleshooting

▶ Makings of a good bird house

▶ Unwanted tenants

▶ Baffling predators

- -

*N*ot all birds nest in trees, and not all birds use bird houses. In fact, a fairly limited number of species use bird houses, but luckily, those species are found all across the continent.

Bird species that nest in enclosed spaces, especially spaces excavated (or dug out) of wood, earth, or some other dense substance, are known as *cavity nesters.* Of the 600-plus bird species that nest somewhere in North America, most of them do so in open nests — that is, in nests that are some variation of the stereotypical cup-shaped bird's nest. Only about 85 of our breeding birds are true cavity nesters.

That's the bad news. The good news is that attracting one or more of these cavity-nesting species to your property is relatively easy when you provide human-made housing. Before you race to the basement for the hammer and nails, consider a few important points about cavity-nesting birds.

Birds in the House

If you have a reasonable amount of woodland habitat nearby, or your yard is well-planted with bird-friendly, fruit-bearing shrubs and trees, you should be able to attract one or more of these house-using species: wrens, chickadees, titmice, and nuthatches. These species prefer woodland habitat for their nesting environs.

Cavity-nesters that need large expanses of open, grassy habitat include bluebirds, tree and violet-green swallows, and purple martins. Great crested flycatchers and flickers (a kind of woodpecker) may use boxes with two-inch entry holes, placed high up. For the really adventurous, you can attract nesting ducks, especially wood ducks, American kestrels, screech owls, and even barn owls with the proper box placed in the proper habitat.

All the species of birds named above are, to varying degrees, limited in their population growth by the availability of nesting cavities. There's stiff competition for suitable nest sites, so by putting up bird houses that are well-maintained and properly protected from predators, you can actually boost populations of these nest-site limited species in your area. Imagine making bluebirds a common sight, where before they were rare. Could there be a better way to make the world a nicer place? (Aside from eliminating war, pollution, and so on?)

Human-made bird housing

Because you may not have a trusty woodpecker working on your trees creating ideal nest cavities for all the birds in your yard, I suggest you consider buying or building a nest box.

With the booming interest in all things backyard, especially birds, many commercial manufacturers began producing bird feeders and bird houses. Backyards all over North America are littered with these early, poor attempts at producing functional products. As bird houses or nest boxes (the two terms are synonymous), most of these loser products were very appealing to the (human) eye, but the birds didn't use them because the dimensions just weren't right. Either the entrance hole was too small and birds couldn't fit, or the entrance was too large and pest species hogged every available house. Or the interior dimensions of the house were too small. I can go on and on.

Birds, like humans, have their specific housing preferences. If you put up a house that seems perfect for a bluebird, but the entrance hole is too small, the bluebird can't use it. It's important to know what the birds' preferences are.

Here's a hint: If you see a bird house that's so incredibly cute that you simply can't live without it, put the bird house up on a bookshelf in your living room. Why waste it on the birds? You're the one who likes it. If the house designer put that much effort into making a cute or pretty house, chances are that it's meant for humans; it's probably not going to be right for birds. Birds don't care about cute. They prefer function over form. Cute can be okay if the other physical attributes of the housing suit the species you're hoping to attract. But remember: Birds don't *want* housing that is conspicuous to predators.

Before bird houses

What did these birds do before bird houses? Well, they're still doing it — using old woodpecker holes. Woodpeckers are the handy carpenters of the bird world. They chisel out new nest holes each spring, and the next season these old nest holes are ready for other species of birds to move in.

Downy woodpeckers are found nearly everywhere across North America, and they chisel out neat 1½-inch diameter holes, with narrow nesting cavities, in dead trees. It's no accident that 1½-inch is the most common and useful hole size for bird houses. A hole of this size lets small birds like wrens, chickadees, titmice, nuthatches, and bluebirds in while excluding bigger hole-nesters like starlings, which aren't very desirable tenants. More on starlings in a bit.

For millennia, before bandsaws and bird watchers' supply catalogs, hole-nesting birds simply relied on woodpeckers to make their homes, and they still do, in large part. Big woodpeckers make bigger nest cavities; flickers make a 2-inch hole and the crow-sized pileated woodpecker, our continent's largest, makes a whopping rectangular cavern that a wood duck can fit into!

Woodpecker nest cavities drilled in trees have a lot going for them, from a bird's standpoint. By looking at natural cavities, you can understand just what properties a bird nest box should have.

Over time, many bird-house manufacturers have gotten better at producing functional housing for birds, thanks to many great ideas and innovations suggested by folks like you and me — people who made their own houses for birds and tinkered with the design until it earned the birds' seal of approval.

Whether you're buying a bird house or making your own, keep in mind these properties of a good bird house/nest box:

- ✔ **Well-insulated:** A typical woodpecker cavity is in a tree that's five inches or more in diameter, giving the cavity nice, thick walls that keep cold out and heat in — important when you're trying to keep eggs or nestlings warm in March! A bird box is best when made of wood ¾-inch thick or thicker.

- ✔ **Weatherproof:** Natural cavities are often on the underside of a limb, sheltered by an emerging branch above, or on the *lee side* of a tree (the side facing away from the prevailing wind). Nest boxes work best when made of wood that naturally sheds water, such as cedar, or wood treated with (on the outside only) waterproof stain or paint, which you renew when needed.

✔ **Deep:** The cavity bottom, where the nest chamber lies, is often eight inches or more below the entrance hole. This depth helps keep predators from reaching in and grabbing the incubating female, eggs, or young. The best nest boxes for woodland birds are at least eight inches deep.

✔ **Protected from predators:** Woodpecker cavities tend to be very inconspicuous — you hardly notice them. Being hard to spot is the cavities' major protection from predators like snakes, raccoons, cats, and opossums. Human box-builders need to rely on more than conceal-ment to protect their tenants, however: You need to put baffles under your boxes. See the "Baffling Predators" section later in this chapter for details on baffles.

Brace yourself for a blunt statement from yours truly: If you're lukewarm about becoming a landlord to the birds, don't put up a bird nest box. Caring for nest boxes and the birds that use them takes commitment (this chapter gives you an idea of what I'm talking about). Poorly placed and maintained housing can actually do more harm than good. I'm done preaching now. Thanks for listening.

Wait, before you buy or build . . .

Before you go out and buy or build a bunch of bird boxes with which to festoon your yard, do a bit of homework. You'll save yourself, and the birds, a lot of trouble if you find out what species of cavity-nesting birds are in your immediate vicinity.

If you're still working on your identification skills, and you don't know whether wrens, chickadees, titmice, nuthatches, or bluebirds, for example, frequent your yard, check out Chapter 3, ask a knowledgeable friend or neigh-bor, or call your nearest nature center. You may luck out and get someone to come visit your yard, appraise the nearby habitat, and advise you on what birds you can attract with what type of houses.

Otherwise, if you're feeling lazy about obtaining that information (or if you have no information alternatives), you can opt for a box that would be appropriate for the maximum number of cavity-nesting species. For example, the box described in the Backyard Tip serves the needs of many different species, from bluebirds (largest) to house wrens and chickadees (smallest).

An all-purpose bird box that's attractive to most small hole-nesting birds has a hole diameter of $1^1/_2$ inches, an interior depth of at least 8 inches (measured from the bottom of the hole downward), and sides at least 4 inches wide (see Figure 9-1).

Figure 9-1:
Tree
swallows
on a nest
box. They
line their
nests with
feathers.

Universal Truths of Bird Housing

There are some universal truths about putting up and maintaining nest boxes. The first is: The worst place you can put a bird box is on a tree! Yep, you read right. Trees make lousy supports for bird boxes. So do fenceposts. The biggest, furriest reason is the raccoon.

A second universal truth is: If you don't baffle a house against nest predators, sooner or later, a predator gets to the nest and devours its contents.

Raccoon reach

You may not realize it, but across most of the country, a nocturnal patrol of raccoons is looking to take birds, their eggs, and young for dinner. No, not out for dinner! The birds are what the raccoons eat for dinner.

Raccoons are smart, and only one successful raid is needed to figure out that bird nest boxes make nifty lunch boxes. Although a raccoon may walk by a tree with a woodpecker hole high up on its trunk, it's hardly likely to overlook a box nailed to the tree or conspicuously placed on a nearby fencepost. And being a raccoon, it investigates and eats whatever living thing is unlucky enough to be inside.

Snake eyes

Snakes are hard on cavity nesting birds, especially black rat snakes in the East and other rat snakes and bull snakes in the West. Snakes are a whole lot smarter than they look. A black rat snake can climb practically anything, draping its length across fine branches and oozing up tree bark effortlessly. These snakes love birds, their eggs, and young. And few nastier surprises exist, even for reptile-lovers like me, than opening up a nest box that you think is full of baby birds to find a black rat snake sleeping off its bulging meal. Do you have chills?

If you find a snake in a nest box, follow these steps:

1. **Remove the snake from the box using a stick or gloved hands (if you're brave).**

   Be gentle and release the snake unharmed. It's just doing what comes naturally, after all. Snakes are an important part of the ecosystem.

2. **Baffle your nest box pole to prevent further reptilian intrusions.**

   Your baffle should offer no space through which a slithering snake can squeeze. I use $1/4$-inch galvanized mesh hardware cloth. (See the "Baffling Predators" section for a simple and effective baffle design.)

Baffling Predators

The best way to keep your nest-box tenants safe from predators is by using pipes and baffles. Pipes and baffles stop snakes, raccoons, cats, opossums, squirrels, chipmunks, and mice — all those nasty little beasts who love to wreak havoc in bird nest boxes.

Pipe-mounting

My preferred way to mount a bird nest box is on a galvanized metal pipe, stuck two feet in the ground, away from overhanging branches. I use a $3/4$-inch inside diameter plumber's pipe in seven- or eight-foot lengths. That way, with two feet buried solidly in a hole, I've got five or six feet to work with to mount the box. Such galvanized pipe is readily available from most hardware stores. This pipe won't rust and it makes a sturdy, permanent support for your bird box. A piece of pipe buried this way becomes a pole (which is how I refer to it from here onward). You can mount the box on the pole with pipe flanges, or use a threaded screw mount for the base, or you can drill a hole in the pole and wire the box to it. The method doesn't matter much, as long as the box and pole don't swing about in the wind. Pole-mounting your nest boxes allows you to put them wherever you want; you don't need to have a tree or fence post handy.

Pole-mounted baffles

A baffle is a guard that you put beneath the box that keeps animals from climbing up to raid the box. Some baffles on the market are meant to keep squirrels from climbing up to feeders, but they won't stop larger animals such as raccoons, cats, opossums, or snakes. You need a different baffle for all these critters.

Basic baffle design comes in many forms, but in just two main shapes: conical and tubular. _Conical baffles_ are created from a circular piece of material, usually galvanized sheet metal or plastic. A hole the size of the pole's diameter is cut in the center of the sheet metal or plastic (to wrap around the pole), and a cut is made from the edge to the center to allow the piece to be formed into a cone.

Tubular baffles are long tubes of either galvanized metal or PVC plastic. Many longtime nest-box landlords prefer to use sections of stovepipe as baffles. This virtually fool-proof design is called a stovepipe baffle (see Figure 9-2) and is good because it can baffle both mammals and snakes. The tubular baffle is fairly unobtrusive, and it won't self-destruct in a high wind as many large conical baffles do. Here's a bonus: You can make the whole thing for under $10.

How to make a predator baffle

Materials used:

Galvanized pipe with ³/₄-inch inside diameter, in a 7- or 8-foot length

Strapping brackets and weatherproof screws (to mount box to pole)

Hardware cloth (¹/₂-inch mesh)

Machine screws with nuts

Hanger iron (in two 7-inch strips)

Galvanized stovepipe (24 x 7 inches)

With tin snips, cut the hardware cloth into a circle 8 inches in diameter. Place it over the stovepipe, bending the edges down so that it will fit snugly into the pipe, about an inch down from the top (A). Close any gaps between hardware cloth and stovepipe, to prevent snakes from squeezing through.

Next, use tin snips to cut three tabs (B) in the top of the stovepipe. Bend these over the hardware cloth. Cut a small hole in the middle of the cloth to allow the assembly to slip over the box-mounting pipe.

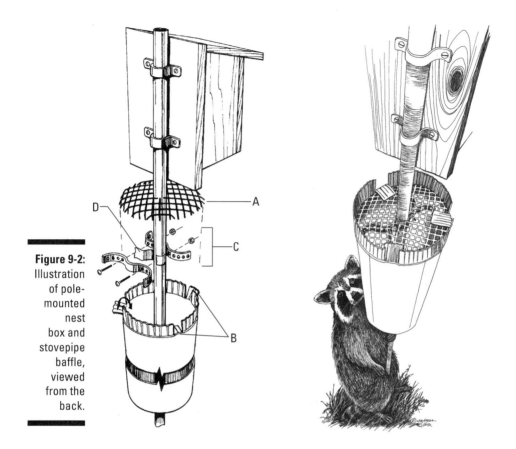

Figure 9-2:
Illustration of pole-mounted nest box and stovepipe baffle, viewed from the back.

Bolt the two strips of hanger iron (C) securely on either side of the mounting pipe, and bend them to support the hardware cloth. Wrap duct tape around the pole (D) to help hold the hanger iron in place. Slip the assembled baffle over the hanger iron bracket, just below the nest box. It should wobble a little; this further discourages climbing predators.

Box-mounted guards

On many boxes available commercially, you see a square of wood perhaps $3/4$-inch thick placed over the entrance hole. This *predator guard* effectively increases the depth of the entrance hole, which is supposed to prevent a predator from reaching in and then reaching down to grab the nest contents. While this guard may work for predatory birds like kestrels, grackles, and jays (which seldom attempt to raid nest boxes), it doesn't work at all for raccoons, cats, opossums, and snakes. A raccoon that finds reaching past the guard into the box difficult, simply chews the guard off, a woody *hors d'oeuvre* before the main meal. And a snake simply glides right through the entrance hole.

Beware of any predator guard that mounts on the box hole. Think of the old analogy: Is it better to put a guard rail along a highway curve at the top of the cliff, or an ambulance at the bottom, awaiting the unlucky souls who drive over the edge? Once a predator is on your bird box, the battle is lost. Baffle them from below, and you'll save more bird lives.

Mounting the Nest Box

If you have a suitable pole upon which to mount a nest box, you're ready to go. But you may have a few other questions.

How high?

It's best to mount boxes at your eye level, about five feet off the ground is a good height for most box-nesting birds. Purple martins, flickers, great crested flycatchers, kestrels, and screech-owls like to be considerably higher. The idea in mounting boxes at eye level is to make looking inside the box and seeing what's going on easy. Five feet is beyond the leaping range of most predators, and it allows you to mount a baffle under the box to prevent them from climbing up.

Get them up anytime

People may tell you that nest boxes must be put up in the springtime, when birds start to sing, mate, and build nests. Actually, nest boxes can be put up any time of year. The longer a nest box is part of your backyard habitat, the more likely birds are to accept and use it. Put a box up in the dead of winter, and it may well serve as a nightly roost for a downy woodpecker, a nuthatch, chickadee, titmouse, or bluebird. The only clue you'll have is a few droppings, feathers, or regurgitated seeds in the bottom of the box, unless you're lucky enough to see the bird enter the box at dusk. Don't be concerned about when you put your nest boxes up; just get them up!

Box Monitoring

If you put a bird box in your yard and then never open it, you're not really sure what went on inside, and you may miss out on a lot of neat stuff. Checking a bird nest box is called _box monitoring_. Monitoring is essential to keeping a bird box habitable, and it enriches your experience as a landlord.

From the time you were very young, you were probably told not to touch bird nests, eggs, or baby birds. "The mother will smell you on her baby, and she won't come back to take care of it," you were warned by some adult. While the particulars are a little off (songbirds have little, if any, sense of smell), this gentle falsehood has done much to protect birds and their young. In fact, birds are so strongly drawn to their nests, eggs, and young that they rarely desert them in the face of the occasional disturbance. This means that you can open a nest box, take a quick peek inside, and even do a little intervention if necessary without fear that you'll cause the birds to desert their nests.

I should emphasize that the box in question needs to be properly mounted, on a pole with a predator baffle, before you attempt to monitor it. The reason for this is, once again, furry. Raccoons and other predators follow human scent trails, hoping they lead to a sandwich crust, some tasty garbage, or something else interesting and edible. They'll follow your scent from box to box, with disastrous results, unless you baffle!

Respecting birds' privacy

Being sensitive to the birds' privacy is important when you monitor your box. You can very well cause desertion if you open the box every day, or raise a commotion by inviting the neighbors over for a viewing. Be discreet, and limit your peeks to one or maybe two per week, and keep them short and sweet.

A baby bird that is still in the nest is called a *nestling*. A young bird that leaves the nest is called a *fledgling*. When a nestling leaves the nest, it is said to be fledging. In most box-nesting birds, the young fledge at the age of 12 to 21 days. The longer the young birds stay in the nest, the better their survival chances are once they leave. This is why I suggest you curtail nest checks when the chicks are about 10 to 12 days of age, so you don't scare them away or hurt their chance for survival.

Remember a couple of caveats when monitoring nests:

- ✔ Stay away while the birds are incubating. Birds are most prone to desertion during this period.

- ✔ Stop your peeking when the babies are about 10 days old. The danger here is that you may frighten the nestlings into leaving the box early. Birds that fledge too soon have greatly reduced chances of survival.

Though the rates of nestling development vary from species to species among cavity-nesting birds, you can use these guidelines, along with species-specific information from a bird field guide or nest reference book, to time your box-monitoring visits:

- ✔ Most small cavity nesters lay one egg per day, often in the morning, until the clutch is complete. Once the clutch is complete, stay away from the nest for a week or more while the adults incubate the eggs.

✔ Once hatching has begun, watch for these signs: Newly hatched birds have closed eyes, little or no feathers, and look like tiny, pink, helpless things. Within a week or so they begin to develop feathers, their eyes open, and they're able to hold their heads up.

✔ As soon as you notice the nestlings becoming mostly covered with developing feathers — especially if the wing feathers are well-developed — cease visiting the nest, fledging time is near. Fledging occurs between two weeks and three weeks from the day the eggs hatched.

As noted previously, after 10 to 12 days, the young birds may react to your intrusion by leaping out of the nest. Once out, they're very hard to put back; they no longer feel safe in their box and keep jumping out. So remember to stop peeking in the box once the babies' eyes are open and the nestlings begin to sprout feathers. Make your observations from afar, and assume that everything's fine as long as the parents return frequently with food.

If you accidentally open a nest box, and find nestlings fully-feathered, bright-eyed, and spilling out of the box, put them back in the box, close it, and plug the entrance hole with a handkerchief or paper towel for a few minutes, until the young birds have settled down. Quietly creep up, remove the barricade, and then leave the vicinity.

Keeping tabs on your titmice

Let's say you've got a nest box in your backyard, and you've noticed a pair of titmice flitting around the entrance. The first thing to do is get a little notebook and start a log of your observations. This process gives you baseline information that can help you in the weeks to come as you monitor your box. Your entries may read:

> *April 15, 1997: Pair of tufted titmice looking in box. Much calling and fluttering around.*

> *April 20: One titmouse entered box with a billfull of moss while the other sat on a nearby branch.*

> *April 21: Both birds coming and going with nesting material.*

> *April 24: Titmice still building nest. Very busy.*

> *April 25: Haven't seen much of the titmice today. Very quiet.*

> *April 27: Still no sign of the pair. What's going on?*

If you combine these observations from a distance with a weekly peek in the box, you'll know exactly what's going on! After a flurry of interest and nest-building activity, nesting birds get very sneaky indeed. They may build a complete nest and then let it sit for a week or so (perhaps to let potential predators forget it's there) before laying their eggs. Even once the female starts laying eggs, you may see little or no activity around the box.

Checking out the chicks

In making your nest checks, it's best to wait until you don't see the adult birds around the box. Perhaps they're off gathering more nesting material, or food for their young. Walk quickly and quietly to the box, open the front or side, look in quickly, close the box, and leave. Write down what you saw, with the date, in your log.

If nesting material is present, note what it is: grass, moss, straw, hair, and so on. Note how much nesting material: a half-inch foundation or a four-inch high nest? Do you see a lined cup for the eggs, or is it just rough material? If you do see eggs, how many? What color are they? Are they warm, or cool to the touch? Any hatchlings? Are they feathered or naked? Are their eyes open?

You may also find it interesting and useful to note the weather conditions, temperature, and any behavior by the birds such as scolding, flitting about you, or even dive-bombing you to drive you away. (It's hard to escape the dive-bomb of a chickadee — they don't miss much!)

After just a few weekly visits, you have a good picture of what's going on in that mysterious box. Cavity nesters have evolved to take advantage of the increased protection afforded them by being hatched and raised in an enclosed space. Whereas most open-cup nesters take only about two weeks to go from egg to feathered fledgling, cavity nesters often take three or more weeks before the young birds are ready to leave the nest.

Good Housekeeping

Lots of reasons exist to monitor your nest boxes, not the least of which is to discover neat stuff about the nesting cycle of birds. While checking, you can also check for interlopers and intervene on the birds' behalf, removing parasites and any infertile eggs or (sad to say) dead young. Even under the best of circumstances some baby birds don't survive. Weekly monitoring allows you to stay on top of potentially unhealthy situations.

Unwanted tenants

Sorry, but not all birds that do nest in boxes should nest in boxes. The top two bird species to discourage from nesting in your boxes are starlings and house sparrows. Both of these species were introduced into this country by well-meaning people. I personally know of three dozen people who would love to get their hands on the folks who brought these mostly unlikeable species to this continent. We could put the encounter on pay-per-view like one of those fake wrestling matches. All the money could go to resettle house sparrows and starlings in their native lands (on the other side of the Atlantic Ocean). But I digress. . . .

It helps greatly if you, as a nest-box landlord, know how to identify and discourage both these pests. See Chapter 3 for help with bird ID.

Starlings

European starlings were brought in by a businessman and literature lover who wanted to introduce to the U.S. every bird mentioned in William Shakespeare's works. One of the first starling nests in this country was discovered in the summer of 1890, under the eaves of the Museum of Natural History in New York City. This nest caused much excitement in the scientific community. Most of the buildings in New York City now line their eaves with prickly wires in an attempt to discourage this messy, aggressive bird, which now numbers in the millions and has spread all across North America.

Starlings are broad-shouldered birds. They fit only in boxes with entry hole diameters of $1^3/_4$ inches or larger. Since most hole-nesting birds can fit into a $1^1/_2$-inch hole, starlings shouldn't pose any problem for you, unless you're looking to attract the larger birds like mountain bluebirds, purple martins, flickers, kestrels, screech owls, and great crested flycatchers. These species require a larger than $1^1/_2$-inch entrance hole for a nest box.

If starlings move into one of your nest boxes, throw out their messy nesting material until they get the idea that they're not welcome. If they persist, plug the box hole to discourage them. Once they find another nest site, unplug the hole. Your target birds may come along.

House sparrows

House sparrows were thought to eat agricultural pests such as wireworms and were introduced from Europe in the late 1800s for pest control purposes. In fact, house sparrows thrive on spilled grain and animal feed. In the pre-automobile days, when horses were the preferred mode of transport, house sparrows made a great living wherever horses, barns, and feed were present. Now numbering in the millions, especially in urban areas and farmyards, house sparrows are vicious competitors for nest cavities. Like starlings, they attack and kill native bluebirds, swallows, chickadees, and others in their usually successful attempts to take over nest boxes.

House sparrows are much more pernicious pests than starlings, since they can easily squeeze into the 1½-inch holes required by most backyard box-nesting species. House sparrow nests are easy to recognize, being composed of long weed stems with the seed heads intact, feathers, trash, and straw. The nest, which is built by the male house sparrow, is usually built so that it curves up the inside back of the box to form an arch over the feather-lined cup.

To discourage house sparrows, haul out the nesting material as fast as the male sparrow brings it in. If the sparrows persist, you may want to catch the male. If a male is removed from the nest site, the female also abandons the nest. Wait until he's finished the nest, because he sleeps in it. After dark, creep up and plug the entry hole. Come daylight, place a plastic grocery bag over the hole, and carefully unplug the box entry. When the male house sparrow sees light, he'll fly right into the bag, and you've got him. Neither house sparrows nor starlings are protected by law (because they are introduced, non-native species), so you can dispose of them as you wish. Be aware that taking these birds for a ride — even one of 20 miles or more — may not discourage them, because they have wings and a very strong homing instinct.

Sparrow traps are available commercially, including ones that fit over the box entrance, and other traps that merely attract sparrows into a cage (cracked corn works best as bait). Either way, you still have to deal with the sparrows once you catch them. What you choose to do is up to you.

Nest pests

As if the nest-box landlord doesn't have enough things to think about, you also have to think about the subject of pests in the nests. These pests are insects for the most part, and you'd think that birds could deal with a few insect pests. But sometimes you need to offer a bit of help.

Box-nesting birds eat bugs, and in turn are eaten on by bugs, that is, insect parasites that live off the birds. Some cavity-nesting birds get more parasites than others, but most wind up with a parasite load of some sort by the time young birds fledge. Whether or not to worry about this is really a fine point; birds have been coping with their parasites for millions of years, and usually come out on top.

The most common parasites of birds are blowflies, mites, and lice. Ants, wasps, and bees are not parasites, but can cause problems in a bird box. Monitoring your boxes allows you to intervene when insects cause problems.

Bluebirds and swallows are the box-using species most commonly affected by blowflies. These insects look like bluebottle flies, with red eyes, and they lay their eggs in bird nests about the same time that the birds are laying theirs. The blowfly larvae, which look like grayish maggots, hatch when the young birds hatch, and they live in the nest lining. Crawling out at night, the larvae suck the blood of the young birds, returning, vampire-like, to their lairs at dawn. The sleeping birds are defenseless against these attacks. Most of the time, this larvae activity doesn't cause a problem, but in times of adverse weather or food shortages, heavy blowfly infestations can weaken and even kill broods of bluebirds and swallows.

Don't mess with (or worry about) box-nesting birds once the nestlings are alert and sprouting feathers (at about 10 days of age). You may cause premature fledging by doing this.

Blowflies

To check for blowflies in a nest box, wait until the female is off the nest (a hot sunny day is best — since she'll likely be gone anyway), gently lift the nest material up, and look for the larvae in the bottom of the box, as well as the brown, coffee-bean-like pupal stage of the blowfly. A soiled, smelly layer of nest material just under the bottom of the nest cup is a sure sign of infestation. If you find these parasites, and wish to intervene, you can gently remove the nestlings from the nest and place them in a grass-lined bucket. Remove the old nest from the box and sweep out the bottom of the box. Fashion a new nest from dry brown (not fresh green) grass that you've gathered beforehand. Replace the nestlings and leave quickly, to give the parent birds a chance to return. The adult birds won't mind the new nest and will set about feeding their young as if nothing had happened.

Mites

Infestations of mites can be so heavy that the nest looks like it's crawling. You can deal with these in the same way you do blowflies, by replacing the nest material. Although some of the nest pests may crawl onto your hands, our skin temperature is too low for them to parasitize us, so don't worry, they don't bite humans.

Ants (not aunts)

Some aunts come for a visit and stay way too long. Nothing you can do, but be nice and smile through gritted teeth. The same is not true for ants. Ants often make bird nests their home, which can pose disaster for hatching young. If you find a nest infested with ants, replace the nest with fresh dry grasses, and smear Crisco, Vaseline, or axle grease in a thick layer on the pole beneath the house, to keep ants from coming back up the pole. I've tried greasing my front doorknob to keep unwanted aunts away, but it doesn't work. Aunt Dot and Aunt Toot, you know I'm just kidding, right?

Wasps and bees

Wasps and bees often build paper nests on the inside ceilings of bird boxes, threatening to sting the birds as they enter. The cause of many a mystery nest abandonment is often a wasp lurking on the box ceiling. I control these pests by crushing them and their nests with a long, stout stick. Persistence pays. Here's another way to discourage wasps and bees: Coat the inside ceiling with a thin film of liquid dishwashing soap. This tactic keeps them from attaching a second paper nest. Make sure you coat only the inside ceiling. Don't put soap anywhere the nestlings or adults may come into contact with it.

Never use pesticides of any kind in a bird house! Baby birds have extremely thin skins, and high metabolisms readily absorb such toxins. Pesticides can stunt their growth or kill them outright. Avoid even supposedly safe poisons like rotenone or pyrethins.

Empty Nest Syndrome

After you're sure the young birds have fledged, it's time to clean the nest box. Wait a few days in case of any stay-behinds — some species have broods that fledge over a period of several days, with the slowest young staying in the box, being fed by the parents, for as much as three days after the biggest and boldest leave.

Cleaning out a nest box is simple:

1. **Open the box and sweep out the old nest.**

   I suggest you not do this on a windy day. Lots of tiny dustlike stuff in the nest can be an unpleasant faceful if caught by a gust of wind.

2. **Make sure that you sweep out the bottom of the box thoroughly.**

   If the inside of the box is especially "decorated" by the birds, give it a squirt of water and a quick brush out.

3. **Leave the box open to dry.**

Winterize it

I live in southeastern Ohio, where winter weather varies from mild, gray, and rainy to freezing, gray, and snowy. I leave our nest boxes up year-round, but I do a bit of winterizing that seems to make them very appealing as night-time roosts for many birds.

After the last brood of bluebirds fledges in late August, I take in our nest boxes a few at a time for cleaning and maintenance. For newer boxes this means a quick rinse out with a light bleach solution (a tablespoon or two of bleach in a two-gallon bucket of water) and a new coat of clear water-resistant stain on the outside (never on the inside) of the box. I keep the boxes in the garage until the stain is totally dry.

For older boxes, I replace any worn-out parts (or sometimes the whole house) and follow the same procedure.

Once the weather starts turning colder, I visit each house with a roll of moldable weather stripping (such as Mortite). I use this to plug up the large ventilation holes at the top of the boxes, just under the roof. These holes are great for keeping nestlings cool in the hot summer sun, but make the house an igloo in winter. I also add some dried grasses or wood shavings to the bottom of the box as added insulation for any overnight visitors.

Several times in the past I've seen our bluebirds — absent from our fields during much of the winter — zip into a house at dusk as a storm approaches. And this winter we have a female downy woodpecker roosting in a nest box by our hillside spring. Perhaps she'll stay to nest come spring.

Rewards

I have to admit that I hardly notice the work we put in to keep our nest boxes in top shape for our avian tenants. Our farm, after four years of nest box landlordship, now has three times the bluebirds it had before. Sure, being a landlord to the birds requires some effort, but the birds repay you in the best possible way. They live their lives all around you. As the old saying goes, "Try it. You'll like it!"

Old nest theory

Some recent studies of nest-box use among birds have spawned some interesting ideas. (Isn't science great?) In several cases, nest boxes that still had nesting material in them from the previous year's use were accepted at a greater rate by cavity-nesting birds than boxes that had been cleaned out. (I know from experience that the same does not hold true for humans when selecting a new house.) The explanation for this higher rate of acceptance is not yet known for certain — only the birds know, and they're not talking. To hedge bets with our birds, I clean out the really messy boxes and fashion a new nest from dried grasses. If the old nest is not too filthy, I leave it in the box.

Chapter 10

Gardening for the Birds

· ·

In This Chapter

▶ Rules of the game

▶ Lose the lawn, lose the yawns

▶ It's okay to be messy

▶ Quick glance plants chart

· ·

No matter where you live, it's a sure bet that you can attract more birds to your yard, garden, or immediate surroundings by including plants, shrubs, trees, and other vegetation that birds love. Beyond providing food to birds, plants provide shelter, nesting material, and nesting sites. And — best of all — trees and plants make your yard and garden more beautiful and diverse.

Throughout this chapter, I list many plants that are exceptionally good for birds. The names of these plants are in **bold-faced type**. Because you may live in a part of the continent where certain plants thrive while others die (such as the desert), I suggest you check with a local garden center, landscaping firm, or your regional agricultural or soil-conservation office for specific recommendations on plants that do well in your growing zone.

Lose the Lawn, Lose the Yawns

Where I live in southeastern Ohio, the lawn is king. People spend most of a day each week mowing vast expanses of bluegrass and fescue, tracing endless back-and-forth paths with riding lawnmowers. Here and there, a small tree may stand, wrapped in white tape and supported by guywires. Carefully clipped shrubs march in rows along the house foundations. This scene is fine, but no birds flit about these cookie-cutter yards, except perhaps the odd robin out prospecting for earthworms on the shaven greensward.

Why are these classic mid-American yards so devoid of birdlife? Because, in a word, these yards are boring. When you plant a lawn, you're tying up the landscape with one or two species of grass. If you mow regularly, these grasses are never allowed to go to seed, and thus have little to offer a bird in the way of food.

Why not rethink things? Plan your yard with a variety of species and types of plant life, from grasses to flowers, vines to shrubs, and bushes to trees.

But how? Well . . . funny you should ask. I've given it some thought and have come up with some rules in the next section that should do the trick.

Cardinal rules for a bird-friendly yard

Creating a bird-friendly yard is easy if you obey these five, basic, bird-watcher-tested rules. I call these the cardinal rules for a bird-friendly yard, but they work for robins and bluebirds, as well. Any kind of bird, actually.

Rule One: Be diverse!

The first rule of planting for birds is: Be diverse! Plant lots of different kinds of plants — annual and perennial flowers, vines, shrubs, and trees. Look at any natural habitat popping with birds and you see a mixture, even a jumble, of different kinds of plants, with different heights and growth habits. That doesn't mean your yard has to look like a Tarzan film set. You can lay things out in a nice, orderly way and still create a paradise for birds.

Rule Two: Choose plants that have something birds like

Precious few plants don't have anything to offer some species of birds. But one that pops into my mind as a loser for birds is a hybrid tea rose. Lovely to look at, this rose offers no nectar for hummingbirds and rarely sets fruit that a mockingbird or another fruit-eater may enjoy. Because many people who are serious about tea roses find it necessary to defend them chemically against insect pests, these plants may even be dangerous to birds! Now that you know my prejudices, let me rush to say that I have a lawn, and I even have roses, but I plant a whole lot of other stuff, too! And some roses are better than others for birds (see the list at the end of this chapter).

A quick scan down the tables in any gardening book shows an endless array of useful and attractive plants you can use to create a bird paradise. Everything from annual flowers, such as zinnias — which attract hummingbirds with nectar as well as tiny insects and goldfinches with their seeds — to the stately oak, with its sheltering branches and tasty acorns, can be of use to birds. The secret is to offer a lot of options for food, shelter, and nesting. A dense shrub like an **arbor vitae** may not have flashy flowers or tasty berries, but it's perfect for a nesting chipping sparrow or a roosting junco. The more options, the more birds you can attract.

Rule Three: Plant lots!

When I first started gardening at about age ten, I used to plant a single specimen of every flower I was interested in, all in a neat little row. I still have that penchant for diversity, but I've learned to plant flowers and shrubs in groups. This is just good gardening sense, but it's also good for the birds (see Figure 10-1).

A goldfinch may not give a single zinnia plant a passing look, but 50 zinnias in a bed gets you a flock of goldfinches, busily stripping seeds from the old flower heads. Flowers planted in masses attract attention with their color. Besides, I think flowers look best that way. This is especially important in a hummingbird garden. Hummers need lots and lots of flowers to feed on so that some flowers are always offering nectar while others recharge their supply. A side bonus is the butterflies attracted to your display.

Rule Four: Don't worry, be messy!

Along about March, my flower and vegetable gardens start looking really, really awful. That's because I don't clean them up in the fall. I have a couple

Figure 10-1: A Carolina wren with nest amidst garden tools.

of reasons for this. First, I'm lazy. Second, I get a lot of pleasure out of watching how the birds use the standing dead stalks of annuals and perennials all winter long.

A bed of annuals left standing after frost is an abundant seed source for sparrows, finches, and juncos all winter. Even with two feeding stations going full bore in February, my old trashy flower beds are still full of birds every morning, stripping the last seeds of zinnias, primroses, sunflowers, and even lettuce plants left to bolt. The birds always drop some seeds, too, and I have the added pleasure of volunteer larkspur, delphinium, marigolds, zinnias, snapdragons, alyssum, and lobelias come spring.

I wait until the weather warms up and new growth starts before I clean all the beds in one sweeping, back-breaking day. By then, the birds hardly miss the old stalks, but they've had all winter to strip them of seeds.

Rule Five: See what the birds are eating!

Buying an 80-acre farm that was rapidly being taken over by "trash" vegetation has been an education in the value of trash! Yes, **sumac** (*Rhus* spp.) looks a little gangly as it leans out over the meadow, but there is no other plant I can think of that has as much to offer birds in the dead of winter. Because its tiny fruits aren't fleshy, they stay edible all winter and are just as tasty in April as they were in October. What sumac fruits lack in fleshiness they make up for in volume. A single sumac tree can help dozens of birds when the going gets tough in late winter. We're greeted every morning by the loud yakking of great big pileated woodpeckers (see Figure 10-2) who cling and dangle like chickadees in the sumac as they pluck each scarlet fruit.

The abbreviation *spp.* indicates the plural of the word *species*. When you see it as *Rhus spp.* it indicates that many species are in the genus *Rhus* (the sumac family) that share the same qualities.

Bluebirds make an electric statement perched atop the maroon sumac heads, and flickers and robins look spectacular in the smooth gray branches as they forage.

You may be surprised to discover what good plants just volunteer in areas of your yard that are left to "go wild." Of course, some are unwanted, but these are more than compensated for by those that pop up unbidden.

I have a suggestion — one which won't endear me to *all* of my fellow humans. Consider keeping your lawn all-natural. That is, save both bucks and birds by *not* drenching your lawn in chemicals and fertilizers. Nature has this amazing gift for doing just fine on its own — which is in direct contrast to the old axiom "better living through chemistry."

Figure 10-2:
Pileated wood-peckers eating sumac and greenbriar fruit.

BACKYARD TIP

If you have the space to spare, let one section of your yard or garden go wild; that is, let it grow up and don't impose your gardener's will on it. You may be pleasantly surprised by the bird-friendly plants that appear. Besides, they'll be free!

Inventory time

Even if you don't know the plants you have in your yard, you can do an inventory of the *types* of plants you have. This can be a simple walk around the yard, noting what's there in terms of flowering plants, seed-producing plants, vines, shrubs and bushes, hedgerows, and trees. Do you see birds feeding on the buds, flowers, or fruits of a certain plant, shrub, or tree? Do the birds seem to spend lots more time in and around a certain part of your yard? If so, try to figure out what is attracting them there. Is it a food source? Is it excellent shelter?

There's no such thing as a useless weed!

The blackberry brambles that tear at my pant legs as I walk our paths offer food in late summer to a great variety of birds, including waxwings, catbirds, brown thrashers, bluebirds, robins, and towhees. Field sparrows, yellow-throats, cardinals, and thrashers nest in their dense tangles. **Blackberries** (*Rubus* spp.) may be a pain in the pants, but they're invaluable to wildlife.

Now I'll really cement myself in the lunatic fringe by singing the praises of **poison ivy** (*Rhus toxicodendron*). It's a great food for birds! Woodpeckers of all kinds seem especially fond of its waxy white berries, as do yellow-rumped warblers and waxwings. Why can birds eat the fruits and flit among the leaves without itching? Because poison ivy is not toxic to birds as it is for most humans. And this plant is so common precisely because birds are so good at dispersing the seeds. Poison ivy certainly isn't a plant you want in the dooryard, but it definitely has its place in the back 40, if you're lucky enough to have a back 40.

My point is simply that you may be tempted to uproot or mow many plants until you take stock of what they offer birds.

To a bird looking for a source of tasty seeds, there is no such thing as a weed. Many of the plants that we, as gardeners, love to hate (**dandelions, thistles,** wild native grasses) are excellent food sources for birds. Consider letting some of these weed species grow in one section of your property.

About Meadows

Meadows come in lots of styles, from *au naturel*, dominated by grasses and native wildflowers, to the so-called meadows-in-a-can, which can create spectacular masses of color. Any meadow is a great habitat for birds, if it's properly cared for — that is to say, not cared for at all!

Although you need to mow to maintain any meadow if you don't have grazing livestock or fire, mowing too much can reduce diversity, in both plant species and the birds they attract. And mowing at the wrong time can be devastating to birds that nest on the ground or in low meadow vegetation.

If you're catering to birds, it's best to mow as little as possible to maintain the clearing. We mow our meadow, which is about 11 acres, in patches. Where there's a lot of woody vegetation coming in, we mow in early spring, before the meadowlarks and field sparrows start to nest in mid-April. That sets the sumac and raspberry canes back for a season, but doesn't dent the herbaceous growth. Some patches we mow in late July, after birds have left their nests, giving the vegetation time to grow back before winter. We thrill to flocks of juncos and tree sparrows stripping the seeds from the little bluestem grasses all winter. The key is to avoid impacting nesting birds and to leave adequate cover over the winter. So we mow early in spring and late in summer, and everybody's happy.

Timing of mowing may vary depending on where you live. If you live in Tucson, you may not need to mow ever unless you water your lawn regularly. You're the best judge of when to mow, and when to let it grow. If you're unsure, use trial and error, and watch how the birds react over time.

Meadows-in-a-can

I've been wooed by colorful ads for so-called wildflower meadows. We put in two 15-x-60-foot strips, with the help of a neighbor who has a tractor and plow, and an obstreperous rototiller that almost tilled us under with the sod.

We took the earth-tilling route in preference to the herbicide route recommended by the seed supplier, figuring that the birds would appreciate a toxin-free meadow. We were glad we did, because the moment we got the seed bed plowed and prepared, our resident nesting bluebirds were busily foraging in the tilled soil for cutworms and beetle grubs for their first brood of nestlings! Using any herbicide at all could have spelled disaster for the babies. We take the organic route and, as my wife's uncle Willard, a corn farmer in Iowa, used to say, "grow enough for the bugs and me, too!"

We spread the wildflower seed, tamped it in with boards, and stood back. Despite a miserably dry summer, we soon had a blaze of color from **Coreopsis, cosmos, wallflower, flax,** and other botanical beauties. They weren't native wildflowers, but they attracted countless butterflies and birds to what would otherwise have been boring old lawn. Late in the summer, brilliant flocks of goldfinches, punctuated by the occasional indigo bunting, were stripping seeds from the flower heads, and tree sparrows, song sparrows, and juncos fed in the meadows all winter.

We had planned to till the meadow the next spring and start over, but life intervened, and we let it go. The perennials in the seed mix, which had been tiny plants the first year, really took off, and huge **gloriosa daisies** and **blanketflowers** reigned all the next summer. For an initial investment of time and effort, we had created a real bird magnet that keeps on bringing them in. We're so glad we never got the chance to till it under because the perennial plants are now as big around as bushel baskets and make a much longer and more spectacular show than the annuals did.

Daisies!

Many of the very best plants for attracting birds are in the composite, or **daisy,** family. These include sunflowers, coreopsis, and purple coneflower, as well as the beloved **zinnia.** These plants are popular because they set fairly large seeds that birds such as goldfinches, sparrows, and juncos find tasty. These plants are also ridiculously easy to grow and cultivate. Most germinate if scratched into the soil as soon as the ground is warm and frost-free.

Sunflowers

Sunflowers (*Helianthus* spp.) are annuals that, thanks to a recent designer craze, have flooded the market with fancy sunflower varieties. For floral designers, pollenless varieties exist, which you should avoid because they never set seed (remember the birds and the bees?). Sunflowers, whether you choose the giant, single-headed varieties or the smaller, multi-flowered kinds, are a sure-fire attractant for seed-eating birds. Goldfinches and cardinals love to pull the maturing, milky seeds from the heads; they fill your garden with color, motion, and sound as they flutter and cling. Cardinals often bring broods of young to sit atop the drooping seed heads as they forage.

Coneflowers

I'll admit that I used to think **purple coneflowers** (*Echinacea purpurea*) were a bit gangly. All right, I'll say it, they're ugly! That was until my dear spouse came home with two gallon pots full of the big, hairy plants as a gift. When they bloomed, the butterflies fought for position, and when they went to seed, the goldfinches did the same. Purple coneflowers are wonderful for attracting birds and butterflies, and once you get used to their size and aggressive growth habits, they make a great statement in the border. Just give them room and they'll do the work for wildlife in your garden. By the way, that's the same *Echinacea* that herbalists tout as a cold remedy. . . .

Don't be a plant snob if you want to garden with the birds in mind. Chances are, what you think is beautiful may not fit with what the birds prefer to eat. Birds may be attracted to the bright colors of the plants, but it's not because they seek beauty. They want to EAT! Don't be afraid to challenge your gardening prejudices. I did it and am a convert to coneflowers!

Zinnias

Zinnias (*Zinnia* spp.) are lovely old-fashioned flowers with brilliant color that lure hummingbirds to probe the tiny yellow "true flowers" ringing their middles. When zinnias go to seed, goldfinches love to strip the petals off and feast. There's no better flower for attracting a wide variety of butterflies, either.

Coreopsis

Several species in the genus ***Coreopsis*** (which includes many species of daisy, and several species of coreopsis) are great bird attractants, too. Hardy and easy to grow, they are a major component in many of the wild-flower meadow mixes and are much appreciated by finches, sparrows, and butterflies. All told, the daisy family has treasures aplenty for bird gardeners.

Hummingbirds and Blossoms

Seed-producing plants in the daisy family are terrific for seed-eating birds. But what about birds that depend on flowers for food? In North America, we're blessed with a number of species of hummingbirds, tiny wonders that feed largely on the nectar of flowering annuals, shrubs, and trees. The main thing to remember when selecting plants for hummingbirds is: RED. True, hummingbirds come to blue, white, pink, yellow, and orange flowers, but red really turns them on. It's no coincidence that many red flowers are tubular in shape (to fit the hummingbirds' long bills) and have stamens that dangle pollen outside the petals, to dab on hummingbird foreheads!

If you only have a little room, or want to simplify things and plant a few flowers that really appeal to hummingbirds, you can't go wrong with these:

- ✔ **Bee balm** (*Monarda* spp.) is a hotly contested resource with its tangy nectar. I've had a male hummer set up a territory around my bee balm, keeping all others away. It's best planted in shades of red or purple (*M. fistulosa*); the pink and white varieties don't seem so popular.

- ✔ **Impatiens** have lots of nectar in the little spurs out behind the petals. Stick to the single-flowered varieties; the double "rose-flowered" impatiens are pretty, but hummingbirds can't get past all the petals to the nectar reservoir. Wild impatiens, or jewelweed (*Impatiens capensis* and *I. pallida*) are irresistible to hummingbirds, and have the added advantage of blooming late in summer when migrants pour through.

When selecting hummingbird flowers, always choose *single-flowered* varieties. Beware of the fancy, ruffled flowers loaded with petals; these often conceal or block nectar-producing parts of the flower, or they simply don't produce nectar at all.

The **mint** family has loads to offer hummingbirds and seed-eating birds. Some of the best plants are in the genus *Salvia*. Go for the red ones with tubular flowers such as *S. splendens* and *S. coccinea*.

Columbines (*Aquilegia* spp.) are delicate, pretty, shade-loving flowers that hummingbirds love, in any color. Planted with coral bells (*Heuchera sanguinea*) and bleeding heart (*Dicentra spectabilis*), you've got a lovely shade garden buzzing with hummers. The eastern wild bleeding heart (*D. eximia*) and western wild bleeding heart (*D. formosa*) are noted for blooming abundantly from spring to frost. The birds will visit and revisit the blossoms, as they produce more nectar all the time.

Vines that bear watching

Any discussion of hummingbird plants eventually twines 'round to vines. There are a couple of vines that hummers just can't resist. They camp out in them, preen, sleep, eat, quarrel, and roost in them. One of the best is **trumpet creeper** (*Campsis radicans*). It has big orange or yellow tubular flowers that hummingbirds literally dive into for abundant nectar.

Another irresistible vine is **honeysuckle** (*Lonicera japonica* and others). Hummingbird fans sometimes comment that their regular feeder visitors disappear in late spring and early summer. This often coincides with the appearance of honeysuckle blossoms which can cause mass desertion of hummingbird feeders when they come into bloom, so abundant and enticing is their nectar. I can't mention these vines without a gardener's caveat. They are AGGRESSIVE. You may nurture your little spindly trumpet creeper along for a couple of years, and the next time you turn around it is inexorably removing the shingles from your roof and sprouting up between the bricks of your walk. Turn your back, and honeysuckle is coming out your ears. Plant these vines where you can keep an eye on them for enjoyment and serious management with clippers and mower.

One really neat thing about vines, for those of us with few trees and scant patience, is that in a short time, you can have an instant tree. Plant a few seeds of red **morning glory** (*Ipomoea coccinea*) under a trellis, and in a single season, you've got a pillar of leaves and flowers that may be abuzz with hummingbirds.

Hanging gardens

For the urbanite with little ground to call garden, hanging baskets can bring hummingbirds in. Coupled with a few feeders, hanging baskets can attract and keep hummers coming.

Fuchsias, the single-flowered varieties (avoid the double ones that look like ballet dancers in frilly tutus), and single-flowered **impatiens** are among the best plants to culture in baskets. In addition, you can find a number of very nice annual **verbenas** with trailing habits and brilliant flowers in the pink-to-red-to-purple range that both hummingbirds and butterflies find tasty.

A Tree, a Bush, or a Shrub

Maybe I'm dating myself, but I love to remember Lady Bird Johnson's Texas drawl as she encouraged the gardening public simply to plant "a tree, a booosh, or a shhrruhb" for the betterment of the landscape. (For the undated among us, Lady Bird was the wildflower-loving wife of U.S. President Lyndon Johnson.) We owe much of Americans' fervor for planting to Lady Bird and her campaign to beautify the country, one shhrruhb at a time. Think of birds, and you think of bushes. Birds love thick shrubbery in which to hide themselves, their nests, and their young. Even better is shrubbery with something to offer in the form of flowers or fruit.

Shrubbery

Viburnums offer both flowers and fruit; one is even called the **highbush cranberry** (*Viburnum trilobum*). Lots of native species form a graceful understory to shade trees, such as hobblebush (*V. alnifolium*). Seek out those that set fruit, and you'll please birds. The **dogwood** family is loaded with useful fruiting shrubs and small trees. The familiar flowering dogwood (*Cornus florida*) calls bluebirds, robins, and other thrushes, as well as woodpeckers, catbirds, thrashers, and starlings, with its fiery red fruit in the autumn. Some of the less well-known small dogwoods like red osier (*C. sericea*), silky (*C. amomum*), and gray (*C. racemosa*) are beloved by fruit-loving birds as well.

Hollies are well-known for berries. One of my very favorites is the native **common winterberry** (*Ilex verticillata*). Its bare branches are laden with brilliant clusters of scarlet berries all winter (that is, before the birds finally strip them). Bluebirds especially love them. This family has lots of decorative imports, like Chinese and Japanese Hollies (*I. cornuta* and *I. crenata*, respectively), that provide both berries and dense foliage for roosting and nesting.

Elderberry (*Sambucus* spp.) is a soft-wooded shrub that, in cold climates, dies back each year. But it makes masses of tiny purple berries that birds really dig. My neighbor likes to come over and pick mine, turning them into a really sweet elderberry wine. I always hope she'll forget to do it, because I'd much rather have flocks of berry-fed birds than the wine!

Evergreens, like **yews** (*Taxus* spp.) and **arbor vitaes** (*Chamaecyparis* spp.), as well as **junipers** (*Juniperus* spp.), are almost as varied in their form and color as birds and people. The ones I've mentioned, though, offer both fleshy fruits and dense cover for roosting and nesting birds. They stop the cold winter wind and the prying eyes of predators and make birds feel safe at night. Planted up against the shelter of buildings, evergreens can mean the difference between life and death for a bird on a night that's 20 below.

When I See Birches . . .

Everyone knows birds need trees to forage, sing, roost, and nest in. There's hardly a tree you could plant that wouldn't attract some bird. Though some have so much to offer that I have to point them out.

> *When I see birches bend to left and right*
>
> *Along the lines of straighter, darker trees*
>
> *I like to think some boy's been swinging on them . . .*

The poet Robert Frost loved **birches** (*Betula* spp.), and so do I, and so do warblers and goldfinches, tanagers, and orioles. Besides having lovely white bark, birches must taste great to every caterpillar known to humanity. Come spring, birches are among the first to unfurl lime-green leaflets, and in turn be chewed on by caterpillars. Close behind come the insect-eating birds. Come fall, birches make little seeds in conelets that siskins and goldfinches love to tweeze apart. They grow quickly and look great planted in threes and fives.

Sassafras (*Sassafras albidum*) is a common species in the eastern half of the continent. It produces blue berries that are loved by thrushes, waxwings, bluebirds, and other berry eaters. Sassafras also seems to be a favorite drilling tree for species such as downy and hairy woodpeckers, perhaps because the wood is fairly soft. I love sassafras trees because I can pluck a twig from one at any time of year and get a flavorful stick to chew on. Pioneers used sassafras twigs as toothbrushes. Maybe that's why George Washington had wooden teeth.

I know they're kind of a mess, but **mulberry trees** (*Morus* spp.) are unbelievably effective bird magnets. The watery, purple berries slide easily down the throats of almost every bird that eats fruit. And the watery, purple . . . just don't plant a mulberry over your sidewalk or driveway, or near your clothesline. My mother never swears, but she does mutter when a bird bingoes a freshly washed pillowcase with processed mulberries. Really, it's a treat to watch birds bring their just-fledged young to a mulberry tree, poke a few fruits in the gaping mouth, and leave them to figure it out for themselves. It's worth the spot washing, Mom.

It almost goes without saying that the larger shade trees — **oak, maple, ash, hickory, elm,** and others — have lots to offer in the bird garden. They are the framework around which you can build your garden. You can attract lots of birds without big trees, it's true, but mature plantings offer lots of nest sites for both open-cup and cavity-nesting birds, and they make seeds, from oak acorns to the winged seeds of maple and ash, that birds as diverse as jays and grosbeaks relish.

I'm often pleasantly surprised by the unusual birds that I find breeding in the mature **sycamores, maples, oaks,** and **gums** planted all around my medium-sized Ohio hometown. Yellow-throated warblers don't mind the traffic roaring beneath them; they're too busy feeding young in cavities in the sycamores lining Third Street! Wood duck hens, wooed by the same sycamore nest holes, can be seen parading tiny ducklings in heavy traffic on their perilous way to the Ohio River each spring. And yellow-throated vireos believe the town green, with its massive deciduous trees, is a perfectly acceptable forest in which to hang their little basket-like nests. Plant them, and they will come.

Get the Picture?

By now, I hope you have a picture of a bird garden that's diverse, colorful, stratified in height, and limited only by your imagination. The key is to design your garden around plants that have something to offer birds. Give each plant room to grow and the light it needs, whether full sun or shade, and let it do its work.

Recently, I visited an acquaintance who had a new house on the edge of a huge woodland. The builders had cleared the house lot right up to the edge of the woods, where the great forest trees made a dark wall. A lawn stretched between the house and woods, innocent of plantings, without a birdbath, feeder, or even a twig to perch on. I sat, making conversation with the homeowners, for three hours, but what I was secretly doing was looking over their shoulders and designing a bird garden in my mind. I could see birds flitting through the woods, and in my mind's eye, I was luring them with plantings and feeders and baths right up to that big (and totally wasted) picture window.

Once you know the joy of having birds at hand, you'll wonder how you survived without your bird-friendly yard.

In the tables that follow, I list some of the trees (see Table 10-1), shrubs (see Table 10-2), vines (see Table 10-3), and flowering plants (see Table 10-4) that are good for birds. The information under the "Good for" heading tells you what these plant species provide for birds. Remember this list is not exhaustive. Many other species exist that may be more appropriate for your climate and soil type. Check with a local garden center or garden club for suggestions specific to your region.

Table 10-1		Trees for a Bird-Friendly Yard	
Common Name	Latin Name	Height/ Size	Good for/ Other Notes
Ash, green	Fraxinus pennsylvanica	50' max.	Seeds, insects, cover
Ash, white	Fraxinus americana	100'	Seeds, insects, cover
Aspen, quaking	Populus tremuloides	60'	Seeds, insects, cover, cavities
Birch, gray	Betula populifolia	30'	Seeds, insects, cover
Birch, paper	Betula papyrifera	40'	Seeds, insects, cover
Birch, sweet	Betula lenta	60'	Seeds, insects, cover
Cedar, eastern red	Juniperus virginiana	50'	Fruit, year-round cover
Cedar, Rocky Mountain	J. scopulorum	50'	Fruit, year-round cover
Cherry, black	Prunus serotina	50'	Fruit attracts 50 species
Cherry, pin	Prunus pennsylvanica	25'	Fruit attracts 50 species
Chokecherry, common	Prunus virginiana	25'	Fruit attracts 50 species
Dogwood, alternate-leaf	Cornus alternifolia	30'	Fruit attracts 35 species
Dogwood, flowering	Cornus florida	30'	Fruit attracts 40 species
Hackberry, common	Celtis occidentalis	50'	Fruit, cover
Hawthorn	Crataegus laevigata	20'	Fruit, cover, nesting
Holly, American	Ilex opaca	50'	Fruit, year-round cover
Maple, red	Acer rubrum	80'	Seeds, cover
Maple, sugar	Acer saccharum	100'	Seeds, cover
Maple, water	Acer saccharinum	80'	Seeds, cover, cavities
Mountain ash, American	Sorbus americana	30'	Fruit attracts many species
Mulberry, red	Morus rubra	70'	Fruit attracts 40 species
Oak, pin	Quercus palustris	75'	Acorns, cover
Oak, red	Quercus rubrum	80'	Acorns, cover
Oak, white	Quercus alba	100'	Acorns, cover
Oak, willow	Quercus phellos	100'	Acorns, cover
Sassafras	Sassafras albidum	100'	Fruit, cover, cavities
Shadbush, or serviceberry	Amelanchier laevis	30'	Fruit, flowers
Tupelo, black	Nyssa sylvatica	100'	Fruit, cover, M,F needed for fruit

Table 10-2	**Shrubs for a Bird-Friendly Yard**		
Common Name	**Latin Name**	**Height/ Size**	**Good for/ Other Notes**
Arrowwood viburnum	*Viburnum dentatum*	20'	Fruit, tolerates shade
Bayberry, northern	*Myrica pensylvanica*	8'	Fruit, M,F needed for fruit
Blackberry, American	*Rubus allegheniensis*	8'	Fruit, dense cover, nesting
Blueberry, highbush	*Vaccinium corymbosum*	15'	Fruit, flowers, cover, acid soil
Chokeberry, red	*Aronia arbutifolia*	8'	Fruit, moist soil preferred
Cotoneaster**	*Cotoneaster lactea, others*	3'	Fruit, low dense cover
Cranberry, highbush	*Viburnum trilobum*	12'	Fruit, shade tolerant, ornamental
Dogwood, gray	*Cornus racemosa*	10'	Fruit, dense cover
Dogwood, red-osier	*Cornus stolonifera*	15'	Fruit, dense cover
Dogwood, silky	*Cornus amomum*	10'	Fruit, ornamental, wet soil.
Elderberry, American	*Sambucus canadensis*	12'	Fruit, dense cover
Firethorn**	*Pyracantha coccinea*	12'	Fruit, dense cover, nesting
Hercules' club	*Aralia spinosa*	15'	Fruit attracts warblers, thrushes
Hobblebush	*Viburnum alnifolium*	5'	Fruit, shade tolerant
Holly, deciduous	*Ilex decidua*	30'	Fruit, M,F needed for fruit
Huckleberry, black	*Gaylussacia baccata*	3'	Fruit, sandy soil preferred
Inkberry	*Ilex glabra*	10'	Fruit, thicket-forming, acid soil
Mahonia	*Mahonia aquifolium*	10'	Fruit, year-round cover
Nannyberry	*Viburnum lentago*	30'	Fruit, shade-tolerant
Pokeweed	*Phytolacca americana*	12'	Fruit, perennial herb
Rose, pasture	*Rosa carolina*	7'	Fruit, many related species
Spicebush	*Lindera benzoin*	20'	Fruit, moist soil
Sumac, smooth	*Rhus glabra*	20'	Fruit, available all winter
Sumac, staghorn	*Rhus typhina*	30'	Fruit, available all winter
Winterberry, common	*Ilex verticillata*	15'	Fruit, ornamental, M,F needed for fruit

Note: All species are native except where starred **; these non-native species are of great wildlife value.

Table 10-3	Vines for a Bird-Friendly Yard	
Common Name	*Latin Name*	*Good for/Other Notes*
Ampelopsis, heartleaf	*Ampelopsis cordata*	Fruit, resembles grape vine
Bittersweet, American	*Celastrus scandens*	Fruit, avoid Oriental species
Grape, wild	*Vitis* spp.	Fruit attracts 100 species, cover
Virginia creeper	*Parthenocissus quinquefolia*	Fruit attracts 40 species

Flowers listed in the following table are for seed-eating birds. Hummingbird flowers are listed separately in the Appendix.

Table 10-4	Flowers for a Bird-Friendly Yard	
Common Name	*Latin Name*	*Good for/Other Notes*
Black-eyed Susan	*Rudbeckia serotina*	Seed
Blazing star	*Liatris* spp.	Seed; flowers attract butterflies
California poppy	*Eschscholzia californica*	Seed
Coneflower, purple	*Echinacea purpurea*	Seed; flowers attract butterflies
Coreopsis	*Coreopsis* spp.	Seed; flowers attract butterflies
Cornflower	*Centaurea cyanus*	Seed
Cosmos	*Cosmos* spp.	Seed
Daisy, gloriosa	*Rudbeckia cultivar*	Seed
Marigold	*Tagetes* spp.	Seed
Primrose	*Oenothera* spp.	Seed
Sunflower	*Helianthus annuus*	Seed
Zinnia	*Zinnia elegans*	Seed; flowers attract butterflies

Chapter 11

Hummers, Bluebirds, Martins, and Hawks

- -

In This Chapter

▶ What's so interesting about these birds

▶ Here's to hummingbirds

▶ Being there for bluebirds

▶ My favorite martins

▶ The wonder of watching hawks

▶ Knowing more

- -

For some of us in the bird-watching game, a special interest in a certain species or family of birds develops. This interest can vary in intensity from general curiosity to single-minded focus.

This chapter includes information on the most popular of the special-focus birds — birds that have large followings and even special organizations devoted to their appreciation and study. Among birds I include in this group are hummingbirds, bluebirds, and purple martins — all of which have strong ties to our backyards. The other group is the raptors, especially hawks, which have their own devotees, known as hawk watchers.

Other bird species and bird families have devoted fans, but the ones I include here are the runaway favorites. If none of these birds interests you, that's perfectly all right. You're normal. But there's no reason you can't start focusing on your own special birds. Most bird watchers have a favorite.

Hummingbirds

You would be hard-pressed to find anyone — even among the general non-birding public — who doesn't like hummingbirds. Of all birds, hummingbirds, or hummers, have generated the most enthusiastic (and clichéd) superlatives among those who watch: "Avian jewels," "The gems of the bird world," "Flying flowers," and countless others.

Why are hummers so fascinating to so many? I think two primary reasons exist:

- ✔ One, humans find it hard to believe that something so tiny, something almost insectlike in its appearance and habits, can possibly be a bird.
- ✔ Two, we can easily attract hummingbirds to our yards, porches, patios, and windowsills using feeders and a simple nectar solution. With hummers in our midst, we can observe their fascinating behaviors and high-energy lifestyles.

Not only are hummers beautiful to look at, they have near-mythic flying abilities. Unique rotating joints close to the body let hummingbirds swivel their wings through figure-eight arcs and do outrageous aerobatics. They need this maneuverability because hummingbirds feed by hovering and drinking nectar from flowers. It's a good thing they can fly so well because hummingbirds have such tiny, weak legs and feet that they aren't able to walk at all. They fly everywhere, even if they only have to go a few inches.

What's a hummingbird?

Hummingbirds, I'm proud to say, are unique to the New World — North America, Central America, and South America. Hummingbirds are the second largest bird family in this hemisphere — 338 species. Most hummingbirds are in the tropics; 16 different species exist in North America.

In exotic Africa and the Old World, hummers' ecological niche is filled with colorful but somewhat clunky sunbirds, who are unable to hover and fly backward like our little buzzbombs, but must clamber about larger flowers for nectar.

Hummingbirds are distinguished by unique, reduced wing bones; whereas most birds flap the entire *arm,* hummingbirds' wings are derived mostly from their *hand* bones. Okay now, flap your arms. Can't do it very fast, can you? Now, pull in your arms and just flap your hands. Wait! You're taking off!

Hummingbirds have a high metabolism; as their name implies, their engines are always humming. What better fuel for a hyperactive little bird than sugar? Sugar burns quickly and cleanly. And always being on a sugar high, hummingbirds have hyped-up behavior to match. A person having as high a metabolic rate as a hummingbird would have to eat almost twice his weight in food every day: 155,000 calories. That's a lotta cheesecake! No wonder hummingbirds are always in motion and are so feisty in defense of their food sources. Their lives depend on it.

Male hummingbirds have absolutely nothing to do with nesting or caring for their young. Their specialty is fancy courtship displays, which in most species involve swinging-pendulum-like flights, special buzzing noises produced by their wings, and breathtaking displays of their colorful throats, or *gorgets*. These gorgets, and their body feathers as well, are cloaked in tiny feathers that have droplets of oil trapped inside them. These oil droplets actually refract the sun's light, bending it to different wavelengths that human eyes perceive as brilliant color. Not for hummingbirds are the pedestrian browns, reds, or yellows of other songbirds. No, hummers go for glory — cerise, magenta, violet, copper, gold, emerald, armor green, cerulean blues — every hue you'd find in a stained glass window and then some.

After a male hummingbird has so dazzled the dull-colored female that she consents to mate with him, they part ways for good. She flies off to gather the softest plant fluff and binds it together with spider webs, often pasting lichens on the walnut-sized nest for camouflage. The thick, fluffy walls of the tight little nest provide great insulation for her two (or, rarely, three) pea-sized eggs. After an incubation period ranging from 15 to 22 days, the chicks hatch. As the young grow, the nest actually stretches to accommodate and cradle them. The female works doubly hard to feed herself and her two young, pumping them full of regurgitated nectar and tiny insects like aphids and gnats, which are often stolen from spider webs! Who needs fairy tales, or fairies, for that matter, when such birds as hummingbirds exist!

Young hummingbirds stay in the nest much longer than most birds; Ruby-throated hummingbirds (the only species that occurs regularly east of the Mississippi) may stay in the nest as long as 31 days! Compare that to robins, who usually explode out of their nest in as few as 15 days. And the female feeds her young much longer after they leave the nest — 40 to 65 days!

Where and when?

Any yard in North America can expect to have at least one hummingbird species visit it during the warmer months of the year (April through late September). In the eastern half of the continent, the ruby-throated hummingbird is the only regularly occurring hummer (see Figure 11-1).

But the lucky folks in the West have many hummers to enjoy, including ten commonly found species. In summer, the hummingbird capital of North America is southeastern Arizona, where a dozen or more species can be found at a single feeding station.

In winter, most of our hummers leave, seeking warmer climes where flowering vegetation and lots of insects sustain them. Along the Pacific Coast, as far north as southeastern Alaska, Anna's hummingbirds are year-round residents, able to withstand the cold and occasional snow.

Figure 11-1:
A female ruby-throated humming-bird, on the nest.

But, for most of us, hummingbirds are primarily a late-spring-through-early-fall phenomenon. As such, their return is eagerly awaited. As I write this, it's early March here in Ohio, and already the hummingbird feeders are appearing, filled with nectar for the birds that return (but not for another month).

Attracting hummers

Hummingbirds are attracted to bright colors, especially red and orange. These colors are a signal in nature that, to hummers, means nectar. A large patch of blooming red or orange flowers is a beacon to hummingbirds. It says "Eat here!" Once they stop to investigate the flowers, your feeder may get noticed. If you keep the feeder filled and clean, the hummingbirds have no reason to look elsewhere.

Hummingbirds feed by hovering in front of nectar-producing flowers and inserting their long bills into the flower. From its bill, the hummer extends its tongue to drink the flower's nectar. This same strategy is used at hummingbird feeders.

Flowers

The very best way to start a hummingbird feeding station is to act naturally. There's no better way to spread the welcome mat for hummingbirds than to plant the flowers they prefer. Most of the flowers are red or orange and have a tubular shape that fits the hummingbird's bill. Flowers not only dress up your yard, but they also provide a constant source of food for the birds that never needs to be washed and refilled, like feeders! Dozens of possibilities are awaiting you at a nearby garden center. Just be sure that you choose flowering plant, shrub, and tree species that thrive in your climate or growing zone.

Among the most widely thriving and popular hummer plants are beebalm, various salvia or sage species, and trumpetvine. For a list of flowers for hummingbirds and other birds, see the Appendix.

Nectar — A recipe for happy hummers

A mixture with a four-to-one (4:1) ratio of water to sugar most closely matches the sugar and energy content of the natural nectar that hummingbirds drink from blooming flowers. More is not better for these tiny birds, so don't assume that you're doing your hummingbirds a favor by putting more sugar into the mixture.

When making the nectar mixture, use refined white sugar (1 part), and add it to boiling water (4 parts). Stir in the sugar until it's dissolved, and then let the mixture cool before offering it to hummingbirds. I keep two gallon jugs of hummer nectar in my refrigerator during the summer. On a busy day, our hummingbirds easily polish off a half gallon from our six feeders.

Don't use anything other than white table sugar when making hummingbird nectar. Molasses, honey, brown sugar, and artificial sweeteners do not match the level of sucrose that hummingbirds get from natural nectars. And some of these other "sugars" spoil very rapidly when placed in a feeder in the sun. Spoiled solution is not good for hummingbirds.

The plants listed in the Appendix are among hummingbirds' favorites. While reds dominate the list, there are plenty of other colors suggested to allow a varied planting. The most important aspect of designing a hummingbird garden is to plan for continuous bloom from spring to fall, ensuring an endless supply of nectar.

Hummingbird feeders

A good hummingbird feeder is easy to clean. The best hummingbird feeders can be taken apart completely in seconds and have no nooks and crannies accessible only by cotton swabs or bottle brushes. You should be able to scrub out the feeding ports and reservoir completely without special tools.

Feeders that have feeding ports facing up toward the sky can't drip; those with feeding ports off the side or pointed down toward the ground invariably drip, attracting insects and often emptying themselves without help from the birds! Look for feeder designs that minimize drippage. If you buy a feeder that leaks, take it back for a refund and try another make or model.

Almost all the good feeders on the market feature bright red parts. This is to attract the attention of thirsty hummers, just as red flowers do. Other bright colors may work, but red is the most eye-catching for hummingbirds.

Sad to say, but those nifty-looking handmade ceramic feeders are rarely cleanable. Stick with clear plastic; it'll let you see how much solution remains and whether or not the feeder needs washing.

If you're starting a new hummingbird feeding station and you don't have blooming flowers already attracting hummingbirds, try hanging a bright red or orange ribbon below the feeder. This flash of bright color improves the feeder's chances of catching the eye of a passing hummingbird.

What to look for and where to put it

Once you've attracted hummingbirds, a feeder's capacity is important. A good rule is to put out only as much solution as will be eaten in a couple of days. If this means partially filling a big feeder, that's fine; you save yourself the expense and trouble of dumping out spoiled solution. Early in the spring, I put out small feeders, switching to the big feeders later on, when the young hummers leave the nest and mob the feeders. A snap-apart base that fits on an ordinary clear plastic soda bottle can be a boon when you have 20 or more hummingbirds vying for limited amounts of solution. When the bottle gets a little scummy, you can recycle it and use a new one.

What to look for in hummingbird feeders:

- Red parts — to catch a passing hummer's attention
- Ease of cleaning — a clean feeder keeps birds healthy
- Capacity: Is it enough for you and your hummingbirds? — you don't want to have to fill it every few hours

A few points should help you decide where to place your hummer feeders. Place them

- ✔ Where they can be seen easily by you and found by the hummingbirds.

- ✔ Out of direct sunlight. Hot sun causes rapid spoilage of solution.

- ✔ Where they're easy to reach for cleaning and refilling.

Hummingbirds are very site-loyal. That is, they return to the same feeder or feeders every day throughout the season, and even year after year.

I dream of hygiene

After getting the 4:1 water-to-sugar ratio right, the most important thing you can do is keep your feeders scrupulously clean. Here's where feeder design comes in. My favorite feeders disassemble in seconds, with as few small parts as possible. The easiest-to-clean looks like a deep-dish pie plate with a big red screw-on lid. In hot, humid weather, I take it down every other day, dump out any remaining sugar solution, and wash it thoroughly in hot, soapy water, rinsing well.

You know when it's time to wash your feeders when the solution turns cloudy or (heaven forbid) begins to grow clumps of gelatinous mold or black scuzz. This reaction can happen in as few as two days in the heat of summer, so err on the side of cleanliness and make washing your feeders a regular habit. Do it each time you refill the feeders. Spoiled solution can harm hummingbirds.

Putting red food coloring in your hummingbird nectar is totally unnecessary. If your feeder has red parts, or if you have bright flowering plants nearby, that should be enough to attract hummingbirds to your yard. Some debate exists about the health effects of food coloring on hummingbirds, so my advice to you is to avoid it. If you have no flowers, and your hummer feeder is faded, tie a bright red ribbon to the feeder. That ribbon does the trick. You can also revive a faded hummer feeder with bright red nail polish applied around the ports. I do this every spring on my older feeders. Be sure to let the polish dry thoroughly before filling and hanging the feeder.

If you want to see a hummingbird eat insects, leave an old banana out until it begins to draw fruit flies. Place the banana and its band of bugs outside near your hummingbird feeder. If the wind isn't too strong (which blows the flies away) you may get to see a hummingbird snapping up these tiny insects. Hummers eat lots of insects, which are a good source of protein. You should try them!

Want more info?

A plethora of good information about hummingbirds is available. Two national organizations devoted to hummingbird study and appreciation are.

- **The Hummingbird Society,** 249 East Main Street, Suite 4, Newark, Delaware 19711
- **Hummer/Bird Study Group, Inc.,** P.O. Box 250, Clay, Alabama 35048

Your local public library probably has several books devoted to hummingbirds. I list some of my favorite information sources in the Appendix.

Bluebirds

"The bluebird carries the sky on his back," according to Henry Thoreau. But bluebirds carry the hearts of many bluebird lovers, too.

What's a bluebird?

Bluebirds are members of the thrush family, which also includes the American robin, the legendary backyard earthworm-eating champion. Three species of bluebirds are found in North America: **eastern bluebird** (found in the eastern portion of the continent, east of the Rocky Mountains), the **western bluebird** (found — you guessed it — from the Rockies, west) and the **mountain bluebird** (found — this is too easy — in the western mountains of North America).

All three bluebirds are blue, but each has color variations on the bluebird theme that make it fairly easy to identify.

Eastern bluebird

The male eastern bluebird has a cobalt-blue back, wings, and head, a grayish throat, a rusty breast, and a white belly. Female easterns are duller versions of the male — or should I say more subtly beautiful versions?

Western bluebird

Male western bluebirds are very similar to male eastern bluebirds, but backwards. In addition to a rusty belly, they have rusty backs, too. Their heads, tails, and wings are a deep ultramarine blue.

The bluebird story

During the middle part of the 20th century, bluebirds were nearly wiped out in North America. Habitat destruction, pesticide use, and increased competition for nest holes from starlings and house sparrows decimated bluebird populations. Bluebirds disappeared from much of their traditional range. This situation drew the attention of a few concerned individuals who started a determined effort to provide human-made housing for bluebirds.

Series of houses were put up in suitable open grassland habitats. This concept became known as a bluebird trail. As trails sprang up across North America (and DDT and other pesticides were banned), the bluebirds made a comeback. Today all three species are doing well, thanks to bluebird lovers who devote their time and energy to providing much-needed housing.

Mountain bluebird

One of North America's only all-blue birds, the male mountain bluebird, is purest cerulean all over, except for a white lower belly. His mate has a more turquoise hue, mixed with ash-gray. The mountain bluebird is larger and longer-winged than other bluebird species, and actually needs a larger nestbox hole: $1^9/_{16}$ inches versus $1^1/_2$ inches for eastern and western bluebirds.

Where and when?

There is a bluebird species (eastern, western, or mountain) in every one of the lower 48 states. Mountain bluebirds even breed in eastern Alaska. Not surprisingly, mountain bluebirds are also the most strongly migratory of the three species, showing up in the winter in Texas in breathtakingly large flocks. Eastern and western bluebirds migrate only as far south as they must to find good food supplies, straggling to the southern states as they are pushed by severe weather. Bluebirds flock in the winter and may sleep together in nest boxes or tree cavities on the coldest nights. Mild winters find flocks staying around their breeding sites, finding sluggish grasshoppers in the meadow grass and feasting on berries and fruits on woodland edges.

Bluebirds always seem to have nesting on their minds, and it's this propensity that makes them such fun to have around. Sunny days in February find them fluttering around nest boxes, singing and waving their electric-blue wings as if it were May. It's heartening, for those of us who mope around all winter, to see the utter conviction in their behavior that spring really is creeping its way back.

Because bluebirds use boxes for nesting in spring and summer and for sleeping year-round, it's never too early or too late to put up a bluebird box. Just get the boxes out there, and if the habitat is right, the bluebirds do the rest.

Attracting bluebirds: Habitat, habitat, habitat

If you've got the proper habitat, you've got a great chance at attracting bluebirds. Here's an example:

I grew up in the classic suburban subdivision: big trees; shady lawns; a patch of woodland behind the house. Once, in late winter, I saw a pair of bluebirds hanging around in the backyard. My dad and I built and put up five bluebird boxes that week. But we never saw those bluebirds again. (We did get nesting white-breasted nuthatches, Carolina chickadees, and some unbelievably cute southern flying squirrels, though, so we came out winners.)

Now, my sister's family also had a house in a classic subdivision. But within sight of the house was this open meadow with barbed-wire fences and scattered small shrubs — all the things bluebirds love. And her bluebird boxes were actually occupied by bluebirds. The moral of this story is: If you're going to get bluebirds in your yard, you have to have some appropriate open habitat nearby.

Bluebirds love open grassy habitat because that's where they're able to find food. Unlike some other species that pursue their food, such as flycatchers or hawks, bluebirds are *perch hunters*. No, they don't eat fish. What I mean is they sit on an exposed perch, such as a fencepost or wire, and watch for movement below. Bluebirds have excellent eyesight, and when motion is detected, the bluebird swoops down to capture the unlucky insect, usually a grasshopper, cricket, caterpillar, or some other denizen of the grass and soil.

If you have a large open grassy area on or near your property (and you live within the range of one or more of the three bluebird species), the best way to attract bluebirds is by offering housing to them.

Bluebirds are *cavity nesters*. Cavity nesters prefer to build their nests inside a hollow or excavated tree, fencepost, or in an artificial nestbox. Because bluebirds don't have strong, chisel-like bills, they depend either on woodpeckers to carve out a cavity in a tree or on people to put up the right kind of nestbox for them. As you may imagine, it can be hard for a pair of bluebirds to find a good nest cavity that's not already occupied by a bird, squirrel, or mouse. So bluebirds naturally appreciate having their options expanded when you put up boxes around a suitable habitat.

Welcome to the color section for Bird Watching For Dummies!

This part should be a treat for your eyes. It's so full of beautiful images that you won't even feel all the helpful and fascinating information that your mind is absorbing as you flip through the next 32 pages.

The first part shows you how to set up an **ideal garden for birds** and other wildlife. It has representative plants of all sizes and types that offer something of value to the creatures that visit your property.

Birding by habitat is illustrated in this color section, too. It shows you how to think ahead about what birds might be found in which habitat type. This can enhance both your bird watching skills and enjoyment.

The **ideal feeding station illustration** shows how a variety of feeders and foods can vastly increase the numbers and species of birds you attract. Variety is the spice of life. As a special bonus, I have also included a photograph showing the most popular types of seed used for bird feeding.

A series of **comparison birds** is included here to help you see how to look at and understand the sometimes subtle differences between similar bird species. You can apply these observation techniques to any other confusingly similar species you encounter.

The icing on the cake is the series of gorgeous bird photographs of my **40 Favorite Birds** of North America. I add a little text about each species to further pique your curiosity.

Garden For Birds

Gardening for birds boils down to one simple thing: *Variety*. Offer birds a variety of choices and you'll attract a variety of birds. Remember that birds need four things to survive: food, shelter, water, and a place to nest. The very best yards and gardens provide these four elements. Please note that although many of the plants, shrubs, and trees shown here are good for much of North America, there may be better choices for your particular region or growing zone. Check with a local garden center, garden club, or government agricultural office for the best matches for your climate and soil.

1. Blue spruce

2. *Butterfly bush

3. Cardinal flower

4. *Butterfly weed

5. Wild bergamot or bee balm

6. *Purple coneflower

7. *Blue pickerel weed

8. Sedum — Autumn joy*

9. *Zinnia

10. *Verbena

11. *C. verticillata* Moonbeams

12. *English lavender

13. Water lily

14. Floating heart

15. Moonbeam coreopsis

16. Lady fern

17. Yellow flag Iris

18. Meadow, mixed wild and cultivated flowers — Field poppy (red), Sunflower, Tickseed, Cornflower

19. Pond — water source for birds; home to frogs, toads, fish, turtles, dragonflies and aquatic insects

20. Stonewall provides shelter for wrens, small mammals, moths, butterflies, toads, snakes, and insects

21. Lawn attracts robins, bluebirds, starlings, blackbirds, sparrows

22. Paper birch

23. Flowering dogwood

24. American mountain ash

25. Highbush cranberry

26. Hosta

27. Gartenmeister Fuchsia

28. Coral bells

29. Columbine

30. Lobelia

31. Hollyhock

*excellent butterfly attractants

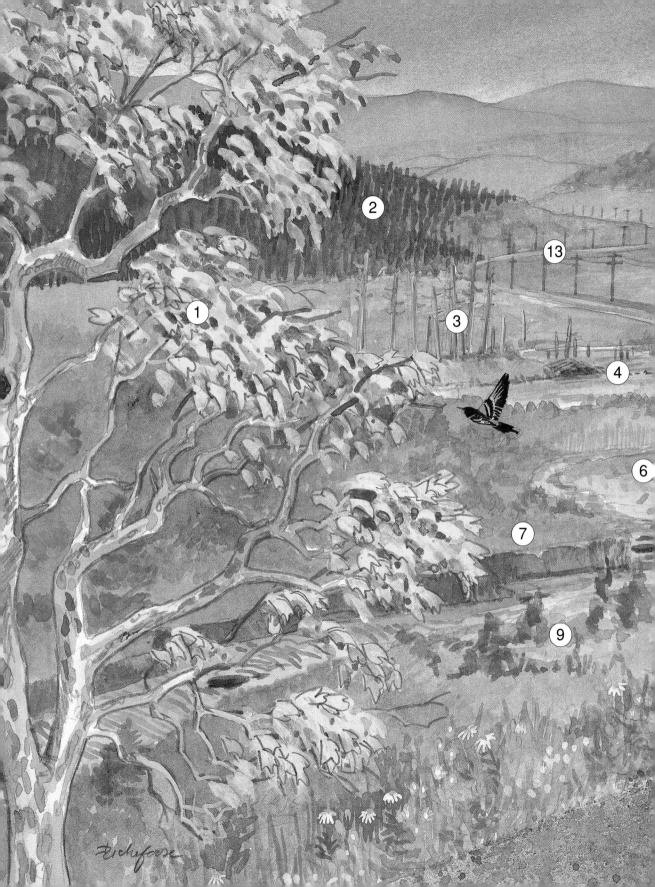

Birding by Habitat

When you look at a landscape as a bird watcher, you can predict what species will be found in each habitat. This illustration should get you thinking in those terms. For more about birding by habitat, see Chapter 17.

1. Sycamore
Orioles
Yellow-throated warblers
Wood ducks

2. Conifer plantation
Owl roosts, nests
Heron nests
Raptor nests
Black-throated green warblers
Pine warbler

3. Beaver swamp
Swallow nests
Ducks
Woodpeckers
Herons
Flycatchers

4. Beaver pond
Ducks
Swallows
Herons
Grebes
Shorebirds

5. Cattail marsh
Rails
Blackbirds
Marsh wrens

6. Tussock (sedge) marsh
Sedge wrens
Swamp sparrows

7. Cut bank of stream
Nesting kingfishers
Nesting bank swallows
Rough-winged swallows
Spotted sandpipers

8. Roadside
Bluebirds
Hummingbirds
Indigo buntings
Sparrows
Common yellowthroats

9. Old field
Common yellowthroats
Prairie warblers
Song sparrows
Brown thrasher
Yellow-breasted chat
Cardinals
Blue-winged warblers

10. Farmyard
Barn swallows nests
Eastern phoebes nests
Barn owls nests
American kestrels nests
House sparrows
Starlings
Cowbirds
Rock doves

11. Hardwood Forest
Tanagers
Warblers
Thrushes
Flycatchers
Cuckoos
Whip-poor-wills
Woodpeckers

12. Haymeadow
Meadowlarks
Blackbirds
Field sparrows
Grasshopper sparrows
Bobolinks

13. Power lines
Hawks
Bluebirds
Indigo buntings
Meadowlarks
Blackbirds
Doves
Kingbirds

14. Pasture
Kildeer
Meadowlarks
Cowbirds
Starlings
Bluebirds
Prairie warblers
Field sparrows

15. Sky
Soaring raptors

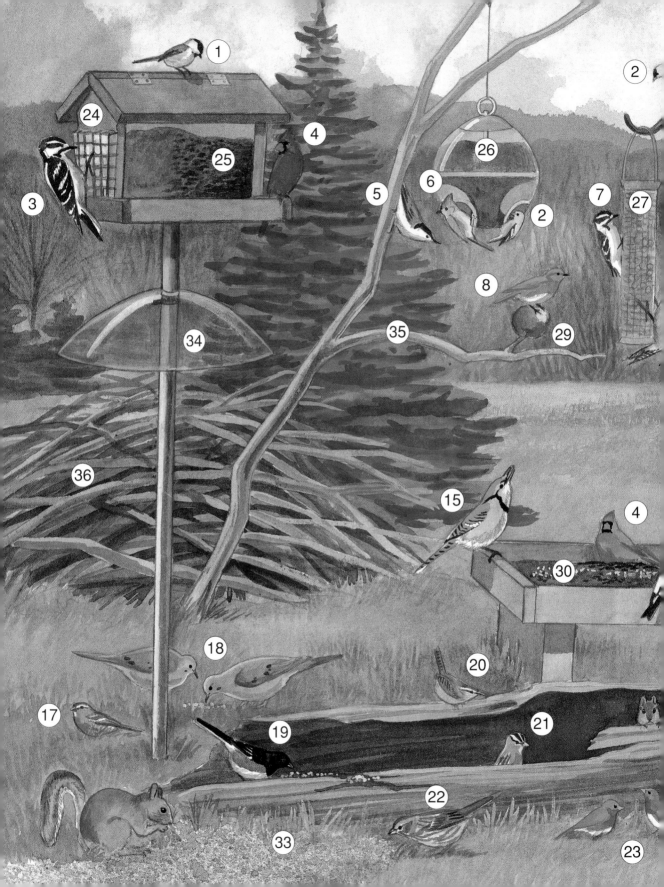

Bird Feeding Station

Offering food for birds can be as simple or complex as you wish it to be. If you want to provide the best-loved foods to each species, you may want to use specific feeders to do so. The scene shown here covers most of the basic feeder types, and the birds that prefer them. For in-depth information about feeders and feeding, see Chapter 7. Not all of the feeders shown here may work for the birds in your backyard. That's when you need to begin experimenting. Think of it as an adventure. Happy feeding!

Birds
1. Carolina chickadee
2. American goldfinch
3. Hairy woodpecker
4. Northern cardinal
5. White-breasted nuthatcher
6. Tufted titmouse
7. Downy woodpecker
8. Eastern bluebird
9. Red-bellied woodpecker
10. House finch
11. Purple finch
12. Common redpoll
13. Black-capped chickadee
14. Pine siskin
15. Blue jay
16. Evening grosbeaks
17. Chipping sparrow
18. Mourning doves
19. Rufous-sided towhee
20. Carolina wren
21. White-crowned sparrow
22. Fox sparrow
23. Dark-eyed juncos

Food and Feeders
24. Suet
25. Hopper feeder (sunflower)
26. Globe feeder (sunflower)
27. Peanut feeder
28. Thistle feeder (tube)
29. Apple
30. Sunflower, sunflower hearts
31. Platform feeder
32. Log feeder
33. Mixed seed (millet, corn sunflower)

Protection
34. Squirrel baffle
35. Snag perch
36. Brushpile

The seed types shown here are the most popular ones used for feeding birds, as chosen by the birds themselves. You couldn't ask for a better panel of judges. For a listing of which foods are preferred by which birds, see the table in Chapter 7.

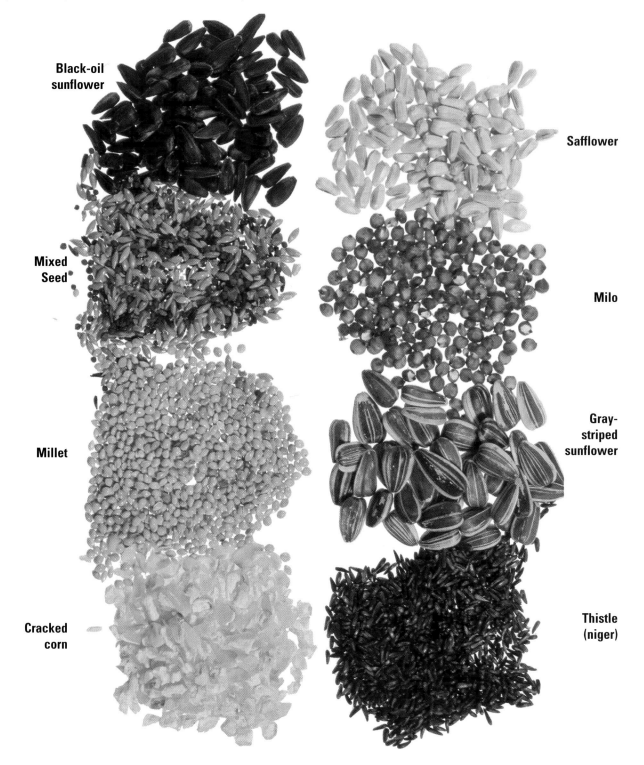

Black-oil
sunflower

Safflower

Mixed
Seed

Milo

Millet

Gray-
striped
sunflower

Cracked
corn

Thistle
(niger)

Name that bird!

Some birds look so much alike that it's hard to tell them apart — especially when they're on the wing. On the following pages are four sets of common bird species that are frequently confused by beginning bird watchers, along with their distinguishing differences. I also offer a few tips that you can use when you encounter any tough mystery bird, whether in your backyard or at some distant hotspot.

Downy woodpecker versus hairy woodpecker

The downy and hairy woodpeckers appear to have almost the exact same black and white plumage patterns. Males of both species have a red spot at the back of the head (females have no red at all). These two woodpecker species are common across much of North America, and occupy much the same habitat. In fact, you can even see them visiting a backyard feeder at the same time. If you're lucky enough to see the two together, you can see that the most obvious difference is size.

Physical differences

The hairy woodpecker is larger than the downy. Here's a trick to help you remember which woodpecker is the larger one: Downy is Dinky. Hairy is Huge.

From bill tip to tail tip, the hairy woodpecker measures 9 ¼ inches; the downy measures just 6 ¾ inches. But an even easier-to-spot size difference can help you decide which species you're seeing. The size of the bill relative to the size of the head is a key field mark. The downy's small bill looks like a tiny black thorn poking out of the bird's small, grape-

sized head. The hairy's bill resembles a large black nail sticking out of a walnut-sized head. The length of the downy's bill is less than half the width of the bird's head, while the hairy's bill is nearly as long as its head is wide.

A more subtle plumage difference between hairies and downies can be found in the white outer tail feathers. On a downy woodpecker, the white outer tail feathers are notched with black spots. On a hairy, the outer tail feathers are white with no black marks at all. If you live in the Pacific Northwest, the hairy woodpeckers you see may be brown and cream colored (as opposed to black and white).

Other differences

These two woodpeckers have similar call notes, both of them say pik! But while the downy's call is soft and sqeaky, the hairy's is sharp and loud. Both birds also give a high whinnying rattle call. The hairy's whinny stays on a single tone, but the downy's descends. I remember this vocal difference by associating the word downy with the downward descent of the call. Generally, hairy woodpeckers prefer more mature woods (ones with larger, older trees) than downies do. Downies are more likely to be found in suburban parks and to visit backyard feeders.

Purple finch versus house finch

The two common "red" finches that visit bird feeders all over North America are the purple finch and the house finch. Of these two, the house finch is the more common. It is also the more commonly misidentified because its plumage can vary from dull red to bright orange.

Male purple finch versus male house finch

The male purple finch is a lovely bird, thanks to the pinkish-purple wash of color throughout his plumage. It looks as if the bird has been dipped in raspberry wine. This raspberry color bleeds onto the bird's back and wings — only the lower sides and belly are clean white.
A male house finch has much more localized color. He is reddish only on his head, breast, and lower back. The upper back and wings are streaky brown, without a wash of color.

Perhaps the quickest way to distinguish the two adult male finches is to look at the birds' lower flanks (the area on the bird's side from below the wings to the tail): If the flanks are streaked with brown, it's a male house finch. If the flanks are white, with a hint of pink, it's a male purple finch.

Female purple finch versus female house finch

Female purple finches look entirely different from males and are much more boldly streaked than female house finches. Look for the sharp contrast in the female purple finch's dark brown and white areas. Female house finches are more muted in color, with fine streaks of brown and tan blending into dull white. This difference is especially evident in the faces of the two female finches. A dark cheek patch encircled in white sets the purple finch apart. The female house finch's face is dull and evenly colored.

Overall appearance

In overall appearance, the purple finch looks more substantial, plumper, and chestier. Purples often appear to have a slight crest of feathers on their head, unlike the flat-crowned house finch. At feeders, purple finches are calmer and perch quietly in one place to eat while the flightier house finches flutter and tweet incessantly.

Songs

The songs of both species are rich, rapid, and musical, but the purple's song lacks the harsh, burry downward slurred notes which the house finch inserts into every song.

Cooper's hawk versus sharp-shinned hawk

These two bird-eating hawks are often first encountered when they are pursuing songbirds at a backyard feeder. In winter in cold-weather regions, these relatively common birds of prey make regular passes at a well-attended bird feeder, picking off sick, injured, or unlucky songbirds ranging in size from tiny chickadees to fairly large mourning doves. In a flash, the hawk swoops upon the birds, scattering them in all directions. One individual is picked out and pursued by the hawk. Neither hawk is at all hesitant about following a targeted bird into deep woods and cover. In fact these species are built for just such aerial pursuit, with strong flight muscles and short, compact wings for maximum maneuverability.

The primary difference between the two hawks is size, but this is not really helpful when the other bird is not nearby for comparison. In both species females are larger than males, and immature birds have brown backs and white breasts streaked with brown, while adults have bluish-gray backs and orange-and-white barred breasts.

The sharp-shinned hawk (length: from 10 to 14 inches; wingspread: between 20 and 28 inches) is the smaller of the two species, and looks to be small-headed for its body size. In flight, it seems to have long narrow (but not pointed) wings and a short tail in proportion to its body length. The end of a sharpie's tail is squared-off, not rounded like the Cooper's hawk tail. Sharpies prefer mixed woodlands and are more likely to prey on smaller songbirds.

The Cooper's hawk (length: from 14 to 20 inches; wingspread: between 29 and 37 inches) is more widespread south of Canada than the sharp-shinned. The Cooper's hawk seems larger headed, with a dark cap that contrasts with its lighter gray back. In flight, the Coop looks like it has a shorter wing but a longer tail in proportion to its body length, appearing stockier and more powerful in flight than the sharpie. Its tail has a rounded appearance when fanned open while the bird is soaring. Cooper's hawks prefer mature woodlands and will sometimes spend the winter in more open country. This species preys upon medium-sized birds such as jays, flickers, and doves, and will also take small mammals.

The best way to become good at telling Cooper's hawks and sharp-shinned hawks apart is to visit a spot through which these species migrate in large numbers (see Chapter 11 for information about hawk watching). Spending time looking at dozens of variations of these two birds will pay off the next time you see a streak of feathers zooming past you through the woods.

Separating Sparrows

Sparrows can drive a birder to distraction. After all, there's a reason why bird watchers coined the term "LBJ," for Little Brown Jobs, to refer to the almost-indistinguishable small brown sparrows that are found all over North America. But take heart! Identifying sparrows is not as tough as it seems. You simply need to know what to look for. Pictured here are three common sparrow species, ones often encountered in the field and at bird feeding stations. Each species is more common in certain parts of the continent, but the most widely distributed of the three is the song sparrow. One of the most helpful things you can do to improve your sparrow ID skills is to fix one particular species in your mind as a reference bird. Then try to ID other sparrow species based upon what you know about your reference bird. Because it's so widespread and common, the song sparrow is an excellent reference bird. Look at its markings in the accompanying illustration.

Song sparrow

The song sparrow has a long tail with a rounded tip. Many color variations of song sparrow can be found, from red-brown to chocolate-brown, but all are brownish, with a brown-streaked breast. In the most basic terms, song sparrows are dark and streaky above, and light and streaky below. All song sparrows (except for juvenile birds) have a dark central breast spot. And all have a dark mustache stripe on each cheek from bill the top of the breast. Song sparrows love thickets and thick underbrush, especially near water. Their song is a series of four clear whistled notes, followed by a bright **chuw-ee** and ended with a buzzy trill.

Fox sparrow

Compared to the song sparrow, the fox sparrow is much larger and more boldly patterned.

I always remember that fox sparrows have a warm rusty (fox-colored) brown on their wings, rump, and tail, with large matching spots on a white breast. In some portions of western North America, however, fox sparrows are a much darker chocolate brown or gray. Many fox sparrows have some dark gray across the back of the head and neck.

When you see a fox sparrow, you immediately notice its size (length from bill-tip to tail-tip is 7 inches). You may also notice its habit of scratching with its feet at the leaves and debris on the ground to find food among the leaf litter. During migration and harsh winter weather, this species may show up at a backyard feeder where it exhibits its scratching feeding behavior on the ground beneath the feeders. The fox sparrow male is a spring singer on or near the nesting territory. Its song is a loud and rich mix of whistles and short, buzzy trills.

Lincoln's sparrow

Compared to either the song or fox sparrows, the Lincoln's sparrow is more subtly marked and delicate-looking. To my eyes, the Lincoln's resembles a song sparrow that's been refined by a semester at charm school. The finely streaked tan breast and warm tan wash across the back are set off by a grayish face and reddish wings and tail, with a white, unstreaked belly. Its bill is smaller than the song sparrow's. The Lincoln's sparrow's overall length is an inch shorter than the song sparrow. Far more common in the West than in the East, the Lincoln's is a solitary skulker in the underbrush; so it is often missed by bird watchers. The call note of the Lincoln's sparrow is a harsh **chup!** and the song is a loud, musical trill.

Bill's Top 40 Favorite Birds

When asked to compile a list of my 40 favorite birds, I was very excited at the opportunity. After finishing a first draft, however, my list of 40 contained 100 species! So the list you see here is a very abridged version of the original.

These birds are listed in taxonomic order — the order in which they appear in a field guide — not by personal ranking. You'll have to guess my top-of-the-trees favorite.

In honor of many joys birds bring me and my family, here are some nice photographs of the birds I love, along with a bit of information about each species. Enjoy!

Common loon

The haunting, yodeling cry of the common loon has been called the sound of true wilderness. Common loons nest along the edges of large,

John Ford

deep freshwater lakes all across the northern tier of the continent. They forage by diving underwater and swimming in pursuit of small fish. In New England, organizations of loon enthusiasts — known as **loon rangers** — work to protect nesting loons and their offspring from human disturbance during the breeding season. In winter, most common loons move to the coastal waters. Breeding-plumage adult loons have a deep green head, a black neck band, and a checkered black-and-white back. Winter loons are a drab mixture of gray and white.

Great blue heron

This bird is no relation to any type of herring, pickled or otherwise. Great blue herons are common all across North America and can be seen standing along the shore of any body of water, from tiny creeks to huge lakes and ocean beaches. Great blues will eat almost anything, from a grasshopper to a young alligator. Because they are large and easily seen, great blue herons are one of the species most likely to be appreciated by non-bird watchers.

Marie Read

Roseate spoonbill

It's probably a good thing that roseate spoonbills, as adults, are tinged with a splash of carmine pink, and a shockingly bright orange tail. Otherwise, their bald head and banjo-shaped bill could be described as homely. They feed by sweeping their bills back and forth through shallow water, snapping up and eating anything that they can catch. Spoonbills inhabit mangrove swamps and wetlands along the entire crescent of the American Gulf Coast. This is a tropical species that we in North America are lucky to have.

Blue-winged teal

The first time I saw a male blue-winged teal, with its gray head and white crescent-moon face patch, and its gorgeous sky-blue wing patch, I thought I wanted to do nothing but watch birds for the rest of my life. This small duck packs a lot of grace and beauty into its compact size. Bluewings are fairly common in spring and summer across most of North America, preferring freshwater lakes, sloughs, and marshes. From a distance, teal appear to have a smaller, rounder head, and a shorter bill than most other ducks.

American avocet

The sleek and slender American avocet, with its upturned bill, is one of North America's most beautiful shorebirds. The bird pictured here is in breeding plumage. In winter, avocets are a blend of dull gray, black, and white. Avocets are primarily a bird of the western half of North America, although some do breed along the mid-Atlantic Coast. Avocets winter along the southern coastal areas of the U.S.

Harold Lindstrom

Long-billed curlew

It's hard to believe that a bird with a bill this long exists, but it does. Although it is a shorebird, the long-billed curlew spends only the winter months near the shore. In spring and summer, you can find it in the dry grasslands of the interior West, where it nests and forages for insects. Bird watchers visiting Florida in winter can see this western species in coastal areas. Longbills also winter in coastal Texas and along the Pacific Coast from Washington to California.

Ron Austing

Maslowski Photograph

American woodcock

Woodcocks are really a woodland shorebird. They use their long flexible bills to probe the soil for earthworms. Each spring at dusk and dawn, the male woodcock performs a spectacular aerial display in an attempt to attract a mate. The nasal **peent** call of the woodcock is given repeatedly by the male prior to beginning each display. Woodcock are common in mixed woodland and meadow habitat all across the eastern half of North America. I love this species because when the males begin displaying in our meadow in early March, I know spring is on its way.

Upland sandpiper

Another example of a shorebird that spends little or no time along the shore, the upland sandpiper prefers to breed in wet, grassy meadows and native grassland from Alaska to New England, and south through the Great Plains. In areas where grassland habitat has disappeared, these birds can be found nesting in the margins of large airports. The call of the upland sandpiper is a wild **whip, wheel, you!** and is often given in flight from high above a male's territory. "Uppies" often perch on fenceposts and telephone poles. This species is declining in the northeastern portions of its range.

Gary Meszaros

Black skimmer

The long-winged, black-and-white skimmer feeds by flying low over water and "skimming" for small fish, using the long, lower half of its bill. When a fish is struck, the bill snaps shut and the skimmer eats "on the wing" or else returns to its nest to feed mate or young. Skimmers are coastal birds, related to the terns, and can be found resting in large groups on sandy beaches, shoals, and sandbars when they are not skimming the shallows for fish. For me, seeing a skimmer working a coastal pool is the ultimate beach experience.

Atlantic puffin

Atlantic puffins nest on rocky islands off the Atlantic coast of North America. Their nests are excavated burrows, or natural crevices, where the female lays a single egg. Puffins were decimated by egg-harvesting in the 1800s, but recent preservation and reintroduction efforts have helped this species recover. I took a puffin-watching trip one June to see these birds on their breeding islands and became a big fan of this species. Atlantic puffins spend the winter far offshore, returning to land to breed.

Cooper's hawk

The Cooper's hawk is the larger of the two bird-eating hawks (sharp-shinned hawk is the other) that sometimes do their hunting near backyard bird-feeding stations. Adult Cooper's hawks have a dark slate back, a breast barred with orange, and a dark crown that gives their face a fierce appearance. The Cooper's hawk hunts small songbirds, often pursuing them into underbrush or through thick woods. If the birds at your feeder scatter suddenly, a Cooper's hawk may have just made a pass at them. An illustration comparing Cooper's and sharp-shinned hawks appears in the comparision portion of this color section.

Ron Austing

Red-tailed hawk

The redtail is the large raptor commonly seen along highways and in roadside fields. In fact, the highway systems of North America have created lots of new habitat for this open-country bird. Redtails often perch in a tree or on a power pole overlooking an open grassy expanse — perhaps resting, perhaps watching for some sign of movement below them, such as a rabbit or a mouse. In flight, the redtail soars in large, lazy circles. As the bird turns in the air, the sun may strike its tail, giving you a flash of the rust-colored tail that gives this species its name.

Ron Austing

California quail

Along the western edge of North America, from southern British Columbia to Mexico's Baja Peninsula, a plump quail with a topknot on its head keeps calling **chi-ca-go**, **chi-ca-go**. This is the California quail, and it's not really crying for Chicago, although its call sounds like it is. A ground-dwelling bird, the California quail is common in brushy and wooded habitat and is a regular at many bird feeders and bird baths. The very similar Gambel's quail inhabits the dry regions of the interior Southwest.

Maslowski Photograph

Snowy owl

Unless you live in the northernmost reaches of North America, the snowy owl is a species you see only in the winter, and perhaps only once every few winters. Snowy owls are thought to come southward only in winters when the lemming populations on the arctic tundra have crashed. Adult male snowies are pure white; females and immatures are white, barred with black. Snowy owls are not nocturnal like most owls, but hunt during the day. I saw my first snowy owl in a front-yard oak tree of my boyhood home in Iowa. Harsh weather and reduced prey populations to the north had driven the bird south, seeking survival.

Maslowski Photograph

Eastern screech-owl

The eastern screech-owl should more properly be called the whinnying owl, because its call sounds like the whinny of a tiny horse. Found over the eastern two-thirds of North America, eastern screech-owls come in two color phases, red and gray. Both color phases can occur in the same brood of young in a single nest. Screech-owls are cavity nesters; they nest almost anywhere there is a nest hole in suitable wooded habitat. Screech-owls also use nest boxes placed high on a tree in a woodland setting.

Bill Beatty

Whip-poor-will

The whip-poor-will calls its name out again and again in a loud ringing voice that can carry for great distances. "Whips" are nocturnal birds of the eastern and southern woods, spending their days sleeping and their nights hunting large flying insects, particularly moths. The nest of the whip-poor-will is no nest at all, but rather a scrape on the ground into which two eggs are laid. The cryptic coloration of the whip-poor-will helps it to blend perfectly with the forest floor, making it almost impossible to see for both humans and potential predators. Spraying for gypsy moths in the eastern United States has wiped out the whip-poor-wills' insect prey and thus greatly reduced the population of this species in many areas.

Ron Austing

Ruby-throated hummingbird

Everybody loves hummingbirds, but if you live east of the Great Plains (and outside of Texas or Louisiana), you must focus all your love on just one species, the ruby-throated hummingbird. Like all hummers, the rubythroat can fly backwards, upside down, and every which way, but spends most of the warm months of the year hovering in front of flowers (or at hummingbird feeders), drinking nectar. In early spring, when the rubythroats return from their tropical wintering grounds, no flowering plants are available for hummingbirds to visit. Instead, these resourceful birds catch flying insects and even visit the small holes drilled in trees by yellow-bellied sapsuckers in order to eat both sap and the insects drawn to it.

Ron Austing

Anna's hummingbird

Many Anna's hummingbirds spend the entire year in the temperate coastal areas of the Pacific Coast, from British Columbia, south to California, and as far east as Arizona. The adult male Anna's has an iridescent magenta crown to match his magenta throat. Anna's are common visitors to hummingbird feeders and garden flowers. You can't ask for a much more beautiful hummingbird than this.

Barth Schorre

Red-headed woodpecker

The boldly patterned red-headed woodpecker is decked out in large blocks of red, black, and white. Once a common sight across much of the eastern half of the United States, the red-headed woodpecker population has suffered due to a variety of factors, including competition from starlings for nest holes, and the use of creosote-treated wooden power poles along with metal and concrete power poles (wooden powerline poles were a common nest site for this cavity-nesting species, but the creosote makes the poles unsuitable for this activity). Red-heads often nest in loose-knit colonies of several pairs. They prefer large, open stands of hardwood trees, particularly oak trees, which produce the acorns that are a favorite food of this species.

Richard Day

Acorn woodpecker

This western woodpecker, with the face that looks like clown make-up, lives communally in colonies of as many as ten individuals. Acorn woodpeckers love acorns so much that they store huge numbers of these nuts in clusters of individually drilled holes. These communal storage areas may be drilled into tree bark, in dead trees, and even in wooden house siding. Acorn woodpeckers also eat insects but, unlike other woodpeckers, do not excavate in wood for insect prey; they capture the insects in flight or on the ground.

Harold Lindstrom

Scissor-tailed flycatcher

Someone once asked a friend of mine if scissor-tailed fly-catchers use their tails to snip the heads off other birds. The answer is no, in case you were wondering. The male of this species does use its gracefully long tail to help him put on an elaborate courtship display flight. A summer resident of the southern Great Plains, the scissortail is often seen perched along roadsides and on power-lines. From these perches the birds make forays into the air and onto the ground for insects. In flight, both males and females show bright pink patches under their wings.

Bill Bevington

Eastern phoebe

One of the continent's most common flycatchers, the eastern phoebe nests under eaves, under bridges, and in barns, almost always making its home near human habitation. Easily recognized by its call of **fee-bee!** and its habit of constantly wagging its tail, the phoebe is such a favorite bird of mine that my wife and I named our daughter after it. Our Phoebe is still just a nestling.

John Trott

Vermilion flycatcher

In the southwestern United States there is a brilliant red flycatcher like no other, the vermilion flycatcher. The male is the more colorful, but the female vermilion is beautiful in her own way, with subtle shades of brown and pink. Along rivers, creeks, and other waterways, the vermilion flycatcher perches in a prominent location from which it makes aerial forays for flying insects. Like the painted bunting, the vermilion flycatcher is a much-dreamed-about bird for bird watchers from all over North America.

Harold Lindstrom

Steller's jay

I really love watching jays. There are two crested jays in North America: the blue jay, east of the Rocky Mountains, and the Steller's jay, which lives from the Rockies, west. Although a bird of the mountains, preferring coniferous forests, the Steller's jay is not shy and retiring by any means. Campgrounds, parks, and mountain resorts are often haunted by a flock of Steller's jays, which sometimes beg food from amused humans. The call of this large, bold, jay with the black crest, is a loud **shook, shook.**

Fredrick Sears

Richard Day

Black-billed magpie

This large black-and-white bird has wings and tail feathers that show an iridescent green in sunlight. Common throughout western North America in woodlands and thickets, especially near water, magpies are one of the most-easily-spotted birds for eastern bird watchers traveling to the West. In some areas, magpies have become common in towns. Their wings and back flash brilliant white patches in flight. Magpies often gather in large, noisy flocks to forage.

Common raven

By far the largest member of the Corvid (crows and jays) family, the common raven is found throughout the western and northern portions of North America, as well as in the highest elevations of the eastern mountains. Ravens in flight can be distinguished from the smaller American crow by their spade-shaped tails (crow tails are fan-shaped) and large head and beak. These birds are adaptable and smart as hunters and scavengers, able to survive both inhospitable habitat and climate.

Gary Meszaros

Maslowski Photograph

Mountain bluebird

Of our three bluebird species in North America, the mountain bluebird is the only one in which the male is all blue. I love all three bluebird species, but I chose the mountain for this grouping because you can find it in such high and lonesome places in the West, from Alaska to New Mexico. In spite of its name, the mountain bluebird is not found only in the mountains. You can also find it in the high plains areas and other open terrain. Because they are slightly larger than either western or eastern bluebirds, mountain bluebirds require nest box entrances that are just a bit larger than the standard entrances on other bluebird houses.

Hermit thrush

Hermit thrushes breed deep in dark coniferous forests all across Canada and the western United States, as well as in the mountainous regions of the northeastern U.S. This habitat preference and their shy, retiring nature earned them the name hermit. Their rust-colored rump and tail make them easy to distinguish from other woodland thrushes. The song of the hermit thrush is one of the most beautiful of all North American birds.

Maslowski Photograph

Gray catbird

Catbirds are friendly, inquisitive birds with a beautiful, varied song. They are good mimics of other birds' songs, in addition to having the cat-like **mew** call for which they are named. Catbirds are slate gray overall, with a black cap and a rusty undertail. Because they prefer skulking in dense underbrush, catbirds are more often heard than seen. When they are singing, catbirds can go on almost endlessly. For this reason (the endless song), an early birding companion gave my mom the nickname of Catbird. My mom, however, is anything but a skulker in the underbrush.

John Trott

American dipper

Sometimes called the water ouzel, the dipper is named for its habit of bobbing up and down while perched on a streamside rock or snag. Dippers feed by walking or "flying" (using their wings) underwater in rushing mountain streams, seeking insect larvae and other aquatic goodies. Dippers are year-round residents from Alaska to the higher elevations in Arizona and New Mexico. Some birds move to lower elevation streams in winter. Though they lack flashy plumage, dippers make up for it with their amazing behavior.

Maslowski Photograph

Mourning warbler

I could not help but include this species on my list of favorites because I spent so many years hoping to see a

mourning warbler. When I finally did see one, at a bird banding station in the mountains of West Virginia, it was handed to me by the bander, and I got to study the male mourning while holding him softly in my hand. The dark gray hood of the male resembles dark mourning clothes, which is why the species is so-named. Mourning warblers breed across a wide swath of northern and northeastern North America. Their preferred habitat is brushy thickets and thorny brambles.

Kentucky warbler

Their black Fu Manchu mustache pattern stands out against a lemon-yellow breast, but Kentucky warblers are surprisingly hard to see. Their chosen breeding habitat is deep hardwood forest, particularly in moist wooded ravines.

Loss of habitat in both breeding and wintering range is reducing this species significantly. The male's

loud, rolling **cherry, cherry, cherry, cherry** is sometimes confused with the song of the Carolina wren.

Indigo bunting

The stunning, all-blue, male indigo bunting sings late into the summer from a prominent perch at the top of a tree. In poor light, his plumage appears to be black. Adult females are an even, tawny brown overall. To get to the small grass seeds they prefer, indigos perch midway on a weed stem, then sidle out to the end until the stem bends enough to let them get at the seed heads. Our farm is named Indigo Hill in honor of all the indigos that spend the summer nesting there.

Maslowski Photograph

Painted bunting

Of all the birds in a North American field guide, the male painted bunting stands out as the one species most lusted after by bird watchers. But what the painted bunting has in showy plumage, it lacks in breeding range. The breeding range of the

Barth Schorre

painted bunting is limited to the south-central United States, from southern Kansas and Missouri south to Texas. Another population of painted buntings nests along the south Atlantic Coast in the Carolinas. Some painteds winter in southernmost Florida. If you want to see this garish bird, you'll have to go looking for it.

Marie Read

Dark-eyed junco

When I was almost two years old, my grandmother put my highchair in front of the kitchen window so I could see the winter bird feeder outside. She claims I pointed out the window at a small gray and white bird, and said "junco!" Juncos are common winter feeder visitors across much of North America, preferring to scratch for seed bits on the ground beneath the feeders. In the eastern half of North America, the junco is gray and white. In the West, several races of this species feature varying amounts of brown on the sides and back, along with the gray and white. At one time these were all considered separate species, but now they are lumped together continent wide as the dark-eyed junco.

White-crowned sparrow

This large, elegant sparrow with the badger stripes on its head is a common sparrow across much of the western portions of North America. The white-crowned carries itself erectly, and its clean plumage and small pink bill make give it a striking and proud appearance. Its song is a long, mournful series of whistled notes that sound like **Oh! Dear me!** In winter, white-crowneds can sometimes be found in large flocks, especially in thick brambles and heavy underbrush.

Marie Read

Maslowski Photograph

Eastern meadowlark

Spring of THE year! That's what the song of the eastern meadowlark sounds like to many bird watchers. This common member of the blackbird family is found in grassy meadows and farm fields. The eastern meadowlark often sings its song from a prominent perch, such as a fencepost, powerline, or the top of a tree along the edge of a field. The lemon-yellow breast and bold, black breastband make this species one of the most beautiful blackbirds you'll ever see. The western meadowlark is hard to distinguish visually from the eastern, but its song is a longer, more bubbly and musical series of notes.

Baltimore oriole

The Baltimore oriole and its western counterpart, the Bullock's oriole, were once lumped together by ornithologists as a single species and renamed northern oriole. In recent years, genetic tests have shown that the two birds are distinct species, so the eastern birds are once again known as the Baltimore oriole, making bird watchers (and baseball fans in Maryland) very happy. Baltimore orioles, which spend the summer months in the eastern half of North America, weave intricate, baglike nests out of grasses, strings, hair, and small vines.

Richard Day

Common redpoll

Maslowski Photograph

The common redpoll — the little red finch with the red cap — lives most of the year in the far northern parts of North America, nesting in scrub trees near the arctic tundra. Some winters, feeder operators as far south as southern Colorado, Kansas, and Virginia are treated to the sight of redpolls at their feeders when harsh weather or a shortage in the natural seed crop push the birds to migrate southward. Both sexes have the red cap or poll all year, but only male redpolls have the raspberry-colored wash on the breast.

Evening grosbeak

Using pressure sensors, scientists have determined that evening grosbeaks possess the most powerful seed-cracking bill of any North American bird. This ability comes in handy for the evening grosbeak, which can crack cherry pits and other hard-shelled seeds. At feeding stations, these birds can devour great quantities of sunflower seed in a short time. Grosbeaks in a flock keep in touch with each other with a loud call of **cleer!** In winter, this species gathers into large flocks that wander nomadically in search of food.

John Trott

Bluebird nest boxes

Here's a good bluebird box design that meets all the requirements of nesting bluebirds. Probably the most important requirement is the right-sized entry hole: $1^1/_2$ inches for eastern and western bluebirds; $1^9/_{16}$ inches for mountain bluebirds. Recent research has shown that a $1^9/_{16}$-inch hole may be best for all three species; even the smaller eastern bluebirds prefer a little wiggle room. But you need to keep the hole size in these parameters because with any hole larger than $1^9/_{16}$ inches, a starling can squeeze in and usurp the box.

If you'd like to build your own bluebird box, you can get free plans from the North American Bluebird Society, P.O. Box 6295, Silver Spring, MD 20916-6295; phone 310-384-2798. A donation to cover costs is appreciated.

If you decide to buy a box, keep the following ideal specifications in mind:

- **Material:** Wood, $^3/_4$-inch or more thick, provides the best insulation from heat and cold. Exterior plywood won't warp or split. Other wood should be protected from the weather.

- **Preparation:** Light, neutral colors of paint, stain, or clear sealer may be applied to the outside of the box only, and allowed to dry and air thoroughly. Pressure-treated wood contains copper arsenate and should not be used. Metal flashing tacked over cut ends of back and roof seams prevents leaks. Nails or screws, not staples, should be used to hold the box together.

- **Access:** Side or front should swing open for monitoring and cleaning, and should be secured at bottom with a screw to prevent tampering. Top-opening boxes are hard to clean and must be mounted low so that one can look inside them. They're less safe against predators because they're closer to the ground.

- **Dimensions:** Entry hole should be $1^1/_2$ inches in diameter for eastern and western bluebirds; $1^9/_{16}$ inches wherever mountain bluebirds occur. Floor: $4^1/_2$ to $5^1/_2$ inches square. The floor should be 8 inches below the entry hole. Perches, favored by house sparrows, should be avoided.

- **Roof:** Should be slanted, with back higher than front, and overhanging 2 inches or more to protect entry hole from harsh weather and direct sun.

- **Interior:** Should be free of sharp projectiles. Inside of front should be deeply scored below hole to give toehold to emerging birds.

- ✔ **Ventilation/Drainage:** Drill holes or gaps near the roof on two sides for cross-ventilation. You should seal the holes with flexible weather-stripping (Mortite is one brand) in cold weather; this should be removed during warm seasons.

- ✔ **Floor:** Should be recessed and completely covered by the sides and front of the box. Rain will seep into the seams of a floor that is nailed flush to the box sides.

Where to put the nest box?

Suppose that you have a box, and you've been lucky enough to see blue-birds around your yard. Why not just run out and nail that box to a tree? At all costs, resist the temptation to bang the box onto the nearest tree or fencepost. Several reasons exist for this; most have fur, and some have slithery scales. Predators. They're out there, and they're hoping to eat bluebird tonight. See Chapter 8 for hints on how to foil them.

Although your yard may not allow it, it's good to put the box as far away (100' or more) from shrubbery and trees as possible. This location discourages house wrens, which like to take over bluebird houses in nasty ways (by puncturing and throwing out bluebird eggs, and then filling the box with packed twigs). If you're lucky enough to have a big open field or yard, put the box up in the middle of it, and do the bluebirds a huge favor by putting up some perches in the field. These perches can simply be tree limbs with the butt ends dug into the ground. The ideal situation is to put a perch or tree about 25 feet from the nest box, directly in line with the entrance hole. This arrangement vastly enhances the field's usefulness for the perch-hunting bluebirds, for fledgling bluebirds making their first flight, and it also increases the chances that your box will be accepted. If you're putting up multiple bluebird boxes, place them at least 100 yards apart to minimize territorial fighting between bluebird pairs.

How high? Which way?

Put the box on its post about five feet off the ground, or so that the nest contents are located at your eye level when you open the box. This is high enough to foil leaping predators, and low enough so that you can see what's going on inside when you monitor the box. The baffle should go right under the box. Face the box away from prevailing winds (that usually means facing it south). Doing that helps keep rain from coming in the hole. Making sure the bluebird nest stays warm and dry is important in rainy springs. I use flexible weatherstrip in all the ventilation holes until it's reliably warm outside.

Check out those chicks!

When you put up a bluebird box, you're starting a crash course in bird nesting biology. What a luxury to have a bird nest in your yard, where you can watch it all happen! Provided you've mounted the box properly and baffled it against predators, you can take a biweekly peek into the box and get involved in your tenants' lives. It's a good idea to be a discreet but nosy landlord. You get lots of enjoyment from it, and the bluebirds can benefit as you keep competitors, insects, and predators at bay so they can raise their young in peace. To find out how to do it, refer to Chapter 8.

Other ways to bring happiness to bluebirds (and to you)

One of the greatest things about bluebirds is how darned appreciative they are. They'll gladly take up residence in a nestbox; while they're at it, they'll perch on your deck railings and garden fence. Give them a bird bath and, on hot summer afternoons, they'll make the water fly. When the young come out of the box, they'll all pile in the bath like kids around a fire hydrant. Bluebirds know how to have fun. Put up a few perches around an open yard and a bright blue ornament will atop them much of the day.

Have mealworms handy

Probably the most fun you can have with bluebirds, aside from having them in your boxes, is feeding them. As I write, a pair of bluebirds is keeping a sharp eye on our kitchen window. When I appear at that window, the blue-birds flutter down to the deck rail closest to the window and fix beady black eyes on mine. Like Homer Simpson with a donut floating in a bubble over his head, they're thinking one thing: WORMS. You see, I buy mealworms for our bluebirds. By the thousand, in bulk, by mail order. And I keep a container of them right on the kitchen counter for those bluebirds, and boy, do they know it!

Bluebirds are really sharp, and it took us only half a day to train them to come in to a little dish where the worms are. Now, they're so conditioned to being fed, they look downright indignant when we miss their cues. The male perches on the empty dish, looking into it again and again, and then hops closer to the window and bobs up and down, all the while keeping eye contact with me. He and his mate barely bother to fly away when we come out to restock the dish. Lots of people train bluebirds to take mealworms from their hand! All it takes is patience and time. Of course, you need a bulk source for mealworms. Try

- **Grubco,** Box 15001, Hamilton, OH 45015; phone 1-800-222-3563
- **Georgia Mealies,** P.O. Box 7724, Tifton, GA 31793; phone 912-382-8874
- **Fae's Mealworms,** P.O. Box 411, Oakland, TN 38060; phone 901-465-2534

You can offer other things to bluebirds, especially in the dead of winter, such as the miracle meal recipe at the front of this book.

Load up on brightly colored berries

Until the bluebirds key into your offerings, a good way to bring them in is with branches loaded with brightly colored berries that they like and naturally seek out. Bittersweet, with its papery yellow bracts and bright orange-red berries, is a favorite. I had a friend who found five bluebirds hanging on her front door bittersweet wreath one winter morning. They picked berries until they stripped it bare, much to her delight.

Drape bittersweet, or a flowering dogwood branch laden with red berries, across your feeder or deck railing and offer mealworms and/or Miracle Meal in shallow dishes nearby. With luck, you'll have bluebirds giving you dirty looks all day, like we do. In some parts of the continent, Oriental bittersweet is a nasty invasive plant. If you'd rather not risk helping an exotic plant, substitute dogwood berries or winterberry holly instead.

Want more info?

One national organization is devoted to the study and appreciation of bluebirds. It is

⊩ ✔ **The North American Bluebird Society (NABS),** Box 6295, Silver Springs, MD 20916-6295

NABS publishes a quarterly journal, *Sialia,* that reports the results of both scientific and casual backyard studies of bluebirds. NABS also sells lots of interesting bluebird paraphernalia, from nest boxes to bluebird earrings (for humans).

In addition to NABS, many state and provincial bluebird organizations exist. Contact NABS for the one nearest you, if you wish to find out more about bluebirds.

Purple Martins

In case you're wondering, purple martins are not the things you see on the cover of a tabloid magazine. Those are *purple Martians*.

What's a purple martin?

Purple martins are birds. They are the largest member of the swallow family in North America. Males are deep, glossy, purplish blue, and females and immatures are dark brown with whitish bellies. Martins soar around on tapered, nearly triangular wings, catching and eating flying insects. Their mosquito-control capabilities have probably been oversold. Being big, beefy birds, martins like big, beefy insects like dragonflies better than itty-bitty mosquitoes. They have a deep, chortling, liquid whistle, and many varied mechanical-sounding growls and trills.

Martins build a nest of twigs, dried grass, and bark in a suitable nest compartment, usually in a martin house or hanging gourd. They line the nest with green leaves, which may help control insect pests and keep humidity high for the developing eggs. A mud and twig barrier near the entrance hole keeps eggs from rolling out in high winds. Three to seven white eggs are laid, and they hatch sequentially; that is, some young are a lot bigger and stronger than the last-hatched in a given clutch. They're fed by the parents on flying ants, bees, wasps, dragonflies, and the like for about 28 days in the nest, and for up to two weeks after they leave. Young martins come back to sleep in the nest for several days after fledging. When late summer comes, the birds all congregate in huge flocks and migrate together to South America.

Like many members of the swallow family, purple martins are sociable birds, and they nest in colonies. What's really neat about them is that they prefer human-provided housing to any other. So those of us fortunate enough to live near good martin habitats (open, short grassy fields, lawns, meadows, golf courses, playing fields, and open water) may be lucky enough to host a colony right in our yard.

Martins are very faithful to their colony sites once they get established. Establishing a colony of martins can take several years, but there's a great thrill in watching the first returning martins swoop in during early spring and take up residence in the same compartment of the same box that they occupied last year (see Figure 11-2). It makes a person feel needed.

Where and when?

As you may expect for a bird that's totally dependent on flying insects, purple martins are highly migratory, clearing out of their breeding colonies in late summer and returning in early spring. This clearing can be as early as January 15 in south Florida, March 15 in North Carolina, or May 1 in northern Maine. They really push the envelope for early arrival, perhaps to take occupancy in their breeding colonies before competitors can. Because of this, martins often suffer from weather-related food shortages and mortality. The first arrivals, often called *scouts,* were once thought to prospect for nest sites and then report back to the flock. We now know that the first arrivals are simply mature, experienced adults. Martins breed across most of the eastern two-thirds of the country, excluding the Rockies, and up the West Coast as well.

Figure 11-2:
Purple martins with natural gourd houses.

Attracting martins

Like bluebirds, martins need a specific kind of foraging habitat near their nestsite. Luckily, they'll accept a wide range of habitats. Marshes, bays, lakes, rivers, swamps, open meadows and pastures, open farmland, golf courses, playing fields . . . all offer ample room and flying insects to eat. They readily colonize areas close to large expanses of open water, but nest in dry areas, too. The only places martins don't frequent are heavy woods, cities, and exposed hills or mountaintops (where the wind blows the insects away).

Assuming you have one or more of these amenities nearby (and hoping also that lots of martins are in the vicinity), you'll want to put your martin housing up in the middle of the biggest open area you can find — no less than 40 feet square. Keep the housing away from tall trees, but near your house — usually within 100 feet. Martins prefer being near people!

Mount the house 10 to 15 feet above the ground, and make sure that the house can be easily raised and lowered for cleaning and inspection.

Housing: Buy it, build it, or grow it

You can take a number of different routes to find good martin housing. You can buy it, you can build it, or you can even grow it, as the Native Americans did. Buying a martin house can be an expensive proposition, and building one, unless (unlike me) you're pretty handy with tools, can be time-consuming. The third alternative, growing your own, can be really fun and can benefit the birds more than conventional housing.

Martin house basics

If you elect to buy or build, make sure that the housing satisfies these basic criteria:

- ✔ Easy access for nest cavity inspection and cleaning
- ✔ White (or paintable) exterior
- ✔ Entry holes the proper size for martins ($2^1/8$ inch diameter hole is best, but martins do accept holes between $2^1/4$ inches and $2^1/2$ inches)
- ✔ Interior cavities the right size for martins (minimum 6 x 6 x 6 inches inside is ideal, but bigger is better, as you can prevent starlings from taking over)
- ✔ Entry holes 1 inch above floor of cavity
- ✔ Housing easily pole-mounted, easy to raise and lower safely. Avoid large, heavy wooden houses, or poles that tip the house over as a means of lowering it
- ✔ Easy maintenance
- ✔ Adequate ventilation and drainage
- ✔ Rainproof and durable
- ✔ Safe for the martins — no sharp edges or splintery wood. No chemical treatment on inside

The Appendix has a list of reliable sources for martin houses.

Gourds

Gourds are naturally attractive to martins. Bird house gourds are a special kind that are big and bulbous, and can be easily dried, scraped out, painted white, and hung from a wire. (The white paint helps reflect sunlight and keeps the interior cool, as well as preserving the gourd for many years. The white paint also makes the dark entry hole more noticeable.) Suspended with as little play as possible, the gourds still swing in a light wind, something martins don't mind at all, but that starlings and house sparrows hate. Because gourds swing, predators have a hard time getting hold of gourd houses. And you can suspend them far enough apart so that you can get a nesting pair of martins in each one. Conventional martin houses, because the compartments are so close together, typically have only 50 to 65 percent occupancy because males may defend more than one compartment.

Any color house, as long as it's white

No matter what kind of martin housing you choose, only choose WHITE houses. Heat is reflected rather than absorbed, as it would be by a dark color, and you'll probably save martin lives during summer heat waves.

In addition, choose only housing that is easy to get into — for you! You need to clean nest compartments at the end of the season and inspect them during the season. Gourds can be cleaned out too, using a long stick and some warm soapy water.

Martins are very picky about the orientation of their nest cavities; it's the only way they know how to find them. When you raise or lower your martin house, be certain it goes back up aligned in the same compass direction and to the same height that it was before. Put a mark on the pole to be sure you've done it correctly, or you'll have some mighty confused martins. See the Appendix for other sources of information on martins.

Competitors

Some birds should never be allowed to nest in your martin housing, or in any bird house for that matter. Both of these species can easily destroy your colony if you let them get a toehold: the house sparrow and the starling. These non-native birds (they were introduced to North America from Europe) are much more aggressive than martins, destroying the martins' eggs and young and even killing the adults.

The best way to prevent these pests from invading your colony is to keep the housing closed off to them using entry-hole plugs, or to keep it down until martins have arrived in your area for the season. This method can take some scrambling around to get the housing up once the martins show up, but it's worth it.

Once the housing is up, you have to make some hard choices if house sparrows and starlings are interested. Most martin landlords either shoot or trap these birds, both of which are legal because these birds are not protected species. Trapped birds should be humanely dispatched; transporting them is useless, unless you put them on a slow boat to China, because they have wings and a strong homing instinct. You can get a variety of live-traps by contacting the Purple Martin Conservation Association, listed at the end of this section.

Predators

Predators in town? Baffle them! That's the only way to be sure that predators won't clean out your colony of martins. See Chapter 9 for a simple baffle that really works against raccoons, snakes, cats, and squirrels.

A more difficult problem is owl predation, which happens at night. Being flying predators, owls can't be baffled from below like climbing predators. You may find piles of martin feathers, or whole wings, under the box if an owl has been visiting. The solution for this situation is to enclose the martin box in a wire cage with openings large enough for the martins to get in and out but too small for an owl to fit through. Some manufacturers of aluminum martin houses sell these cages to fit specific house models.

Gourds, hung from a wire, offer much better protection against owls and climbing predators because they're just too wobbly and slippery for the intruder to get a good foothold on them.

Parasites — yuck!

In your nest checks, you may find nasty creepy-crawlies in the nest material, or even attached under the young birds' wings and legs. These creepy-crawlies are likely martin blowfly larvae, which look like grayish maggots. They suck the blood of the young birds and, in large infestations, can weaken them. The easiest way to help is to replace the nest. Just put the young birds in a shoebox with the cover on loosely. Remove the old nest and replace it with a new nest of dried, not green, grass. (Having a supply of this grass gathered in advance is handy). Shape it into a shallow, tight cup and replace the young into the new nest. They'll be much more comfortable, and the adults won't mind. Don't worry. These parasites are harmless for humans.

Want more info?

Two national organizations are devoted to martin study and appreciation. They are

- ✔ **The Purple Martin Conservation Association,** Edinboro University, Edinboro, PA 16444
- ✔ **The Nature Society,** Purple Martin Junction, Griggsville, IL 62340

A plethora of good information is available about purple martins. Your local public library may have some publications devoted to purple martins. I list some of my favorite information sources in the Appendix.

Hawks, Raptors, Birds of Prey

Hawks, eagles, falcons, owls, and other birds of prey are sometimes called *raptors*. They are natural-born predators that make their living by killing other animals. Birds of prey have fascinated humans since the dawn of time.

What's a hawk?

A hawk is a powerful bird that preys upon other animals (see Figure 11-3). All birds of prey have sharp, hooked beaks designed for tearing flesh and for administering a killing bite. Most birds of prey also are very strong fliers and have powerful feet tipped with razor-sharp talons. These talons are used for gripping and killing prey.

To use the term hawk to describe all birds of prey is not really accurate, sort of like calling all motorized vehicles cars. More all-encompassing terms are raptor (a carnivorous bird that preys upon other living things), or bird of prey.

What's cool about hawks?

Hawks are strong and powerful creatures. They're born to kill and are equipped accordingly. Humans admire their swiftness of flight, their agility, their keen eyesight, and their deadly hunting skills. This fascination with birds of prey led to what we today call *falconry:* hunting by means of trained captive birds of prey. Falconry was practiced by the ancient kings of Egypt and by King Arthur and his pals, but today you must have a permit to practice this ancient activity. All birds of prey are protected by federal law from interference by humans.

Figure 11-3:
Cooper's
hawk
chasing
birds at a
feeder.

Types of raptors

Falcon: Strong, rapid fliers, capable of extremely high speeds when diving on prey. Long wings tapered to a point. Bill sharply hooked. Seven falcon species are found in North America. Examples: peregrine falcon, kestrel.

Buteo: Large, soaring raptors with wide, rounded wings. Large head and broad shoulders make these birds look huge when perched. Examples: red-tailed hawk, rough-legged hawk, Swainson's hawk.

Accipiter: Woodland birds with long tails and short, rounded wings. Typical flight pattern is *flap, flap, sail . . . flap, flap, sail . . . .* Examples: sharp-shinned hawk, Cooper's hawk, northern goshawk.

Eagle: Huge birds of prey with large, hooked beak and large yellow feet. Long rounded wings show primary *fingers* when soaring. Examples: North American eagles: bald eagle, golden eagle.

Osprey: Also called *fish-hawk* for its feeding method of diving into water to capture fish. This white-headed, black-masked bird is eaglelike in appearance, but smaller, with a distinctive crook in its swept-back wings. The osprey is classified in its own family and is found all over the world except on Antarctica.

Vulture: Large dark birds most often seen soaring high in the sky. They resemble eagles in flight, but lack an eagle's large, protruding head (vulture heads are small and unfeathered). Even though vultures only eat dead animals (carrion), they're still considered raptors.

Where and when?

Raptors are found almost anywhere in North America throughout the year. Though many species migrate to warmer climates in the fall and winter, species such as the red-tailed hawk, bald eagle, red-shouldered hawk, several accipiter species, and rough-legged hawks, remain in North America all year long.

Most of the larger-winged raptors spend a lot of their time soaring in the sky, especially on warm sunny days. Don't forget to look up and scan the sky — even from your backyard; sooner or later you'll see a soaring raptor. Figure 11-4 shows a selection of raptors in flight.

Another good place to keep your eyes out for raptors is along roadways. Eagles and several hawk species use these human-made openings to their advantage as good places to hunt for small mammals and the occasional free meal provided by roadkills.

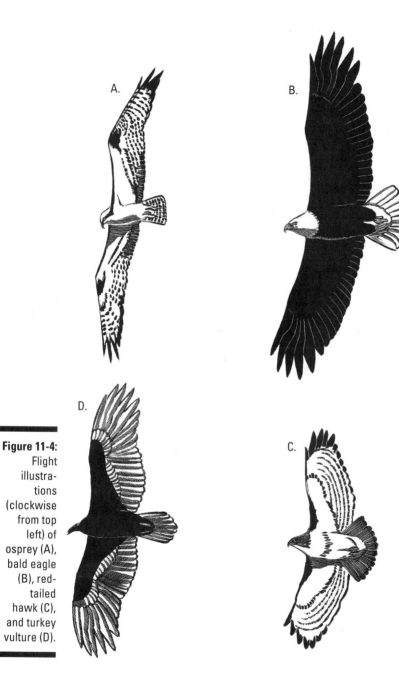

A.

B.

D.

C.

Figure 11-4:
Flight
illustra-
tions
(clockwise
from top
left) of
osprey (A),
bald eagle
(B), red-
tailed
hawk (C),
and turkey
vulture (D).

FIELD TIP

Raptor facts

When diving, the **peregrine falcon** can reach speeds of more than 200 miles per hour.

Bald eagles are adept hunters but also often scavenge for dead fish, or rob other birds of their food. This is an energy-saving, survival strategy.

Northern goshawks do attack and strike humans that venture near their woodland nests.

The two most common predators at backyard feeders are **Cooper's hawks** and **sharp-shinned hawks.**

Broad-winged hawks and **Swainson's hawks** (found in western North America) sometimes form soaring flocks (known as *kettles*) of several thousand birds during spring and fall migration. You can see a kettle of broad-winged hawks in the figure below.

The Hawk Mountain story

Of the many hawk-watching sites in North America, none is more famous than Pennsylvania's Hawk Mountain Sanctuary. Years ago, this site, a bare outcropping of stone along the Kittatinny Ridge in east-central Pennsylvania, was famous as a place to hunt hawks. The southward running ridge of this part of the Appalachian Mountains creates powerful updrafts of warm air. Migrant hawks use these updrafts, or thermals, as well as the air currents deflected off the high mountain ridges, to assist their soaring flight, and take advantage of the air currents by migrating along the high ridges of mountain ranges. As the migrant hawks passed through each autumn, hundreds of hunters would line the ridgetops to get a shot at these hawks. Such gunning was stopped on Hawk Mountain by the determined efforts of conservationist Rosalie Edge, and the mountain was declared a sanctuary. Today, the shooting or harming of any bird of prey is illegal.

Hawk watching

Spring and fall migration are the best times of year to observe hawks because their seasonal movements concentrate them in large numbers. Such concentrations can occur along natural migration routes, such as along mountain ranges, coastal areas, and peninsulas. Concentrations also occur in habitats where there's an abundance of food, such as when bald eagles congregate near a large dam in winter. The dam's spillway provides open water and also many fish that are stunned by the rapidly flowing water and become easy meals for the eagles.

Each autumn, thousands of hawk watchers gather atop Hawk Mountain's lookouts to watch passing raptors. On a really good day, nearly 1,000 migrating birds of prey may pass.

The thrill of hawk watching has spread to many other parts of North America, and today places like Hawk Ridge, Minnesota, and the Goshute Mountains in Nevada, are just as synonymous with hawks as Hawk Mountain.

Hawk migration, whether in the spring or the fall, is very weather dependent. A good front for hawks may mean lousy weather for humans, but you can bet the dedicated hawk watchers will be out there on the ridge, counting birds as they fly past.

Want more info?

Several national and regional organizations are devoted to hawk study and appreciation. A few of the largest ones are

- ✔ **Hawk Mountain Sanctuary Association**, 1700 Hawk Mountain Road, Kempton, PA 19529

- ✔ **Hawk Migration Association of North America**, 377 Loomis Street, Southwick, MA 01077

- ✔ **Hawk Watch International**, P.O. Box 660, Salt Lake City, UT 84110

Interested hawk watchers can discover more by consulting any one of the many hawk books and guides that are available commercially. Your local public library is a good place to start looking, and I list some of my favorite information sources in the Appendix.

Stay Focused

Focusing your attention on specific birds can add much enjoyment to your bird watching. A vast amount of information is available on specific species or groups of birds, so don't be shy about seeking it out. Your local bird club and public library are excellent places to start looking. The Internet is another source that's increasingly valuable. For hints on where to search for good bird info in cyberspace, see Chapter 25.

Part III

Bird Sighting 101: Using Your Tools

The 5th Wave By Rich Tennant

"Gee, those are light binoculars."

In this part . . .

1In this part you get the specifics on how to use your bird watching tools. You also get insider tips on improving your birding skills and on keeping records and lists of the birds that you see. For the beginner wishing to move to the intermediate level, this part is a big help. After reading this part, you'll be able to watch birds anywhere in the world (and look like a pro while you're doing it).

Chapter 12

Optics and How to Use Them

*T*he binocular is the tool of the bird watching trade. You can watch birds without the magnifying power of binoculars, but you won't always get a satisfactory look at the birds.

A myth about binoculars is that they're expensive. They can be, but they don't have to be. Recent advances in lens technology and the manufacturing process have resulted in very affordable binoculars for bird watchers.

In this chapter, I discuss what binoculars are, how they work, and how to choose them and use them most effectively for watching birds. Plus, I offer some tips on cleaning and loving your binoculars, because if you have decent binoculars, you *will* learn to love them, especially if they show you lots of neat birds.

Optics Defined: What You See Is What You Get

When birders talk about their optics, they're referring to their binoculars or spotting scope. Because the vast majority of the bird watching public has binoculars (a.k.a. *binocs*, or *bins*), this is usually what is meant by the term optics.

Spotting scopes — higher-powered, single-tube (telescope) viewing devices — are used primarily for viewing distant birds, such as waterfowl or shore-birds. These high powered scopes are becoming more popular as the number of avid bird watchers grows. But almost no one starts out with just a spotting scope — while everyone starts out with binocs of some sort. For more on spotting scopes, see Chapter 22.

Binoculars are composed of two optical tubes, joined side by side, much like two miniature telescopes. Inside each tube is a series of lenses and prisms that reflect, magnify, and transmit light (see Figure 12-1). When binoculars are held up to your eyes and pointed at a distant object, a magnified image of that object is transmitted to your eyes — it looks bigger and closer than if you had no binoculars.

Types of binoculars

Two basic types of binoculars are used by modern bird watchers: Porro prisms and roof prisms. You can tell them apart by how they're constructed.

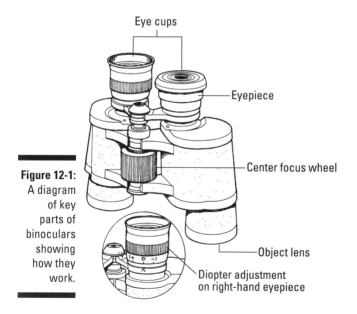

Figure 12-1:
A diagram of key parts of binoculars showing how they work.

Eye cups

Eyepiece

Center focus wheel

Object lens

Diopter adjustment on right-hand eyepiece

Porro-prism binocs

Porro-prism binoculars were first designed in the mid-1800s by some Italian fellow named Porro. His concept of placing two right-angled prisms in each barrel of a set of binoculars is still used today. Porro-prism binocs are the stereotypical angled-body binocular design. When standing on their barrels, or hanging from a strap around someone's neck, Porro-prism binoculars appear to form an M shape (see Figure 12-2).

Porros focus by relying upon an external focus wheel which, when turned, causes the eyepieces for each side to slide forward or backward along an external tube. This type of focusing allows for sharp images of close birds and other objects, as well as precise focusing on objects as close as six to ten feet.

The advantages of this binocular design are

✔ Brighter images due to greater transmission of light

✔ Fast focusing

✔ Close focusing

✔ Wider field of view (the amount of area you see when looking through the binoculars)

For low-to-mid-range priced binoculars, Porro-prisms offer the best value.

The disadvantages are weight (the better transmission of light is due to large prisms, which are weighty) and bulkiness, which can make Porros hard to use for small-handed folks. In addition, the external focusing mechanisms of many Porros can make for less-durable binoculars, that is, ones that can be more easily jarred out of alignment.

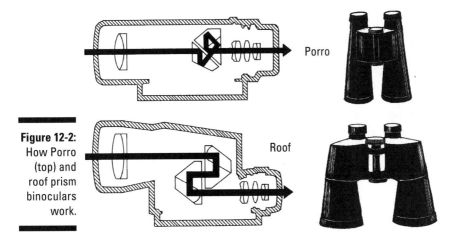

Figure 12-2: How Porro (top) and roof prism binoculars work.

Porro

Roof

Roof-prism binoculars

Roof-prism binoculars were first developed by a German binocular manufacturer in the mid-1800s. This design features two straight barrels, giving it an H-shaped appearance.

The design reflects light through a series of five small prisms in each barrel. Roof-prism binocs have grown in popularity among birders in the last few decades, primarily because many leading optics manufacturers are producing excellent optics in this format for the bird watching market. Because of the way roof-prisms are designed, most of the focusing hardware is enclosed inside the body of the binoculars. This hardware is adjusted with an external focusing knob or wheel.

The advantages to roof-prism binoculars are

- ✔ Ease of handling
- ✔ Fewer external moving parts (which means increased durability)
- ✔ A better ratio of power-to-weight; that is, in general, a 10x roof-prism weighs less than a 10x Porro

At the mid-to-high price range for binoculars, roof-prisms dominate the market.

The disadvantages are that roof-prisms tend to be more expensive than Porros, and they often don't focus as closely, making it hard to see nearby objects clearly. Because of the additional prisms required to reflect incoming light, roof prisms often do not offer as "bright" an image as Porros.

Choosing Binoculars

You need to consider a number of factors when choosing binoculars, but the most important three are *cost, power* (or magnification), and *comfort*. When selecting binoculars for yourself, bear these three factors in mind. Neglect any one of them, and you'll almost certainly regret your decision later.

For example, if you decide to buy an inexpensive pair of binoculars even though you like a more pricey pair better, you may find at a later date that you wished you'd made the additional investment. Or if you purchase a large pair of bins that seem heavy when hanging around your neck in the store, imagine your agony months later when you're out on a long bird walk? Talk about a pain in the neck.

Before you buy, I suggest you gather all the information you can about binoculars. The best sources for information and advice on bird-watching optics are your fellow bird watchers.

Ask your friends and fellow birders about their binocs. What brand and power do they have? What do they like about them? What do they dislike? How much did they pay? Where did they buy them? Would they do anything differently the next time they buy binoculars? If you can get answers to these questions, you'll begin to get a picture of what *you* would prefer in a binocular.

BIRDY WORDS

Binocular terms

These terms are helpful to know if you wish to be fluent in binocular-speak.

✔ **Armoring:** An outer coating, often rubber or synthetic, that makes binoculars more water-resistant (or even waterproof), more durable, and easier to hold.

✔ **Close focus:** How closely a pair of binoculars can focus (between 8 and 12 feet is ideal). Many high-power binoculars can't focus on objects that are nearer than 20 feet. This limitation is a disadvantage for birders wishing to look at nearby birds or butterflies. To determine the close focus of a binocular, try to focus on your feet, or another nearby object. The distance to the closest object upon which you can focus clearly is the close focus value of your binocular.

✔ **Eye relief:** The distance from your eyes to the outer surfaces of the eyepiece lenses. You don't want your eyes or eyelashes to touch the lenses, but if the eye-relief distance is too great, you lose field of view. Imagine peeking through a hole in a fence: the closer your eye gets to the hole, the more area you can see through the hole.

✔ **Eyepiece:** The lens nearest your eyes (the end of the binoculars that you look into).

✔ **Field of view:** The amount of area that can be seen when looking through a pair of binoculars. A larger field of view makes finding a distant bird through your binoculars easier. Higher powered binocs (10x and up) often have a reduced field of view.

✔ **Lens coatings:** Treatments applied to binocular lenses to increase image clarity, brightness, and color quality. Coated lenses are one of the things that make expensive binoculars expensive, but also better.

✔ **Objective lens:** The lens nearest the object at which you're looking. The diameter of the objective lens, measured in millimeters, is the second number in the two numbers used to describe optics (see "7x35" below).

✔ **Power:** The amount of magnification provided by the binoculars. Usually listed as 7x, 8x, or 10x.

✔ **7x35, 8x42, 10x40:** Pronounced "7 by 35," and so on. The common model designation for binoculars. The first number is the power or magnification (a 7x or 7-power binocular magnifies a distant bird 7 times, making it appear 7 times closer). The second number indicates the size of the objective lens (the larger end, not the one you look through). The larger this number, the larger the objective lens (and wider the field of view), and thus the more light enters your binoculars. More light means a clearer, brighter image.

After you get answers to these questions (and if you feel you can pester them a bit more without endangering your friendship), ask to try their binoculars for a few minutes. Try to avoid asking for the binocs just as a peregrine falcon flies overhead — your friend may get cranky. While trying your friend's bins, it's time to ask yourself a few questions: How do they feel in your hands? Are they easy to focus? Are they too heavy for you to hold steady?

Cost

It may seem hard to believe, but binoculars are one of those few items for which a higher price actually means higher quality. Another way to say this is: You get what you pay for. So the guiding rule for binocular-buying birders has been: "Buy the best optics you can afford."

But what's the price range for good binoculars? I'm glad you asked that question. But the answer depends on you and how you use the binoculars.

The low end of the price range for a new pair of adequate birding binoculars is $100. You can get some compact (small and lightweight) binocs for slightly less than that, but not all of these are ideal for in-the-field bird watching. The high end of the price range for binoculars is in the thousands of dollars! But you need not spend this much to get good optics.

Why not shoot for the mid-range of $150 to $350? In this price range, you can get a pair of binoculars that will be well-suited to you and your mode of watching birds. Dozens and dozens of binocular brands and models are available to choose from in this mid-price-range. If you choose to get mid-priced binoculars, you can always invest in a better (more expensive) pair at a later date.

"But," you ask, "isn't a $100 pair of 7x35s the same as a pair of $350 7x35s?" "Probably not," is my answer. A lot of competition exists among binocular manufacturers, and the not-worth-the-money brands and models are quickly taken off the market or greatly reduced in price. Perhaps the more expensive 7x35s have coated lenses, thick rubber armoring, and come with a manufacturer's warranty of several years.

Here's an interesting thought: A new pair of fairly expensive binoculars, costing, say, $750 would, over the course of a year, average out to only about $2.05 per day. Over five years, the figure becomes $0.41 per day. Not much to pay, for what you get in return.

Don't, under any circumstances, buy any binoculars that are marketed without a recognizable brand name or that are marketed at unbelievably low prices. These optics stink! Believe me, you'll be sorry. One warning sign of El Cheapo binoculars is a prismlike halo of colors around any object you view. This effect is caused by inferior optics inside the binoculars.

Power

The best binoculars for bird watching come in the 7x to 10x range (that's 7-power to 10-power). Binocs in this range provide enough magnification to make distant birds look bigger, without being too heavy to hold steady or to have hanging around your neck. Three of the most common powers are 7x35, 8x42, and 10x40.

Power is as much a matter of personal preference as anything. You may like the high magnification of 10x binoculars, but their increased weight may make your arms tired after holding them to your eyes for only a few minutes. Try several different binocs, either at a camera/optics store or at a gathering of bird watchers. You'll notice a difference in weight between binocs of different powers. Any binoculars above 10-power are likely to be too heavy to hold still, but can be used successfully when mounted on a tripod.

Recent advances in binocular design have helped make binoculars lighter and better balanced in the hand. For many bird watchers, a new well-designed 10x binocular is now as easy to hold steady as an older pair of 7x's. The mantra is "Try before you buy!"

The first number in a binocular description (7x35) refers to the power or magnification of the binocular. The higher the number, the more powerful the binoculars (which means a 10x binoc makes a distant bird appear much closer than a 7x one does). The second number in the description refers to the size (in millimeters) of the objective lens. The larger this number is, the more light is allowed into the optics. Lots of light means a bright, clear image is presented to your eyes.

Using the logic that more is better, wouldn't a 12x50 binocular be great? Lots of magnification and lots of light? The answer is an emphatic *no!* Such powerful binocs require large lenses and internal prisms, which makes them almost impossibly heavy to use without mounting them on a tripod.

Never look directly at the sun through binoculars. Magnified sunlight can seriously damage your eyes. When bird watching, always be aware of the sun's position so you don't inadvertently point at or swing your binocs past the sun. Ouch!

Comfort

"The best binoculars" an optics expert once wrote, "will disappear from your awareness while you are using them."

When you try binoculars, ask yourself if they feel comfortable to use. Comfort is a combination of factors: Are they easy to raise to your eyes? Does your forefinger automatically rest on the focus wheel? Can you easily adjust the settings to fit your needs? Do the binocs feel very heavy around your neck? Do they feel good in your hands?

You can have the best optics money can buy, but if you're not comfortable using them, they may as well be a lead doorstop. Here's an analogy for you: I'd love to own a racy sports car. There's one problem though (besides lack of money): I am six feet four, and there's no way I can fit into a sports car. Sexy and stylish though it may be, I am miserably uncomfortable in a tiny car.

If you have trouble holding a pair of binoculars steady (if the image is constantly moving and jiggling), the binocs may be too heavy for you to use. Try using a friend's lighter or smaller binoculars and see if you have a more stable image.

Other considerations

If I haven't confused you yet about how to choose binoculars, here are some other things to think about.

Field of view

Make sure the binoculars you choose have a reasonable field of view (the amount of area you can see at one time when looking through the binocs). Binoculars with narrow fields of view make it hard to find the bird when you raise the optics to your eyes.

Close focus

An ideal pair of binoculars focuses on objects as close as 12 feet away. Some compact models focus on closer objects, but you may sacrifice power and field of view. High-powered binocs, such as my own 10x40 wonders, may only focus to about 20 feet. This limited focus is a drag when a warbler perches 10 feet away and I have to *naked-eye* it while my wife *oohs* and *ahhs* at the close look she can get through her 8-powers. For butterfly watching (a natural spin-off of birding), close-focusing is a must. Nothing is worse than having to *back-up* to get a good look at a resting butterfly!

Brightness

The level of image brightness produced by your binoculars is a factor of how large the objective lenses are (x35, x40, x42,and so on) and the quality and coatings of the optical elements (lenses and prisms). Larger objective lenses produce brighter images.

Lens coatings

Coated lenses and high-quality prisms reduce the amount of light lost and thus transmit more light, which makes a brighter image. Test several models with coated and uncoated optics and you can see the difference. But remember, the better the coatings, the more expensive the binoculars are likely to be.

Armoring/waterproofing

If my binoculars weren't armored, I'd have smashed and dented them at least 400 times since I got them ten years ago. Armoring is a rubberized coating that encases the binoculars (but not the lenses), providing protection from bumps and knocks, as well as providing some protection from moisture. Most binocs are not water*proof*, but they are water *resistant*. So if you drop them in the pool, call your insurance agent. Armoring is a very good thing, and I recommend that you buy rubber-armored binoculars.

Avoid zoom binoculars, which may have inferior optics to regular non-zoom models. Avoid fixed-focus field glasses, which are simply impractical for watching birds. Avoid binoculars that lack a center focus wheel — meaning they can *only* be focused by turning the two individual eyepieces. These binocs are too hard to use in the field, if you only have two hands.

Using Binoculars

For several years after I started watching birds, I didn't know how to focus my binoculars properly. I'm going to save you from a fate such as mine (and save you from some painful headaches). When a friend finally showed me how to *really* focus binoculars, I couldn't believe how 3-D the birds looked all of a sudden! And I had no moment of dizziness after lowering my binocs. My next move was to beg my parents for new and better binoculars.

Using binocs isn't as simple as raising them up to your eyes. But the process is pretty simple nonetheless. Because not all eyes are created equal, binoculars are designed to be adjusted to accommodate your needs.

Setting the eyespace

All good binoculars are made in a way that allows the two optical barrels to pivot so that the space between them can be adjusted. When using binoculars, it's key that you get the two halves of the binocs the right distance apart to get the maximum image size. This spacing should match the amount of space between your eyes.

That statement may seem overly obvious to you, but you'd be surprised how many bird watchers use binocs for years without getting the eyespace aligned properly for their eyes. (If you've ever appeared in a Picasso painting and both of your eyes are on the same side of your nose, please ignore this section.)

To set the eyespace of your binoculars correctly, push the two barrels together so that they're adjusted to their minimum spacing. Raise the optics to your eyes and slowly expand the space between the barrels until you have the maximum amount of view or image space. If the barrels are too close together, the image area you see is circular and you may be able to see your hands or lots of black space out of the corners of your eyes. If the barrels are too far apart, you see two separate image circles with a black area in between.

If you've got the proper eyespace for your eyes, your image area appears oval-shaped and you notice the large, clear image space.

If you wear glasses, beware of older model binoculars that have metal or hard plastic eyecups. These eyecups not only scratch your glasses, they also greatly reduce your field of view because your eye is farther away from the eyepiece than is ideal. Think of it this way: Isn't it easier to see more through a keyhole if your eye is right up next to the hole?

Using the diopter: The eye equalizer

Almost everyone has one eye that is stronger than the other. This means that when the eyes focus on a distant object, the images transmitted to your brain from each eye are different. To test this, stick out your thumb as though you are about to be fingerprinted. Raise your arm and cover up a distant object, such as the light switch across the room, with your thumb — that is, block it from view. Now close your eyes alternately. See how the image jumps around? In addition, many people suffer from near-sightedness or far-sightedness. If your eyes aren't a perfectly matched 20-20, you may have a difficult time using binoculars because you can't focus clearly.

The word *diopter* is used by optometrists to measure the amount of correction needed for eyeglass prescriptions. The diopter (sometimes spelled dioptre) adjustment on binoculars compensates for these differences between eyes, as well as for any near-sightedness or far-sightedness. Adjusted properly, the diopter helps you to focus clearly on your target image.

You can use two basic configurations for adjusting a diopter. One is controlling the diopter adjustment with a second focus wheel, mounted in front of the primary focus wheel. Many roof-prism binoculars use this method. The other configuration has the diopter adjustment in the right eyepiece (refer to Figure 12-1) of the binoculars. In either case, the diopter scale appears on the focus mechanism. Once set, these markings, with 0 as a center point, allow you to remember the best setting for your eyes.

Using a diopter is an intrinsic part of focusing your binoculars.

Focusing

To focus your binoculars properly, follow these easy steps:

1. **Turn your main focus knob all the way to the right.**

   Locate your diopter focusing piece (either another focus knob or a movable eyepiece (usually the right eyepiece).

2. **Choose a distant stationary object on which to focus.**

3. **Close your left eye (or cover the left objective lens with your hand) and quickly turn the diopter focus piece so that the image is clear and in sharp focus for your right eye. Lower the binoculars and rest your eyes for a moment.**

4. **Looking through the binoculars once more, open your left eye (or uncover the left lens) and, using the center focus wheel, adjust the focus until a clear image appears.**

   You may need to adjust both wheels slightly to achieve the sharpest degree of focus.

5. **Once you've achieved maximum focus, look at the settings for your diopter adjustment (most binocs have symbols or numbers to indicate settings).**

   Remember where your optimal setting is, so you can automatically readjust your binoculars to that point should the setting be changed by another user.

Once you get your binocs focused and the diopter adjusted for your own eyes, the only focusing you have to do is with the center focus wheel. For most birds that appear in the middle distance, say 30 to 60 feet away, you don't need to refocus at all. Closer or more distant birds require some focus adjustment with the center wheel, however.

Properly focused, your binoculars give you a crystal-clear image. When I first discovered this, I thought that sharply focused binocs made birds appear almost three-dimensional. At any rate, the birds seemed clear and sharply defined to my eyes for the first time.

You can get fast at focusing by practicing on stationary objects. To set my binocs, I always pick an object with lots of contrast, such as a dark tree branch against a light sky or a black-and-white highway sign or billboard. Before long, focusing becomes second nature to you.

Trouble in Paradise: Balky Bins

If you're new to this binocular-toting hobby called bird watching, you may be having some less-than-heavenly experiences using your optics. This is normal, even for veteran bird watchers! The happy news is that all these problems are easy to remedy.

Focus problems

If you can't seem to get your birds in focus, even after following the steps in the section on "Focusing" in this chapter, here are two suggestions:

- Clean your binoculars thoroughly and try again.
- Take or send your binoculars to a trained optics repair professional and ask that the alignment be checked.

Binoculars go out of alignment from a hard bump or knock, just like the tires on your car. Out-of-alignment binocs are impossible to focus precisely, so your eyes try to adjust to make up for the lack of focus. The result is headache, dizziness, and frustration for you.

To find a person trained to fix optics, call your binoculars' manufacturer, ask the company that sold you the optics, or inquire at your local camera store. The Appendix has a list of major optics manufacturers.

Dizzy eyes

If your binoculars are not truly in focus, or if they're out of alignment, you may experience a moment of dizziness after you lower the binocs from your eyes. Believe me, it's better to solve this problem than to continue to use the binocs as they are. If you can't eliminate the problem by refocusing, or by using your diopter adjustment, take your binoculars to someone who can adjust the alignment. If you don't have an optics specialty store in your area, call the manufacturer of your binoculars and inquire about certified repair shops.

Here's a quick way to check the alignment of your binoculars. Look at a horizontal line, such as a telephone wire. Slowly move the binoculars away from your eyes and watch to see if the lines in the two eyepieces stay lined up. If one appears higher than the other, get thee to an optics repair shop — your bins are out of whack.

Glasses

If you wear eyeglasses, you have to suffer through some reduction of image space or field of view because your glasses prevent your eyes from getting as close as possible to the eyepieces of the binoculars. Today, most quality binoculars feature rubber eyecups that improve comfort for users, whether bespectacled or not. For the glasses-wearer, these rubber eyecups can be rolled down, allowing you to place the binoculars up against your glasses. This permits your eyes to be as close as possible to the outer lens of the eyepiece, which gives you an enlarged field of view. It also prevents the binoculars from scratching your glasses. Avoid older (and cheapo) binoculars that have hard plastic or metal eyecups.

 With a little practice you can raise your binocs to your glasses without jamming your glasses into your nose. Always make sure the eyecups are squared-up with your glasses, so that you're not cheating yourself out of the largest possible field of view. You may find that it helps to have a second pair of glasses, specifically for bird watching. Find a pair that allows you to get as close as possible to your binoculars' eyepieces. If your regular glasses are bifocals, ask your optician to move the bifocal line as low as possible on your glasses' lenses. This step makes using your binocs easier.

 If you don't wear glasses, extend the eyecups to help block out side light from entering your view.

Warbler neck

Warbler neck can happen with or without binoculars. It's caused by looking up for long periods, perhaps at some treetop warblers or soaring hawks. To avoid it, stretch out on the ground. This way you can scan the skies while your aching neck gets a rest.

Can't find the bird

You set your sights on the bird and you can't find it. This is by far the most commonly made rookie mistake. You see a bird. You lift your binoculars to your eyes. You start moving your head around crazily looking for the bird. Relax, will ya?

Here's a trick. See a bird. Note where the bird is in relation to a nearby (to the bird) landmark, such as a red leaf, a crooked branch, a clod of dirt, or whatever. LOCK YOUR EYES ON THE BIRD AND DON'T MOVE THEM! Bring your binocs up to where your eyes are. Line up the binocs on the landmark that you spotted, and the bird should be easy to find. Unless the bird has flown.

Fogging

There are certain times when you just have to put up with your bins fogging up, such as when you walk into a warm house after being outside in very cold weather. But if your binoculars fog up all the time, try cleaning them, using some anti-fogging lens fluid. This fluid is available at any camera store and at many pharmacies.

If your binocs fog up on the inside, you need to seek professional help (for them). Good binoculars don't fog internally. If they do, some moisture is inside them, which is not good. Get them looked at by the manufacturer or by an authorized repair person.

How to Carry Your Bins

Strap it up, I'll take it! *Always, always, always* use some kind of strap with your binoculars. If you don't — mark my words — you'll be sorry. And even if you do have a strap on your bins, but you tend to get lazy and hand carry them by the strap, beware! You will drop them at some point.

Now that I have all that gloom and doom out of my system, let me mention that you should have a strap for your binoculars and you should wear it around your neck. A strap is not just a convenient, hands-free way of carrying your optics, it's also a kind of safety belt for them.

My favorite kind of strap is the stretchy kind made from wide neoprene. This strap spreads out the weight of my heavy binocs and never gives me a sore neck from too much friction. An added bonus is that it comes in flashy colors.

A good neckstrap is soft, hooks securely to your binoculars, adjusts to fit your length preference, and feels comfortable holding *your* binoculars around *your* neck.

A word about the thin, shiny plastic straps that sometimes come with binoculars: they stink! Not all included straps are worthless, but most are. If you buy an expensive pair of binoculars, you usually do get a decent strap with them. Excellent straps are available, by mail order or in any store that sells cameras, that fit any model of binocs. Invest in a strap that is comfortable for you.

A variation on the around-the-neck theme is the binocular harness. These units *really* spread out the weight of your optics by means of criss-crossing shoulder straps. Though they take some getting used to, I know several harness users that claim to have been free of neck and back problems since adopting one of these alternative straps.

When watching birds from a car that has automatic shoulder seatbelts — the kind that slide automatically into place whenever the car is started or the door is shut — be careful of where your binoculars are. If you're behind the seatbelt strap, but your binoculars and strap are in front, watch out when the strangulation device — I mean the seatbelt — begins its unmerciful trip to its destination. You can find your neck in the most uncomfortable viselike grip of an object intended to save your life. When I'm in a rental car with this feature, I either unlatch the shoulder belt (if I'm birding in a no-traffic area) or take my bins strap from around my neck.

If your binoculars bounce around and pound against your chest or stomach when you walk, here are three solutions:

- ✔ Change the way you walk, or quit birding from a pogostick. If this isn't practical . . .

- ✔ Shorten your binocular strap; most straps have a slip-through buckle for making this adjustment on either end, near where they connect to the binoculars. Or . . .

- ✔ Purchase one of the harness-type straps that holds your optics snugly against your body. The added benefit is that a good harness distributes the weight evenly across your back and shoulders.

Cleaning and Caring

Clean binoculars are happy binoculars. If your binocs are like mine, you can practically recall every meal you've ever eaten over them. The hard-to-reach areas around the lenses hold a veritable food-museum's worth of crumbs and UFO's (unidentifiable foodlike objects). There's no time like the present to clean up your act.

Spotting Scopes

For 85 percent of the bird watching you do, your binoculars likely give you adequate performance in magnification and image clarity. However, for some birding situations where the birds are quite distant, you can enjoy better looks at birds by using a spotting scope. A spotting scope is one optical tube (binoculars have two) that generally offers greater magnification (above 20 power) than binoculars (usually between 7 and 10 power). For more on choosing and using scopes, see Chapter 22, "Better Optics and Other Fun Gear."

Here's how:

1. **Get lens-cleaning fluid and lens paper from a drugstore or camera store.**

2. **Blow forcefully on each lens to loosen bits of dirt, bread crumbs, or hardened mayonnaise.**

3. **Using a crumpled lens tissue, brush lightly across each lens.**

4. **Wet a clean lens tissue with lens cleaning fluid and lightly wipe each lens in a circular motion.**

5. **Use a clean and dry lens tissue to wipe excess moisture from the lenses.**

For especially mayo-covered lenses, two rounds of cleaning may be in order.

To clean the body of your binoculars, which may be coated in french-fry grease, dampen a cloth with water and wipe. Be careful not to get your binocs too wet, and be sure to dry them promptly.

Don't wipe your binocular lenses with your shirt tail. Take the time to clean them properly and they'll pay you back with great vision for years to come. Take the sloppy way out and wipe them with your sleeve and you'll put thousands of tiny, light-bending scratches on the lenses. This type of behavior puts you on the road to binocular ruin. Breathing on the lenses and then rubbing them with your shirt tail or a facial tissue is also not good. Only resort to such "seat of the pants" cleaning methods in an emergency.

Chapter 13

Choosing and Using Field Guides

*T*he arsenal of the bird watcher includes two primary weapons: binoculars and a field guide. Binoculars (see Chapter 12) let you see a bird well enough to identify it. A field guide helps you to identify what you see.

A field guide is a great companion to have alongside you in the field. At home, it can be a rich source of daydreams as you flip through it and fantasize about all the birds you've never seen. A field guide can also be your record book, a place where you note important sightings, dates, and locations.

What's a Field Guide?

A field guide is a book, usually small enough to fit in your pocket, that has illustrations of all the birds that regularly occur in a given area. Most field guides used on this continent show all the birds found in North America. A few guides are limited to the eastern or western halves of the continent. You also have scores of regional guides to birds of places such as Texas. Which guide you choose depends, in part, on what part of the country you live in and how much you're going to travel. You can also find field guides to the birds of Europe, Mexico, and most South American, Asian, and African countries. No matter where you live or go — at least on this planet — you can almost certainly find a field guide to the birds of the region.

A field guide has only one purpose. A field guide enables the user to identify a bird. Nothing else matters if it doesn't fulfill that purpose. A field guide doesn't ID a bird for you. You can't take a field guide, point it at a bird and expect the guide to fall open to the right page. It's a tool, not a miracle. But good field guides, like good tools, are designed well. They make the job easier.

Just as you're good with some tools and some tools you should never be allowed to touch, different field guides work better or worse depending on the user. If the field guide you're using is not producing results (that is, you aren't able to identify *anything*), don't punish yourself. Get another field guide. You wouldn't use a hammer if the head kept falling off and hitting you on your big toe. Don't use a field guide that leaves you scratching your head and saying, "Well, I wonder what *that* was?" each time you spot an unusual bird.

The order of the birds — what does it mean?

New bird watchers frequently ask why field guides are organized the way they are. Why are the water birds in the front half and land birds in the second half? Well, it's not as arbitrary as it first appears. The answer is taxonomy.

Most field guides use the same sequence that scientists use. This sequence reflects what scientists think is the evolutionary relationship between birds. But taxonomy is not a simple timeline of bird evolution.

My first field guide

When I was just starting to watch birds, at about age 10, I was given a field guide to the birds. Actually, it was the family's guide, but I felt very possessive about it. One of my favorite things to do was to write in the date and place each time a new bird was seen. One of my younger brother Andy's favorite things to do was to try to beat me to the field guide so he could write the stuff in. One day, Andy decided to write our family life list on the first page of the guide. His large, second-grade handwriting filled the entire page after just six birds, one of which was "rock dove." I had never heard of this, the more appropriate name for the city pigeon. I exclaimed, "Where did *you* see a rock dove?" feeling very smug and much smarter than my little brother. I was sure he'd made it up, that a rock dove was some exotic dove from somewhere else. When our mom explained that rock dove was the real name for pigeon, Andy really teased me. He still does, 25 years later. We've still got that field guide, though it now lacks its cover. Every so often, Andy comes into my office, pulls the old guide off the shelf, and stares at it with great concentration. I go for the bait, of course, and say "What are you looking for?" He says, "Just wanted to make sure ROCK DOVE was still on our list!"

The problem is that any sequence is the result of trying to cram a complicated set of relationships into a linear format. Taxonomists (the scientists) do this because field guides and other books are two dimensional (flat page, words) rather than three dimensional, which would allow the scientists to show the many branches of simultaneous evolution.

Almost all field guides are organized by taxonomy. Be wary of field guides that choose a different system of presenting the birds. At first glance, a guide that organizes birds by habitat or color or size may seem appealing, but first glances can be misleading, and ultimately these guides can prove much harder to use.

Taxonomy 101

Taxonomy has nothing to do with April 15 and taxes. When ornithologists talk about taxonomy, they're talking about the relationships between birds. For bird watchers, two aspects of taxonomy are important.

Relationships

First is the relationship between groups of birds. It's fairly obvious that hummingbirds are not closely related to pelicans, except that they both have feathers and fly. On the other hand, gulls and terns are clearly closely related. One aspect of taxonomy is trying to determine which groups are closely related and which are not. The result is the sequence of birds found in most field guides and checklists.

The sequence, which starts with loons and ends with sparrows, is an attempt to put in order our best understanding of those relationships between and among species. It's an imperfect and constantly changing system. If you look at the order of birds in your field guide, you'll notice that the hawks are next to the ducks, but the closest relationship between ducks and hawks is that one sometimes eats the other. The problem again is that field guides try to put the oldest birds (ones that evolved long ago to their present form) first and the newest (most recently evolved) at the end of the list. It's generally thought that ducks evolved very early and sparrows evolved more recently. Hawks also evolved fairly early, so they end up near the front of the book.

Species

The second part of taxonomy is the question of what is a species and what isn't. Go back to the hummingbird and the pelican in the previous section. It doesn't take a bird scientist to know that these two are different species. It isn't too hard to see the differences when you look at the two kinds of pelicans that occur in North America; one is brown and the other is white. But when you try to tell the differences among the sparrows, the problem gets harder. Why are birds that look almost identical considered separate species?

Before the advent of modern science, bird species were identified based pretty much on what they (the birds) looked like. Birds that had a similar appearance were considered one species. Over time, as more information was discovered about birds, the rules changed. Early ornithologists were able to consider subtle characteristics like song and habitat, and many species that were once considered one were split into two or even three species. Later came focused, scientific field ornithology with its more careful observation of birds in the field, and the rules changed again. If two groups of birds interbred successfully, ornithologists called them one species, no matter how different they looked.

The last big change in the rules came less than two decades ago, when scientists developed the ability to look at the DNA of birds. Now ornithologists decide which birds are species based on how similar their DNA is. Each species has its own DNA signature.

All this sounds complicated, and the rules are still changing and always will change as the amount and type of information scientists use changes. Don't worry about it. As the science changes, so do the checklists and field guides. Don't think of the changes as irritations, think of them as scientific advances.

Looking into a field guide, you see that birds are grouped together in clumps: the ducks, the geese, the hawks, the swallows, and so on. These groupings of very similar species are known as *bird families*. The field guide also groups similar families together (ducks and geese, swifts and swallows, and so on). This grouping process is very helpful to the bird watcher. Once you have an idea about a bird's general family, you greatly narrow the possibilities so that you don't have to look through the entire field guide. Flip through any field guide organized taxonomically, and you can easily see the delineations between bird families.

What's in a name?

Bird names can be strange. Beginning bird watchers frequently ask why birds are called pipits, warblers, or loons. They also wonder why, for example, a certain sparrow is called Henslow's sparrow. Who is Henslow, anyway, and why does he or she have a bird named after him/her? And what is a prothonotary warbler? And why is a bird with a red hood, a black-and-white striped back, and a tiny spot of red on the belly called a red-bellied woodpecker? Who thinks up these things?

Bird naming is a quirky and inexact science. In fact, despite the existence of some rules, it's not a science at all. At its best, bird naming is an art. Some of the time it's a mess. Here's how birds get their names.

Name games

First, the scientist who initially discovers a new species gets to name it, sort of like a game of finders-keepers. The only serious rule is that if you discover a new bird, you can't name it after yourself. Of course, if you have a friend who owes you a favor — well, you get the idea.

Second, most birds were discovered more than two centuries ago, back in the time when scientists didn't have ready and immediate communication with each other. They were left creatively free when choosing names. A great many of North America's birds were named by early ornithologists and explorers. These guys (they were almost all men) tended to take one of four roads when choosing the name for a bird.

My sponsor's warbler

One of the most popular ways to name the bird is after a friend or sponsor. A lot of the early ornithologists were poor, and they relied on the largesse of rich patrons to fund the pursuit of their passion. Ornithologists rewarded those patrons by naming birds after them. They also named birds after people to whom they owed money or favors as a way of settling the debt. (They also named birds after wives, girlfriends, and distant relatives.) So John James Audubon named a warbler and a sparrow after his good friend and sponsor, Reverend Bachman. If you want your name immortalized on the name of a bird, sponsor an otherwise indigent ornithologist doing field work in the tropics, which is the only place where new birds are still being found.

Name that feature

Just as popular was the practice of naming birds after some distinctive characteristic. White pelicans and brown pelicans were named because they are, well, white and brown, respectively. Ditto black-and-white warblers, blue grosbeaks, and vermilion flycatchers. Hundreds of examples exist. Sometimes birds were named for obscure characteristics because early ornithologists, not having binoculars or field guides, carried shotguns in the field so they could capture the bird and study it closely. The ring-necked duck, for example, has a subtle chestnut ring around its purple neck, easy to appreciate in a hand-held bird, but usually invisible in the field.

Name that place

The third large category of bird names consists of habitat and location. The first Cape May warbler known to science was collected in Cape May, New Jersey. The fact that the bird is fairly rare there doesn't matter. Ditto Connecticut warbler, which is rare in Connecticut. The generic form of this type of naming concerns geography, and includes names like mountain bluebird (found in the mountains), eastern kingbird (found in the East), western kingbird (guess where); you get the idea. Habitat is also popular. The seaside sparrow is found along the seaside. The pine warbler is found in pines. The cedar waxwing likes cedar berries.

Sounds and symbols

The fourth category is sounds. Pewees are called pewees because that's the sound they make. Chickadees say *chick-a-dee*. Bobwhites say *bob-white*. A warbling vireo warbles, sort of.

Some names are more imaginative. The prothonotary warbler was so named because its golden color reminded an early scientist of the color of the robes worn by the prothonotary, an officer of the Catholic Church. Harriers were named because they were known to *harry,* or harass, poultry and gamebirds in Europe. Limpkins have a limping gait as they move about in the marsh.

Names that stick

No matter how inappropriate the bird's name may be, it's not likely to change. Rules agreed on by scientists all over the world say that the initial name that a bird or any other organism is given is the name that it has for all time. At least most of the time. If scientists decide that two species, like Audubon's and myrtle warblers, are really one species, they have to come up with a new name. They chose yellow-rumped warbler, despite the fact that a half-dozen warblers with yellow rumps exist. When ornithologists decide that one species is really two, they have to come up with two new names. What was, until recently, the brown towhee, is now the canyon towhee and the California towhee.

What's in a Field Guide?

All field guides are different, but all do have basic components necessary to the bird watcher. These components are

- **Illustrations** using color artwork or photographs of birds.
- **Maps** showing the birds' range and distribution.
- **Text** that augments the visual depiction and gives other information unique to each species.
- **An introduction** that tells you about the guide, how to use it, how to interpret the maps, what the special characteristics of the book are, what unique symbols are used, and so on.

✔ **An illustration** of the parts of a bird that allows you to see quickly what the author meant when talking about superciliums or primaries.

✔ **An index** that enables you to find the right pages quickly if you already know the bird is a hawk, or a duck, or whatever.

Pictures of birds

An illustration of a bird, whether it's artwork or photography, is a visual representation of thousands of facts. Each feather (and birds have lots of feathers) is a fact. The color of the bill, the length of the legs, and the shape of the tail are all facts. The more facts the illustration shows, the better the illustration. An illustration that shows only a few key field marks (and this can happen with photographs as well) can leave you frustrated. A field mark may help you decide which bird it is, but you need to see the whole bird, in all its glory, before you get to the field mark stage.

Be wary of guides in which the birds look awkward or ill-formed to you. If the artist doesn't have a feel for what a bird looks like, he or she is likely to get a lot of the facts wrong, too. Of course, photographs, being a frozen moment in time, can present some very distorted views as well. All of us have seen at least one photograph of ourselves that we would pay big bucks to have burned.

Field guide range maps

The maps in a field guide to the birds show, in general terms, where each species can be found at different times of the year. The area over which a species can be found is known as its *range*. The easiest-to-use field guides place the range map on the same page as the text and an image of the bird. Maps are terrifically useful, telling you whether the bird is supposed to be in your part of the world or not.

Not all maps are equally well done, but all maps in field guides are generally accurate. Each guide's maps can be a little different, reflecting the changing state of knowledge and the personal interpretation of the author.

A map can tell you whether a bird should be in your state, but it can't tell you whether it ought to be in your yard. You discover that fact by watching the birds in your yard.

The field guide may say that a certain bird is common and show it occurring all over your state. But if it's a woodland bird, and you have no woods where you live, the bird is likely to be rare for you. Because they cover a vast area, range maps in field guides simply can't provide that kind of detail. Field guide maps are pictures painted with very broad brushes.

Field guide text

The text in a field guide interprets the picture of the birds and tells you which field marks of each species are important. The text also tells you which species are similar and how to tell them apart. Some field guide authors are more adept at this than others, so reading the text for a few species is important before you choose which guide to buy. What you're looking for is text that seems clear and easy for you to understand. If the text confuses you, try another guide.

Many people don't read the text, even after they've bought a guide and are using it in the field. Most people trust what they see rather than what they read. Remember, the text is supposed to be a help, not a hindrance. Eventually, you'll need the text to identify a bird, so get in the habit of reading it.

The text is a detailed guide to the illustration. Not reading the text is like trying to find your way in a strange city without using a map. Sparrows offer a good example because they have a fascinating and subtle collection of streaks, spots, bars, and patterns to their plumage. If you're trying to identify a sparrow that you've seen, you can spend hours poring over several pages of sparrow illustrations trying to figure out what is important. Don't bother. The field guide author has already figured it out and put the information in the text. You paid good money for the information, so go ahead and use it. The information tells you immediately whether the streak on the head, the spot on the breast, or some other field mark matters most when identifying each bird.

Abundance Terms: How Common is Common?

All field guides use words like abundant, common, uncommon, and rare to describe how numerous a bird is. These descriptions aren't precise, scientific terms; they're generalizations, and different authors mean different things when using them. The only way to interpret what is meant by *common* in the field guide that you're using is to read the author's definition of common in the introduction.

These terms are an attempt to relay what we think is known about real bird populations. They have nothing to do with the likelihood of your seeing the bird. For beginning bird watchers, a conversion table is helpful:

✔ Abundant birds are, at best, common or fairly common, meaning you're apt to see them regularly in small numbers.

✔ Common birds are at best uncommon, but you probably run across some once in a while.

✔ Uncommon birds are definitely rare.

✔ Rare birds don't exist. At least that's how it can seem.

The more experience you have, the more the definitions in the field guide make sense. Seeing an uncommon or rare bird requires experience in finding birds, an understanding of the bird and its habitat requirements, and often, knowing which pond or field in which to look. Sometimes luck can compensate for a lack of all that knowledge.

Variations Among Field Guides

Unlike humans, not all field guides are created equal. Each guide that's ever been published has one or more traits that set it apart from its competitors.

A field guide is a delicate balancing act between three competing interests: cost, size, and knowledge. Publishers know that they can't sell $100 field guides. They impose limits on the author, limits designed to make the book affordable. Field guides can't be the size of an unabridged dictionary, and they can't come in 10-volume sets. A field guide has to be one book, small and light enough to carry and use in the field.

The information gets distilled to fit the requirements of cost and size. The distiller is the author. Different authors have different ideas about what makes a good field guide, what information is most important, how it should be presented, and what will make users happy.

The differences among authors, and thus the field guides that they write, are the reason so many bird watchers own more than one guide. They don't carry them all in the field, but these field guides are great back-up references for the library shelf. No matter how attached you get to the field guide that you choose to take into the field, eventually you'll need a piece of information from one of the other guides.

Coverage

The big decision for most bird watchers is whether to choose a guide that shows all the birds found in North America or to go with one that shows only the birds found in either the western half or the eastern half of the continent. Each choice has advantages.

If you live in the middle of the continent — from the northern parts of the western Great Plains to South Texas — you either have to go with a single guide or carry both the eastern and western versions when you go out.

Specialty field guides

In the past two decades, a new arena of field guides has emerged, focused on single families or groupings of families of birds. These specialized guides go into great detail on the species they're covering, especially in plumage variations among individuals. Among the new crop of specialized guides are those covering the warblers of the world, seabirds, shorebirds, hawks, owls, hummingbirds, and many others. If you find that you're particularly interested in one bird family or another, a specialized guide can place a vast amount of information about the family at your fingertips.

The closer you are to the middle, the more likely you are to see birds that are found in one book, but not the other, and vice versa. The problem is that you can find eastern field guides and western field guides but no middle field guides. Sorry about that.

What's the advantage to using an eastern guide or a western guide? Well, let's say you live in Salt Lake City, or San Diego. The western guide has almost every bird you'll ever see (except, of course when you're visiting relatives in Miami). But because such a guide covers fewer species than an all-of-North-America-guide, it can include more in-depth information about the species it covers.

What's the advantage to owning a field guide that covers the entire continent? Well, eventually you're going to see a bird that isn't in the western field guide. Sometimes western birds show up in the East, and sometimes eastern birds show up in the West. Few things are as frustrating as seeing a bird and then discovering it isn't in your limited-coverage field guide. So if you own a western guide or an eastern guide, you really have to own both, even though you'll only be carrying one guide around most of the time. On the other hand, if you have a guide that has all the birds, this problem almost never comes up, unless you did not get a sufficiently good look at the bird to ID it.

Which should you choose in an all-the-birds field guide? Your choice depends on what you want — more information or more birds? It depends on whether you travel a lot. The best solution is to persuade your wife, or husband, or boyfriend, or girlfriend, or significant other, to take up bird watching too, and then you carry one guide and your companion carries the other. It's nice to share!

Photographs versus art

This is the *big* question — the hottest argument in the field guide galaxy. Do you choose a guide that uses photographs or one that uses art to depict birds?

Experienced bird watchers overwhelmingly favor guides with art. Beginners overwhelmingly favor guides with photographs. What are the differences, and which should you choose?

A field guide, ignoring for the moment that it includes text, is a collection of bird pictures. The illustrations are supposed to show the birds in a way that demonstrates the characteristics that make each bird distinctive. Both paintings and photographs can accomplish this goal. I open the debate with a statement from the proponent of photographs.

Photographs show real birds, just like the ones you see in the field. Photographs give a real sense of the bird that an artist can rarely, if ever, capture. This realism inspires confidence in the field guide user. Photographs don't filter the image of the bird through the artist's eye.

Thank you. And now a word from the proponent of paintings.

Available photographs often don't show the key field marks. Too often a distortion in the photographic or printing process results in an incorrect coloration shown. Sometimes the only decent photograph available of a given species is blurry, or shows a slightly weird plumage variation, or subspecies. Getting comparable photographs of large groups (such as warblers) is impossible, where all the images are equal in quality, image size, and brightness. An artist can show exactly the same pose, typically in profile, for a large group of similar species. This art allows the user to make direct comparisons between similar species. An artist can create a picture that shows every part of the bird the user needs to see. Artists' renditions are composites, showing the most typical plumage.

Which should you choose? It depends in part on what is available. In the Appendix is a list of the most widely used guides, the ones that have stood the test of time and use in the field. Try choosing a guide from that list to start with. Better yet, choose two, one with photographs and one with paintings. Over time, one becomes your primary source, and one becomes your backup.

Size does matter

You're going to be carrying this field guide around with you. Two, three, and four-volume field guides turn you from a bird watcher into a pack mule. Worse, you never know which volume to grab.

A guide that is too big to fit in the pocket of any pair of pants or any jacket that you own can be a burden. The only thing you want in your hand when you're watching birds is your binoculars. (And perhaps a cookie.)

On the other end of the scale, a variety of compact pocket guides are small enough to fit into any pocket. Most of them cover only a sampling of the birds that you're likely to see, or the information in them is somewhat limited. Try for the middle ground — single volume guides that cover all the birds of the continent or at least the half of the continent in which you live.

Durability

Do you know what the life expectancy of a poorly made field guide is? Probably about two years of moderate field use. It will be crammed into pockets and backpacks. It'll fall under car seats and into mud puddles. Your field guide will be left out in the rain and baked by the sun. It'll tumble onto the road after being left on the car rooftop. It'll be bent around pencils and forefingers, pressed on flowers, and closed on mosquitoes and bits of tuna fish sandwich. And it'll be opened a thousand times, at least.

Most guides today come with some variation of a coated-paper cover. This kind of cover adds some durability and flexibility to the guide. Hardbound field guides put up a noble defense in the back pants pockets of birders everywhere, but they ultimately lose their covers. Flexible is where it's at.

Also check a field guide's binding (where the pages are glued together and joined to the book's spine). If the binding looks like the pages are barely held in there, put the guide down and back away slowly. If you buy a field guide with a bad binding, plan on chasing those pretty pages of bird pictures across a windblown field in a few months (or years).

Drying out your field guide

If the worst happens and your field guide gets totally wet, here are a couple of suggestions:

✔ Immediately get a roll or two of paper towels and begin wiping each page dry.

✔ For really soaked pages, close a section of paper towel in between pages and let the guide sit until the towels draw out most of the water.

✔ Hang the book on a plastic-coated wire coat hanger (uncoated wire hangers will rust) so the pages hang down from the

book. Place a fan beneath the guide so that it blows the pages dry.

It's important that you get each page as dry as possible to keep the pages from sticking together. I have an old guide that got soaked. It used to have 300-plus pages. Now it has about three really thick pages.

If all else fails, get a new field guide and start over. Face it, your old guide is never going to be the same.

Format

Early field guides featured text first; farther along in the book, the color plates (illustrations of the birds) were grouped (which made it cheaper to print), and then in the back came the range maps. This formatting made for clumsy reference. You spent a lot of time flipping from one section to another. Today, most available guides clump all the pertinent information about each bird together on facing pages.

Field guides that don't have the maps, the text, and the illustrations on the same page may have other virtues, but they're harder to use. If you believe that you have the dexterity to hold a field guide open to two or three different pages, using the fingers of one hand, while flipping back and forth, while holding binoculars in the other hand, while looking first at the bird and then at the guide, go ahead. But don't try it while standing over a puddle. Or anywhere near a puddle. The world record for how far a field guide can be thrown was set by a bird watcher trying just that trick.

The Mythical Perfect Field Guide

No such thing as the perfect field guide exists. The search for the perfect field guide is the equivalent of the search for the Holy Grail or the Fountain of Youth. The *perfect* field guide is the one that you're comfortable using, the one that you most easily understand, and the one that enables you to identify birds. Your perfect guide may be someone else's nightmare.

Here is the basic field test for a field guide. It's just you, the guide, and the bird. Consider the following:

- Are the illustrations easy to interpret?
- Are similar species easy to find and compare?
- Is the typeface large enough to be readable?
- Is the text clear and easy to understand?
- Can you read the map quickly and without a magnifying glass?
- Does the bird in the book look like the one in the bush?

The answer may not be yes to every question, but if more than one or two is no, you're headed for frustration and an attempt at breaking the field-guide tossing record.

If you buy a guide and then find that it isn't the right one for you, I suggest you buy another guide. After all, practice makes perfect. The first guide you bought can be a handy reference at home or at the office.

Using Your Field Guide

You have a brand-new field guide. Now it's time to get out in the field and use it. First of all, write your name and address in indelible ink on the inside front cover. I know this seems like a first-grade thing to do (and if your handwriting is like mine, it's a little too much like first grade) but believe me, you'll misplace your field guide at least once between now and that big field trip in the sky. You'll be so very happy when a conscientious bird watcher turns your field guide in to your first grade teacher.

For the first few weeks or months, you'll baby your new guide. That's okay. But soon your guide evolves into a trusted, slightly worn field companion, and you won't leave home without it.

Read the introduction

Field guides are semi-technical. If you're a new bird watcher and have never used a guide before, read the introduction to the guide. Don't worry — introductions are almost always short.

The introduction is the basic operating instructions, the user's manual. Just as you wouldn't consider operating a new microwave, automobile, or camera without reading the instructions (actually, a lot of us do, with predictable results), you shouldn't consider using a field guide for the first time without making sure how best to use it.

The introduction provides several key pieces of information. It tells you how to interpret the range maps, which can be confusing because all the guides seem bent on using different colors. Some guides use special keys to speed you to the right section or bird family, and the introduction tells you how to make the key work for you. Introductions often provide basic backgrounds on bird families, bird behavior, optics, appropriate bird watching clothes, bird migration, bird finding, and bird identification.

The introduction is a quick and dirty seminar on birds and bird watching, written for the beginner. Taking a few minutes to read it can save hours later. It's a good investment.

Read the text

Don't just look at the pretty pictures of the birds. Once you've found the bird that you're trying to identify in the field guide, take a moment to read the accompanying text for that species. This step is another way to firm-up (or totally negate) your identification of the bird. The text contains many gems of information that can't be conveyed visually in a painting, photograph, or range map. And the text tells you about confusingly similar species, which you may want to check out, just in case your identification sleuthing has led you to the (slightly) wrong bird.

Use the maps

Range maps are key field marks to a bird's identity. They tell you where a bird occurs, or at least where it ought to occur. Often, the final identification of a bird is based on the discovery that the only other species possibility is found in a small area on the opposite coast.

Range maps typically show where you can expect to find a bird in the summer, in the winter, and year-round (see Figure 13-1). Each map appears as a different color or pattern, and the introduction (remember to read the introduction very carefully) provides the key to the colors or patterns. Remember them so that a quick glance lets you know how likely the bird is to be in your area.

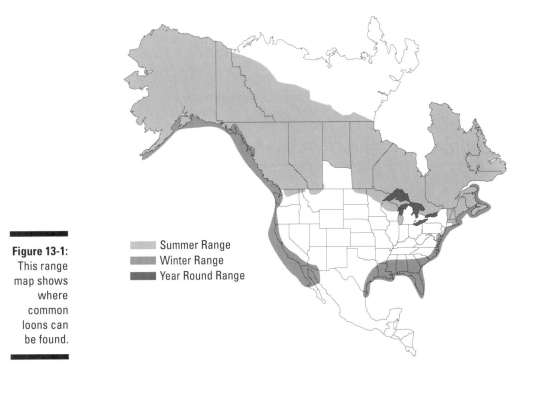

Figure 13-1:
This range map shows where common loons can be found.

Summer Range
Winter Range
Year Round Range

Range maps are a snapshot, a picture of the range of the bird at the time of the guide's publication. But sometimes ranges change. No current guide has maps that accurately reflect the explosive growth of the range of house finches in the East. And no map accurately reflects the disappearance of loggerhead shrikes from much of their former range. Use the maps as a guide, but be prepared to see changes over time.

Carrying your guide

Although your back pocket may suffice for a small guide, what about a larger guide? What about those days when you're wearing your pocketless Spanish bullfighter's pants? How do you carry your guide then, amigo?

The obvious answer to the too-big-for-the-back-pocket conundrum is to tuck the guide into your waistline, either in front or in back. But this, too, has its drawbacks, such as when the guide shifts position, dropping all the way inside your clothing or out onto the ground, magically staying airborne long enough to plop into the nearest puddle.

I much prefer giving the field guide its own little place in which to ride along with me. My current favorite is a handy waistpack that comes with its own wide belt. In this pack I can fit the field guide, several pens and pencils (I lose them constantly), a small notebook, sunscreen, lip stuff, and some snack or other. The belt holds the pouch snug against my hip, and the guide is right there whenever I need it, no matter how far from the car I wander. Of course, I still drop the field guide into the occasional mud puddle as I fumble with my bullfighter's cape and binoculars.

BIRD TALES

Up on the rooftop

One place that my field guide often ends up is on the roof or hood of the car. This happens most often in warm weather when I'm in and out of the car a lot. Here's how:

I'm watching birds with family or friends. A bird flies past the car, catching somebody's attention. We all pile out of the car and realize the bird is an unusual sparrow. We watch the bird for a bit until it decides we've had enough of a look and it disappears into the tall grass. Everyone begins stating the field marks they noticed on the bird as I reach for the field guide. We discuss the bird, pass the field guide around, and settle on an ID. Grasshopper sparrow — pretty nice! The last person to touch the guide (probably me) forgets and leaves it on the roof. Happy as a herd of oblivious oxen, we load into the car and leave, not hearing the soft thud of the field guide as it blows off the roof and hits the road. As we drive off at a high rate of speed, the guide begins inching its way over to a roadside puddle. Two hours later we're back with a flashlight, looking for the field guide.

Chapter 14

Expanding Your Skills

. . . .

In This Chapter

▶ Practice, practice, practice

▶ Hit the books

▶ Discover spishing

▶ Keep notes

▶ Satisfaction at last

. . . .

*B*ecoming proficient at identifying birds gives you a real sense of satisfaction. Being able to put a name on most of the birds you see is thrilling, and over time, you can feel your confidence growing. It's not all that hard to get good at naming birds, either. Like the guy who asked a New York City cab driver, "How do I get to Carnegie Hall?"

The answer: "Practice, practice, practice."

Practice, Practice, Practice

Practicing to improve your bird-watching skills doesn't have to be as agonizing as practicing your piano lessons, or as scary as using your high-school French lessons for the first time in Paris. All you really need to do to improve yourself as a birder is to — you guessed it — watch birds.

Okay, I admit that you can do a few other things to be all the bird watcher you can be.

Practice with binocs

Binoculars (a.k.a. "binocs," or "bins"), in the hands of a bird watcher, can be either a clumsy annoyance or a deadly accurate weapon. Have you noticed how veteran bird watchers can get their binoculars on a distant flying bird before you can even get your hands wrapped around your optics? This fluid, skillful use of binoculars comes from practice. There's no reason why you can't also become every bit as smooth when wielding your binocs.

It takes practice. Hunters perfect their aim with target practice. Basketball players shoot warm-up shots before each game. But most bird watchers don't practice the most basic of field skills: putting your binoculars on the bird.

This move is easy to practice:

1. **Lock your eyes on a distant object, such as the top of a tree or a church steeple.**

2. **Slowly bring the binoculars up to your eyes, without moving your neck, head, or eyes.**

As you practice this move a few times, you get quicker on the draw. This, in turn, can make you faster at getting your bins on birds in the field.

I use a trick to help me get on distant birds. As I see the bird's movement with my unaided eyes, I try to locate something else in the vicinity of the movement — a bare branch, an unusual leaf, a knot on the trunk — and I note the relationship to the place where I saw the movement (for example, just left of the knot). As I raise my binocs to my eyes, I may notice the object before I can locate the bird that is moving (or by now, not moving), but I know where I saw the movement, so I shift my focus to that point. Unless the bird has moved away, or is *totally* concealed, I'm almost always able to locate it. This technique works just as well for birds hopping along the ground, soaring in the sky, or swimming on the surface of the water, but reference points vary according to the location.

Practice on the clock

Out in the field, if you're with a group, you may hear the field-trip leader say, "There's a kingbird at 11 o'clock in that large cottonwood tree." Do you know what this means?

Look at any tree and imagine a large clock face superimposed over it (see Figure 14-1). The most vertical, top point of the tree, would be 12 o'clock. Straight below this point, halfway down the trunk, would be the "dead center" of the tree, and at the bottom, six o'clock. Three o'clock and nine o'clock would be at the outer right and outer left sides of the tree, respectively, and so on.

The clock technique is a very helpful way for one bird watcher to direct others to a hard-to-spot perched bird.

Figure 14-1:
Clock face diagram for locating a bird in a tree. There is an indigo bunting at 1 o'clock in the outer canopy. Really.

Because you may hear the bird before you can see it, try listening to bird-song recordings — concentrating especially on those species you expect to see on your field trip — and you'll see how helpful it can be. See Chapter 5 for more information on bird sounds.

Get used to the field guide

Flipping through your field guide in a frantic search for the right bird is a big frustration. You never find the bird right away, and sometimes you've forgotten what field mark you were looking for by the time you find the right bird.

Lots of field guides also provide a quick-reference index, sometimes color-keyed to each family of birds. This helpful feature shortens the frantic searching somewhat.

No substitute replaces using the guide regularly to help you get familiar with where the birds are.

Look at the bird, not at the field guide. The field guide is always there, but the bird isn't.

Book learning is fine, but the best is in-the-field training. When you get bored being a bookworm, get outside and look at some birds.

Create fantasy field trips

If you can't be outside looking at actual wild, living birds, why not play Fantasy Bird Trip? *Fantasy Bird Trip* involves leafing through your field guide until you see a bird that fascinates you, likely one you've never seen. Read up on the species and then figure out where you'd have to go to see it. I used to do this all the time.

By the way, while you're fantasizing, you're also ingesting lots of good information about birds.

Develop Other Helpful Skills

If you just can't get enough of this refining-your-skills business, you have lots of other things you can do to improve yourself as a bird watcher. Some of these activities even involve making funny noises. Who can resist that?

Try spishing

Many variations on spishing for birds exist. *Spishing* is named for the sound it makes, a *spssh, spssh, spssh* noise made when you hiss through clenched teeth. Some folks call it pishing, some squeaking (made with puckered lips, or by kissing the back of your hand), and some call it evil.

Spishing is meant to attract the attention of curious birds, and it sometimes does. Sparrows, some warblers, wrens, chickadees, titmice, and nuthatches are often attracted to these birder-generated sounds.

There's a limit to how much you should spish. If spishing doesn't appear to work after a minute or so, give it up. Some bird watchers, indeed whole cultures of bird watchers in Europe and elsewhere in the world, believe that spishing is harmful to birds and shouldn't be done. I can see the point. If a bird along an oft-birded path responded to every spish it heard, it would have no time to feed, mate, or sing.

Keep the sun at your back

To get the best color out of the birds you see, keep the sun at your back. A male indigo bunting singing from the top of a tree at 3 p.m. on a hot summer's day can look totally black unless you get the sun behind you. Tricks of light can be very confusing. Use light to your advantage and minimize its effects. If you see a bird but can't see any color on it, try moving around to get a better-lit view of the bird.

Even before you see a bird, you can approach a good bird habitat with the direction of the sunlight in mind. For example, you may want to wait to visit a large lake until the sun is in your favor. Bright light gleaming off the surface of the water directly into your eyes can be both annoying and painful. Knowing that — at least on this planet — the sun rises in the East and sets in the West may help you to determine when to visit a certain locale. Morning light and evening light are often the best times to see bird plumage colors at their most brilliant.

Gently stalk your bird

Low and slow and steady as you go. That's the best way to sneak up on a bird that you're stalking. Many birds — sparrows are one example — rely on staying still and quiet to avoid detection. When stalking a bird, you don't always want to spook it into moving, also called *flushing* the bird.

Suppose that you're trying to see a grasshopper sparrow, which is a sneaky, flat-headed sparrow that prefers old meadows with tall grass. You hear the grasshopper sparrow's insectlike buzz (hence its name), and you see the bird fly to land on the middle part of an old weed stem, but you can't quite see it.

It's time to become a bird stalker:

- ✔ Without trampling over all the habitat (and perhaps the sparrow's nest), move carefully around the spot where the bird is, to a better vantage point.

- ✔ If you need to get closer, move slowly and quietly, with your binocs at the ready.

- ✔ Avoid noise and sudden movement.

Add a dose of patience, and you may see your bird.

If several minutes of bird stalking don't produce the desired view of the bird, be willing to accept defeat until next time. At all costs, avoid disturbing or harassing the bird. It's not necessary, and it's not kind to the bird. You'll get another chance to see this species at some point. Wild birds have enough to worry about without a bunch of birders harassing them.

If stalking a bird fails, try just sitting patiently for a half-hour or so, a short distance away. When I've tried this strategy, I've often seen the bird return to the area where I first saw it and have gotten good looks. Birds that aren't stressed, or don't sense they're being watched, are unknowingly cooperative.

Avoid shiny, flashy clothes

We recently ran a short news item in *Bird Watcher's Digest* about how bright clothing worn by birders can scare away birds. It seems that today's clothing is made with artificial brighteners to make the colors more attractive to human eyes. Because brighteners affect the ultraviolet range of the colors in the clothing, even dull-colored clothes can be "brightened." Birds see color and brightness differently than humans do, so the artificial brighteners in your new clothing may startle or scare the birds you're trying to see. For this reason, I suggest you wear older clothes, especially ones that have been washed many times. These clothes are less likely to have active brighteners. Besides, they're more comfortable, having been broken-in already.

Don't be ashamed if you make a bad call when identifying a bird. Everyone does it. I just did it this morning. A mourning dove flew past our kitchen window at blazing speed. I shouted "Falcon!" as it came to rest on our platform feeder and bent down to peck at some mixed seed. Julie said, calmly, "Yes, dear. That's the rare mourning falcon. Only found on one ridge-top farm in southeastern Ohio." Fortunately you'll not be subject to such ridicule if you make a bad call. Most bird watchers are kind about it (if you're not married to them).

Keep Notes

If you're the kind of person who keeps lists and reminder notes about stuff like the grocery list, to-do projects, and the like, you may enjoy keeping notes about the birds you see. Note keeping is an ancient form of bird watching, but don't think you need to be a scientist with a pocket protector full of pens and slide rules to keep notes. You can keep whatever kind of notes you want to keep quite easily.

Just a few notes can help you remember clearly the details about a bird or a particular experience. When you see an unusual bird, you think you'll never forget the moment. But if you try to recount the experience just a few days later, lots of the detail gets lost. Keeping notes can be a big memory helper.

Even if you can't draw a stick bird, making a rough sketch and jotting down a few important notes can help you later identify a mystery bird that you encounter. (Chapter 24 has lots of field sketching tips.) I try to carry something to write with and something to write on whenever I go on a field trip.

Chapter 15

Writing It Down

- -

- -

*N*early all bird watchers are record keepers. Only the level of involvement in record keeping varies. Some folks are content with the occasional note stuck on the refrigerator saying something like, "I saw a bluebird in the backyard today." Some bird watchers catalog every bird they see, along with the date, time, location, weather, phase of the moon, and whether the coffee was decaf or high test.

Most bird watchers fall somewhere between these two extremes. We make notes about those things that interest us, or about things that we think interest others, or things that we're afraid we'll forget. No experiments prove that people who watch birds have a gene for compulsive record keeping, but it's widely accepted as truth.

Two forms of record keeping are most prevalent. The first form is making lists. The second is keeping a notebook or journal. Each form has its pleasures and advantages. Which you choose depends on your own interests. Some bird watchers do both. If you're very diligent and very detailed in your record keeping, you'll find that you almost have enough time left over to watch birds (occasionally).

Keeping a Life List

Bird watchers can be obsessive about keeping lists. The number of lists is limited only by your imagination, as you'll see by some of the lists that are kept by bird watchers that I know.

The list, the one every bird watcher keeps, even if only mentally done, is the life list. All other lists are secondary.

The birds of your life

A *life list* is a list of all the species of birds that you've seen. Some cynics claim that this list is really a list of all the birds you THINK you've seen, and is therefore a lot longer than the list of birds you actually HAVE seen. Ignore those people. They're just jealous. A life list is a very personal document. People who are obsessed with the life lists of other bird watchers are the same sort who, when you mention that your neck is sore, top it by telling the story of the time they were in traction for a week. They need professional intervention.

A *life bird* is a bird that's new to you — one you've never seen before in your life. A life bird gets added to your life list. For most North American bird watchers, the term life list refers to their North American life list. That is, all the bird species they've seen in the United States and Canada. Even though Mexico is geographically part of North America, its tropical bird life and difference in language set it apart. For birders, North America is everything north of the Mexican border.

Even if you don't keep your list in written form, you'll know what your life list is. When you see your first bald eagle (those appearing in car commercials don't count), you know that it's a new bird for you, something that you've not seen before. You've started a life list. Unless you can forget seeing a bald eagle (and most of us cannot) your life list has become a reality, a part of your bird watching.

What do you include?

The simplest form of a life list is just a list of the birds you've seen, either written down somewhere or checked off on a pre-printed list. Most people like to add a little more information, such as the date and the location of the sighting. This information allows them to check not only what they've seen, but when and where.

My life list gets updated once every few years. I keep it in an old nature notebook that lists all the birds of North America. The problem is, with the changes in bird taxonomy and nomenclature that our scientific friends have created, many of the birds on my list are out of date. (See Chapter 13 for more about bird taxonomy.) Still, I know that my life list includes somewhere around 600 birds for North America. I'm ashamed to say that I have no idea exactly how many my world life list includes (a list of *all* the bird species I've ever seen, including those seen on trips outside North America). I've never tallied it, though I keep threatening to do so. It's more than 1,000 but less than 1,500.

Where do you keep the list?

There is no right way or place to keep a life list. You can use a simple notebook, a pad of paper, a book, a pre-printed checklist, or computer software designed for just such record keeping.

Some people keep their life lists in their field guides. Many field guides provide little boxes in the index that can be used to check off the birds after you've identified them.Other people write the date and place next to the species account in the field guide. This information allows you to see the picture of the bird at the same time you're checking your list, letting you see at a glance which birds you've recorded and which you haven't.

Many people prefer a pre-printed checklist for keeping their life list. These checklists are small, folded cards that fit easily into a pocket or the back of a field guide. They are also easy to leave at home, where they're safe and sound.

BIRD TALES

Starting my life list too late

Two years before I started watching birds actively, my family spent several weeks in Mexico touring the Yucatan peninsula. I remember the iguanas on the Mayan ruins, the giant cockroaches running around the swimming pools, and the scrawny dogs everywhere. But I can't remember seeing a single bird, though I know they were pointed out to us by our guides and by other turistas. My point is: I missed seeing a lot of birds because I was unaware. I was unaware because I had not yet gotten into identifying birds, so I didn't make any notes about what we saw. If I had, I would have several more Mexican species on my life list today. Do yourself a favor and start your list this minute.

Lots of various pre-printed checklists are available. Most states and many local bird clubs produce a checklist for the region or local area. These checklists typically cost less than a dollar. The disadvantage is that they often don't contain all the birds you'll eventually see, especially if you travel a bit. What's more, these checklists are small, so you don't usually have enough room to make notes about where and when you first saw each bird.

You can also find notebooks designed to be used as life lists. These notebooks are often 50 to100 pages long and include plenty of space to record additional information. Almost all of these notebooks cost less than $20.

What about computer lists?

Computers have made listing easy for those bird watchers familiar with technology. A wide variety of computer list programs exists. These programs enable you to keep an almost unlimited number of lists, sort them any way you want, and provide space for writing notes.

Computerized bird-list programs come in two forms: List-keeping software and CD-ROMs.

List-keeping software has been evolving constantly over the last decade. Not only are the available programs changing to meet increased user demand for speed and ease of use, but list-keeping software is changing to keep up with changes in bird names and in bird taxonomy.

Most available programs function like an electronic checklist: You put in the information, and the software stores it and sorts it out. So if you want to know all the birds you saw on September 11, 1993, the program can sort all your entries and select those that contain that date. The amount of data you can enter and the level of sorting vary from program to program. But if you enjoy entering data and playing with it on your computer, list-keeping software is for you.

CD-ROMs for bird watchers have emerged in recent years, some of them based upon list-keeping software and some based upon field guides to the birds. All of these CD-ROMS offer some of the bells and whistles that make using CD-ROMs fun, such as recordings of bird songs, short video clips of the birds, and bird ID quizzes and tutorials. List keeping is a component of most of the CD-ROMs currently available, although accessing your bird list may require that the CD-ROM disc be running.

See Chapter 25 for information about online bird watching. See the Appendix for a list of companies that produce birding list-keeping software and CD-ROMS.

Lists Breed Lists

Lists breed lists. Once you've started your life list, you'll probably begin other lists. This process is natural. The trick is not to let it get out of hand. Listing can become an obsession that dominates your bird watching. It doesn't have to be that way. A few lists are a good idea, and most people are sufficiently balanced to keep lists in perspective. If you have an addictive personality, however, you'll want to keep a close watch on the tendency to create new lists. Or just indulge it and enjoy this fascinating new cranny in your personality.

Yard list

After the life list, the second list that almost every bird watcher keeps is a *yard list*. This list is exactly what it sounds like: a list of all the birds that you've seen in your yard. Yard lists are popular because they're simple. Yard lists cover an area you're in almost every day, and they're a way of documenting the diversity of bird life in your area. Yard lists can be kept the same way as life lists, except that the list of birds is likely to be much shorter. Many bird watchers keep their yard lists on a small pre-printed checklist and stick it to the refrigerator door along with shopping lists, drawings by small children, and traffic tickets.

Keeping a yard list has one tricky part. Even if you have several bird feeders, a bird bath, and a brush pile, the list stops growing rapidly after a year or two. After that, each new addition becomes a red-letter event because you've already seen all the common and regularly occurring birds.

There are some rules to list keeping that a few bird organizations and some competitive birders try to live by. Two examples of these rules are:

- ✔ If you only *hear* a bird, but don't see it, you cannot count the bird on your life list, no matter how certain you are that you know the species' song or call.

- ✔ If you're bird watching with another person or persons and somebody else identifies a bird and shows it to you, you cannot count it on your life list. You did not identify it yourself.

I think both of these rules are for people who are overly competitive about how long their bird list is. When bird watching starts getting rules, it begins to lose its appeal as a relaxing, enjoyable activity. If you want to count birds that you have heard rather than seen, and you want to count the obscure shorebird that somebody ID'd for you, I say do it. But if you don't feel right about counting a bird you did not see well, or did not ID yourself, that's okay, too. It's all about what you're comfortable doing.

What's in a yard

Anywhere in North America you can go out in the yard, look up, and see a vulture or a hawk flying over. The bird flying overhead definitely was not in the yard, but you were. Should you count it?

Unless you've entered into a contest with one of your friends over who has the largest yard list and have negotiated a complicated set of rules over what counts and what doesn't (don't laugh — it happens), the answer is entirely up to you. It's no one else's business. Do whatever brings you the most pleasure, or do what you think is right. Most birders keep a yard list

that includes anything they can see or hear while they (the observers) are standing in the yard. They do this because it's easier and because it means a bigger list. Other bird watchers like to do it the hard way, where each bird has to be physically in the yard. You can define the boundaries as you see fit. For me, if I could keep one toe on my Ohio property and see a spotted owl in Oregon, I would count it. Dratted curvature of the earth is a problem there, however.

Remember, a bird watcher's yard is a bird watcher's castle. You make the rules.

A list of lists

After the life list and the yard list, the sky is the limit. Commonly kept lists include state lists, county lists, and North American lists. Some people keep lists for their favorite bird watching sites, places like National Wildlife Refuges and local parks. The number and type of lists is limited only by your imagination and interests.

To see how varied lists can be, and how far some people can go, here's an annotated list of some lists that are regularly kept by bird watchers. (Some lists are not so regular, but they give you an idea of the possibilities.)

- ✔ **County List:** All the birds that you've seen in one county, usually the one in which you live.

- ✔ **State List:** All the birds that you've seen in one state, usually the one in which you live, but some well-traveled bird watchers keep a list for every state.

- ✔ **North American List:** All the birds that you've seen in North America.

- ✔ **Lower 48 List:** All the birds that you've seen in the lower 48 states. Popular with bird watchers who travel but are unable to get to Alaska or Hawaii, where many birds exist that you cannot see anywhere else on this continent.

- ✔ **World List:** This list is important for folks with the money, time, or the obsession, to travel often to birdy places such as Africa, the Far East, and Australia. But anytime you venture outside North America, you can add to your world life list.

✔ **U.S. List:** North America minus Canada, for jingoistic bird watchers. Canadians have similar lists.

✔ **Country List:** Like state lists, but for each country you've visited. For *very* well-traveled bird watchers.

✔ **Regional List:** For less far-ranging bird watchers, typically covering several states; for example, a Midwest list.

✔ **Day List:** All the birds that you've seen each day. Although time consuming, many bird watchers keep day lists, at least for the days they spend actively bird watching. One advantage of day lists is that they reveal the changes of the seasons. You can look back at them and tell exactly what day the first white-crowned sparrows showed up at your feeder and what day the ruby-throated hummingbirds returned in the spring.

✔ **Year List:** A list of all the birds seen in a year, in any locality you choose. Year lists are popular because they allow you to start over every January 1. These lists can also be compared from year to year. Did you see more birds in your yard this year than last? It's a question you'll ask yourself some day, and a year list is the only way to answer it.

✔ **Television List:** Now I'm getting into some of the stranger lists. This one includes all the birds you've seen on television. Some bird watchers watch golf tournaments solely to increase their TV bird lists. The advantage is that golf tournaments are held outdoors, with trees around, and everyone is quiet. It's amazing how many bird species you can identify by sound if you're familiar with the songs. Nature shows are another popular source for TV birding. Some purists won't count any bird that the announcer identifies for them, while others count them all.

✔ **Dream List:** Some people dream about birds. This is not a cause for concern. Some people dream about birds constantly. This may be a cause for concern, but it's between themselves and their therapists. Some people keep lists of birds they have dreamt about. You can decide for yourself what that means.

Dreams can be very real, though. I once had a dream of finding a rare bird and the dream was so real, and so persuasive, that it took several hours after I had awakened to convince myself that it hadn't actually happened. I was even to the point of calling people and telling them about this bird and where to find it.

✔ **Heard-Only List:** This is a list of birds that the observer has heard but never seen. Usually it contains owls, rails, and a few other night birds. The primary purpose of this list is to target birds that you need to see.

✔ **Christmas Card List:** All the birds the observer has seen on holiday cards. Birds are popular, and if you have a lot of people sending you cards, this list can grow quickly. One advantage is that card manufacturers include birds from all over the world, some of which are the figments of an artist's imagination.

Many more lists do exist, of course, some of which are too strange for a family publication such as this. Feel free to invent your own. If it brings you pleasure, keep a list of all the birds you've seen while standing on one foot, while at baseball games, or while lying in your hammock. It's probably not a good idea to share these lists with other bird watchers, at least until you know them well.

Listers, Twitchers, and Just Plain Birders

Listing has become an obsession with some bird watchers. They live for the chance to add a bird to any of their various lists. They seldom venture afield unless they think they're going to pump up a list. These folks are called *listers*. They represent a small portion of the bird watching community. Everyone keeps lists, but few let it take over their lives.

How do you know lists have gotten out of hand? Well, here's a true story. One lister (now completely recovered) reached the point where he had to create a list of his lists because he had so many lists that he could not keep track.

Listers and twitchers

In Great Britain, listers are called *twitchers* because of the uncontrollable twitching that takes over their bodies at the prospect of adding a new bird to the list.

Listers and twitchers take themselves very seriously, which is good because if they didn't, who would?

A lister is a collector, no different from collectors of matchbooks or beer cans. Their pleasure is not in the birds themselves, but in the opportunity to add one to a collection. It's easy to recognize obsessive listers. They see a new bird and immediately begin to gush: "Wow, that's not only a state and county bird, it's my first March record, a new park bird, a new bird seen only in flight. . . ." When the list of lists gets too long, it's time to break away, lie down, and have a cool drink. Try leaving the list at home for awhile and go back to looking at birds.

Obsessive listing is not contagious, unless you hang out too long with listers. The vast majority of bird watchers handle lists the way the vast majority of people handle drinking alcohol — in moderation and with easy control. A yard list is a nice glass of wine with dinner. Ten or twenty lists is binge listing and can lead to blackouts.

Real birders versus listers-only

Bird watchers fed up with obsessiveness, and occasional nuttiness, of out-of-control listers sometimes try to argue that listers aren't really bird watchers. They even claim that they themselves never keep lists. This attitude is the opposite extreme. Avoid list-aversion as determinedly as you would avoid list mania.

Lists are merely a way of organizing information. They are catalogs and reminders. Make them work for you.

Don't let a fear of being obsessive interfere with the pleasure of seeing a new or rare bird. If, very rarely, you arise at three in the morning, drive for several hours, and stand around a garbage dump in freezing weather to see a rare bird, you are not, by definition, a compulsive lister. Rare birds are fun to see, mostly because they are rare. Going the extra mile once in a while is not nutty. On the other hand, if you do all that to see a bird you've seen many times before, and you do it only because it's a new bird for your Friday the 13th list. . . .

Two lists that you can get fairly nutty about without raising other bird watchers' eyebrows are the life list and the yard list. It's possible to go too far even with these lists, however. One obsessed bird watcher used the rent money to fly from the East Coast to the West Coast to see a new bird. He returned home to find that he, and his family, had been evicted. Still, he felt the new bird was worth it.

Keeping Notebook Records

A notebook is a form of list, but it's much more detailed. Many bird watchers keep notebooks in which they record a variety of observations about birds. Notebooks are more than lists, although they can include lists. Notebooks are bird watching diaries.

What goes into a notebook is entirely up to you. Notebooks are by nature quirky, reflecting the interest of you, their author. They can be full of unanswered questions, speculations, humorous stories, the names of people that you've met, and descriptions of places that you've been.

Most bird watchers who keep notebooks use them to record descriptions of unusual birds they've seen or birds that they've had a difficult time identifying. These entries include notes about birds in unusual plumage, or interesting bird behavior. Later, when home, these notes are valuable in helping the bird watcher to recall the field marks of hard-to-identify birds. There's nothing like a quick sketch or a few observations jotted down to help refresh your memory long after the bird is gone (see Chapter 24 for more on field sketching).

What kind of notebook is best? Whatever you like, but consider the following requirements:

- ✔ It should be large enough to write in easily, to sketch in, and to draw maps in. The tiny, two-for-a-dollar notebooks that you find in the supermarket aren't big enough.

- ✔ It should be portable enough to travel with you, both on business trips and for a day in the field. The large, loose-leaf binders that kids lug to school every day are just too bulky, and the paper tears and falls out.

- ✔ It should be durable. Flimsy covers eventually tear.

Many birders use one of the hard-backed diaries found in stationery stores. They usually measure about 5 x 8 inches and hold 100 to 200 pages. These diaries are small enough to fit in a suitcase, briefcase, or even a large coat pocket. They are hardy enough to tolerate the occasional splash of coffee or blob of doughnut icing. The hard backs make writing in them easy when you're sitting in the car or standing in a field.

Your own rules

Keeping a notebook is no more work than you want it to be. No rules exist. The notebook is yours and should accomplish only what you want it to. Try keeping one, but don't let it become a burden.

Keeping track of what you've seen and where you've been is an important part of the pleasure of bird watching for most people. Even if you're just starting out, try keeping at least a simple list and a few notes. If keeping records is not right for you, quitting is easy. But if your notes turn out to be a source of pleasure, you cannot go back and recreate them a year or two later. Too many bird watchers don't start keeping lists and notes until they've been bird watching for several years, and they always regret not having started sooner.

Part IV
Beyond the Backyard

The 5th Wave   By Rich Tennant

Pterodactyl COSTUME

"Alright you two—one time around the field and then leave those poor people alone!"

In this part . . .

One of the neat things about bird watching is that you can do it virtually any place in the world — with new bird sights and sounds awaiting your discovery. This part introduces you to life in the field, beyond the comfort of your home base. In addition, I present a selection of field trips, festivals, tours, and other events to help get you out into the wider world of birding.

Chapter 16

Taking a Field Trip

. . . .

. . . .

A field trip — it's what makes bird watching exciting, especially when you visit new places in search of new birds. Depending on the extent of your trip and the type of habitat you plan to visit, a field excursion can be as simple as throwing your binocs and field guide in the car and going to a new spot to watch birds, or it can be something akin to Hannibal and his elephants crossing the Alps. It's up to you.

In this chapter, I cover the basic stuff that you need to consider when taking a bird-watching field trip, whether you go alone or with your local bird club. Over the years, I've discovered the hard way what to leave in and what to leave out when setting out on a birding adventure. Some of my experience may be helpful to you. If nothing else, you can laugh at the examples of my own stupidity.

What's a Field Trip?

A *field trip* is defined as going afield — that is, beyond your immediate home surroundings or backyard. For many beginning bird watchers, their first organized field trip is with a bird club. This field trip can be an educational experience as you observe how other bird watchers act in the field, how they spot and identify birds, and where they go to find birds.

In the more traditional sense, a bird-watching field trip is going to some good birding area for several hours or several days. I even know some folks who decided to go see some birds in Montana, which was a long drive from their Pennsylvania home. They liked it so much, they stayed. Now that's the field trip of a lifetime!

My definition of a field trip is loading the car with food, coats, boots, and other gear, more food, cold drinks of all types, the optics, a field guide or two, and ourselves, if we can fit. Then we head off to see what we can see. We often come back after a long day of bird watching exhausted, sunburned, and happy.

I love the adventure of going somewhere to see what birds you can see. Sometimes at the start of a day-long field trip, my wife, Julie, and I make a bet with each other about how many species we'll see. The loser usually gets to buy or fix dinner, or gets to change all of daughter Phoebe's diapers for the remainder of the day. I try *very* hard to guess correctly.

Sometimes your luck just runs out and you get to a birding spot that has *no birds!* This happens a lot in the heat of a midsummer's day, or in the dead of winter. I have a suggestion for keeping yourself interested on a birdless summer day. If it's sunny, look for butterflies. I got into butterflies in exactly this manner. If it's the middle of winter, I suggest you go find a warm, greasy-spoon diner and get a cup of hot chocolate. You can count the days until spring. For more on butterflies, see Chapter 26.

Planning Your Field Trip

If you've got common sense, you can plan a field trip just fine. Here's a quick checklist to help you:

- ✔ Plan where you want to go.
- ✔ Plot your route and determine your schedule (early wake-up and departure to get there for prime dawn birding, and so on).
- ✔ Gather binoculars, spotting scope, field guide, and bird checklist (if you use one).
- ✔ Check the weather and plan the clothing and outerwear you'll need. Then take one extra layer.
- ✔ Make sure that you have the right footwear (boots, rubber boots, extra socks).
- ✔ Pack or wear a hat with a visor.
- ✔ Add food, glorious food. Take some even if you plan to eat in restaurants or at quickie-marts.

Access for everybody

For information on areas that are accessible for bird watchers who use wheelchairs, motorized carts, and other devices that facilitate mobility, contact: The National Parks Service Accessibility Program (FMD), Room #7243, P.O. Box 37127, Washington, D.C. 20013-7127. Or call 202-565-1244.

✔ Get stuff to drink. You'll be thirsty more often than not.

✔ Take money. You may need cash for an emergency (especially coins for a phone call).

✔ Include other gear for comfort or necessity. Depending on the weather, the gear can include sunscreen, lip balm, sunglasses, binocular rain guard, emergency survival kit, and other stuff.

✔ Tell someone where you're going. You can't be too safe.

I was doing a birdathon once in New Jersey. Our team had rented a giant boatmobile of a car to fit all six of us, plus our gear, for the 24 hours of frantic bird-chasing. We left our safe house at one minute past midnight and drove out a dirt road into the middle of a huge, dark marshland. We piled out of the car to listen for any rails or other marsh birds that might be vocalizing. Thinking we'd want to make a hasty getaway to our next stop, the driver, who shall ever remain nameless, left the keys in the ignition. One of the others in our group accidentally brushed against the electronic door lock switch as he got out. We all heard the car lock just before the last door slammed. A locksmith came and opened the car about two hours later. I think our complaining drowned out any birds that may have been calling.

Lesson: Get a magnetic key-holder and put an extra set of keys in it for your vehicle affixed under the front bumper. When traveling, always pocket the keys before you slam the doors. The aggravation you save may be your own.

Dressing for Birding Success

Do you recall the scene in the movie *The Graduate* where the father is telling Dustin Hoffman that the key to his future was one word, "Plastics!"? Well, the key to your bird watching comfort is just as easy: layers. As in, dress in layers of clothing.

Nothing is more miserable than being underdressed in cold or damp weather. Take my 25 years of experience in wearing the wrong thing to go bird watching, and put it to good use for yourself.

There are things I always wear or take no matter the season when I go bird watching.

Layers

I always dress in layers, whether it's 110 degrees or -10 degrees. Layers allow you to peel off or add on clothing as needed. In winter, my layers start with thermal underwear — long johns — top and bottom and end with a wind-and-waterproof outer shell. In summer, my upper body layers are a T-shirt and a light-colored (reflects the sun), long-sleeved shirt with a collar. Two reasons exist for this long-sleeved, collared shirt: I'm fair-skinned and can't take much sun, and my neck is already red enough without the combined effects of sun and a rubbing binocular strap. I'll take a collar and sleeves, thanks.

Hat

Even before the thatch on my roof was getting a bit thin, I always wore a hat to go bird watching. Now that I have an additional part of my body to get sunburned, as well as an additional place for body heat to escape, I'm always the cat in the hat. Utility-minded as ever, I go for a baseball-style cap with a nice brim.

Some folks with whom I bird watch swear by the wide-brimmed Australian or African bush hat. Those hats are nice looking on some heads, but I still prefer the ball cap. In winter, if an insulated ball cap won't cut it, I abandon any pretension to style whatsoever and go for the very goofy (but oh-so-warm) fur-lined hat with earflaps. It's very Elmer Fudd-like, but I still have all the fleshy parts of both my ears.

Comfy footwear

You do experience times when you can get away with wearing tennis shoes for bird watching. Heck, even times when you can get away with loafers or sandals. But my experience has shown me that the best way to stay comfy while birding is to have warm, dry, unsore feet. That's why I always wear (or at least take along) some sturdy but lightweight hiking boots when I go on a field trip.

Hiking boots have come a long way from the heavy leather styles of just a decade or so ago. I recommend that you get a pair of lightweight hikers and break them in well before you wear them for any extensive hiking or walking. The best hiking boots for birding are lightweight, have stiff ankle support, rugged shock-absorbent soles, and sufficient tread to help you clamber up a muddy hillside.

The tennis shoes I sometimes wear are hightops. These give me much-needed ankle support. Believe me, you need ankle support if you do any *off-road* bird watching. All it takes is one molehill to make you aware of inadequate footwear.

My wet weather boots are a pair of calf-covering green waders. I love these things! They let me feel like an English lord in his *Wellies* when I'm walking my farm fields in the rain. An added bonus of such boots is their impenetrability to things other than rain: thorns, ticks, and snakes are three things I laugh off when I'm wearing my green boots.

Sunscreen/lip balm/lotion

The sun is a dangerous thing, even in small amounts. All avid bird watchers can take precaution against overexposure to sunlight by using sunscreen. If I plan to be out in the sun for more than two hours, I dab some sunscreen on my ears, neck, face, and hands. All other parts of my body are covered with clothing. Yes, I know I'll never win the Mr. Suntan Universe contest. I've conceded that.

Chapped lips are a regular thing for field birders. But you can stay kissable by regularly protecting your lips with lip balm. I carry some in all my bird-watching coats and in my field guide pouch.

If you're on an extended trip and are outside birding a lot, you'll notice the effects of sun and wind on your skin as a whole. Don't forget to lotion-up! Why lose your skin like a snake?

Pockets

The pants and shirts that I wear to go bird watching must have pockets, and lots of them. Notebook, pens, pencils, snacks, maps, owl pellets, somebody else's litter — all kinds of stuff ends up in my pockets. Pockets hold all my stuff and keep my hands free for my binoculars.

You may find that you don't need pockets, or you may find that a birding or safari vest works just as well. It's up to you to find your own comfort level.

Other stuff I always take

Just because you're dressed to go birding doesn't mean that you're ready for action. Being ready for anything means taking along a few extra things. Here are some of the items I choose to tote:

✔ **Field guide pouch:** I like the kind of pouch that hooks to your belt and is wide enough to accommodate a field guide and notebook plus other assorted junk, like car keys. Even though I don't always need a field guide to decide what it is I'm seeing, whenever I *don't* have a field guide I *really* need it! With a belt-mounted pouch, you can keep your field guide with you wherever you go without having to cram it into your back pants pocket.

✔ **Pen or pencil and paper:** Writing notes is part of bird watching. A ball-point pen (ink won't run in the rain) is handy for notes about birds, people, or places. Pencils always work (except when you break the point, so take spares).

✔ **Pocketknife:** I've done everything from fixing eyeglasses to cutting open watermelons with my beloved pocketknife. Everybody has the occasional screw loose. A pocketknife — so useful, so outdoorsy. Sterilize your knife blade over a match and you're almost ready to remove somebody's appendix.

✔ **Pocket munchies:** I *never* pack enough food. So to trick myself, I stash munchies in my coat pockets and field guide pouch. This trick allows me to start snacking as soon as we're out of the garage. Believe me, you'll get hungry sooner than lunch, and you'll be ravenous for dinner by 3:00 p.m.

✔ **Tissues:** You have every chance that you'll see some bird that is so beautiful that it reduces you to tears. You have an even better chance that you'll have a runny nose. In either case, having tissues handy is a good thing. Besides which, there aren't well-stocked public restrooms at every bird-watching spot you'll visit.

✔ **Bandanna:** The bandanna cleans your binocular lenses! It dries your sweaty brow! It keeps the black flies from biting the back of your neck! It wipes the mayonnaise off the windshield after you sneeze! I could go on.

✔ **Four quarters:** While you're standing at the pay phone calling the tow truck to come and drag your car to the shop, you can enjoy a cold can of soda — that is, if you remember to bring four quarters. In the age of cellular phones and phone cards, this old safety trick is losing its meaning.

✔ **Wallet:** You may think that you won't want to risk losing your wallet while out bird watching. But you may get pulled over for speeding, or you may be stopped in a routine rounding up of suspicious characters. In such a situation, it's good to have a picture ID on your person. Besides, you never know when you'll need that rarely used credit card to scrape ice off your windshield.

Where the Birds Are

The whole point of taking a field trip is to find birds. If you don't have a local bird club with which you can take field trips, you'll have to find the birds yourself. Here are some places to look for information:

- ✔ **Check out your own county:** Get a county map and check out all the places that have water, extensive woodland, or preserved natural areas. Some birds are bound to be in some of these places.

- ✔ **Pile in for a few hours' drive:** State or provincial parks, preserves, and wildlife management areas are great places to explore for birds, and to find information about birds. Scan a map of your area to find government-run sites that can offer you assistance. Apply what you know about bird habitat preferences to your searching.

- ✔ **Ask around:** Your birding acquaintances may have suggestions for good birdy places. If you don't know any other birders, call your local extension office, conservation office, or department of the environment. They may even be able to put you in touch with other bird clubs or bird watchers in your area.

- ✔ **Use bird-finding guides:** More and more states and provinces are being covered in detail by specific bird-finding guides. If a guide hasn't been published for your specific area, check on titles for adjoining regions. See the appendix for mail order sources of bird-finding guides and other bird books.

- ✔ **Visit the big hotspots:** Feel thwarted by the lack of field trip sites in your region? It can happen. That's when you need to pack up and head for a really big hot spot. Entire books are written just on North American bird-watching hot spots, and most bird magazines feature at least one prime location in each issue. See Chapter 18 for more about birding hotspots, and Chapter 28 for a list of my personal favorites.

For more suggestions on how to find birds when you get there, see Chapter 17.

Using Field Skills

When you encounter birds on a field trip, you need to get your binoculars on them, listen to their calls or songs, and then, with any luck, identify them. This is the time that your field skills as a bird watcher come into play.

Nothing substitutes for years of experience looking at birds in the field. But if you're a beginner, you can make major strides in your field skills with just a bit of practice. For more on general birding field skills, see Chapter 14. Here are some field-trip specific things you can do to improve your performance in the field:

✔ **Anticipate and study:** If you plan to go to a place known for its spring migrant fallouts, where warblers, orioles, tanagers, grosbeaks, and the like are dripping from the trees, you can prepare by reviewing what you know about the species you're likely to see. I still do this every year, especially if I'm leading a bird-watching trip or participating in a birdathon or Big Day.

First of all, I read through the species accounts in the field guides that I have. This sparks my rusty memories of the previous spring. Perhaps I have a few notes written in my field guides — things that help me remember something about a particular species. Once I have my eyes and brain synched up, I move on to another one of my senses: hearing. For more on birding by ear, see Chapter 5.

✔ **Scout the spot:** If you plan to go on a field trip with a bird club, and you want to have a bit of a head start over the other participants, visit the location a day or two ahead of the trip and scout it for birds. Scouting helps you gain valuable insight into what to expect in terms of terrain, climate, birds, and other important information, such as where to eat or where to get a cold drink.

I always try to scout locations, especially when leading a field trip. The process helps me be a better field trip leader.

Field Trip Etiquette

Believe it or not, there are rules of etiquette — both written and unwritten — that guide the behavior of bird watchers. For a quick read through of the semi-official written guidelines, get a copy of the American Birding Association's Code of Ethics. The address is listed in the Appendix.

In some ways, the unwritten rules are more important. Nearly all of them deal with common sense notions and modes of polite conduct. You probably remember all those types of rules either from your mom or some strict school teacher.

Following are a few helpful hints from me — just a bird-watching fool who has broken most rules of the hobby at least once, and some rules many times. But I'm better now.

Following the leader

When out with a group that's being led, by all means follow the leader. It's pretty annoying for everyone else if one person decides to forge ahead of the group to find the good birds. What ends up happening, usually, is all the birds — good or bad — get scared away.

If you want to get away from the group, stay behind and wait for the birds to reappear. But don't move ahead. Besides, you may miss something good if you wander off.

Spishing

On a field trip, ask the leader, or your fellow bird watchers, how they feel about spishing before you commence. *Spishing* is a bird-attracting sound birders make by hissing through closed teeth. If your fellow watchers don't endorse this activity, don't spish. If they're pro-spishing, spish away, but do so with moderation, and not all at once. One spisher at a time is plenty.

Calling out birds

Sooner or later you'll get good enough to identify most of the birds you encounter. On many field trips, particularly those organized outings with a trip leader, you may not need to call out the identities of the birds you spot. In some cases, your fellow bird watchers may not *want* you to call out the IDs because they want to try their own hands at reaching a conclusion. The proper tactic for you is to hold back until you see how the trip is going. If folks are calling out birds left and right, there's no reason you can't, too.

On my first trip to Costa Rica, my wife Julie and I were anticipating lots of new birds. Even though Julie had been to Costa Rica several times before, she told me that she was not going to call out the birds, but was going to let me try to ID them myself. "There's more satisfaction that way," she said. Just our luck, on a guided part of our trip, we were stuck with a very knowledge-able guide who called out every bird he saw and every bird song he heard. I may as well have stayed home and watched a nature special about Costa Rica on TV. We soon peeled away and made our own outings. We did encounter some mystery birds with which we could have used some help (and I did ask Julie to reactivate her bird-ID-calling), but we enjoyed being our own guides. There's more satisfaction that way!

Pointing out others' incorrect IDs

Somebody on a field trip with you sees a red-tailed hawk soaring overhead, but calls out "immature bald eagle!" What do you do? You have three choices:

- ✔ Say nothing.
- ✔ Say: "I don't see your eagle, but there's a red-tailed hawk soaring overhead."

✔ Say: "I don't know the field marks of an immature bald eagle, can you explain them to me?"

How you respond depends on the tone of the field trip and the level of expertise of the participants. I personally never like to point out somebody else's misidentifications out loud (and I don't like having mine pointed out). So any one of the above responses could be fine.

Just be sensitive to the other person's feelings. What goes around comes around, and if you make somebody else feel stupid, you can bet that your turn will come soon.

Maybe the best thing to do is to get everybody else looking at the bird. Then the collective skill of the group can come to a conclusion as to the bird's ID.

Asking questions

When I was a beginner, I always made it a point to ask questions of the better bird watchers with whom I was in the field. I still ask questions, especially when I'm with someone who knows more about a bird, plant, butterfly, or some other natural phenomenon than I do.

Never be shy about asking questions of others on a field trip. Almost everyone you encounter is thrilled to pass along the information you seek. If you get rebuffed, you just received a very important answer to the question: Is this a nice person to go bird watching with? Answer: No!

Providing gas money

An unwritten rule of the bird watching field trip is this: When riding as a passenger on a long field trip in another birder's car, offer to help defray the cost of gasoline. Or you can treat for an ice-cream cone, or lunch, or something. Even if your driver accepts nothing, you've held up your end of the bargain simply by offering.

Dealing with the jerk

Most field trips you go on are trouble-free. Once in a great while — about as often as a rare bird shows up at your bird feeder — you find yourself on a field trip that's cursed with a jerk. This jerk can be somebody who's having a bad day, who's crotchety by nature, or who's plain and simply just hard to be around.

Knowing what to do is hard when you've got a jerk on your hands. Confrontation is not always helpful, nor is ridicule. If at all possible, hint to the jerk that he or she is being unpleasant. You can do this with a stare, without a word. If the message isn't received, you may have to put up with the jerk until the trip is over. Then make sure that you don't include this person again. If you're on an expensive, prepaid bird-watching tour, ask the leader to deal with the situation.

I've been on a few trips with a jerk — not the same jerk each time, mind you. And I've tried all the obvious tactics. Once I even told a jerk that she was being a jerk, and the transformation was amazing. But I'm not so naive as to think that's the magic solution.

Here's a theory of mine: Don't be a jerk yourself, and you'll encounter fewer on your bird-watching adventures.

Taking Precautions

Some people argue that bird watching is not a sport. Well, maybe it's not a *contact* sport, but, like any other sport, bird watching can take a lot out of your body. Not only do you, the bird watcher, have to concentrate on locating your quarry, you must also deal with the natural elements in all their fierce glory.

I know people who've gone to the hospital after an intense session of birding. I know others who should have gone to the hospital. I even know some who never should have been let out of the hospital — but that's another story.

Here are some of the dangerous and painful things that may await you and the precautions you can take to avoid them.

Sun

If the ozone layer is getting thinner, our sunscreen lotions should be getting more powerful. And they are. Even on cloudy days the sun can burn your skin, so you can't be too careful about applying sunscreen — at least SPF 15 — to exposed areas of your skin.

I always wear a hat when I go out birding. I gave up on the idea that a tan is desirable years ago, after a decade of sunburns followed by several layers of peeling skin. The sun is our friend in that it gives us light with which to see birds. Beyond that, I avoid the sun like a vampire does.

Temperature extremes

Too cold at dawn, too hot at noon, too cold at night. This is the pattern of temperatures that bird watchers encounter across much of North America between April and October. In some areas (Arizona, South Texas, southern California), the pattern is hot, hot, hot. And in winter the temperature can be cold everywhere. This variation in temperature is why the concept of dressing in layers was invented.

When you're birding afield in these so-called warm locales, remember to have adequate clothing for the conditions. No bird, no matter how rare, is worth losing appendages to frostbite or risking your life to heat exhaustion.

Always drink plenty of liquids (plain water is best) whenever you're out bird watching. You can be overcome by heat exhaustion or dehydration very quickly, even on seemingly balmy days.

Insects

Of all the insects that can really get at a bird watcher, ticks, mosquitoes, biting flies, and chiggers are the four worst pests. I have, in the past, used chemical deterrents to ward off biting insects. These products almost never work for me. Other bird watchers I know swear by a certain brand. My strategy with the aerial biters is to cover up as much of my exposed skin with clothing as possible. Of course, in some places that you seek birds — in a swamp, for example — biting insects are unavoidable and you're vastly outnumbered. In this case, you can put up with it or not go.

Chiggers

Chiggers are a tiny biting mite most often encountered in areas of tall grass. Some chiggers only bite you. Other chiggers crawl up your legs and embed themselves beneath the surface of your skin, particularly in areas where the skin is constricted, such as waistbands and around the tops of elasticized socks. Once embedded, chiggers (and chigger bites) cause intense itching. Getting rid of chiggers once they're embedded is difficult. One of the methods used by Texas birders, where chiggers are fairly common, is to soak your legs and torso in a hot bath. The hot water kills the chiggers.

Ticks

The problem with ticks is that they can carry two potentially harmful diseases: Rocky Mountain Spotted Fever and Lyme Disease. Both diseases have become fairly widespread in North America, but they can be avoided if you're careful. For both ticks and chiggers (which are too small to see), I use the trusted tuck-the-pant-legs-in-the-socks method. This forces these critters to crawl all the way up my legs to get to their beloved goal: my skin. I regularly look over my pants legs to see if I can find any ticks before they can find me. Once home, I change clothes right away so any unseen pests cannot find their way to my flesh.

If I know an area is heavily infested with ticks or harbors chiggers, I stay out. This may mean staying on a road or path, avoiding nearby brushy or grassy areas. Or it may mean avoiding the areas altogether. After visiting an area where ticks are present, always check yourself thoroughly for these small, dark insects. If you find a tick embedded, use tweezers to pull the tick out, head and all. If you become sick or ill, see your doctor and ask to be tested for these two tick-borne diseases.

Fire ants

In some areas of the South, a new source of pain for bird watchers is the fire ant. Fire ants are aggressive colonial ants from Central and South America that have invaded North America. When their large, conical earthen nest is disturbed, fire ants swarm the perceived threat and deliver an exceedingly painful sting. If you plan to visit a southern state, ask local officials about fire ants. And ask a local birder to point out a fire ant mound, so you know what to avoid. I did this backwards. First, I stepped on a small fire ant mound and got stung, and then I found out about fire ants and what to avoid.

This all sounds horrible, but it really isn't. Most insects you encounter while bird watching do nothing more than annoy you. Hundreds of insect repellents, insect-proof suits, and even folklore cures (eat a banana the night before and the bugs won't bite you) are available. You can find one that suits you.

Trespassing

My rule about trespassing is: *don't.* Wandering onto somebody's property without asking permission is never okay. That you're only bird watching won't make a difference to a landowner who decides to be a hardcase about his property lines. I discovered this lesson:

One June, I was with a group doing a Breeding Bird Survey high in the mountains of West Virginia when we came upon an old barn alongside the remote road we were covering. I thought the barn looked like a prime spot for barn owls, and said as much as I walked over to the barn and then through the open doorway. What I saw inside was a neatly arranged line of glass jugs and plastic buckets. Steam was coming up through the floorboards. Copper tubing was running to a large vat. I was putting all this together when one of my colleagues said, "Bill. Come out slowly as if nothing unusual is going on. We've got to get out of here." I did so. Only after we were down the road a mile did he tell me that, in scanning the hillside opposite the barn, he had seen another ramshackle building. Only this one had a man sitting in the doorway, with a rifle pointed at me, ready to shoot the people who'd discovered his moonshine still! In some states, it's legal to shoot trespassers. I've never unthinkingly trespassed since.

Hunting seasons

A hunting season exists for almost everything. In some cases, this coincides with good times of the year for bird watching. Always keep yourself aware of any active hunting seasons and active hunting areas.

When Things Go Wrong

Sometimes things just go wrong. What starts out as a bird-watching adventure can become a nightmare, or at least no fun at all. A twist of fate may be unavoidable, but you do have ways to cope when things go wrong.

BIRD TALES

A toehold on pain

When Julie and I went on our honeymoon, we chose Belize, because neither of us had ever been there. What was meant to be a splendid week of snorkeling, birding, and sightseeing turned ugly in a hurry. After many trials and tribulations with lost luggage and bad plane tickets, we finally reached our tiny island destination off the coast of Belize. Getting to the island in an open fishing boat, we got thoroughly soaked from head to toe.

Once ashore, I couldn't change into dry clothes (my luggage was still lost), but I decided to take off my shoes and socks to go barefoot. Julie, to her credit, warned me about hurting myself — splinters from the dock, stepping on some nasty bug, and so on. I glibly replied, "Dear, sweet wife. This is the

tropics! I'm *supposed* to go barefoot!" Two hours later, as I was stepping out of someone's way on the unlit verandah-dock, I fell into the ocean. But I caught a toe in the dock as I fell. There was pain. There was blood. I was soaked for the second time (still no luggage) and rapidly descended into shock. Back on the boat and into Belize City, I went to see a doctor.

Threat of infection. I must go back to the U.S. Six weeks on crutches and a few "I told-you-so's." Later I was limping along, almost as good as new. Our tropical honeymoon had devolved into ten hours of pure hell. Accidents happen. Especially if you're as foolish as I was. Now I *always* listen to everything my lovely, slightly smug wife says to me.

Lost

If you're lost in the wilderness, and can't retrace your steps, the best thing to do is to stay put. Sooner or later somebody will come looking for you, or someone will happen along the same path you took. If you keep wandering aimlessly, you may be making it tougher for someone to track you down.

Foul weather

I don't want to sound like a nagging parent, but please don't go outside to watch birds when a major storm is either happening or about to happen. Especially avoid lightning, hail, blizzards, tornadoes, and hurricanes. You can go look for birds *afterwards*. Do I really have to tell you this? I could also tell you to avoid Mothra and Godzilla, but would you really listen to me?

If you're going to be out in the rain, you may wish to have something to cover your binoculars (as well as your head and feet). A hasty binocular rain guard can be fashioned out of a zippable plastic sandwich bag. You can use the one in which you packed your snack. It's cheap and it works.

I've found that a moderately priced rain suit, like those sold at camping stores or outdoor outfitters, can be very handy for foul-weather birding. I was once on an island off Alaska where it rained every day for a week. The birds didn't mind the weather, and I didn't either, all comfy and warm inside my rain suit.

Flash floods are deadly and happen unbelievably fast. Do not, under any circumstances, attempt to drive your car or walk through rapidly moving water, particularly if you're in a flash flood zone.

Sickness

If you start feeling ill when you're out in the field, don't keep pressing onward thinking that it will go away. Seek help, or get home as soon as you can.

If you're feeling dizzy or have a headache, stop using your binoculars for a while. Sometimes you can give yourself a headache by straining to see through binoculars for long periods. And if your binocs are even a little out of alignment, your eyes work extra hard to keep the images aligned and in focus. This extra effort gives you the feeling of wearing someone else's prescription glasses.

If the problem goes away while you're not using your optics, consider getting your binocs checked out by an optics professional. The optics may be out of alignment. Realignment is simple and usually inexpensive.

Accidents

It's a good idea to let somebody know where you're going before you leave for a long field trip. If you're unfortunate enough to have an accident, someone can eventually come looking for you.

Most birders take precautions against accidents: wearing heavy boots to guard against injuries to ankles or feet; avoiding areas of unsafe footing; balancing periods of strenuous walking with periods of rest. Common sense can be your guide.

I always carry an emergency kit in my car in case of a breakdown. I always carry coins for pay phones. I always advise someone of my travel plans. And I *never* run with scissors.

Special Trips

Field trips take on new meaning when you have target birds. Target birds are birds that may be the goal of a given field trip. Certain groups of birds can be relied upon (usually) to put on a show at certain times of the year. Here are a few of my favorites.

Warblers and migrants in spring

Spring migration is the best time of the year to be a bird watcher. On a good fallout day (a day when lots of migrant birds are present during spring or fall migration — seemingly fallen from the sky),when brilliantly colored birds are everywhere and their songs are filling the air, you thank your lucky stars that you're there with your binocs. And you'll wonder how you ever ignored birds before you became a watcher.

Legendary spring migration hotspots exist, such as Point Pelee in Canada and High Island in Texas, but you can also do quite well near your home. You need to find a prime habitat to which migrant birds are attracted. Wooded areas along large bodies of water, or high points of the landscape, such as ridges, are likely spots for migrants, as are geographical features such as islands and peninsulas that concentrate migrating birds.

You also need to have cooperation from the weather. The relationship between the weather and bird migration is not entirely understood. But, put simply, in spring, northbound migrants tend to move when they have a strong tailwind — winds from the south, southeast, or southwest. This pattern makes sense. The wind helps the migrants on their way. Many species won't migrate northward if faced with a southbound wind. Monitor how the weather in your area affects local migration spots. This information can help you predict the best mornings in late March, April, May, or early June (depending on where you live) to be outside looking for migrants.

Hawks in fall

September, October, and November are peak months for fall hawk migration. Many bird clubs and other nature groups organize special hawk-watching field trips at this time of year. In recent years, many important hawk migration sites have been established all over North America. Even at places where official hawk counts are being conducted, the public is almost always welcome. Do yourself a favor and get to a hawk watch in the fall. You'll gain a new appreciation for the birds of prey.

Shorebirds in late summer

The only good thing about the end of summer (besides the fact that the kids get to go back to school) is that this is when the majority of the migrant shorebirds migrate southward through North America toward their wintering grounds. If you're within driving distance of any shoreline on a large body of water, July and August are the prime months for watching shorebirds, many of which are still in breeding plumage as they migrate from their breeding grounds in the Far North. If you want to study shorebirds and improve your ID skills on this often confusing group of birds, late summer is the best time of year to do so.

Owling

Owling is cool. It helps you to get to know *whoooo's whoooo* in the woods at night. Most bird clubs run owling trips, sometimes called *owl prowls*. These prowls are usually held in mid-to-late winter when the owls are at their most vocal, during courtship, just prior to settling down to breed.

You can do your own mini owl prowl if you have a suitable wooded habitat near your house. Go outside late at night in midwinter and listen for the low hoots of the barred or great-horned owl, or the whinnying whistle of the members of the screech-owl family. Not all owls are denizens of the woods. Some owls prefer prairie, or desert, or tundra. Your field guide can help you determine which owls may be found in your area. If you're curious about owl sounds, check out the bird-song recordings at your local library. Almost every modern set of bird vocalizations contains some material on common owl species.

Pelagic trips

Get on a boat in the wee hours of the morning. Head out to sea in search of seabirds. Maybe you'll see thousands, maybe you'll see none. You may get seasick. What is it that bird watchers find so fascinating about pelagic trips? The birds!

Pelagic is a word derived from Greek, that means "of the open sea." There are many seabird species — called *pelagic birds* — that only come to land to nest. These birds spend the majority of their lives roaming the surface of the briny sea.

If you're interested in building a long life list of birds, sooner or later you'll hear the siren call of the sea. On the East Coast, most pelagic trips are aimed at getting out as far as the Gulf Stream, the warm ocean current in which seabirds find abundant food. Because this trip can be quite far offshore, you can spend several hours getting there, do a bit of birding, and spend several more hours getting back. I've been on several pelagic trips off the East Coast, and I've been lucky to see lots of birds and never get seasick. Most of my friends can't say the same.

The West Coast is blessed with rich, life-sustaining ocean currents near to shore, so the pelagic trips get to the birds faster. But the Pacific Ocean, some would say, is misnamed. It can have mighty large swells, which are anything but peaceful on your stomach.

If you wish to go on a pelagic trip, by all means go on an organized one. Don't ride along on a fishing charter boat. You'll see far more birds and smell fewer fishes and tackle boxes on the all-birder trip. Most bird magazines feature listings for pelagic trips in their advertisements.

For me, taking my first field trip was the start of a lifelong passion for birds. Now, on land or on sea, I enjoy nothing more than my friends of the air.

Chapter 17

Birding by Habitat

• •

In This Chapter

▶ Thinking like a bird

▶ Knowing what to expect

▶ Habitat types

▶ Bird preferences

▶ Habitat as an ID clue

• •

*I*magine yourself as a bird, flying high in the sky. You're a spring migrant songbird, returning from the mountains of Costa Rica where you spent the winter. Instinct is propelling you to the place where you were born so that you can seek a mate and produce offspring yourself. But how do you know when you get there? You're a bird and can neither read a roadmap, nor stop to ask for directions. Of course we all know that *male* birds never stop to ask directions. Hmmm. . . .

The answer for a bird is that home can be wherever the habitat is. But the habitat must be right, or the bird may not survive. Being extremely mobile creatures, flying around in search of a suitable place to rest, feed, seek shelter, and reproduce is pretty easy for birds.

For you, the bird watcher, bird habitat preferences are an excellent clue to help you know what species to expect in certain types of habitats. This chapter helps you make the connection between habitat type and bird type.

Thinking Like a Bird

When looking at a particular piece of habitat, ask yourself: "If I were a bird, where would I go within this area? Where's the best shelter? Where am I likely to find food? Water? If I wanted to hide from nosy bird watchers, where would I go?"

See the color section for an example of how to view a landscape (as a human) when you're birding by habitat.

Birding by Habitat

Birding by habitat (BBH) is not only a neat way to find birds, it's also easy. Here's a test to check your BBH IQ: In which of these two habitats would you most likely find a wood duck: Along a river? Or in a tree in the woods?

If you said along a river, your score is 75 out of 100. If you said in a tree in the woods, you score 25 out of 100. But if you said **both,** you scored a perfect 100! Wood ducks feed along rivers and streams, but they nest in hollow trees (hence their name)!

Preferred habitat

Every bird species has habitat preferences, and some of them are very specific. Bird families have broad habitat preferences, which makes generalizing about ducks preferring water to land easy. As you become more familiar with the habitat preferences of birds, you begin to see some of the specifics among bird habitat preferences as well.

Birding by habitat allows you to know what to expect in a given habitat before you enter it. This knowledge gives you a distinct advantage. You won't be fooled or surprised to hear a yellow warbler singing from a willow tree on the edge of a wetland. You know that this species loves willow trees and wet areas, and so you expect to find a yellow warbler in this area.

But when something unexpected shows up, you're ready. If a bird isn't in your mental reference for this habitat, you know you'd better take a closer look.

Knowing where and when

Another advantage of being able to bird by habitat is knowing where birds can be found during different times of year, as many birds use different habitats at different times. That yellow warbler in the willow tree may not be there from December through April, but you know that it will be around from May through July.

If you're like me, from time to time you get an urge to see a certain species. For me, lately, it's been red-headed woodpeckers in the summer and short-eared owls in the winter. Neither species is common here in southeastern Ohio, so I have to know when and where to look. In both cases, I know precisely where the best habitats are for these species (red-headed woodpeckers love big stands of oak trees; short-eared owls love large old grassy meadows), so I can get my annual fix if I visit these spots at the right time of year.

Birds need four basic things to survive: food, water, shelter, and a place to reproduce. Look for these things when you're birding by habitat, and you'll find birds.

Habitat Types and the Birds that Love Them

What follows is a very general list of some common North American habitat types and the bird families and species you commonly find in them. Remember that the birds in your part of the continent may differ somewhat from those listed here, depending on factors of climate, available habitat type, and season. This list is not all-inclusive, but it does contain some representative species for each habitat type.

You can use this general round-up of bird habitats to help form your own ideas of what birds to expect in the habitats in your region.

Lakes, rivers, and wetlands

Anywhere in North America where you find water may be considered a wetland. Where there's water, there's bound to be birds. Why? Because wet habitats support a vast diversity of life, from microscopic aquatic insects to huge animals such as humans, bears, and the Loch Ness Monster.

Bird watchers are drawn to water because birds are drawn there, too. All birds need water to survive, but some birds prefer to make their homes in, on, or near water. These are the species and families of birds that you can expect to find in wetland habitats:

- ✔ **In open water:** ducks; geese; swans; loons; grebes; cormorants; phalaropes

- ✔ **Along the water's edge:** herons; egrets; shorebirds (sandpipers, plovers, and the like)

- ✔ **In the marsh vegetation:** bitterns; rails; yellow-headed, tricolored or red-winged blackbirds; boat-tailed grackles; marsh wrens; swamp sparrows; common yellowthroats

- ✔ **In wooded edges and flooded bottomland:** willow flycatchers, alder flycatchers, Acadian flycatchers; prothonotary warblers; yellow warblers; woodpeckers; kingfishers; red-shouldered hawks; barred owls

- ✔ **Flying overhead:** northern harriers; swallows; swifts; flocks of waterfowl

The key: Sneak up on 'em

Finding birds in habitats with water can require some stealth on your part. Ducks feeding and resting on a wooded pond won't stick around long if you appear suddenly on the shore. Nor will any other species on or near the water.

Find a distant vantage point from which to scan the pond and then choose a discreet route to get closer for a better look. I've had amazing luck watching birds from a canoe. For some reason, a slow moving canoe with two bird watchers in it doesn't seem to threaten waterbirds as much as if those same two birders popped out of a car and walked to the edge of the water. (Make sure you observe all boating safety rules. Just because you're a bird watcher in the middle of a calm lake doesn't mean you won't tip the canoe over.)

Special places: Dams and reservoirs

In winter, when much of the fresh water may be frozen, birds congregate wherever the unfrozen water is, such as directly below a dam or reservoir — anywhere that has moving water. Ducks, geese, swans, loons, grebes, gulls, and other waterbirds can be found using the open water. Hanging around nearby may be several bald or golden eagles, or possibly red-tailed hawks, looking for an easy meal among the many waterbirds.

Woodlands: From clearings to deep, thick forests

Four hundred or so years ago, the eastern half of North America was so thickly forested in virgin old-growth timber, it's said that a single squirrel could have traveled from Maine to the eastern edge of the Great Plains without ever touching the ground. Although this is no longer the case (due to the effects of human industry and agriculture on the landscape), many parts of the continent are more tree-covered than they were even 60 years ago. Besides, all the squirrels are too busy at our bird feeders to attempt an historical reenactment of this epic mammalian trek.

These are the species and families of birds that you can expect to find in various woodland habitats:

- **Clearings and cut or burned-over areas:** feeding areas for flycatchers; bluebirds; kestrels; flickers; robins; swallows; many other species

- **Scrubby zones, with a few saplings:** warblers (such as prairie warbler, yellow warbler, orange-crowned warbler); white-eyed vireos; sparrows; grouse

✔ **Riparian areas (wooded waterways):** wood ducks; hooded mergansers; herons; woodcocks; barred owls; red-shouldered hawks; magpies; crows; some warbler species (prothonotary warblers, American redstarts, waterthrushes, and the like); phoebes; flycatchers

✔ **Secondary growth (medium-sized trees, with thick underbrush):** towhees; sparrows; gray catbirds; thrashers; northern cardinals; buntings; and warblers such as mourning, hooded, Kentucky, MacGillivray's warbler

✔ **Deciduous forest:** red-eyed vireos; many warblers; tanagers; grosbeaks; thrushes; grouse; turkey; nightjars; jays; woodpeckers; great-horned owls; screech owls; broad-winged hawks; white-breasted nuthatches; black-capped or Carolina chickadees; titmice

✔ **Coniferous forest (pine, spruce, fir):** crossbills; grouse; finches; red-breasted, pygmy, and brown-headed nuthatches; mountain, boreal, and chestnut-backed chickadees; blackburnian warblers; pine warblers; yellow-rumped warblers; Townsend's warblers; black-throated green warblers

✔ **Mixed coniferous/deciduous forest:** solitary vireos; chuck-will's-widows; woodpeckers; jays; many warbler species

The key: Listen up

Cheers, big ears! Use your ears when birding in wooded habitats and you greatly increase your chances of finding birds. Even if you don't know what the bird is that's singing, that's okay. Use its song to help you locate it. With visual and audio clues, you can identify the bird accurately. For information on identifying birds by their songs, see Chapter 5.

Succession: The process of regrowth

After a thickly wooded area is cut or otherwise destroyed, regrowth begins in a process called succession. Each stage of succession has certain characteristics that set it apart from other stages, just as each stage has particular bird, animal, and plant species associated with it. For example, golden-winged warblers prefer to nest in old neglected fields where brush and saplings have begun to grow. A farm field, if left alone, goes through these stages: grassy meadow; brushy meadow; overgrown meadow (brushy with some saplings); secondary woodland (medium-sized trees, thick underbrush); climax forest (large trees, sparse undergrowth). The first few stages can occur over just a few years. The last two stages take longer, even centuries. For the golden-winged warbler, the habitat may only be suitable for two or three years before it becomes too wooded. Then it's time to move on to another old meadow.

Special places: Edge habitat and waste spaces

An *edge habitat* occurs where an open habitat such as a meadow, meets a wooded habitat. This mix of habitats is very attractive to birds of both areas, and is almost always productive for bird watching. Plus, the birds are easier to see than if they're deep in the woods. Test this theory out the next time you're in an edge habitat. See if it isn't birdier than either the meadow or woods habitat alone.

Believe it or not, *waste spaces* — areas that are unsightly or even ugly — can be very good places to find birds. Old abandoned farmland, clearcuts, old cemeteries, and even old industrial land can have lots of birds simply because they have successional habitats and no people.

Grasslands, prairies, and farmlands

Before the central portions of North America fell under the plow, they were part of a vast sea of grass stretching from present day Ohio to Colorado, and from northwestern Canada to Mexico. It was the proverbial "home where the buffalo roam." Patches of the native prairies remain, and in these patches you can see what the trip list of a Westward Ho pioneer may have included: prairie-chickens, bobwhite, several grouse species, sandhill crane, long-spurs, bobolink, many sparrows, larks, and so on.

But even in areas that are heavily farmed, you can see many birds. Some birds are prairie species that have adapted to take advantage of available habitats, while other birds are immigrants that prefer living in this altered habitat.

These are the species and families of birds that you can expect to find in various grassland habitats:

- **Native grasslands/prairies:** special sparrows, such as LeConte's, grasshopper, vesper, Henslow's, and others; lark buntings; upland sandpipers; mountain plovers; long-billed curlews; ferruginous hawks; golden eagles; short-eared owls

- **Fences and roadsides:** *on fences* — Dickcissels; lark buntings; bluebirds; nighthawks; meadowlarks; sparrows; upland plovers; burrowing owls; *along roadsides* — killdeer; horned larks; longspurs; quail; pheasants

- **Telephone/electric poles and wires:** *used for hunting, eating, and resting* — hawks; eagles; vultures; kingbirds; shrikes; swallows; flycatchers; *used as song perches* — meadowlarks; bluebirds; buntings; sparrows

- **Farm fields:** *plowed fields* — killdeer; mountain, golden, and black-bellied plovers; snow buntings; Lapland longspur; larks; gulls; blackbirds; *pastures/cultivated fields* — crows; blackbirds; swallows; sparrows; goldfinches; kestrel

> ✔ **Woodlots and windbreaks:** great-horned owls; barn owls; screech owls; nesting hawks; woodpeckers; crows; jays; orioles; tanagers; flycatchers; warblers; chickadees; song sparrows; goldfinches

The keys: Look sharp and listen

The key to watching birds in vast open, flat areas, such as in the middle of the Great Plains, is to scan for perching birds on any tall, exposed perch, such as a telephone pole or fencepost, a lone tree, or a tall weed stem. In treeless areas, any perch is regarded as valuable real estate to the birds living there. Although many of the grassland species sing while in flight (horned larks, upland sandpipers, bobolinks, pipits, and longspurs), others, such as sparrows and meadowlarks, sing from the best perch. Raptors hunt from the perch. Other birds use perches for resting or preening.

Be sure to use your ears, too. Many grassland species sing from the ground. Rather than diving into the grass to attempt to flush these birds out, wait patiently. Eventually you'll see the birds that you're seeking.

One final key is to look for water. Farm ponds or natural wetlands can be teeming with ducks and shorebirds.

Special places: Prairie potholes and booming grounds

In the north-central portions of the Great Plains, you can find thousands of small ponds, pools, marshes, and wetlands called *potholes*. In and around these potholes, the majority of North American ducks and a few species of shorebirds nest and raise young. When birding in the northern plains states or in central Canada, be sure to look for waterfowl and shorebirds in these wet areas.

Leks and *booming grounds* are other locations. Early every spring, males of certain gamebird species gather to perform their breeding rituals in hopes of attracting a mate. These gathering spots are called leks or booming grounds (for the booming sound the males make in their displays).

The males (all of one species) arrange themselves in a given area and begin their individual displays. Females select a male from all the hopefuls, mate, and then leave to begin nesting. By using a concealing observation blind, in some places you can observe this incredible behavior without disturbing the birds. In North America, the species that perform these breeding displays are the greater and lesser prairie-chickens, sage grouse, and sharp-tailed grouse.

Bird-finding guides for Great Plains states, the Rocky Mountain region, and the Southwest can help direct you to some of these special places. See the Appendix for a list of sources for these guides.

Coastal areas

Humans love going to the ocean and so do birds, but for different reasons. Instead of sun, sand, and surf, birds go for the more mundane: food and flyways! The coasts of the Atlantic and Pacific oceans and the Gulf of Mexico have an enormous variety of habitat types associated with them, and with these habitats come a similar abundance and variety of birdlife. Here are a few of the most common coastal habitats and some of the bird species and families that may be found there:

- ✔ **Beaches:** shorebirds of all kinds but especially sandpipers and plovers; terns; gulls; black skimmers; pelicans; some herons and egrets; blackbirds; fish crows; American crows

- ✔ **Rocky shorelines and breakwaters:** harlequin ducks; eiders; scoters; loons; grebes; turnstones; surfbirds; wandering tattlers; purple sandpipers; oystercatchers; surfbirds; cormorants; pelicans; gulls; terns; osprey; bald eagles

- ✔ **Brackish marsh:** herons; egrets; terns; black skimmers; swallows; shorebirds (especially whimbrel, plovers, dowitchers, stilts, and avocets); rails; bitterns

- ✔ **Freshwater inlets:** osprey; bald eagles; gulls; terns; belted kingfishers; ducks; grebes; shorebirds; pelicans; herons; egrets

- ✔ **Seacliffs:** puffins; guillemots; murres; auks; cormorants; gannets; kittiwakes; gulls; peregrine falcons

The key: Scan the horizon

Bird watching along the seacoast is like standing along a very busy street in New York City. Sooner or later, everything passes by you.

My favorite thing to do when birding along the coast is to find a comfortable place to sit and then spend a while just scanning to see what I can see, on the sea. In winter, when lots of ducks, loons, scoters, and gannets are moving offshore, I can sit and watch for hours (provided I'm out of the cold wind). In summer, plenty of terns, gulls, and shorebirds are around. During the spring and fall migrations, you can never tell what's going to fly past.

Special places: Winter coastal birding and pelagic species

I love visiting the seacoast in the northern parts of North America during winter. There may not be warm water and sunshine, but there are bound to be lots of birds.

Depending on where you go, you can encounter thousands of birds along the coast in winter. As a bonus, you encounter few people on the beach and little or no competition for hotel rooms. Dress warmly in layers, take your spotting scope, something hot to drink, and you're ready to rumble.

Winter is a good time to see *pelagic species* (birds that spend most of their time far out to sea, perhaps coming ashore only to breed) from shore. Changes in water temperature and currents bring food resources near shore, and the birds follow. Among the species you may glimpse are murres, gannets, shearwaters, kittiwakes, jaegers, murrelets, and auklets. If you're very interested in seabirds, consider taking a pelagic trip on a boat that's specially chartered for birders in quest of pelagic species. For more information on pelagic trips, see Chapter 16.

Deserts and scrublands

If you think that the desert is a barren wasteland, you haven't been wasting enough time in front of the television watching nature shows. The desert regions of North America are wonderful places for watching birds. The key is knowing where to look.

Water, being a scarce commodity in the desert, is an obvious attractant for desert birds, but vegetation, especially lush vegetation, is also appealing to birds. Vegetation offers shade, a place to hide from predators, and a place to nest for many species. For example, the saguaro cactus of the Southwest is a source of food, liquid, shelter, a place to nest, and a place to perch for a variety of birds. These cactus plants take the place of trees in a spot where no tree can survive.

Here are some of the many desert habitats in North America:

- **Sagebrush flats:** *in areas where sage predominates*: sage grouse; sage thrashers; Brewer's sparrows; sage sparrows

- **Brushy desert with mesquite bushes and cactus:** roadrunners; Gambel's quail; elf owls; Costa's hummingbirds; phainopepla; cactus wrens; thrashers; black-throated sparrows.

- **Canyons, cliffs, mesas:** nesting areas for golden eagles, prairie and peregrine falcons, and several hawk species; as well as vultures, canyon and rock wrens, and Say's phoebes

- **Cultivated/irrigated areas:** anyplace with water may have shorebirds; larks; ducks; gulls; flycatchers; cattle egrets; many other birds

- **Streams, rivers, water holes:** kingfishers; flycatchers (vermilion flycatcher); gray hawks; Cooper's hawks; migrant shorebirds; yellow warblers; Bell's vireos; yellow-breasted chats; black phoebes

The key: Go early or late

Besides looking for sources of water and cooling shade, you'll further enhance your chances of finding birds if you time your outings for early and late in the day. Avoid high noon and the hot hours immediately preceding and following noon. Take my advice and find a nice cool bar or hotel swimming pool where you can work on your bird list or clean your binocs. Fewer birds are out and about during these times, I promise. Take a siesta.

Look along rivers, in shaded canyons, or even in town parks (especially those with ponds or lawn-sprinkler systems).

Whenever you venture out in the desert, take a few precautions. Wear a hat, cover your exposed skin with sunscreen, carry and drink plenty of water, watch where you step and place your hands (remember that snakes and scorpions live in the desert), and don't venture anywhere remote without letting somebody know where you're going and when you plan to return. Call me a mother hen, but it beats getting bitten by a rattlesnake or frying yourself in the sun — both of which can be easily avoided.

Special places: Sun, rocks, sand, and oases

Hot sun on rocks and sand make for rising hot thermals upon which raptors soar. Don't forget to look up when birding in the desert. You may see an eagle, falcon, Harris' hawk, zone-tailed hawk, common black hawk, or some other interesting bird of prey.

Gardens and backyards of desert communities are also good spots: Anywhere there's water in the desert, you can find lush vegetation that draws birds like a wiggling worm draws a fish. Some of my most productive hours on desert bird watching trips have been spent roaming through sidestreets of small desert cities and towns, looking at the birds in the trees, lawns, ornamental plantings, and at backyard feeding stations.

Knowing What to Expect

As noted earlier in this chapter, birding by habitat helps you to know what to expect when you get there. It may seem like a lot of work to study-up ahead of time, but after the first few visits to a habitat, you automatically know what birds are likely to be seen. Soon you begin to feel as though a visit to a familiar habitat is akin to going to a party where you see all your old friends.

Here's a way to hone your BBH (birding by habitat) skills. Before visiting a particular habitat, make a list of the species that you think you'll see. Keep a list during your visit to the habitat and compare the two afterward. Believe me, your accuracy improves over time.

Chapter 18

Birding Hotspots

· ·

In This Chapter

▶ What and where are hotspots?

▶ How do you find these places?

▶ When should you go?

▶ What use are bird-finding guides?

▶ Life after hotspots

· ·

*F*or humans, a hotspot is often defined by the fact that others go there. Consider a trendy nightclub: Even if the drinks are expensive and the music is mediocre, people may continue to show up, just because that's "the place to be."

Birds are smarter than that. They may pause to check out a place where they see other birds (that's why ducks, for example, will drop in to a pond with decoys), but if that spot doesn't supply their basic needs (food, water, shelter, a place to breed), they quickly move on.

Birding Hotspots: What and Where Are They?

Temperature has nothing to do with defining a hotspot. What you're really looking for is a place where the birding is hot. (And that can happen even when the weather is downright cold!) You want a place with a lot of birds, preferably a place with a lot of different *kinds* of birds. Even better is a place that offers not only numbers and variety, but also an element of surprise: the kind of spot where odd birds sometimes show up, far from their normal haunts.

Hotspots for bird watching are scattered all over the world. No matter where you live, there are bound to be some hotspots nearby, others that you can reach with a little effort, and still others that you can dream about visiting someday.

Location, location, location

Typically, what makes a place great for birding is either its location or its habitat. Geography turns some places into big concentration points for migrating birds. A peninsula on the coast or on the shore of a major lake can be a place where birds pause before setting out on their next flight, especially under certain weather conditions. A wooded park in the middle of a large city may have the same kind of concentrating effect during the migration season.

One of the best migration hotspots in the Northeast is Central Park in New York City. It doesn't offer an expanse of habitat, but what it does have — green trees and thick underbrush, water, and shelter — is the only choice migrant birds have. The park is surrounded by miles of concrete, skyscrapers, bustling traffic, and people. During spring migration, incredible concentrations of birds can be found on this green island in the center of Manhattan.

Habitat

More reliable for birding at other seasons is a place with really good habitat. Of course, no two kinds of birds will see "good habitat" in exactly the same way. A horned lark may be happy in a plowed field, while a wood thrush seeks out the forest shadows. Therefore, habitat variety is a key point. It helps to have lots of plant life: A woodland with a brushy understory is likely to hold more birds than a park with nothing but mowed lawns under the trees. Water is almost always an element of good bird habitat. A stream or small pond attracts certain types of birds while a large marsh or lake attracts many more. For some additional insight about birds and habitat, see Chapter 17.

Odd spots

Some kinds of hotspots for bird watching can seem bizarre to normal people. I guarantee that if you pursue birds for long, you'll find yourself comparing notes with other birders about your favorites among the sewage ponds and garbage dumps you've visited. But if you're trying to get a friend interested in birds, it's probably best not to take them to such a place on the first date.

Finding Hotspots

Trial and error is one way to find hotspots. You can pick a random spot and hang around to see if any birds show up. But birds are practically everywhere, so it can take a while to figure out whether a spot is average or great.

FIELD TIP

Unusual usual places for birds

Birds can commonly be found in spots you wouldn't think to look. Here are some of them:

✔ **Sewage treatment plants and ponds:** Fertile water means lots of food for birds.

✔ **Landfills:** Gulls are legendary garbage pickers. Sometimes the regular gull species attract their rarer fellow gulls.

✔ **Urban boating/shipping harbors:** Lots of handouts for gulls, ducks, geese, and swans.

✔ **Urban/suburban lakes, ponds, reservoirs:** Calm water with little or no disturbance from watercraft. Birds like that.

✔ **Vacant lots or old industrial sites that are overgrown:** Hawks, owls, killdeer, swallows, sparrows — lots of species move in when humans move out.

✔ **Arboretums and tree farms, even in urban areas:** Great habitat for attracting all kinds of birds. Can be especially good for owls in winter and warblers in spring.

✔ **Cemeteries:** Quiet places with good habitat where birds can feed and rest in peace.

✔ **Roadside rest stops:** Ornamental plantings and the presence of water attracts birds. Convenient bathrooms attract bird watchers.

✔ **Powerline right-of-way cuts:** These often pass right through dense woodland habitats. Poles and lines provide perches for birds.

✔ **Edge habitats along highways and roadways:** Any edge habitat is good for birds. Notice how many red-tailed hawks you see along the highway. The grassy medians are perfect for mammal-hunting birds of prey.

In most parts of North America, good birding spots are already known. Nearly all bird watchers are willing to share the good places. It's not like fishing — if too many people go fishing at one spot, they may use up the fish. You're not likely to use up all the birds.

Go clubbing

Unless you live in a really remote region, a bird club is probably located somewhere near you. (For more information about finding a bird club, see Chapter 21.) Bird watchers with local experience can give you a big head start in finding the hotspots. They may be able to recommend a nearby park, lake, refuge, or other location where the birding is great.

Read up

You also may be able to find published information on where to go birding. Hundreds of bird-finding guides are available for North America — some cover large areas, such as several states or provinces; others detail the birding spots in a small area, such as a single county. If you don't know any bird watchers who can advise you about such guides, your local library may be able to steer you to these publications.

Lewis-and-Clark It

You can, of course, discover your own hotspots. If you develop an eye for habitat, you may recognize productive spots at first sight — you may predict, for example, that a marshy pond next to a forest is likely to be good. You may predict that an empty parking lot is likely to be a lousy bird habitat — unless it happens to be next to a fast-food restaurant, in which case the gulls are probably going to show up soon.

Timing Your Visit

Some places are great for bird watching at all times of the year. Those are the exceptions. A lot of birds move around with the seasons, so the birding spot that's great in the summer may be dudsville in the winter, or vice versa. If you don't want to find yourself sitting in the swamp, waiting for birds that won't show up until three months later, you need some advance information.

Check the local checklist

A very useful source of such information is a local checklist that tells you the seasonal occurrence of each species. Some such checklists use simple codes: "W-c, S-r" may mean "common in winter, rare in summer." Other checklists use bar graphs to show seasons of occurrence, and these can give you a really precise idea of when to expect each bird.

Looking at bar graphs, you may see, for example, that many of the sandpipers are represented by thick black bars across late July, August, and early September. This would be a sure sign that late summer is the time to go to that hotspot for shorebirds. The same bar graph may show you that most of the ducks do not pick up in numbers until October, so you can plan to hit that great pond for waterfowl later in the fall.

Use bird-finding guides

Bird-finding guides can be a real boon to birders. They may be simple pamphlets published by the local bird club, or they may be professional productions. Regardless of how they look, they can lead you to great birding spots.

Bird-finding guides often give specific notes about the best times to look for particular birds at any given place. These notes are a good reason to read the fine print — to read the whole text and not just the road directions.

The guides vary in format, but typically they include detailed road directions to a wide variety of birding spots, and they often have at least simple maps. To make the best use of a bird-finding guide, you should study it before your birding trip and then take it along to check directions as you go.

In your pre-trip studying, you need to decide which spots to visit. Authors of bird-finding guides usually are not shy about saying which spots they think are best. If your time is limited, you may want to hit only the high points. Check the calendar and try to figure out which spots will be best at that season. You may be after a particular bird; if so, check the guide's index to read up on it and see where that bird is likely to be.

Of course, even the best directions can leave you lost if a certain road is temporarily closed, or if a sign has been changed. You should always carry a road map and check the guide's directions against the map. Also remember that directions do go out of date, especially near cities or other developing areas. Even if a bird-finding guide is recently published, you should be mentally prepared for the possibility that local conditions might have changed.

Life After Hotspots

I love using bird-finding guides when I visit an unfamiliar area and want to see some of the local specialties. But I have learned that you can't put all your birding eggs in one basket when you take a trip. I did this on three different trips to Florida. On each trip, I took a different bird-finding guide in hopes of seeing a snail kite, a resident bird found in South Florida. The guides gave very specific directions to kite spots, but I never found kites when I got there. Was it bad luck? No, just a case of my being too focused on the guide. If I'd read up on the kites, I might have learned that they're regularly found around the north shore of Lake Okeechobee. Instead, I was following the dotted lines on maps to specific spots deep in the Everglades, where all I found were lots of mosquitoes. And, in my single-minded quest to reach "THE SNAIL KITE SPOT," I probably missed snail kites and other birds en route. My lesson? In the immortal words of the Beatles: *Think for yourself, cause [the bird-finding guide] won't be there for you.*

This kind of thing has happened over and over, all over the continent. It's tempting to go for the sure thing rather than explore on your own. Maybe the best approach is to do some of both.

Go to that famous birding spot — but then look around for the unknown places. Follow the crowd for a while — but then go off the beaten track. There's a special pleasure in watching birds at a hotspot that you've discovered for yourself.

My Faves

I have not visited all the hotspots of North America. In fact, there aren't many people who have, because it's tough to define what a hotspot really is. Is it a place with lots of birds, or a place with rare birds? Or is it just a place where the birds are easy to watch, and thus lots of bird watchers visit it regularly?

I think a hotspot is whatever and wherever you want it to be. Then again, I think there ought to be an international holiday devoted to bird watching. And we ought to have World Peace while we're at it.

In Chapter 28, I list my very arbitrary selections for the top 10 or 11 North American hotspots. Before you write me an angry letter because I did not include your favorite spots, stop to think how much better that time would be spent if you just went bird watching. See you out there with the birds!

The "Patagonia Picnic Table Effect"

Isn't it amazing how rare birds seem to show up right where the bird watchers are, instead of someplace else? Actually, there's a name for this phenomenon, and the name has a history.

Back in the 1960s in Arizona, an active birder stopped to look for birds at a roadside rest stop near the little town of Patagonia. In the trees above the picnic tables, he found a couple of rose-throated becards — a rare species — so he began making regular checks of the area. Soon he found more rare birds there — thick-billed kingbirds, and then the first nesting five-striped sparrows for the United States. At that news, other bird watchers started going there as well. They discovered more rare birds, notably the first black-capped gnatcatchers ever found north of the border. More birders started going there, and they turned up even more rare birds, including yellow grosbeak, yellow-green vireo, and others. So then, even more birders started going there. . . .

True, that roadside rest stop was located in a good bird habitat. But it continued to produce rare finds partly because all the bird watchers went there and looked for rare things. And every time another rarity was discovered, it made other birders want to go there, so the coverage stayed intense. You can see how this sort of circular cause-and-effect would continue.

Similar things have happened at other birding hotspots around North America, but the phenomenon — of rare birds attracting more birders, who then find more rare birds, which then attract more birders, *ad infinitum* — is now known as the "Patagonia Picnic Table Effect."

Chapter 19

Birding Tours: On Site with a Pro

Mention "bird tours" to your neighbors, and they might imagine a bus rolling down the highway with lots of birds inside, looking out at the scenery. In fact, bird tours are for bird *watchers*. They are trips designed for fairly small groups, traveling with one or two expert birders who know the area and its birdlife. Such guided tours can offer great opportunities to see new species in new surroundings under the guidance of a real pro.

In this chapter, I take you on a tour of bird tours.

The Good and the Bad

Even on their trip to Oz, Dorothy and her pals had both dazzling fun and crushing disappointment. Bird tours are no different, except you won't be attacked by flying monkeys and will encounter very few green witches. Green birds, on the other hand. . . .

Downside

Let me give you the bad news first (because there's less of it). On a tour, you don't have much control over what happens: You have to go along with a pre-arranged itinerary and go along with what the leader and the rest of the group want to do. Sometimes you can skip a morning, or skip a side trip, but going off to do something completely different is usually difficult and often impossible.

You also spend a LOT of time with the group; the days are long on a typical tour. If the group happens to include someone who sings *Ninety-nine Bottles of Beer on the Wall* every time he or she sees a new bird, the days can seem even longer.

Birders in general tend to be really nice and fun and easy to get along with. But if you have very limited tolerance for people, you could be doing cuckoo imitations by the end of a two-week tour.

Upside

So what's good about a tour? Lots of things. You don't waste any time going to unproductive places or getting lost. You save yourself weeks of research about where and when to go, where to stay, and how to travel. You don't have to do any of the driving, or worry about meals or other details.

Best of all, you almost always see a lot more birds than you would on your own. The leaders know just where to go, they know the habits and hangouts and calls of each bird, and they can identify those tough little mystery birds that might be nothing but question marks for you otherwise.

Vive la Difference!

Many different kinds of trips are being offered to bird watchers today. They range from casual nature trips that take in a few birds, all the way up to gonzo marathons where sleep and sanity are sacrificed in a mad dash to tick off as many species as possible.

Most professional bird tours are somewhere in between: You see a lot of birds, but you do so at a pace that allows you some time to actually look at them. However, the pace won't allow for much else. Days usually start very early, lunch is often a picnic in some birdy spot, time for trinket-shopping is limited or nonexistent, and lodging is usually in a place where there's no night life available (except maybe standing around in the dark and listening for owls).

Your non-birding companion

The nothing-but-birds aspect of birding tours can be of critical importance if you're thinking of taking along a spouse or sweetheart who is not interested in birds. This can be a Big Mistake. (As the wife of one avid birder said after a particularly intense trip, "I don't know how he's going to pay for the tour and the alimony too.") If your Significant Other has not caught the birding bug, you should either consider a solo vacation, or look for a tour that will cater to wider interests. Fortunately, there are a number of possibilities of the latter type. Some companies and organizations offer trips that combine bird watching with other pursuits: music festivals, history, holidays in exotic spots, and so on. There are also nature tours on small ships, to places like the Galapagos or the Amazon, that might appeal to people with more general interests.

If you peruse the back pages of any bird magazine, you are likely to see ads for a score of tour companies and hundreds of tours. Start writing away for information, and a blizzard of material may land in your mailbox. The choices can seem overwhelming.

North America has a few large, well-established bird tour companies, each running dozens of trips every year. There are also many smaller companies that run fewer trips. By looking at ads in several magazines, you can usually tell which are the big companies by the amount of advertising they run. You can find a partial list of tour companies in the Appendix.

Big or small company?

Both large companies and small "independents" can offer you a good value for your money.

With a big, long-established tour company, you may pay a little more, but you can be pretty sure of what you're getting: their trips are consistent in quality.

Smaller, newer companies may be able to charge less for a comparable tour, but you have to research these cheaper trips more carefully. Some of these start-up tour companies run outstanding trips so that you're really getting a bargain. Others don't know what they're doing yet, so even a very cheap trip might not be worth what you're paying for it.

Ask around before choosing

One of the best ways to find out about a tour outfit is to talk to someone who has traveled with them. Ask around among members of your local bird club. Chances are good that you know someone who has taken guided tours. Personal recommendations are worth more than any amount of advertising.

Choosing a particular trip is a different kind of challenge. After reading a tour company catalog, you may want to go on all of them! But if you've never gone on a tour before, you should start with a relatively short excursion in North America to see how you like the experience, rather than leap into a three-week marathon trip to some exotic country. You should also consider the pace and intensity of the tour. Some trips are relaxed; others are more gung-ho. The descriptions provided by the tour company should make that clear.

Take me to your leader

Experienced tour-takers often say that the leader is THE most important factor in a successful bird tour. (Tour leaders, in rare moments when they aren't being modest, will say the same thing.)

Leaders have to be more than just expert birders: They also must be very good at handling logistics, resourceful in dealing with emergencies, and flexible in interacting with a wide variety of people. In fact, "people skills" are just as important as birding skills for a leader. Individuals who succeed as bird tour leaders are usually friendly, fun, outgoing types who enjoy sharing birds with others.

Ordinarily, a company will proudly advertise its tour leaders. If a company plans and advertises a tour without having chosen the leader first, this may be a warning sign. Although not all tour companies list the leader for a given tour in their advertisements, when you inquire and get additional

---

Big bucks for birds

You can spend a lot or a little money when taking a bird tour. The most basic one-day or weekend trips can be as little as $100. A weeks-long safari to Africa may set you back $5,000, not including airfare, tips, and cocktails. I know some birders who like to figure out how much each new species will cost them before they take a big trip. They might consider $200 per species to be a worthwhile endeavor. Before you decide to take a tour, rough out a budget with the planned expenses; then add a few hundred dollars on top for unplanned expenses and emergencies.

information about the tour from the company, the leader's name should be included. Ask the company about the leader. Is he or she experienced in leading tours, and are they familiar with this tour and area?

Finding yourself in the middle of nowhere with an inexperienced leader can be worse than being lost in the same place all by yourself. You don't want to quit the tour, because you've paid good money to take it.

As with choosing a tour company, one of the best ways to find out about a particular leader is to talk to someone who has taken a tour with him or her.

Questions to Ask the Tour Company

Usually a bird-tour company maintains an office staffed with people who know the tour business. If you can't find out what you need to know by reading the published information, you have a right to call the office and ask questions.

With an established tour company, these questions usually are answered in the brochures, so be sure to read the material before calling to ask about these points:

✔ **Has the company run this tour before?**

Often it's wise to avoid a company's very first trip to a new region. The tour will probably be held anyway — eager bird-listers will pile on to go check off the specialty birds of that area before their friends get them — and you can go next year, after the bugs are ironed out of the itinerary.

✔ **Is the leader familiar with the area?**

The company may have a long history of trips to West Wombat, but that's slim comfort if THIS year's leader has never been there before.

✔ **What's the maximum group size?**

Group size can make a big difference in the quality of the experience. If you have 50 bird watchers following one leader, birder number 47 is not going to see anything but dust. But effective group size can vary with the terrain. In very open surroundings, as on a trip to the Antarctic, one leader might be enough for 20 participants. On narrow forest trails, a group of more than eight or nine with one leader is probably too large.

✔ **What is included in the tour cost?**

What the tour cost covers can vary widely. Some North American trips can look surprisingly cheap until you find out that meals are not included in the price. On foreign tours, airfare from the United States sometimes is included, but usually is not. As a general rule, tour prices don't include laundry costs, alcoholic beverages, personal phone calls, or a private secretary to write down all the birds for you.

A friend of mine once went to lead a trip that was to spend a week visiting a whole series of small, uninhabited islands. The tour brochure had given glowing descriptions of putting ashore on these isolated islands where few other visitors were privileged to tread. At the beginning of the trip, my friend met the group at the airport, and they all were transferred by bus down to the coastal town where the docks were located. As the crew started to carry luggage onto the small ship that the group would be inhabiting for the next week, one of the participants came up to my friend, wild-eyed, and said, "You mean we're going on a BOAT??!! I can't travel by boat!"

Be sure you read the tour information ahead of time.

Be Prepared

I can't say this too often: Before you sign up for any tour, read the published information about it with great care. Most tours are not physically challenging, but there are exceptions. It is supremely disappointing to go on a strenuous trip and discover that you're not up to it. Ask yourself if you're up to the physical challenges of a birding trip to the high altitudes of the Peruvian Andes.

Note: You don't have to ask these questions to yourself out loud, or even look in the mirror when you ask them, although this technique often helps me.

You may also ask yourself whether you're *mentally* prepared for a particular tour. On a big trip to East Africa or tropical South America, you may feel bombarded with more than 500 species of birds, most of which are unfamiliar to you. This could be either a dream or a nightmare, depending on your outlook.

Suppose you really want to go on a tour, but there's a slight possibility that you may have to cancel for some reason. Should you sign up or not? Most tour companies won't give you a refund, or at least not a full one, if you bail out at the last minute. You can, however, purchase trip cancellation insurance, which will pay back most of your tour cost if you do have to cancel. About the only insurance people CAN'T offer is to provide the birds that you miss by not going on the tour.

Even a tamer trip may expose you to a lot of birding challenges. Before you head out to join the group, make a few preparations. Practice finding birds in your binoculars. Take a look at a field guide to the birds of the area you'll be visiting, so that at least you'll be familiar with the names of the birds when the leader calls them off.

Physical challenges

Many tour companies specify that tour participants be able to hike, climb hills, and crawl in and out of tour vehicles many times per day. If you're someone who has difficulty walking or hiking moderate distances, or if you have trouble breathing at high altitudes, or if you think you may not be up to the physical challenges of a given tour, ask the tour company in advance for their advice. Most tour companies ask participants to complete health questionnaires prior to registration so that health emergencies and accidents can be avoided as much as possible. Rather than assume that you'll be okay on a long, strenuous birding tour, do yourself, your fellow tour participants, and the tour company a favor, and ask for a detailed description about how physically challenging a given tour will be. The tour company may be able to offer suggestions for alternative tours and birding destinations better suited to your abilities.

Plan Ahead, Reserve Early

Wouldn't it be great if you could call up out of the blue and sign up for a major trip that starts in three days? And while we're at it, wouldn't it be great if someone rang your doorbell and gave you a check for $10 million? Meanwhile, back here in the real world, neither of those possibilities is very likely. If you want to go on a bird tour, your mantra should be: plan ahead.

Birding tours have limits on group sizes, and popular tours may fill up months ahead of time. Even if the trip has not filled to capacity, things like hotel reservations must be established well in advance; last-minute registrants may have the tour office scrambling to find rooms for them.

On the other hand, advertised tours don't always run. They are canceled if no one signs up, of course. But they may have to be called off a couple of months ahead of time, so that the companies can cancel hotel and vehicle reservations without penalties. Operators have sometimes gotten numerous calls to ask about a tour, just AFTER they have officially canceled that trip for lack of participants.

The moral of the story: Register for a tour well ahead of time!

What if you suddenly are given vacation time, you have money to spend, and you run across a notice of some great tour that's just about to depart? Go ahead and call — it doesn't hurt to ask. Maybe they will have room for some reason, perhaps because some participant has canceled at the last minute.

And for that matter, maybe somebody WILL ring your doorbell with a $10-million check. If that happens, you can hire me to come along on the tour and carry your telescope for you.

Rules of the Road

Bird tours tend to be pretty informal. Dress is casual throughout — indeed, a cocktail dress or black-tie-and-tails can be a real handicap on a muddy forest trail — and people usually don't dress up for dinner. Some leaders ask that participants not wear brightly colored clothing in the field (with the idea that such clothing might alarm the birds), but they won't ask you to go naked if bright colors are all you've brought. And they probably won't roll you in mud.

The rules for taking part in a tour can be summarized in just two points: common sense and courtesy. Practice these, and you'll never go far wrong. It's common sense to keep conversation down while birding, because the leaders may find many birds by sound and because noise may scare birds away. It's a matter of courtesy to be considerate of your fellow participants — not blocking their view at critical moments, for example, and not hogging the group's telescope.

You'll soon find that it comes naturally to be courteous to the other birders: On most tours, within a day or two, you'll have the strong feeling that you're traveling with a group of your best friends.

You Can't Take It with You: Pack Light

Packing for a birding tour is not that different from packing for a field trip. For more on what gear to take with you, absorb the fascinating information provided in Chapter 16.

Whereas on a field trip you can chuck a bunch of stuff in the car, on a bird tour you might be hauling (or watching some poor tour leader haul) your gear through airports, hotel lobbies, and up mountainsides. You want to have enough of the vital things (clean socks, underwear, toothpaste, proper outerwear); you definitely don't want to take anything unnecessary. For example: If you can't sleep without your grandfather clock ticking next to your bed, perhaps you can find a replacement noisemaker. Don't take the clock on a tour. It won't have a good time anyway.

Keep the tip

To tip or not to tip? That IS a question, and the answers vary from one situation to another.

During the tour, if meals and lodging are included in the trip price, the leaders generally take care of tips in restaurants and hotels.

But should YOU tip the leader at the end of the trip? It depends. In some areas of the world, where local driver-guides cater to ecotourists — such as in East Africa or Costa Rica — they expect to be tipped, and your goodbyes at the end of the trip can feel very awkward if you don't catch on. In these cases, it helps if you've checked with the local outfitters or tour operators ahead of time to ask what would be an appropriate amount.

On the other hand, on bird tours run entirely by leaders based in the United States, the leaders generally don't expect tips and may be surprised to receive them. Again, if you're unsure, check with the tour company office ahead of time or talk to other participants during the trip — seasoned travelers may be available who have gone with this company before.

As a consumer, though, you should remember that gratuities are just that, and they are ALWAYS optional. If your leader or guide has been a total jerk (it's rare, but it can happen), there's no reason to give him or her anything. And if some leader has really gone out of his or her way for you — has gone way beyond the bird-call of duty — he or she probably won't turn down a tip or a small gift.

On a trip to Costa Rica one May, I was faced with the age-old question: rain boots or hiking boots? I could not take both. I was told by everyone _but_ the tour company that I should plan to get soaked by rain at least twice a day. They said, "It's the rainy season there!" The tour company guy told me "We call it the _green season_. It doesn't rain that much." I took rain boots. It rained once in about 10 days. We hiked all over the place, me wearing knee-high green waders. Yes, they were hot on my feet. Yes, I got blisters. Yes, Costa Rica was green at that season — almost as green as I was, gazing with envy at my fellow tour-takers who had brought sturdy light, cool, hiking boots.

Your best bet is to follow the guidance offered by the tour company regarding what to take on a given bird tour. Ask specifically about weather extremes, footwear needed, and luggage allowances. Also ask about any local customs or social taboos. In some countries you can get looks of horror and disdain (or worse) from the local populace simply for wearing short pants.

Final Stop

Taking a bird-watching tour can do lots of things for you: Show you new and wonderful birds, allow you to make new friends, let you test your bird ID skills in a new place, and even lighten your bank account. Some birders are lifelong tour takers. They prefer to visit far-flung hot spots with a guide who helps them maximize their experience. Others like to take the occasional tour to spice up their bird-watching life. No matter which side of the scale you think you'll end up on, plan to take a birding tour at some point. If nothing else, you'll see lots of new birds and lots of other bird watchers.

Chapter 20

Festivals and Other Events

. . . .

In This Chapter

▶ Party time!

▶ Finding festivals

▶ Big Days, Big Sits, and the like

▶ Going to school

▶ Spreading the word

. . . .

*I*t has been said that bird watching is the number one spectator sport in North America, which means it's bigger than professional sports such as basketball, baseball, football, and hockey, as well as other spectator events such as auto racing and golf.

How does this affect you, the bird watcher? It means that as the interest in birding has grown, so has the number of organized activities for bird watchers. In this chapter you'll find out about some of the events that are specially designed for bird watchers. This includes everything from birding competitions to festivals to seminars and workshops. In fact there are so many such events that I can only cover a few of the most prominent ones here. As you become more involved as a bird watcher, you'll find out about other events both near to home and far afield.

Let's Party!

It can be fun sitting alone in your backyard or on your deck, watching the birds that pass by. But if you're like me, gregarious by nature, you may find yourself longing for somebody else with whom to share your bird watching experiences. Sure, maybe that somebody else is your spouse or best friend. And then there's your local bird club. But maybe you still want more. What to do?

We bird watchers have been referred to as a "clan" many times by fellow birders, and by those outside the loop. "Flock," "family," and lots of less flattering terms have also been used. Even though I wince every time somebody tells me that I am "for the birds," like birds, bird watchers do like to flock together from time to time.

To satisfy this flocking urge, gatherings of bird watchers happen, sometimes spontaneously, all over North America. Some of them start as informal parties — groups of friends gathering to have a good time and look at birds. Others are started by communities wishing, quite literally, to attract more tourists and their tourist dollars.

No matter what the initial impetus, the good news is that you have lots to choose from among the many festivals, Big Days, and other events for bird watchers.

The first organized gathering of bird watchers I attended was at a hawk watching and banding site. It wasn't even an open-to-the-public event. These were hardcore bird bums running this deal, and I was just a lowly high school kid interested in birds. I was very nervous. I didn't know the lingo or any of the other people there. And I certainly wasn't up to their speed as a birder. But I found that, in spite of a few cold shoulders, most of the people there were willing to explain things to an interested beginner (me). In fact, they were proud to get to show off their hawk know-how. I ended up having a great time.

So don't be shy! Don't assume that a hotshot won't want to share his or her knowledge with you. Likely the exact opposite is true.

Birding Festivals

Birding festivals come in all shapes and sizes. Some are held near locales where birds naturally have been gathering for eons. Many of the best festivals are organized around a natural phenomenon such as the gathering of sandhill cranes on their wintering grounds, or the return of the Kirtland's warbler to its breeding grounds in Michigan. Other festivals are just excuses to get together with a bunch of bird watchers to talk shop and have fun. A few are even bird festivals in name only. Such events aren't really for birders at all, but rather for general tourists.

New birding festivals are starting up all the time, and as can be expected, a few fold. But most keep steaming on, getting better with each year. The bird watchers in North America have an enormous economic impact. This is why many communities are working so diligently to come up with some "hook" to draw visiting bird watchers. A study done in 1992 showed that bird watchers added more than $155 million to the economy of Texas in 1991. That's big bucks!

Finding festivals

When my family began publishing *Bird Watcher's Digest* in 1978, there weren't any well-known festivals for bird watchers. In fact, the only large gatherings of the bird-seeking crowd were when there was an abundance of birds such as during fall migration at Hawk Mountain, Pennsylvania, or in the spring at High Island, Texas, or in the winter at one of the Florida refuges. Once or twice a year there would be an extremely rare bird found somewhere on the continent and that would attract the hardcore contingent. But beyond the local bird club, bird watchers had few organized activities which they could attend.

Today, there is a birding festival held every month of the year somewhere in North America. Nearly every state and province has its own "Festival of the Something or Other." There are festivals for cranes, ducks, geese, shorebirds, warblers, vultures, swans, eagles, hawks, hummingbirds, and swallows. You name it, and there's probably a festival for it, or there will be soon.

The best method for finding festivals is to read through a few bird magazines. I can think of at least one bird magazine I'd recommend especially. Most festival organizers — sooner or later — advertise their event in a publication for bird watchers. Look particularly in the classified ads section of the magazine.

An excellent source for information is a pamphlet published annually by the Fish and Wildlife Foundation, called *A Guide to Birding Festivals*. This publication lists many of the festivals held for birders each year. To obtain a copy of the pamphlet, contact: NF&WF, 1120 Connecticut Avenue NW, Suite 900, Washington, DC 20036.

Attending festivals

Here's some good advice to heed when attending a festival: **Book early.**

Although not all festivals limit the number of attendees, some do. Others may limit the number of attendees in particular seminars, or there may be limited seating in an auditorium where a well-known speaker is appearing. For your own sake, call the festival organizers and get the schedule of events in advance to see what's happening. There may be a can't-miss presentation, seminar, or speaker that you'll want to take in. Alternatively, there may be entire days that have little interest to you. That's the time to spend watching birds away from the hubbub of the festival.

In addition to ensuring your place at the festival events, you may also want to make your travel and lodging arrangements in advance. Many long-running festivals have a high number of repeat attendees. These folks book their flights, rooms, and rental cars as much as a year in advance. The local chamber of commerce has a listing of accommodations and eateries. Ask about festival discounts on airfare and rental cars. Because birding festivals tend to be where the birds are (away from major airports and metropolitan areas), your airline and rental car choices may be limited. Book early! Did I say that already?

While you're preparing to attend a festival in a distant state or province, find out about the weather at festival time. I learned this the hard way.

Several years ago, I was to be the featured speaker at a bird festival in a western state. I was so excited about visiting the region in April, thinking about all the life birds I'd see, that I completely forgot to ask about the weather. Oh, somebody from the festival told me in passing that April was when things started warming up, but that was all the info I had. So I packed for semi-warm spring weather and headed out west. As I got off the plane, my breath was taken away by a blast of freezing air. Before I chipped the ice off my rental car, I was nearly a human Eskimo Pie. As I drove out of the parking lot, the snow started flying thicker than the iceworms on a polar bear. I asked a policeman where I could find a camping outfitter. He said, "Not from around here, are you?" A few hours and $245 later, I was on my way to the festival, looking like some scary vision from the L.L. Bean catalog. What the festival rep meant by "warming up" was that the water wasn't still frozen solid at festival time, and you could actually stay outside for minutes at a time.

Just a few festivals

More than 50 active bird festivals take place in North America. Here are descriptions of just a few of them.

Avocet Festival, near San Francisco, California   **late fall**
San Francisco Bay National Wildlife Refuge is the setting for this autumn festival. The refuge is a wintering area for the American avocet. P.O. Box 524, Newark, California 94560-0524; 510-792-0222.

Buzzard Sunday in Hinckley, Ohio   **March**
This is not really a festival for bird watchers as much as it is a fun event — something like Ground Hog Day in Punxsutawney, Pennsylvania. In this case, this is the day that the vultures return to Hinckley in the spring. Legend has it that the vultures began appearing on the day that a local witch was hanged. Hinckley Chamber of Commerce, P.O. Box 354, Hinckley, Ohio 44233; 216-278-2066.

Copper River Delta Shorebird Festival, Cordova, Alaska   May
Millions of shorebirds, heading for their Arctic breeding grounds, converge on this important river delta area each spring. Cordova, reachable by plane or ferry, has a small, frontier-town charm. Cordova Chamber of Commerce, P.O. Box 99, Cordova, Alaska 99574; 907-424-7260.

Hummer/Bird Celebration, Rockport, Texas   September
The Texas Coast is home to an ever-increasing number of wintering hummingbirds. Aside from hummers, this part of the state hosts lots of other bird species, and is at the crossroads of two migratory flyways. Rockport-Fulton Chamber of Commerce, 404 Broadway, Rockport, Texas 78382; 800-242-0071.

Festival of the Cranes, Socorro, New Mexico   November
Thousands of sandhill cranes, geese, and ducks galore make this festival a feast for the eyes. Socorro Chamber of Commerce, 103 Frincisco De Avondo, Socorro, New Mexico 87801; 505-835-0424.

John Scharff Migratory Bird Festival, Burns, Oregon   April
Spring in southeastern Oregon means dancing sandhill cranes, displaying shorebirds, and lots of migrant waterfowl. Harney County Chamber of Commerce, 18 West D Street, Burns, Oregon 97720; 541-573-2636.

Kirtland's Warbler Festival, Mio, Michigan   June
There is a very limited part of the planet that hosts breeding Kirtland's warblers. This festival is in the heart of Kirtland's country. Chamber of Commerce for Oscoda County, P.O. Box 426, Mio, Michigan 48647; 800-826-3331.

The Loon Festival, Moultonborough, New Hampshire   August
Common loons are the focus of this one-day festival. Loon Preservation Committee, P.O. Box 604, Lee's Mills Road, Moultonborough, New Hampshire 03254; 603-476-5666.

Eastern Shore Birding Festival, Kiptopeke, Virginia   October
Fall migration is reaching its peak when this festival opens its doors. Peregrine falcons, merlins, and other birds of prey are a specialty along the Eastern Shore at this time of year. Eastern Shore of Virginia Chamber of Commerce, P.O. Drawer R, Melfa, Virginia 23410; 804-787-2460.

Swan Days, Swan Quarter, North Carolina   December
Tundra swans, which spend the winter in this region, are the featured species at this festival. Mattamuskeet NWR, Route 1, Box N-2, Swan Quarter, North Carolina 27885; 919-926-4021.

Eufaula's Fins, Fur, Feathers and Flowers,   **March**
Eufaula, Alabama
Boat tours are offered on Lake Eufaula to see bald eagles, and many water-fowl. Eufaula NWR, 509 Old Highway 165, Eufaula, Alabama 36027; 334-687-4065.

Grays Harbor Shorebird Festival, Montesano, Washington   **April**
Most of the shorebird species that live on the Pacific Coast can be found along the shores of Grays Harbor at this time of year. Grays Harbor Audubon Society, P.O. Box 444, Montesano, Washington 98563; 800-321-1924.

Midwest Birding Symposium, Midwestern United States   **September**
This gathering of midwestern bird watchers takes place every other year, and the sites where it is held also vary. The 1997 and 1999 events will be held in Ohio, during the peak week of fall songbird migration. MBS Information, P.O. Box 110, Marietta, Ohio 45750; 888-844-6330.

Snow Goose Festival, Tofield, Alberta, Canada   **April**
A three-day festival dedicated to the appreciation of these elegant white waterfowl. Town of Tofield, Box 30, Tofield, Alberta TOB 4JO, Canada; 403-662-3269.

Wings Over the Platte, Grand Island, Nebraska   **March**
The Platte River is covered in thousands and thousands of migrating sand-hill cranes each March. Geese, ducks, bald eagles, and even a few whooping cranes are also present. This large festival helps participants experience the magic of this migration spectacle. Grand Island Visitors Bureau, 309 West Second Street, P.O. Box 1486, Grand Island, Nebraska 68802; 800-658-3178.

Thinking BIG!

For the bird watcher who likes to compete, whether with himself/herself or against others, there is another brand of event: the competitive bird count, sometimes called a Big Day.

Bird watchers love to think big, as in Big Day, Big Sit, and Big Year. "What's a Big Day?" I hear you mutter. It's a day during which you try to see or hear as many bird species as possible. Big Days are usually conducted within a set geographical area, such as a state or county, and must be accomplished within a single 24-hour period, often midnight to midnight.

On a Big Day bird count, you're supposed to count the number of species, not the number of individual birds you see. I was at a count once where a guy came to the tally gathering and said he'd seen more than 2,000 birds. He thought he'd surely be the winner. Then someone explained that the competition was to see how many *species* he could see. Oops!

Big Days: What's the big deal?

There are four reasons for doing a Big Day:

- ✔ To get a big list of birds. This allows you to brag to your friends.
- ✔ To record the migratory birds present in your area for scientific purposes.
- ✔ To raise money for bird conservation, your local bird club, or another worthwhile cause.
- ✔ To have fun.

I've done Big Days every spring for almost 20 years. Initially I did them strictly for fun. It was a chance to see lots of migrants in their colorful breeding plumage — lots of these species were ones I could see only during spring migration as they passed through Ohio on their way to breeding areas to the north. Later, I began to think I was a studly birder, and a hefty Big Day count was proof of this. That charade got old after a few years. I'd rather take my time and enjoy the birds. Today I still do Big Days for the fun, but I also send my count results in to the North American Migration Count, which compiles results of spring migration. Although the NAMC is only a few years old, it has an impressive amount of data collected on timing and patterns of migration and how things like weather and temperature affect it.

For more on the NAMC and other organized bird counts and census projects, see Chapter 21.

Organizing your own Big Day

You can create your own Big Day count. You don't need to pay an entry fee or have your veracity checked by a board of governors. Pick a date on which you know lots of bird species will be present in your area and go for it! You don't even need to stay up for 24 hours. In fact, the tendency in recent years has been for groups to conduct "sane" Big Days. These involve maximizing the number of hours spent in the field and reducing the number of hours spent slumped behind the wheel of your car straining to hear a bird — any bird — and wishing you were home in bed.

A sane Big Day typically starts at or just before dusk with the participants searching for night birds such as owls, rails, and nightjars. After a few hours, everyone heads for home and bed. The count resumes before dawn the next morning and carries on until nightfall. At dusk, the participants meet someplace for a *tally-rally* and dinner.

Bird watching competitions

It was inevitable that, with the (usually) friendly competition that exists among birders, an organized event for teams of birders be created. The most successful of these competitions is the annual World Series of Birding that is run by the New Jersey Audubon Society and its Cape May Bird Observatory. Teams entered in this 24-hour birdathon are racing the clock, the elements, and each other to try to see or hear the maximum number of bird species within the state of New Jersey between midnight and the following midnight on a weekend in early May. This date coincides with the projected peak in the spring bird migration, which can be an absolutely awesome phenomenon in New Jersey and elsewhere along the East Coast. Northbound migrants flying along the Atlantic Coast are funneled across Delaware Bay to the southern tip of New Jersey. In recent years, the winning teams' totals have surpassed the 200 species mark, and the event has attracted corporate sponsorship. Best of all, many teams raise money for conservation through per-bird pledges. The success of the World Series has prompted spring birdathons in other parts of North America. For more information about the World Series, contact: CMBO, 600 Route 47 North, Cape May Court House, New Jersey, 08210.

A more recent player on the scene of competitions is The Great Texas Birding Classic, a three-day set of birding events held in three separate parts of the Texas Gulf Coast. Because Texas boasts the most species recorded for any state or province in North America, participants in this competition are certain to see lots and lots of birds. Most of the sites covered by the participating teams are found along the Great Texas Coastal Birding Trail, a 500-mile driving route planned and marked specifically for bird watchers. For more information, contact: Texas Parks & Wildlife Dept., 4200 Smith School Road, Austin, Texas 78744.

The Big Sit

"For every action, there is an equal — but opposite — reaction." Some famous brainiac like Newton or Einstein said that, and he surely was correct. For those who dislike the race-around-ticking-off-birds-on-your-checklist mentality of the Big Day/birdathon set, there is the Big Sit. Not just a birding event for the La-Z-Boy crowd, a Big Sit can be every bit as much fun as a Big Day. What's truly amazing, however, is how many birds you can tally simply by staying put and watching and listening — in some areas Big Sitters can tally more than 100 species without ever leaving the count circle.

The concept for a Big Sit is to do just that: sit. You're also trying to see or hear as many birds as possible while sitting. Some Big Sitters have elevated this event to a high art, bringing barbecue grills, entire carloads of provisions, portable heaters, electric generators, and other camping gear. A group of Big Sitters from Connecticut has even organized a national Big Sit Count, held on a mid-October weekend day. The popularity of this event is growing as quickly as the waistlines of overindulgent Big Sitters. The totals of species seen or heard for some of the North American Big Sit counts are quite comparable to many Big Day efforts.

The rules for a Big Sit are simple. Choose a good site, one with a variety of habitats. Mark off a circle with a 15-foot diameter. Set up your Big Sit site with all you need and you're ready to go. You may count the birds you see and hear from the circle, but you may not leave the circle to find new birds. You are permitted to leave the circle to confirm the identification of a bird.

For more information on the national Big Sit, contact John Himmelman, 67 Schnoor Road, Killingworth, Connecticut 06419. Or via e-mail: `jhimmel@connix.com`

Going to School

Some events for bird watchers are more educational in nature. A plethora of birding schools, weekend seminars, and skill-building workshops are available for bird watchers. Some are offered as part of annual festivals, while others are from accredited colleges and universities or offered by bird clubs, bird observatories, state and federal refuges, parks, and nature centers.

Among the most popular topics for bird watchers are field identification courses or seminars, particularly those dealing with the sometimes difficult groups of birds, such as fall warblers, hawks, sparrows, and shorebirds, especially peeps (small sandpipers). Also popular are courses in beginning bird watching, bird song identification, and anything having to do with birds in the backyard (feeding, gardening for, housing for, and so on).

Inquire with festival organizers about educational seminars. Ask your local college or university about a bird watching course. Call your Department of Natural Resources and ask if they offer bird courses or classes. Even mail-order courses in ornithology are available. Read through the ads in a bird watching magazine (see the Appendix for a listing of magazines), and you'll be sure to find something that can help you to become a better birder.

Schools for bird watchers

The organizations listed below are but a few of the many places you can find classes, seminars, and workshops to help you improve your bird watching skills.

Cornell Laboratory of Ornithology
159 Sapsucker Woods Road, Ithaca, NY 14850; 607-254-2400

Cape May Bird Observatory
600 Route 46 North, Cape May Court House, NJ 08210; 609-884-2736

Institute of Field Ornithology
University of Maine at Machias, 9 O'Brien Avenue, Machias, ME 04654; 207-255-1200

Manomet Observatory
Box 1770, Manomet, MA, 02345; 508-224-6521

Pocono Environmental Education Center
PEEC, RR2, Box 1010, Dingman's Ferry, PA 18328; 717-828-2319

Point Reyes Bird Observatory
4990 Shoreline Highway, Stinson Beach, CA 94970; 415-868-1221

Roger Tory Peterson Institute of Natural History
RTPI, Dept. BW, 311 Curtis Street, Jamestown, NY 14701

Spreading the Word

When attending a festival you may have the opportunity to do your part to promote an awareness of the economic impact of bird watching. Rather than leave your binocs and field guide in your car, take them into a restaurant or shop with you. If you're asked about them, explain that you are visiting the area to watch birds. Here's how such a conversation might go:

You: "Hi, I believe I'd like the eggs Benedict and a cup of coffee, please."

Waitress: "Are you taking pictures with those?" (points to your binoculars)

You: "No, these are binoculars. They're for looking at birds. I'm here in town attending the Starling Festival."

Waitress: "Are you a bird watcher?"

You: "Yes, I am. And you have a lot of wonderful birds in this area!"

Waitress: "I saw a blue crane once" (as she sets a plate of scrambled eggs and a cup of tea in front of you).

Even so, it's important that bird watchers let our economic presence be felt. Some bird clubs even provide members with small business cards that say "Your business has been patronized by a bird watcher. Preserve habitat for the birds. Bird watching is big business!"

Chapter 21

Birding that Makes a Difference

. . . .

In This Chapter

▶ Helping track the birds

▶ Counting more than crows

▶ Acting locally

▶ Using Bird Hotlines

▶ Joining Bird Clubs

▶ Teaching kids

. . . .

*E*veryone has his/her own reasons for watching birds. Perhaps you're captivated by the beauty of birds. Or maybe you're fascinated by the variety of birds and the changing of the guard from season to season. Perhaps you love the rush of chasing a rarity, or the numbers on your life list. Maybe bird watching for you is an excuse to get outdoors, or an opportunity for social interaction with other bird watchers. There are nearly as many reasons as there are people who participate.

Many bird watchers find satisfaction by participating in data-collecting projects. *Ornithology* (the science of bird study) has been called the last great amateur science. In recent decades, more research has required experts to study the technical aspects of DNA (the genetic fabric that makes each living thing unique), but unlike other sciences, ornithology has been built upon the incredible mass of data collected by amateurs — bird watchers. The opportunity to contribute, even in a small way, appeals to a lot of people, and many opportunities exist for all of us bird watchers to add to the science of the study of birds.

In this chapter, I provide information on many of the most popular bird watching projects and ways of finding out about others. I also provide information about bird clubs and how to find one that's right for you.

Doing Field Work that Matters

Bird watchers who participate in projects think of them as a way of giving something back for the enjoyment birds afford them. Bird watching is a source of great pleasure, and bird watchers are pleased that they can contribute to the study of birds. They recognize that their individual contributions are not necessarily significant, but as part of a larger effort, bird watchers help scientists understand birds and may help save some species.

Bird watching also makes people more aware of the natural world, and bird watchers are among the first citizens to notice when a habitat is destroyed, when bird populations decline, and when the landscape changes. In a small but significant way, the data that bird watchers collect helps scientists and public officials make more intelligent decisions about land use and preservation.

Who, me?

You can make a difference to birds. Absolutely. You don't need to be an expert or a scientist. Everyone can play a part.

As I mention earlier in this chapter, almost everything we know about the real lives of birds — as opposed to, say, the chemical composition of their eggs — comes from information gathered by amateurs. It is the amassed data of amateurs that tells us which bird species are declining and which are increasing. And the great bulk of what we know about the migration of birds has come from the amassed data of amateurs.

You don't need to be a hot shot or hair-trigger quick with field identifications. To a scientist, the family of woodpeckers at your feeder may be more interesting than the rarity an expert finds. If you're interested, you can participate in gathering and sharing this information on any level.

How to find out what's going on

Projects for interested bird watchers are everywhere. The trick is connecting with them. The place to start is with your local bird club. The local club is nearly always the organizer of field projects in a given area. As soon as you make it clear to others in your bird club that you're interested, you'll be contacted to help, because, as in so many things, there are always more projects than there are volunteers.

Finding your local bird club is often harder than finding a project on which to work. Sometimes clubs are listed in the local phone book under "Birds" but most are not. If your newspaper has a nature column in it, contact the writer for information about a local group. If you don't have a local club, I tell you later how to start your own.

Both the National Audubon Society and *Bird Watcher's Digest* can provide you with information about how to get in touch with the bird club closest to you. In addition, the American Birding Association publishes an annual list of volunteer opportunities, plus a list of members and bird clubs from all over North America. For more on locating a bird club, see "Finding or Founding a Bird Club?" later in this chapter.

No matter what your special area of interest — bird banding, bird feeding, hawks, puffins, purple martins, or whatever — a project is going on that you can be part of. All it takes is a bit of enthusiasm for birds, and I think you've got that covered.

In this chapter, I outline a few of the major ongoing projects, ones that attract thousands of birders to participate, as well as some other projects you can get involved with.

The Christmas Bird Count

The Christmas Bird Count is the granddaddy of all field projects. About 50,000 bird watchers participate every year, and the Christmas Bird Count (CBC) has been going on for almost a century. Most of what we know about the winter distribution of birds, and about winter bird populations, comes from the CBC. The nice thing is that *everyone* can participate — there's even a category for feeder watchers (folks who just count the birds seen at their feeders). This category is wonderful if you live in the Yukon and don't like being out in the howling wind and snow, or if you live in Hoboken and still hate howling wind and snow.

The Christmas Bird Count is exactly what it sounds like — a count, or census, of birds held around Christmas time. The CBC, which is sponsored by the National Audubon Society, is held all across North America (and even in some parts of Central and South America) in designated circles 15 miles in diameter. The purpose is to try to find and count as many individual birds as possible in each given circle in a given time frame. About 1,200 counts are held continent wide, so surely you have one near where you live.

Each CBC is organized and run by a local bird club or state bird group. Each group decides the boundaries of the count circle, and a count compiler works to make certain that everyone has a territory to count within that count circle.

Each count lasts 24 hours, from midnight to midnight, but almost nobody is crazy enough to spend the whole 24 hours in the field. Very few birds can be found in the dark, especially in winter in the colder parts of North America! Most people start at dawn, when birds are most active, and continue counting until late afternoon or evening. Counts are held during the annual count period, which runs from late December to early January.

A nice part of most CBCs is the *tally-rally*. At the end of the count day, the counters gather, usually at a volunteer's house or local greasy-spoon diner, for a couple of hours of sharing the experiences of the day, warming up with hot soup, and tallying the results. The tally-rally is one of the most anticipated social events of the bird-watching year.

At the tally-rally, the count compilers tally the day's sightings and send the results to the National Audubon Society, along with the CBC fee that each participant pays (about $5.00), in order to help defray the publication costs of the results. About half a year later, the results of all the year's CBCs are published in a huge volume of *Field Notes*. If you paid your fee, you get to see your name right there in black and white, under the results from your CBC. Of course, you can also see your name in black and white on your driver's license, along with a picture! But hey, you're contributing to science.

The data collected by Christmas Bird Counters is invaluable in assessing changing bird populations. Many counts have been going on for more than 25 years. With so many counts scattered across the country, it's possible to see which birds are declining and which are increasing. The spread of the house finch throughout the eastern parts of North America showed up first on Christmas Counts. Similarly, the decline in many waterfowl species was first noted by CBC participants. As a matter of fact, whole books have been written analyzing the results of the Christmas Bird Counts. Your little corner of the local count circle may not seem important, especially after you discover that they've put a shopping center in your favorite field, but in Christmas Bird Counts, every bird matters, whether it's there or not!

The most important thing to remember about participating in a CBC is that you don't have to be an expert. Others on your count can help you with bird identification. All you really need to be able to do is count. To find your local Christmas Bird Count, get in touch with your local bird club, or contact the National Audubon Society, 700 Broadway, New York, NY 10003; 212-979-3000.

How the Christmas Bird Count started

The Christmas Bird Count started in 1900 as an alternative to the *sidehunt*. The sidehunt was a fairly common custom until the early part of the 20th century. It involved going out for several hours on Christmas morning and shooting every bird and animal that one came across. Frank Chapman, one of the great early ornithologists, started the Christmas Count to counter the hunt. He encouraged a few friends around the country to go afield on Christmas morning and count, rather than kill. For the first two decades, the counts grew slowly, but in the second half of the 20th century, the counts have exploded in popularity.

The North American Migration Count

The North American Migration Count (NAMC) is to spring bird watching what the Christmas Counts are to bird watching in winter. Started by an interested birder in Maryland, the NAMC has become one of the largest volunteer bird-watching projects ever. The NAMC is conducted at the county level, and its ultimate goal is to cover every county in the United States.

The field work is the same as for the Christmas Counts. You go out and count everything with feathers (except for domestic fowl, exotic dancers, and feather pillows) that you can find in one day. The difference is that the NAMC is always held on the second Saturday in May. Everyone goes out on the same day, rain or shine. Every state has a coordinator for the NAMC, but you can find out more about the count and the names of the local coordinators by writing to NAMC Coordinator, P.O. Box 71, North Beach, MD 20714. You pay no fee for participating in the NAMC.

The NAMC provides a snapshot of the progress of spring migration. With thousands of bird watchers counting birds all over the continent, the results, once tallied, show where the northernmost members of a given migratory species are located on that particular day. In theory, you can then draw a line saying, "This is how far all the bobolinks had migrated thus far in spring migration."

The data collected on the NAMC is becoming increasingly important as an assessment of how birds are doing. It will take a few years before there is enough information to analyze completely, but that only means that you can get in on the ground floor of one of the biggest volunteer projects ever conceived!

Although the organizers of the count knew that the data collected would be important in the future, they began the count so that they could see the "shape" of migration for given species of birds. Because hundreds of counties participate, mapping the results for each species is possible, showing exactly where the center of the migration is at that point. Despite all the information collected about birds over the past two centuries, we didn't really know this before.

The success of the spring NAMC has led to the logical next step, the fall NAMC. This organization is newer and smaller, but is growing, and in a few years may be just as big as the spring effort. Information on the fall count is also available from the NAMC coordinator.

International Migratory Bird Day

International Migratory Bird Day (IMBD) began in 1993 as a celebration of the return of more than 350 migratory birds to North America from their wintering grounds to the south. IMBD is meant to focus attention on the plight of migratory birds, many species of which have been declining in numbers in recent decades, and to encourage birders to get involved in bird conservation.

IMBD is a designated day in mid-May on which bird-oriented events, such as bird counts, conservation fundraisers, and bird habitat seminars, are held all across North America. For information on IMBD, contact: The National Fish & Wildlife Foundation, 1120 Connecticut Avenue, NW, Suite 900, Washington, D.C. 20036; e-mail info@nfwf.org.

Atlasing

Many states and provinces, including almost all those east of the Mississippi River, have conducted Breeding Bird Atlas projects. A Breeding Bird Atlas is just what it sounds like, an effort to map the breeding distribution of all the birds in the state. In almost all atlases, the state is divided into a grid of blocks, and volunteers survey the blocks during the summer to find breeding birds.

The Breeding Bird Atlas is another project that requires no particular expertise, especially in finding nests. Most atlas work is done on the basis of the mere presence of the birds, not on nest finding. If you can recognize the local breeding birds, you can be an atlas participant.

A lot of bird watchers love atlas work because it's another reason to go afield in the summer, the slowest season for most watchers. Atlas field work is also an opportunity to observe birds in their home life, not as migrants or winter visitors. Atlas field work is a whole different way of looking at birds, and many people have become nearly addicted to it.

Many of the atlas projects are finished, but some states and provinces are just beginning or haven't yet started. The way to find out about atlasing is to contact your local or statewide bird club or ornithological organization. If neither of these sources works, contact the state/provincial department of natural resources. This office may be able to tell you the status of any ongoing atlasing projects.

Atlas field work is conducted entirely by volunteers, and local clubs are always at the center of recruiting volunteers. If your state has not had an atlas project, volunteer to help get one off the ground. Or, if getting the project started at a state level isn't possible, start the way many other projects did, with a local atlas covering one or more counties.

Atlas projects have turned out to be very useful to state governments as they try to make land-use decisions and plan for long-term development. The results of atlas projects allow state governments to see at a glance where the greatest numbers of birds are, along with the locations of certain key habitats.

Hands-on Experience — Banding

Banding birds is another activity in which a beginner can participate. Thousands of people across the continent band birds, many in their backyards.

Banding birds means capturing the birds and placing a band on one leg. Bird banders usually use fine mist nets designed for the purpose. The process doesn't hurt the birds, and the bands put on the birds' lower legs are lightweight aluminum or plastic. One advantage to banding for the beginner is that having the bird in the hand makes identification simpler. Almost every part of the country has active bird banders who are looking for volunteer help. The easiest way to find them is through the local bird club. To become a bird bander yourself requires working with a licensed bander until you qualify. The bands come from the U.S. Fish and Wildlife Service, which requires that you demonstrate some experience before you can be licensed.

Banding has provided scientists with critical information about bird migrations, longevity, and habits. If you want to discover more about banding before getting in touch with one of the local banders and volunteering, write to the Bird Banding Laboratory at: U.S. Fish and Wildlife Service, Laurel, MD 20708.

Other Volunteer Projects

Many opportunities exist to volunteer and participate in bird-related projects. Some of them are research-based scientific studies, while other opportunities only require your enthusiasm, willingness to help others, and perhaps a little elbow grease. A very good resource for interested volunteer bird watchers is the *Guide to Volunteer Opportunities for Birders* published by the American Birding Association, P.O. Box 6599, Colorado Springs, CO 80934.

The American Ornithologists' Union (AOU), c/o Division of Birds, National Museum of Natural History, Washington, D.C. 20560, also publishes a newsletter, *The Ornithological Newsletter* that lists current volunteer and paid opportunities. Ornithology professors at universities usually subscribe and can be a source of information on other opportunities.

Breeding Bird Survey

The Breeding Bird Survey, run by the U.S. Fish and Wildlife Service, uses volunteers to monitor breeding bird populations. It requires familiarity with bird songs, and most participants are moderately experienced bird watchers. However, even the newest beginning bird watcher can help out with keeping records, running the time clock, or driving the vehicle used for the survey. Volunteering for this survey can be a great way to find out about bird song from experts at birding by ear.

A Breeding Bird Survey (BBS) is a 25-mile route along secondary roads with 50 stops, each stop one half-mile apart. At each stop, the observers count all the birds heard or seen during a three-minute period.

These surveys are conducted in late spring, when migrant species have already passed through the area, and breeding birds have set up territories but haven't entered the less active period during nesting. At this time, which varies with the advent of spring at different latitudes, male birds are most vocally active, singing to advertise themselves and their chosen territories to interested females. BBS runs are begun in the early mornings, just before dawn when the bird song is at its peak. Because it's often not yet light, and because of the short time at each spot, almost all the birds tallied are heard rather than seen. The results of the hundreds of BBS routes run all over the continent provide the best data available on changing songbird populations.

To find out about BBS routes near you, contact Patuxent Wildlife Research Center, Laurel, MD 20708-4038. No fee is charged to participate in a Breeding Bird Survey.

Project FeederWatch

Project FeederWatch is run by the Cornell Laboratory of Ornithology, 159 Sapsucker Woods Road, Ithaca, NY 14850. This watch involves thousands of people from all over the continent who report how many birds visit their feeders every week, year-round. The project is easy and you can do it in your backyard.

The information from Project FeederWatch is being used to monitor populations and migrations. The Cornell Lab also operates other volunteer-based research projects, including, among others, Project Pigeon Watch and Operation Tanager. All these programs have a fee for participation.

Refuge volunteer

Virtually every National Wildlife Refuge (NWR) is looking for volunteers for a variety of projects, from building and marking trails to counting birds. If you live near a National Wildlife Refuge, simply drive in and ask the refuge staff about volunteering. Chances are they'll be thrilled by your offer, and you can bet they'll find something for you to do. Because of budget limitations, many NWRs are staffed primarily by seasonal employees with just a few permanent staff.

State and local parks

State, county, and city parks are always looking for volunteers to help with bird-oriented projects. Many of the programs at these parks — including bird walks, school outings, bird watching seminars, and bird censuses — are run by volunteers. You can get information from any local park or by calling your state department of natural resources, department of recreation, or wildlife office.

Bird rehabilitation centers

If you want real hands-on experience, try volunteering at a local bird rehabilitation center. These are the facilities where people bring injured or sick birds. Often run entirely by volunteers, usually with donations and a willing veterinarian or licensed rehabilitator, rehab centers are constantly in need of people willing to make the commitment to help individual animals.

Dealing with injured animals is not for everyone. It's time-consuming (try feeding baby birds every 20 minutes from dawn to dusk!). Sometimes, no matter how dedicated the rehabilitation effort, the bird doesn't recover, which is disheartening. But for the people who participate in rehabbing birds, the satisfaction of successfully saving a bird outweighs all other considerations.

Bird rehabilitation centers exist all across the continent, but not every community has one. Rehabilitation centers must be licensed by state and federal wildlife protection authorities and must meet strict standards for the care of wild animals.

All native birdlife, except for a few so-called pest species such as starlings and house sparrows, is protected by law in North America. You need to have federal and state (or provincial) permits to handle birds, even if you have the best intentions. Believe it or not, you need permits even to pick up bird feathers! This may sound strange, but it's the only way to protect birds from exploitation or irresponsible handling.

The first place to check for a rehab center near you is the local bird club. (Where have you heard that before?) You can also check with the state agency that deals with wildlife, because it licenses and oversees the operations of the centers. One other potential source for information about nearby bird and wildlife rehab centers is your local veterinarian. Vets are faced with many injured and sick birds found and brought to their offices by well-meaning souls, so it's a good bet that your local vet knows where the nearest licensed rehab center is (not all vets are trained to treat wild birds and animals). Another source for information on rehab centers is the International Wildlife Rehabilitation Council, Box 3007, Walnut Creek, CA 94598.

Acting Locally

Along with the national projects, thousands of local projects run by local bird clubs exist. After you get in touch with your local club, you will find no shortage of opportunity and no shortage of work to be done. For example, many parks, refuges, and nature preserves are created because of lobbying by local bird watchers and other nature enthusiasts who have recognized the importance of the site. In addition, many local clubs have bird counts beyond the traditional Christmas Count and spring migration count. Some local clubs sponsor special waterfowl or raptor censuses, some monitor grassland birds, some bring bird watching to retirement homes, and so on.

No matter what sort of project you volunteer for, being a part of it brings you considerable pleasure and adds something to your experience. Bird watching is a hobby, a pleasurable way of putting the pressures of the world behind you, but it can also be a way to contribute. Contributing can be a source of pleasure in itself.

Compile a local checklist

With the advent of home computers, more and more bird watchers are able to create localized checklists of the birds for a given area (see Chapter 25 for more about computers and bird watching). It used to be that you'd have a checklist for the birds of North America, or perhaps one for the birds of a National Wildlife Refuge, but nothing that reflected the diversity and status of your local birds.

If this sort of work intrigues you (and it doesn't appeal to everyone), I suggest that you gather the records of local birders and begin by creating a file on every bird species found in your area. This process can be most easily done electronically, on a computer, but it can also be accomplished using the traditional pen-and-paper method.

A good checklist shows a listing of all regularly occurring species along with an indication of their seasonal status. Terms used to describe a species' status are: abundant, common, uncommon, and rare. Often a checklist has four columns, corresponding to spring, summer, fall, and winter, next to each bird. A letter (A=abundant; C=common, and so on) is placed in each column to indicate whether or not a species is to be found in the checklist region in each season. No letter indicates that the species is entirely absent during that season.

You can make the checklist anything you wish it to be. I suggest you begin your checklist simply and get more complex as your desire for information grows.

Two things to remember when working on a checklist project: The checklist is always going to be a work in progress, so change is normal as species are added or notations altered. And you'll need the help, input, and advice of lots of your fellow bird watchers, so be open to suggestions.

Assist the Bird Information Line/Rare Bird Alert

Every state and province in North America has at least one rare bird alert (RBA) or bird information line. These telephone-based services are sometimes run by bird clubs and sometimes by avid bird watchers who enjoy getting and sharing information on bird sightings. Here's how they work:

A telephone number is selected and an answering machine or voice mail system is set up to play a pre-recorded message about recent bird sightings. Interested birders can call this number at any time to hear what's been seen recently and where sightings have occurred. Increasingly, this information is also being shared via the Internet and e-mail. At regular intervals, often weekly, the message is updated with new sightings and information.

Rare bird alerts tend to focus primarily on the most unusual sightings and rarities, birds that would create much excitement among avid listers and birders who keep life lists.

Bird information lines are not limited to rarities or unusual birds, but rather to sharing recent sightings of common birds and perhaps other aspects of nature, such as signs of spring, meteor showers, and other natural phenomena.

You can contribute to this information sharing system in a few ways. The obvious one is to share your sightings. The less obvious one is to offer help in maintaining the messages. Better yet, why not start your own information line for your local area? Sharing information with others is at the heart of what makes bird watching enjoyable.

Spread the phone tree

Bird clubs often have another form of rare bird alert — the *phone tree*. A phone tree works like this:

- ✔ You, or someone else in the local group, finds an interesting bird, one that some members of the club would like to know about.

- ✔ Instead of calling a machine somewhere, leaving a message, and hoping someone else will call and hear about it, the phone tree swings into operation. Each person is assigned three other bird watchers to call.

- ✔ In turn, each of those people has three others to call, and so on, down the line.

Pretty quickly, the word gets around to everyone in the local club (usually within an hour — scientists remain baffled by the speed at which news of a good bird can spread through the bird watching grapevine!).

Being part of the local phone tree (or starting one) has two main benefits. First, you help make certain that the lines of communication remain open. Second, you get to hear all the local hot news almost as soon as it happens.

Report your sightings to your birding friends, your local bird club, or regional bird records compiler. You don't have to be an authority on birds to contribute important information. Besides, telling your pals about a neat bird you saw means that they'll return the favor the next time they see something good.

Take a friend out to watch birds. You can open somebody's eyes to nature with the simple act of showing them a bird and telling them what it is. Pass it on!

Finding or Founding a Bird Club?

Several thousand bird clubs exist in North America, and these clubs come in many sizes, forms, and intensities. Some are well-run, venerable institutions staffed by paid professionals who operate the club, produce the club's publications, hold events, and handle the chores associated with large membership rolls. Perhaps a few dozen clubs operate like this in North America.

The vast majority of bird clubs are local groups of like-minded bird watchers who get together occasionally for field trips and social events. These clubs are mostly run by volunteers, and the dues paid by members cover the club's expenses. These clubs focus on enjoyment.

Finding a Bird Club

Finding a bird club in your area can be as easy as asking another bird watcher whom you encounter in the field. But clubs can also be as hard to find as a dropped contact lens, and, like finding a lens, the key is to know where to look. If you don't know anyone else who watches birds, ask anyone you know who is interested in nature if they know of a club.

Some other likely sources of information are garden centers where bird seed and feeders are sold; a local environmental official, agricultural officer, or game warden; a local veterinarian (they receive lots of injured birds and may know a local bird authority); your local library; or your local newspaper, which may have a nature columnist. You have many potential contacts. Almost everybody knows at least one bird watcher (sometimes you have to ask to find out, though). Any gathering of more than two bird watchers can be considered a bird club!

The following list covers some of the most successful and prominent bird clubs from across North America. It's by no means all-inclusive, so don't be disheartened if you do not see a club near you. The most prominent national organizations of birders are

- **The American Birding Association,** P.O. Box 6599, Colorado Springs, CO 80934; 800-850-2473 or 719-578-1614
- **The National Audubon Society,** 700 Broadway, New York, NY 10003; 212-979-3000
- **The Association of Field Ornithologists,** OSNA Business Office, Allen Press, P.O. Box 1897, Lawrence, KS 66044; 913-843-1221
- **Cornell Laboratory of Ornithology,** 159 Sapsucker Woods Rd., Ithaca, NY 14850; 607-254-2473

The following are prominent regional and local organizations:

- **Audubon Naturalists' Society of Central Atlantic States,** 8940 Jones Mill Rd, Chevy Chase, MD 20815
- **New Jersey Audubon Society,** 790 Ewing Ave., Franklin Lakes, NJ 07417
- **Whitefish Point Bird Observatory,** HC 48, Box 115, Paradise, MI 49768
- **Point Reyes Bird Observatory,** 4990 Shoreline Hwy, Stinson Beach, CA 94970

- ✔ **Manomet Observatory,** P.O. Box 1770, Manomet, MA 02345
- ✔ **Tucson Audubon Society,** 300 E. University Blvd #120, Tucson, AZ 85705
- ✔ **Los Angeles Audubon Society,** 7377 Santa Monica Blvd, Los Angeles, CA 90046
- ✔ **Florida Audubon Society,** 460 Hwy 436 #200, Orlando, FL 32707
- ✔ **Du Page Birding Club,** 405 Washington Street, Elmhurst, IL 60126
- ✔ **Maryland Ornithological Society,** Montgomery County Chapter, P.O. 59639, Potomac, MD 20859
- ✔ **Massachusetts Audubon Society,** Stony Brook Nature Center, 108 North St., Norfolk, MA 02056
- ✔ **Linnaean Society of New York,** 15 W 77th St., New York, NY 10024
- ✔ **New York Birders,** Maxwell C. Wheat, Jr., 333 Bedell St., Freeport, NY 11520
- ✔ **Cincinnati Bird Club,** 7066 Wesselman Rd., Cleves, OH 45002
- ✔ **Audubon Society of Portland,** 5151 NW Cornell Rd., Portland, OR 97210
- ✔ **Delaware Valley Ornithological Club,** Academy Natural Sciences, 1900 Benjamin Franklin Pkwy, Philadelphia, PA 19103
- ✔ **Houston Audubon Society,** 440 Wilchester, Houston, TX 77079
- ✔ **Texas Ornithological Society,** 201-A Big Joshua Creek Rd., Comfort, TX 78013
- ✔ **Virginia Society of Ornithology,** 520 Rainbow Forest Dr., Lynchburg, VA 24502
- ✔ **Seattle Audubon Society,** 8050 35th Ave. NE, Seattle, WA 98115
- ✔ **Brooks Bird Club,** 707 Warwood Ave., Wheeling, WV 26003
- ✔ **Long Point Bird Observatory,** P.O. Box 160, Port Rowan, ON N0E, 1M0, Canada
- ✔ **Toronto Bird Observatory,** 10 Bateman Ct., Whitby, ON L1P 1K2, Canada
- ✔ **Club des Ornith. de Quebec,** 2000 Boul., Montmorency Quebec, PQ G1J 5E7

Every bird club, even a small one, has a variety of committees. Someone has to organize the field trips, set up the programs, oversee refreshments, inspire letter-writing campaigns, serve as liaison to local government and other groups, and fill the offices of president, treasurer, editor of the news-letter, and on and on. If you really want to feel loved and needed, show up at a bird club meeting and ask: "Is there anything I can do to help?"

Starting a bird club

If you have no local bird club, start one! Don't worry, you won't have to memorize *Robert's Rules of Order*. Starting a bird club is easy. All you need to do is locate a few other bird watchers and declare yourselves a club. If you want to be more organized, that's fine. What's important is that you get together with the other members from time to time and watch birds, talk about birds, and so on. If potluck dinners turn you on, go for it.

First, make sure that that your town or county has no existing bird club; the members of an existing club (even one that hasn't met since the last passenger pigeon expired) may accuse you of poaching members!

Follow these steps for starting a bird club in a place where no bird club exists (also known as a bird-club-free zone).

1. **Contact any other bird watcher about the club.**

   If you know absolutely no other bird person, call your local newspaper and ask to be included in the social club news (or coming events/public meeting) section. Set a date for interested bird watchers to meet at a neutral site.

2. **Choose a local site that offers good bird watching and schedule your first club outing.**

   This can be the site of the first meeting for interested parties.

3. **Meet people. Watch birds. Have fun.**

4. **Pick a name for your club. Then spread the word.**

As your club grows, you can decide if you want it to be more formalized (dues, regular meetings, committees, and so on) or if you prefer it to be less formal and more social. Both methods (and all variations in between) work equally well.

Teaching the Kids

You can have a profound impact on young people if you are willing to spend some time with them and encourage their interest in the natural world. Volunteer to give a short talk about birds or bird feeding at a local school or scout group. Kids are fascinated by birds, so be prepared to answer lots of questions. Invite those who are very interested to attend a bird club outing or lend them your copy of *Bird Watching For Dummies!*

To work individually, wait until the child's around age 10 for more than the most casual bird watching (younger children don't have a long attention span). Begin by pointing out easy-to-see birds. Canada geese, great blue herons, and mallards may all be present on a nearby pond or lake. Crows, turkey vultures, and large hawks can be seen along almost any road in North America.

Once you get the youngster to see the bird, you can add a tidbit of information about it (it's okay to cheat and peek at your field guide for this info). This tidbit will be a helpful reminder for the child the next time he or she sees the bird. Remember to keep things at a pace the child can handle.

Field guides designed for younger users are available from most bookstores, public libraries, or nature centers. Take a few minutes to study the guide with the child and read the introduction together. Show the child the basic technique for identifying a bird and go through the process once or twice.

Spend a few minutes showing the child how to use the binoculars. Remember that small hands need small binoculars, so if the child shows a real interest, consider getting an inexpensive child-size pair for your outings.

Share the chores: If you feed birds, let the child participate in filling and cleaning the feeder or the bath. Turn a chore into a treat (like Tom Sawyer white-washing the fence). Create projects, such as building a simple bird feeder or nest box together. Encourage list keeping; each time the child identifies a new bird, have her (or him) check it off the list or write it down, adding other information, such as the date, how many birds were seen, and the weather.

A number of other opportunities exist to involve a child in projects, depending on the age and interest of the child. For example, if you have a bird house, let the child determine how many days it takes the eggs to hatch, or how many times an hour the adults bring food to the babies. The range of projects is limited only by the birds' need for privacy and the child's imagination. And you can have an avid bird-watching companion for life.

Part V
Once You're Hooked

The 5th Wave   By Rich Tennant

"Well, let's see where we're spending this year's vacation."

In this part . . .

Once you begin bird watching, it's easy to become addicted to it. Fortunately, bird watching is completely legal, not very expensive, and wonderfully fulfilling when you see a new and beautiful bird for the first time in your life. This part offers several outlets for the extremely interested bird watcher, along with ways to improve your optics, advance your identification skills, sketch birds like an artist, and go online to find more birds and bird enthusiasts. I even provide advice on extending your passion to other flying creatures, such as butterflies and bats.

Chapter 22

Better Optics and Other Fun Gear

In This Chapter

▶ Upgrading your optics

▶ Spotting scopes

▶ Tripods

▶ Other binocular stuff

▶ Packing it in

▶ High-tech gadgets

▶ Bird finding guides

*J*ust like any other hobby, bird watching has a never-ending ocean of doodads, gadgets, gear, and stuff that you can buy to enhance your experience. Some of the things I swear by. Some of them I swear at. It's all a matter of personal preference.

I'm not going to name products by their brand names in this chapter. That's a path to sheer madness. Instead, I give you general descriptions of birding gear, and you can make your own decisions as to the make, model, and brand name. Much of this stuff can be purchased in the usual places or via mail-order houses. Another good way to learn about new and/or improved products is to check out the advertisements in any bird or nature magazine.

Enough yakking. Here's the stuff.

Non-Commercial Message

Let me say this before you get out your wallet or purse: Buying more gear does not necessarily make you a better bird watcher. Nor does it guarantee that your bird watching is any more enjoyable than it already is. I have a pile of unused bird-watching products in my garage to prove this.

The things that do enhance your birding, or help you to be better in the field, are the ones you can't believe you ever lived without. Finding those gems can be tough, but it's worth the search.

Upgrading Your Optics

About ten years after I started watching birds seriously, I realized, with a start, that the reason my friends could see and identify birds more quickly than I could was that they had *better binoculars*. Soon after, I got a mid-priced pair of binocs to replace my old El Cheapos, and I could see the difference immediately. It was as if I'd taken a pill that allowed me to see birds really well for the first time. The only other time such a vision transformation had happened to me was in fifth grade when I got eyeglasses and began my so-called four-eyed life.

Better and cleaner binocs

My new binocs were not only better optically, but they were also clean and properly aligned! No more gazing through years-old mayonnaise- and jelly-coated lenses. No more squinting and straining. No more accompanying headaches. It was the best $250 I had ever spent.

You may feel that now is not the time for you to upgrade your optics. At some point, you may want to consider it, however. Buying new binoculars is the same as buying your first pair. But now you have some experience using birding optics upon which you can base your decision.

Consider the following things when you are ready to upgrade:

✔ Can you afford the new pair? You should buy the best binocs that you can reasonably afford.

✔ Do you want a lighter pair of binoculars?

✔ Do you want more power?

✔ Are you very comfortable with your new optics? Do they feel good in your hands?

✔ Are the new binocs easy to use and clean?

✔ Do the new optics come with a warranty?

✔ Who will service your new optics?

For more on the basics of choosing binoculars, see Chapter 12.

Extra binocs

If you do buy a new pair of binoculars, you have a bonus in store. Now you have an *extra* pair of binoculars (your old ones) that you can leave in a convenient place. I leave an old pair under the seat of my car, for those avian encounters along the road of life.

Should you so disdain your old bins that you can't bear to have them near you, consider donating them to a young bird watcher or to your bird club as a "community" pair of binocs.

A program sponsored by the Manomet Observatory sends old binoculars (which are donated by North American bird watchers) to young bird watchers in Central and South America. If you'd like to send your old optics in as part of this program, contact: The Manomet Observatory, P.O. Box 1770, Manomet, MA 02345, or call 508-224-6521.

Strapping on

More variations are on the binocular strap than there are toes on a foot.

- First, you have the standard thin strap that you get with any pair of binoculars. It's made of plastic or "pleather" (for plastic leather) and begins cutting into your neck flesh about 15 seconds after you don your binocs.

- The next level is the wider cloth or plastic strap, which spreads the weight more evenly but is still very hot on sunny days.

- One step above the wider strap are the specialty straps. Specialty straps come in two styles, which I lovingly refer to as bungee and harness.

  - Bungee straps are made of springy neoprene. They distribute the weight of your optics and have some "give" to them, which makes your optics feel even lighter than they are. These straps also "breathe" better than all-cloth, nylon, or leather straps, which makes them more comfortable on hot days.

  - Harness straps are great for folks who can't stand the weight of binoculars around their necks. The harness system distributes the optics' weight across the shoulders and back, keeping the neck unencumbered. The harness also holds the binocs snug against the chest, preventing them from bouncing when you walk. Of course the harness still permits you to raise the binocs to your eyes.

Most specialty bird stores and camera stores carry binocular straps, as do most birding gear mail-order companies.

Spotting Scopes

The spotting scope is a serious investment for folks who are serious about bird watching. I can think of only two disadvantages to owning a spotting scope: they're expensive, and you can't use them in every birding situation.

You can spend more than $2,000 on a spotting scope if you want a top-of-the-line product. The best low-end scopes usually sell for about $300–500, and that doesn't include a tripod for mounting. That may sound like a lot of money at first, but if you average your investment cost over the years of birding you'll get from a scope, you realize it's only costing you pennies per day.

I never go anywhere without my spotting scope, even when I know I'll have little use for it, such as when I plan to hike several miles along a woodland trail. Why lug it along? Because if I don't take it, I'm sure to need it. (I don't claim to be brilliant. It's a lot like what happens when you decide to leave the umbrella at the house or in the car when you go to the mall.)

Scopes are best for viewing distant birds, such as shorebirds, waterfowl, and perched birds of prey, and for scanning vast areas. But you can also use scopes to get breathtaking, up-close views of cooperative birds that are not so distant. Put a spotting scope on a pied-billed grebe that is 50 feet away from you, and you'll be able to see the bill marking that gave this species its name. And you'll see the droplets of water on the grebe's head feathers.

As more optics manufacturers enter the spotting scope market, your choices for models, styles, powers, and prices of scopes multiply. This is good. You have lots more from which to choose.

When choosing a spotting scope, I suggest you consider price first of all. Decide how much you want to spend, and then look at the scopes within your price range.

If you're lucky enough to live near an optics dealer, or if you can get to a place where lots of birders are using spotting scopes, test as many models as you can before you buy. Within your price range, buy the best you can afford.

Next, decide on the features you want to have.

Aperture

The aperture is the measurement (in millimeters) of the diameter of the lens on the big end of a scope. This lens is called the objective lens, and its measurement is how scopes are named: a 70mm scope has an objective lens measuring 70 millimeters. The larger the aperture, the more light is allowed in to carry the image to your eye. Larger aperture scopes — those in the 70-80mm range — are more expensive, but their light-gathering capabilities give them superior resolution to smaller scopes, so your image is much sharper.

Erecting prisms

Some scopes you encounter — especially those very high-powered models — don't have erecting prisms. They show you a backwards image. For example, if you're looking at a Canada goose that is facing left, the image in this type of scope shows the bird facing right. This set-up can make finding a distant bird very difficult, because you must pan backwards. It's like being in an optical fun house. Erecting prisms flip the image back to normal.

I would not consider buying a scope that does not have erecting prisms. I like to see things facing the right way.

Eyepiece

The eyepiece is probably the most important part to consider when choosing a scope. It's the eyepiece that gives a scope its magnifying power. On most spotting scopes used for bird watching, you can change the eyepiece to suit your viewing situation. A more powerful (higher magnification) eyepiece can be used for viewing distant birds, while a less powerful eyepiece is better suited for scanning a wide area because it gives you a wider field of view (the amount of area you can see at one time through the scope).

When considering buying a spotting scope, ask whether or not the scope comes with an eyepiece, and what power that eyepiece is. Not all scopes come with eyepieces. If you need to buy an eyepiece, or if you want to buy an additional eyepiece, the power ranges commonly used for bird watching are between 15-power and 40-power.

You have some other things to consider about eyepieces.

To zoom or not to zoom?

As an alternative to switching between eyepieces of different powers, *zoom eyepieces* offer a variety of powers, often from 15-power to as high as 45-power. Because they're more complex to produce, zoom eyepieces are often more expensive than fixed-power ones.

The advantage to zooms is the ease with which the birder can switch powers to suit a situation. One drawback to zooms (other than price) is that they don't offer the superior resolution provided by fixed eyepieces. Think about it: the image must travel through a greater number of lenses, prisms, or mirrors within a more complex zoom lens. Each time the light strikes a surface, the overall amount of light is slightly reduced, causing a slight decrease in image quality.

Zoom lenses don't always offer excellent results when zoomed to their highest power, especially under the low light conditions you may encounter at dawn or dusk. When I use a zoom eyepiece with a spotting scope, I find that I almost always dial back from the highest zoom to get a sharper image of the bird I am viewing.

Angled or straight?

The eyepiece/scope configurations most commonly used by bird watchers have either a straight-through alignment or have the eyepiece mounted at a 45-degree angle to the scope.

You may naturally assume that the straight-through format is better and easier to use. I always assumed that, until my wife and I got a scope with an angled eyepiece. She preferred this format for using the scope while drawing birds. It's easier on the neck to look down into a scope than to crane the neck to look into a straight eyepiece.

We found the angled eyepiece even easier to use when sharing the scope. With our difference in height (more than a foot), our old, straight-through eyepiece was a real drag. One of us always had to contort to get a good view through the scope.

After a few weeks of using the angled eyepiece, we were both able to get the scope on distant birds quite quickly. It took a little getting used to, but now using it is second nature. I suggest you try both formats and see which you prefer.

Extra options

Among the extra options you may wish to consider for your spotting scope are the special lenses designed to improve optical quality. Often called ED glass, SD glass, or fluorite glass, these lenses don't disperse the color spectrum of light as much as regular glass lenses do. This means a clearer, sharper, brighter image for the scope user.

At low powers, most birders claim there is little difference between scopes that have this fancy glass and scopes with regular lenses. It is at the higher magnifications that the difference is apparent.

Now the bottom line: High-quality lenses such as these can almost double the price of a new scope. The choice is yours to make. The bank is yours to break. And the birds are out there, waiting.

Protecting your investment

I would not consider buying a new scope without getting a protective case for it. You can get one from your scope's manufacturer. It looks like a mini down jacket for your scope, and usually has Velcro or zippered covers for both ends of the scope and for the tripod-mounting attachment. You'll be bumping and maybe even dropping your scope accidentally. A protective case helps cushion these potentially harmful blows.

If you don't want to fool with a protective covering, then at least get good lens caps for your scope. Nothing reduces optical quality like dirty, scratched lenses.

The lens caps I got with my first scope were very loose fitting, so I soon lost them. I fashioned replacements out of an empty film canister (for the eyepiece) and the bottom of a large plastic yogurt container (for the objective lens—the big end of the scope). Both of these fit more snugly, and thus protected better, than their predecessors. Believe me, there is *some* size of plastic container that will fit each end of your scope. Besides, you'll be recycling, which is always a good thing.

Tripods

You really can't use a scope without a good tripod. I have seen bird watchers try to hand-hold scopes and try to use scopes mounted on gun stocks. Face it, nothing works as well as a tripod. Tripods hold the scope entirely steady so you can get a good look at the birds. Think of a tripod as legs for your scope.

Lots of tripods are available on the market. The best ones for birding have these characteristics: sturdy (won't blow over in moderate winds), not too heavy, quick and easy leg extension, solid scope mount, and easy to use when panning in all directions.

Next time you're out with a group of bird watchers, check out the tripods in use and ask the scope-users about their preferences. Avoid inexpensive, lightweight tripods. These fall over if you look at them or talk too loudly in their presence. If you've just invested many hundreds of dollars in a scope, invest a bit more in a good tripod. A good new one will cost you between $75 and $200.

High-Tech Birding Gear

If you thought that granola bars were the highest-tech items ever used by bird watchers, think again, my friend. Computers and satellites now have as much business being a part of bird watching as bird feeders and binoculars. And I have a feeling that we are just at the start of birding's technological revolution. Just think about when all the little kids who have been using computers from age two start becoming avid bird watchers. Look out!

Birding software

The first uses of computers for bird watching involved tabulating results from bird counts on huge mainframe computers. A natural extension of this number-crunching ability is list-keeping software. Birders love keeping lists of the birds they see. Keeping this information in a computerized database makes your life list interactive. That is, you can sort your list any way you wish; by species, by locale, by date, and so on. This is both fun and informative. If you want to look for owls in Canada in winter, you can sort your list to show you all the owl species you have and have not seen. Then you can plan your trip accordingly. Pretty cool, huh?

Suppose you want to print out a list of all the birds you've seen in Tennessee. Or all the birds that have the word "blue" in their name. List-keeping software lets you do all this and more.

At least a dozen excellent list-keeping software programs are on the market. Each one has different features and options. Most of the companies advertise regularly in the bird magazines, and some will even let you sample a demo of their program. A list of birding software companies appears in the Appendix.

CD-ROMs

The explosion in popularity of the home computer has fueled the CD-ROM market. Bird watchers have several excellent CD-ROMs from which to choose. When it's crummy weather outside, you can take a virtual field trip by cruising through a CD-ROM. Most CD-ROMs offer an interactive field guide format, but some add dynamic features such as video and audio clips of birds. Some of the CD-ROMs also offer list-keeping software, a skills quiz, and even an encyclopedia of bird information.

When buying a birding CD-ROM, make sure that your computer has what it takes to play CD-ROMs. You need a CD-ROM drive (not just an audio CD player), perhaps a sound card (if you want to hear birds singing) and a video memory card, and lots of RAM (memory). Many wild bird specialty stores and computer and book stores sell these products. Their sales people can help you sample the products and determine the technology you need to play CD-ROMs.

Global positioning

I was once on a bird tour, deep in the tropical jungle, when I heard a strange, screechy call that sounded like "Wurryaat." I found Julie, my wife, and asked her what was making that call. She was just as puzzled as I was. The call kept up, and it was getting closer. We thought it was a large bird, perhaps a ground-dwelling fowl of some sort. But we couldn't pinpoint it. Then, from around a giant tree trunk, came another member of our tour group. She had lost her husband and was screaming "Where ya at?" at the top of her lungs.

The moment was both funny and scary, as you can imagine.

If our fellow traveler had had a *global positioning system* unit, she would have known exactly where *she* was at, but her husband still would have been lost. And who could blame him? Global positioning systems, or GPSs as they sometimes are called, rely on signals from orbiting satellites to determine one's exact position on the planet. These small, hand-held units are very useful for birders doing breeding-bird surveys and other field work. GPS units are often used to pinpoint locations where rare birds have been spotted. A GPS unit can not only tell you exactly where you are in terms of longitude and latitude, it can also help you navigate back to a pre-chosen point by giving you directional information.

Not all bird watchers will find GPS units useful. The price for them is rapidly dropping into the affordable range (under $500). No doubt these little bits of technology will find wider applications among birders in the future.

Hearing aids

No longer does a loss of hearing prevent you from enjoying the dawn chorus of bird song on a May morning.

Loss of hearing in the high frequency ranges — the frequencies at which most warblers sing, for example — is very common among adult male bird watchers. In fact, many men begin to notice a loss of high frequency hearing in their late 30s. Fortunately, excellent options exist to enhance human hearing in these frequency ranges. Small hearing aids that fit completely inside the ear are available, as are units that combine a small microphone with earphones or headphones. Many of these products are advertised in bird, nature, and camping/outdoors magazines.

Other gear

Sometimes I look at all the gear I take with me when I go bird watching, and I have to laugh. I mean, you'd think I was planning to go on a month-long safari or something. If you want to become a gearhead like me, check out this stuff.

- A *scope pack* holds your scope and tripod safely and securely on your back; a *fanny pack* straps around your waist for storing stuff; a *field guide pouch* hold books vertically.

- *Bird-finding guides* give you precise directions to specific places where you can find birds, along with local birder information.

  In North America, almost all the well-known bird-watching areas, and many lesser-known spots, have guides specific to them. Some of these areas are sponsored by local bird clubs or state organizations; others are sponsored by national organizations. All the guides have helpful information for the traveling bird watcher, often including local birding hotline numbers and the names and numbers of local birders.

- To lure birds into the open for a better look with a bird caller, consider a *bird squeaker*. The most common version is a little red peg rotated around a metal shaft to produce a high-pitched squeak.

Field computers for the future

My dad used to say he wanted to develop a magic, gunlike device you could point at a distant bird. The device would have sensors to analyze the bird's size, shape, color, and song. After obtaining this info, the device's internal computer would tell you what species the bird was. I tried to explain to Dad that this would take all the fun out of watching birds. He said: "But we'd be millionaires!"

With the powerful hand-held computers of today used by traveling business people, such a device may not be all that far from reality. All it will take is an enterprising bird expert computer guru, and lots of developmental money. . . .

Chapter 23
Advanced Bird ID

. . . .

In This Chapter

▶ What's so advanced about all this?

▶ Get to know the common birds

▶ Look for more field marks

▶ It's in the details; train your eyes

▶ Get your birding into shape

▶ Molt and wear: Good for them, bad for us

▶ Beware of the common pitfalls

▶ The thrill of victory (not to mention that other stuff)

▶ Know when to say when

. . . .

*A*fter you're hooked on bird watching, you want to seek new and different birds in new and different locations. Many of the new species you encounter present challenging identification puzzles. This chapter gives you some shortcuts on the path to becoming an advanced bird watcher.

What's Advanced Bird ID?

What's advanced bird ID? That's a fair question. Bird ID is not rocket science. Because there are no birds in outer space, rocket scientists rarely even have to think about tough identifications. Any bird can be tough to name if it's a mile away, or hiding in dense shrubbery, or flying away rapidly in the fog.

But I'm talking here about the kind of bird that is genuinely hard to recognize: One that you see perfectly well, one that even sits around patiently while you haul out the field guide, but one that doesn't quite match anything in the book.

Get to know the common birds

The birds probably don't want you to know this, but I'll let you in on one of their rotten little secrets. When you and I have big troubles identifying a bird, the problem usually is not caused by some really rare species. No, the majority of the time, it's the common birds that cause all the trouble.

It makes sense if you stop to think about it. Common birds have more chances to trip us up, just because there are more of them. Besides, they need to do something to entertain themselves, and what could be more fun than causing confusion for bird watchers?

One of the best ways to avoid being confused by strange birds is to get to know those common birds better. After you've identified a bird, don't just walk on immediately in search of something novel; spend some time watching it, committing it to memory.

Look for more field marks

Beginners often hope to find "the one diagnostic mark" for each species of bird — sort of a "magic bullet" that will nail it every time. (Not to mention those occasional frustrating days when it seems like any kind of bullet would help.) Unfortunately, any time you rely on just one field mark, there's a good chance that it will trip you up eventually.

For example, you may latch onto the fact that the snowy egret has yellow feet contrasting with black legs, and decide that you don't need to look at anything else about that bird. Doing this sounds fine in theory. In the field, though, exceptions may loom:

✔ Egrets spend a lot of their time wading, so at times you just can't see their feet.

✔ Snowy egrets that have waded in especially black and sticky mud may appear to have dark feet when they emerge.

✔ Some young snowy egrets have legs that are mostly greenish-yellow, not black.

✔ If you're really lucky/unlucky, you may run into a stray of a European species, the *little egret*, which also has yellow feet and black legs. Or you may encounter a hybrid between snowy egret and little blue heron.

In all of the preceding cases, you'll have problems if you haven't paid attention to other field marks besides the supposedly "diagnostic" one.

It's in the details; train your eyes

Many years ago, I was out with a more experienced older birder, and he spotted a gull that looked suspicious to him. It was one of those motley younger gulls: a medium-sized one, all brown, sitting on a sandbar in the river.

"We ought to take some notes on it," my friend opined. So I whipped out my pocket notebook. "Medium-sized gull," I wrote. "All brown."

As I was putting away the notebook, I noticed that my friend was still writing. He continued to write — stopping to look at the bird, then writing some more — for another 20 minutes while I stood around, self-consciously shuffling my feet and twiddling my thumbs. Finally, as a last resort, I started looking at the bird some more, to see if I could spot something else to write about. But I couldn't see anything else about the gull's appearance that seemed to stand out to my eyes.

My friend's eyesight was no better than mine, but he had trained himself to look for details beyond that first impression of "medium-sized and all brown." The gull turned out to be a first-year California gull, a pretty unusual bird for the area.

Get into shape

Although most field guides don't mention this, some of the most important field marks involve the shapes of birds.

Sometimes you use shape as a field mark without even thinking about it. Not even a beginning bird watcher is likely to confuse a brown duck for a brown owl: Those birds may be the same size and color, but they are differently shaped.

Shape is useful beyond such general divisions. Pick up any bird guide and look at the sandpipers in winter plumage. Most of them are brownish gray on the back and whitish underneath, but no two species are exactly the same shape. Their legs may be long or short. Their bills may be straight or curved, stubby or elongated. Their heads may be hunched down on their shoulders, or they may have long slender necks. The practiced bird watcher can recognize many of these shorebird species by silhouette alone.

Molt and wear: Good for them, bad for us

Birds are covered with feathers. (If they weren't, nobody but a poultry farmer or butcher would enjoy looking at them.) Feathers are amazing things, very lightweight and very strong; but they do gradually wear out. And then they have to be replaced.

As a rule, a healthy bird replaces all of its feathers at least once a year. Not all at once, though — a few at a time. This orderly replacement of feathers is called *molt*. Each kind of bird goes through its molt at a predictable season.

To take an example that may be outside your window right now, the house finch goes through its annual molt in late summer or early fall. By mid autumn, the house finches all look crisp and fresh, with neat pale edges on all the wing feathers. Their feathers are then subject again to the very gradual process of wear. Over the next ten months or so, their feathers very gradually become worn and faded, so that by mid-summer the birds can look pretty ratty before they molt again.

Another finch, the American goldfinch, goes through two molts each year. In the fall it gradually molts all its feathers, leading to a fresh winter plumage with crisp black wings and tail and pale tan body feathers. In the spring it molts again — but just the feathers of the head and body this time, not those of the wings and tail. This spring molt produces the summer plumage, in which the body of the male is bright yellow with a black cap.

So, the same bird that looks crisp and fresh at one season can look dull and faded at another, and it can look patchy when it is molting in feathers of a different color. A bird's tail can look oddly short when its tail feathers are molting, and the shape of its wings can look funny. There's no need for you to memorize the molts of all these birds. But if you're aware of such things as molt and wear, you won't find their effects so mystifying.

Be Aware of Common Pitfalls

If you go out and look for them, you may or may not find common loons, common grackles, or common mergansers. But you don't have to seek the common pitfalls: they come looking for you.

The following sections describe ways in which a bird can look unexpectedly odd, problems that are seldom mentioned in field guides.

Illusions of size

Consciously or unconsciously, you often start the process of identifying a bird by considering its size: classifying it as smaller than a sparrow, larger than a crow, and so on. This is great if you have judged its size correctly. If you haven't, you're off on the wrong track immediately, and you may take a long time to figure out what's wrong. Unfortunately, it's easy to be misled by illusions of size, especially when a bird is seen alone with nothing nearby for easy comparison.

I've had people give me a perfect, feather-by-feather description of a common bird — a meadowlark, for example — that left them completely puzzled. When I suggest the obvious, their emphatic answer is something like, "Oh, no, it was definitely too large for a meadowlark." Chances are good that the bird was a meadowlark, and that its larger size was an illusion. There's really no one good way to compensate for this illusion, except to be aware that it is a possibility. If all the field marks, except size, point to the bird being one species, don't rule out the obvious answer.

Tricks of light

As my pal Isaac Newton once pointed out, what we see as color is really an effect of light. Because light can do really strange things, birds often look odd, through no fault of their own.

Under the glare of noon, colors can be washed out, and dark blue can look like black. Near sunrise or sunset, the low-angled sun can make birds look redder.

Other kinds of illusions are equally likely. A group of birders I was with once saw a mystery bird dash into a thicket — a bright greenish bird, with lots of stripes. For five minutes we peered into the bushes, racking our brains, trying to figure out what rare visitor this might be. Finally we saw it well. It was a song sparrow. A very common bird, brown, with stripes. The greenish color had been nothing but an illusion.

Stained or discolored birds

Birds get messed up in a variety of ways. Some of them are messy eaters, and it shows — in stains on their plumage.

I can remember flipping through the field guide in consternation, looking for the hummingbird with a big yellow spot on its forehead; what I had seen, of course, was a spot of yellow pollen that the bird had picked up from a flower. Then there were those birds that looked just like white-crowned sparrows, except that their faces were variably black from feeding on fallen over-ripe olives. And the herring gull with the odd greenish face — I don't even want to think about what that bird may have been eating.

In Costa Rica, I once spent hours looking in a field guide for the plain greenish-gray warbler with a peach-colored face and throat that I had seen. Finally, I saw a winter-plumaged Tennessee warbler feed at a red *Combretum* flower and get pollen all over its face. I thought I had discovered a species previously unknown to science. Instead it was a sloppy, pollen-faced warbler. Was my face red!

Odd or aberrant plumages

Question: What bird looks just like an American robin, but has big white patches in its wings? Before you start rummaging through the foreign bird guides, I'll give you the answer: It's an American robin. Just a partial albino American robin, with some extra white in the plumage.

You don't see such albinistic birds every day. But if you do much bird watching, you're going to see them eventually — or maybe birds with other kinds of weird, or aberrant, plumages. Occasionally a bird is oddly dark, or more reddish than usual. Sometimes a bird has all of its red pigment replaced with yellow. A few years ago there was excitement over a bird (coming to a feeder in Kansas City) that looked like a cardinal except that it was bright yellow. Bird watchers searched through the foreign field guides, to no avail — the bird was a cardinal.

Oddly plumaged birds are not as uncommon as you may think.

Bill deformities

Very often the shape of a bird's bill is an important field mark. But on occasion, you see a bird with a funny bill — twice the usual length, or oddly curved, or deformed in some other way. A robin with a real long bill isn't a funny plumage of the *long-billed dowitcher*; it's just a funny-looking robin. If you know that such birds are possible, they're less likely to trip you up.

Escaped birds

Visit a zoo with a big aviary, and you may be amazed and impressed by the wide variety of birdlife from other parts of the globe. Then try to imagine what would happen if some of those birds got away and showed up in your local woodlot.

Some such escapees are obvious. If you see a scarlet macaw — three feet long, flaming red — you may immediately suspect that it won't be in your field guide to North America. But a lot of bird fugitives look less exotic than that; they even look superficially like they may belong here. You need to avoid the temptation to "stretch" these birds to fit something in the book. It helps to know where and when you are most likely to encounter such escapees. Southern Florida, south Texas, and southern California are three regions where lots of escaped exotic birds are found. Many of the species found in these areas are from the tropics and have done well enough to reproduce successfully in their new homelands. Some species are accepted now as legitimate North American breeding species. Field guides to these regions contain the most often-encountered exotic bird species.

Hybrids

It's sad to say, but when mating season rolls around, birds don't always behave themselves. Sometimes a bird will pair up with a member of another species. The offspring of these pairings can be very confusing in their appearance.

On one occasion, a bird reported as a black-chinned sparrow in an odd place turned out (after much careful study) to be a hybrid between dark-eyed junco and white-throated sparrow. In another case, a duck that looked a lot like a Baikal teal — a very rare visitor — was actually a hybrid between a northern pintail and a green-winged teal.

Some Strategies for Handling Tough IDs

What's the best approach to handling a tough bird identification? Sometimes, your approach depends on the type of bird with which you're dealing. Here are some suggestions for particular groups of toughies.

- **Fall warblers:** Fall warblers are really confusing little creatures. The dullest and drabbest are tough to identify even if they pose right in front of you, daring you to guess their identity. But if you focus first on the pattern of the wings and the face, you'll go a long way toward recognizing the birds.

- **Immature gulls:** Immature gulls are always bad news, but they get worse and worse in late spring and through the summer, when their feathers are in worn condition. The best strategy is to ignore these ratty and faded gulls of summer, and then (if you feel up to it), focus on them again in late fall, when they are in fresh plumage.

- **Sparrows:** Often called LBJs for Little Brown Jobs, these are sneaky birds that are hard to see and hard to identify. Often a good approach is to go beyond the illustrations in the field guides — read the text! Read about each sparrow's habitat and habits, which are often more revealing than their markings. For example, Savannah sparrow and Lincoln's sparrow are both little streaky birds, but one lives in open fields (Savannah) while the other hides in thickets (Lincoln's).

- **Flycatchers:** Some flycatchers are just impossible to recognize when they're not singing — and during migration they may be unlikely to sing (though they give their call notes more often, which can be a help). Sometimes it's best to ignore the flycatchers in spring and fall and then focus on them in summer, when they are on their nesting grounds and singing their trademark songs.

The Thrill of Victory

You may be asking yourself this question: What's the point to pursuing these challenging identifications?

The point is this: You can't beat the feeling of accomplishment that comes when you can look at a field full of sparrows, or a pond full of ducks, or a beach covered with gulls, and you KNOW THE NAMES OF ALL THOSE BIRDS. That ability comes with experience in the field. Sitting at home and memorizing the field guide may help you some, but it won't do as much for your bird ID skills as looking at actual birds will do.

Know When to Say When

You'll never be a real bird expert until you can be comfortable saying three little words: "I don't know."

Not even the top experts in the world can name every bird they see. If you feel as though you have to put a definitive label on every single bird, you're likely to wind up frustrated — or, worse yet, trying to fool yourself. It's better to admit that you just don't know.

It's *always* okay to walk away from a confusing bird and go looking for something else. No one can fault you for saying, "It's an unidentified flycatcher." (Even if it's really an unidentified vireo instead, you're still half right.) Bird watching is supposed to be enjoyable. If you make yourself unhappy by struggling too long with impossible birds, you're missing the whole point.

Chapter 24
Field Sketching

• •

In This Chapter

▶ Why sketch?

▶ Becoming a quick sketch artist

▶ Tools you'll need

▶ Finding birds to sketch

▶ You're an artiste!

• •

When I started writing this chapter of the book, I was faced with a decision: Learn how to draw birds, or find someone who knows how to write about field sketching. So I did the only reputable thing I could — got somebody else to do my work for me.

In this chapter, you find out about field sketching from one of North America's preeminent bird artists — expert field sketcher, Julie Zickefoose. Her artwork can be seen throughout this book. Now you'll discover her trade secrets.

Take it away, Julie!

Field Sketching: A Bird in the Hand

As you look through this book, you see drawings of birds, pieces of birds, and birds doing lots of different things. Drawing birds is my job. I illustrate books, and I've done covers and interior illustrations for *Bird Watcher's Digest* since 1986.

You may be surprised to find out that I also draw birds for fun — in the field. And it's that exercise that informs all my work, makes it accurate, and gives it feeling. Because I make a habit of drawing birds from life, I can draw any bird doing any particular thing that a publisher may request. Field sketching is a powerful tool, but it's also a lot of fun.

You don't have to sit in a field to field sketch. In fact, you can do it in a park, a zoo, or in the comfort of your own home as you look out the window. I use the term *field sketching* to describe the act of drawing a living creature — not just birds. You may come away with a finished, detailed portrait of a bird if you're sketching while the bird is sleeping, sitting on a nest, or preening. If your bird is hopping about, however, you may end up with hurried little bits and pieces of bills, legs, eyes, and wings dashed all through your sketchbook. Either way, sketching the bird helps you understand much more about how that bird is built, how it behaves, and what it truly looks like than if you'd never tried to draw it at all.

Why Sketch?

When you draw something — anything — you have to ask yourself a lot of questions, among them things like:

- How does my subject look?
- What colors can I see in it?
- How does the light strike it?
- Why am I asking myself all these questions?

And in answering those questions, you discover volumes about how the subject is constructed. Drawing makes you a much better observer; it makes you a better bird watcher, and it may even make you an artist!

Sketches can be better than photographs

Suppose you're birding, and you see a strange-looking sandpiper. You whip out your pad and pencil and start to draw, making notes about the bird as you go along. You watch the bird closely, noting tiny details, making mental measurements of bill, legs, wings, and tail. You see subtle shadings of color. As long as the bird stays, you sketch and make notes. When that bird finally flies away, you may have all you need to make a positive identification.

Had you tried to take a photograph, bad lighting, equipment failure, distance, wind, and shutter noise may all have conspired against you. Maybe your sketches aren't perfect, but you're bound to have found out more about the bird and its behavior than you would have had you simply snapped a picture and moved on. Before cameras and photography were invented, sketching and painting were how all naturalists committed their sightings to paper, and communicated them to others.

Sketching makes you a better bird watcher

If you make a habit of sketching the birds you watch, no matter how common they may be, you may be surprised at what you come up with. And your bird watching skills do improve because of it.

I know a number of artists who, like me, spend a lot of time drawing birds — both common and rare — in the field. When we get together, we trade observations that may sound funny to others, like this:

> "What do you think about the ID on that peep (sandpiper)?"

> "Kind of looks like a western to me."

> "No, I don't think so. The face is too sweet. Westerns have a kind of sourpuss look about them. I'd lean toward least sandpiper."

> "Really? With that big an eye? I think of leasts as kind of squinty. . . ."

> And so on.

Drawing birds makes you notice the smallest things, and more importantly, it helps fix details and overall impressions in your mind like nothing else. It all adds up to greatly heightened powers of observation (see Figure 24-1). When the really rare bird shows up, you'll be ready for it, even if (as I have on a number of occasions) you wind up sans equipment, scrawling the bird's image on the back of an ATM envelope with a golf pencil. I once even used eyeliner when no pencil could be unearthed.

Like a Boy Scout — always be prepared. Keep a sketchpad, pencils, and erasers in your car, your backpack, or your purse. Just keep them with you wherever you go, and you'll be a lot more likely to use them. The more you sketch, the more you'll want to sketch, until it becomes second nature. That's when you'll know you're hooked.

Tools to Get You Started

If becoming a bird watcher is cheap, becoming a field sketcher is even cheaper. A spiral-bound sketchpad that's not too big or too cumbersome (I prefer an 11 x 14-inch down to 8 x 10-inch size format), some pencils, and some erasers are all you really need. (I'm assuming here you already have the binoculars.) Of course, the pointers in the following sections can make it easier for you.

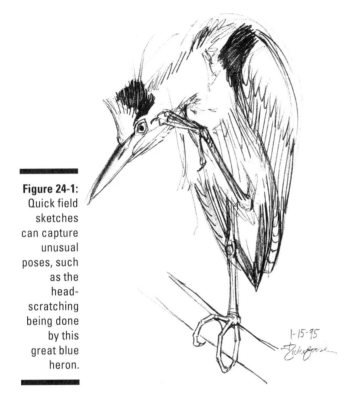

Figure 24-1:
Quick field sketches can capture unusual poses, such as the head-scratching being done by this great blue heron.

Paper (your sketchpad)

In choosing a sketchpad, find one that's lightweight but that has a strong cardboard backing for support. You'll be standing, supporting it on one forearm, and bearing down as you draw, so you want something that won't bend. You can also retrofit a flimsy backing by gluing a stronger piece of corrugated cardboard to it.

Paper surfaces are a matter of taste, but I like something fairly smooth, without much texture to it. That way, your images won't be so smeary, the pencil will travel more easily over the surface, and you won't dull your point as fast. Stay away from extremely thin paper, which can tear in a sudden gust of wind.

Pencils

Pencils that need to be sharpened all the time can cut into your sketching (or provide a great excuse to let your focus wander while you sharpen them). There are a couple of ways around this:

✔ You can invest in an electric pencil sharpener and leave the house with about two dozen pre-sharpened pencils in a zippered pouch, ready to be changed out as you work.

✔ You can use a mechanical pencil, whose lead advances with a click.

I switched to mechanicals a long time ago when I found I was spending more time fussing with pencil sharpeners than drawing.

One thing I've found is that mechanical pencils with a metal ferrule (a tube that encloses and protects the pencil's lead) that protrudes from the body of the pencil, effectively lengthening the lead at the tip, are no good for me. I get so passionate about drawing that I constantly break the lead where it leaves the tiny ferrule. I buy cheap plastic mechanical pencils (which lack the metal ferrule) by the box, and I love them.

Whether you choose soft, medium, or hard lead is up to you. I like B leads, of medium softness, but I also bring a couple of pencils loaded with HB or H leads for the finer details. I wrap a bit of tape around the pencils that have harder leads so that I know what I'm grabbing.

I always draw in regular gray lead pencil. If you prefer a more colorful approach, sets of colored pencils are available commercially. If I really like a sketch I've done in pencil, I may take it back to my studio and "colorize" it using my watercolors.

Erasers

You can't draw a living creature without creating a few flaws. Fortunately, you have an easy way to deal with them: erasers. Next to your pencils, erasers are your most important tool. Erasers are essential; I keep one in my left hand all the time. My favorite kind are the white, soft erasers that are housed in a plastic casing and advance with a click. They won't scuff your paper surface like the hard rubber erasers that come on the end of most pencils, and they erase much more cleanly, without crumbs. I don't know how they do it, but these erasers are wonderful!

Packing to go

After you get your gear, you can throw it all in a backpack or rig up a strap that hooks to the spirals of the sketchbook. That way, you can hang it over your shoulder and have it always at your side. You can get spring-loaded rectangular clips at a stationery store that will hook into the spiral binding, but allow you to turn pages in the sketchbook. Run a length of nylon webbing or cord through them, and you're ready to roll.

A word about wind. It's nasty. Almost as nasty as rain for would-be bird artists. When I take sketching trips to Newfoundland, where the wind seems never to stop, or to any beach (ditto), I put a sturdy rubber band around my sketchbook near the bottom of the page, to keep it from blowing apart in the wind.

Optics for the sketcher

If you're planning to draw wild birds, you need some optics to get you a close look at your subject. Binoculars are fine for most sketching. You quickly get used to raising them, taking a look, and lowering them to draw.

If you really want a revelation, though, try sketching through a scope. Set it up so that it's focused on a bird that's resting or preening and isn't likely to move much. You can stand, or sit if the tripod allows. Suddenly, you have both hands free to hold the sketchbook, nothing hanging around your neck to get in the way, and a better, more magnified view to boot.

Even if your first efforts don't look like very much, be encouraged. Don't be ashamed of your drawing. I know it's hard, but you've got to take it easy on yourself. You're asking a lot of your eye-hand coordination to draw a living bird that's moving around, especially when the last thing you may have drawn was a jug or a bowl of fruit in your high school art class. Look at field sketching as a process, and don't expect to come out of it with a perfect, finished portrait of a bird. Be happy with a decent foot, bill, or eye. I am!

Finding Birds to Sketch

Warblers in treetops will always be somewhere, but you may want to save them for when you get your sketching chops going. When I'm teaching an introductory field sketching class, I like to find a city park that has a bunch of freeloading mallards, lazy Canada geese, or even domestic ducks who will sell their souls for a loaf of stale bread. The idea here is not to overwhelm beginning field sketchers with the notion of drawing tiny, skittish birds through binoculars. So we start slowly, with big, tame, chunky birds that sit still for long periods.

Another potential place to sketch is a zoo. Besides offering exotica like crowned cranes and secretary birds, zoos also let you get up close, which allows you to dispense with the optical aids in many cases. There are drawbacks, however.

One relaxing venue for field sketching is home. If you have a bird feeder and a kitchen table, you have the ideal sketching setup. Move a feeder close to your window, get yourself a cup of something hot, and spend a relaxing morning discovering the chickadees at your feeder.

When you have a cooperative bird, observe it closely and carefully (see Figure 24-2). Don't worry about whether it's a bird worth drawing, such as a rare bird; any bird is worth drawing. You can learn everything you need about field sketching from drawing house sparrows. If the bird sticks around and you can get a good, long session with it, draw it! Seize the moment!

Sketching in very cold weather can be a drag unless you make sure to stay warm. I find that the more comfortable I am, the more likely I am to make good sketches. If I'm to be out for even a few hours, I layer my clothing and take lots of snacks and hot drinks. For extremely cold weather, I use thin gloves with the fingertips of the right hand cut off to help keep my hand warm. Very thin silver glove liners are great, too, and you don't have to cut the fingers off. Seat warmers, which generate heat when compressed, are wonderful, and electric socks look silly but really help those popsicle toes.

Figure 24-2: Try sketching birds from unusual angles, such as from the back. This is a broadwinged hawk.

Basic Sketching Techniques

Take a good, long look at the bird before starting to draw. Try to get a sense of what it is doing, or about to do. Watch for repeated behaviors or poses that may be good to draw. Relax and allow yourself to become absorbed in watching your subject before starting to sketch.

A bit at the start!

Perhaps the most useful bit of advice I can offer to start is: Start with bits!

Beginning sketchers often block out a detailed portrait of a bird, only to erase and erase again as the bird changes position. Birds move constantly, and you're only setting up frustration if you try to represent your subject in a single pose. So draw the bill, the eye, a wingtip, a foot — just study with your pencil, and before long you'll feel up to assembling a whole bird.

Birds begin with an egg

Lots of people like to start drawing birds with a basic egg shape for the body — adding head, legs, wings, and tail as they go. If that works for you, fine.

I tend not to start with the body; I generally start drawing whichever part is moving (usually the head), deciding on the attitude of the rest of the bird based on what the head is doing. It often helps to draw a couple of quick lines along the vertical, horizontal, or oblique axis of the bird.

- ✔ Is the bird standing bolt upright, or at an angle?
- ✔ If the bird is walking, is the head well forward of the body or tucked back into the shoulders?
- ✔ If the bird is flying, are the wingbeats deep and slashing, or are the wings held stiffly?

What I'm going for is a quick impression of the movement (see Figure 24-3). I can add details later; the important thing is to record an overall impression of what the bird is doing at the moment I've chosen to record.

The value of a field sketch is its ability to capture a moment in the movement of a bird. If you want to make a detailed portrait of a bird, you can sit down in front of a zoo specimen or even work from a photograph. If you want to make a field sketch, try to capture the bird in an activity. Do several dozen of these, and you have a record of how it moves and behaves that's ultimately much more interesting than a still life.

A word about erasers: Although I keep an eraser in my left hand at all times, I try not to get too caught up in making each sketch perfect. It's better for your hand and eye to simply move on to another sketch than to try to refine each one to perfection. Think of sketching as an exercise, a process of learning how a bird looks and moves. Your sketches are little signposts along the way to understanding.

As the great British field sketcher Eric Ennion once advised, "Do not worry a bad sketch right!" Move on!

No hard and fast rules

The truth about field sketching is that it can't be done by hard and fast rules. It's learned simply by doing. Each person develops a style that works best, getting more proficient with practice. The important thing is not to be too much of a perfectionist; just settle for an impression of your subject.

You needn't draw birds all the time to be a good field sketcher. Anything — and I mean anything — you draw adds to your powers as a sketch artist. I often do my best field sketches after a few sessions with a human model in a friend's studio. It's all grist for the mill.

Contour drawing

Contour drawing is a really interesting exercise, and it's a technique that finds its way into most of my best sketches.

In *contour drawing,* the student looks steadily at the subject, not at the paper, and allows the pencil to travel around the outline of the form. Using this technique, it's absolutely amazing how easy it is to create a passable image of something you didn't think you could draw. Try it by drawing your hand (a devilishly hard thing to draw, if you think about it). If you're right-handed, just look at your left hand and let your pencil trail over the paper as if tracing its form (you won't actually be outlining your hand, just drawing its outline). I think you'll be pleased with the result.

After demonstrating contour drawing to a beginning field-sketching class, one of my students sat down in front of a resting sheep and, without taking her eyes off the animal for a moment, produced a lovely image, far nicer than mine. She had never drawn in her life, and the tears rolled down her cheeks as the "secret" of drawing was unlocked. I had very little to do with it; she taught herself through doing.

Figure 24-3:
Highly patterned birds such as these black skimmers can be captured with just a few lines.

You're an Artiste!

Try sketching some birds. Think of it as you might think about riding a bike. It's a little wobbly and frustrating at first, and you don't see how you're ever going to get that two-wheeled thing up and rolling without killing yourself first. Then, one fine day, you set off, pedaling like mad, and before long, you're riding with no hands — it's second nature. Keep your sketch pad and pencils around, use them as much as possible, and field sketching may become second nature to you, too (though you may want to keep a hand on your pencil).

Chapter 25

Birding Online (Nesting on the World Wide Web)

. . . .

In This Chapter

▶ Roadkill along the information superhighway?

▶ Getting there

▶ World Wide Jargon

▶ Commercial online services

▶ Some favorite Web sites

. . . .

*T*he Internet — the vast information highway that circles the globe via telephone cables — offers bird watchers with computers access to more information about birds and bird watching than they can possibly absorb in a lifetime.

The Internet enables you to talk to other bird watchers, visit museums, get news from scientific organizations, see bird checklists from parks and refuges, discover meetings and organizations, keep up with the latest news about rare birds, see tens of thousands of pictures, ask questions, and get answers. And that's a small fraction of the information available. New Web sites (Internet locations that are graphical sources of information) are being created every day. If you have a computer and a modem, you'll love birding on the information superhighway.

If you need help in how to access, navigate, and even master the Internet, see *The Internet For Dummies* by John Levine and Carol Baroudi, or *The World Wide Web For Dummies,* 2nd Edition, by Brad Hin, both from IDG Books Worldwide, Inc. If you're already cyber-savvy, read on and enter the wonderful world of online birding.

Bird Talk: Chat Groups

A chat group is just what is sounds like — a group of folks chatting, just as they would in the backyard during a summer barbecue. What's different about chatting on the Internet is that some of you are in New York, some in California, a few in Texas, and maybe one in Australia.

A chat group can either be live — where a bunch of online birders log on to the same Internet location at the same time and type comments to each other — or the chat group can operate as a bulletin board, where people post comments, questions, and so on, that can be seen by others when they log on to that location.

Rec.birds

One of the oldest and most active of the Internet bird bulletin boards is `rec.birds`. This bulletin board can get several hundred postings per day. And the postings aren't necessarily sorted by topic, which may mean that you have to wade through lots of postings on subjects that you don't care about. However, `rec.birds` is neat, if only because it's a meeting of bird brains from all over the world.

Listservs

Some bulletin-board-type discussion groups have an automated feature that sends all postings electronically to a list of subscribers. This subscriber list is known as a listserv.

Hundreds of bird-oriented listservs are on the Internet and WWW. The oldest and most popular of the bird chat groups is called BIRDCHAT.

To join the BIRDCHAT discussion group, send an e-mail to: `listserv@listserv.arizona.edu`

In the message area of your e-mail you should type:
Subscribe BIRDCHAT (your name)

In a few seconds, you get a message back via e-mail asking you to confirm that you want to join BIRDCHAT. This step prevents someone else subscribing you to various groups. Once you've confirmed, you're in. No fee or secret handshake is needed.

Birdy Web Sites

Navigating the ocean of Web sites that is available to the online bird watcher can be as confusing as finding your car in a crowded shopping mall parking lot during the winter holidays. I suggest that you start by visiting some of the major Web sites listed in this chapter, and use the active links contained in these sites to help you find other sites of interest.

✔ **Major ornithological organizations:** Most major ornithological organizations have Web sites. Lucky for the online birder, these major Web sites are listed as links on hundreds of other Web sites. For example, if I'm an avid birder in Ohio, my Web site may offer links to other Ohio bird Web sites, as well as to my favorite bird magazine, and to my favorite sites from all over the WWW.

✔ **Government agencies:** The U.S. Fish and Wildlife Service has a Web page that provides access to all their information on bird population trends, as well as maps of species distribution (see the "Some neat birding Web sites" section). They even have a quiz about birds. Lots of national wildlife refuges and parks have Web pages as well. Some of these sites include checklists of the birds found at the park or refuge. This use of a Web page is very helpful if you're planning a birding trip or outing.

✔ **Personal Web pages:** Personal Web pages are a very mixed bag. Some pages are interesting, some are slightly nutty because you can put anything you want on a personal Web page. No rules exist. I have visited some of the personal Web sites and Web pages put up by bird watchers. Quite a few provide interesting information, beautiful images, and even bird videos and bird sounds. Other sites give you way more than you ever wanted to know about somebody. Thank you for sharing.

✔ **Bird families and species:** Believe it or not, some bird species and even some individual birds have their own Web pages. Obviously they didn't create these sites themselves. As an example, consider the rare seabird (a marbled murrelet) that showed up in Ohio. Naturally, a lot of people went to see the bird, and a lot of people took pictures. Two days after the bird's discovery, the bird had its own Web page. It was full of photos of the bird, directions (including maps), and all sorts of discussions about why a seabird would go to Ohio (they never settled that one). The bird is long gone, but the Web page is still there.

Creating a thorough listing of all the fantastic Web sites for bird watchers is impossible. Literally thousands of sites are of interest to a bird person. Here are a few of the most popular, most helpful, or most interesting ones I've run across. Caveat: Web site addresses sometimes change. If an address listed below doesn't work, try using your Web browser's search engine to find the site's new address.

www.petersononline.com

Operated by Houghton-Mifflin, publishers of the Roger Tory Peterson field guide series. Also offers bulletin boards for posting questions on many subjects, and has regularly updated reports from most rare bird alerts of North America.

www.petersononline.com/birds/bwd/index.html

This is where you can sample material from the pages of *Bird Watcher's Digest*, *The BWD Skimmer* newsletter, and some of the backyard booklets produced by BWD Press.

www.audubon.org

The Web site for the National Audubon Society includes some chapter pages and a chapter directory (helpful for finding a bird club near you).

www.learner.org/content/k12/jnorth/

A great site for teachers who want to teach students about bird (and animal) migration. The site tracks the migratory progress of certain species and offers links to participating schools.

www.nmnh.si.edu/BIRDNET

Listings of all the North American bird publications and ornithological journals.

http://nbhc.com/birdmail.htm

The home site for BIRDCHAT, the very active listserv for online birders who like to share information, gossip, complain, and eavesdrop electronically on the online discussions of thousands of bird folks from all over the world. Post a question here and you're likely to get several hundred answers.

http://www.ntic.qc.ca/~nellus/links.html

This site from Canada features hundreds of links to bird sites all over the world, but with a special emphasis on North America. Includes links to bird clubs, ornithological societies, checklists, and many other fascinating WWW destinations.

www.mbr.nbs.gov/bbs/bbs.html

Offers an analysis of 30 years of data from North American Breeding Bird Surveys. Included is information on 500 bird species with distribution maps, and population trends for each species. Operated by the National Biological Survey.

```
http://users.aol.com/jimmcl/index.html
```
and
```
http://www.WSD.com/WSD/nabluebird
```

Both are great sites for bluebird information. The second site is operated by the North American Bluebird Association. Both feature links to other important bluebird sites.

```
http://www.derived.com/~lanny/hummers
```

This site bills itself as the most complete hummingbird site of the World Wide Web (visit it and you can be the judge of this claim). It has a regular column by hummer expert Nancy Newfield, and lots of information about hummingbird research, natural history, feeding tips, and links to other hummingbird sites.

```
http://www.gorp.com/gorp/activity/birding.htm
```

The Great Outdoors Recreation Pages (GORP) has an extensive amount of birding information, including lots of links to other sites around the world.

```
http://www.Webdirectory.com/
```

A site that provides information on the Web sites of loads of environmental organizations.

Commercial Online Services

Several major commercial online services have bird content available for users. Unlike the information on the Internet and World Wide Web, which can be viewed by anyone with Internet access, commercial services limit access to those folks who subscribe to their service.

Here are three commercial online services and the directions to their bird content.

America Online

Keyword: *Nature* gets you to The Nature Conservancy's area, which features an area called the Birding Forum. Inside the Birding Forum are bulletin boards listed by topic. A bulletin board for bird watchers is also available in the Hobby Central section of Life, Styles, and Interests, which is part of AOL's main directory. The Bird Watching Folder in Hobby Central features links to other important bird sites on the Internet.

The American Birders' Exchange is an informal group of AOL users who hold weekly live chat sessions. Schedules and contact names are listed in the Birding Forum (keyword: nature). An e-newsletter, *The Beakly News*, is available for a nominal fee and contains news from the world of birds, humorous accounts of birding adventures, and excerpts from other bird publications. To subscribe, send an e-mail note to MamaDuck1@aol.com, or to Kestrel923@aol.com.

Prodigy

You can reach the Birding Bulletin Board on Prodigy Classic (the commercial online service formerly known as simply Prodigy) via the jump word: **Hobbies BB**, and then by selecting the topic: Birding. The board's subjects are determined by participants, and include backyard birding, field birding, bluebirds, purple martins, and other subjects. On Prodigy Internet (which offers access to the WWW), the Good Birding community Web site can be accessed via the Go Word: **Birding**, or at: http://lifestyles.prodigy .net/hobbies/good_birding/index.htm.

Other services are offered by Prodigy as well, including an e-mailing list named Feathers, and weekly chat sessions. For more information, contact the Prodigy Birding Community Moderator, Hank Thompson, at: h_thompson@prodigy.net

CompuServe

CompuServe hosts the Birds Forum as part of its Petsforum group of forums. It's devoted to all areas of bird and avian life, from family pets to wild birds worth watching. The message sections and libraries cover such topics as large and small parrots, finches, pigeons, waterfowl, wild birds, and bird watching. To access the Birds Forum, type **GO BIRDS.**

Final Frontier

The Internet and World Wide Web offer unlimited possibilities for bird watchers. In the future, the amount and type of information you receive via an online computer will be greatly different from the current situation. People communicating about birds more efficiently and more rapidly can mean good things for the future of bird conservation, and for the future of bird watching.

Chapter 26

Other Flying Creatures

*T*he late bird master Roger Tory Peterson often referred to warblers as the butterflies of the bird world because of their striking beauty. I often refer to butterflies as the silent warblers of the insect world. Well, they *are* beautiful like warblers, but of course they can't sing. Or maybe they just sing very, very softly.

In this chapter, I explain why lots of bird watchers have gotten into looking at flying things other than birds — such as butterflies, dragonflies, and bats. And I offer advice on how you can get into these things, too, if you so desire.

Enjoying Butterflies

If you tried, you'd be hard-pressed to find somebody who doesn't like butterflies. And if you did find such a person, that person would probably be some world authority on dung beetles who thought butterflies were simply too gaudy to be serious insects.

Most of the serious bird watchers I know also enjoy butterflies, and why not? Butterfly watching is a natural extension of birding. Butterflies fly. They're beautiful to look at. You can identify them as to species. And you can attract them to your backyard with many of the same plants you offer to birds.

What's more, butterflies are active and flying during the sunniest, hottest times of the day, when most birds are quiet and resting. These noontime hours are the best times to shift your focus to the insect world (assuming you're not sipping something cool in the air-conditioned comfort of the indoors during the sunniest, hottest times of the day).

Even if you don't plan to get as deeply involved with butterflies as you are with birds, you may want to keep your eyes open for butterflies while you are out looking for birds.

Where butterflies fly

Where there are plants, there are butterflies. During the warm season, almost any habitat in North America features several species of butterflies. Even though you may think of butterflies as fragile creatures, they are actually very hardy insects. They are found all over the planet, in all types of habitat and climate. In fact, some parts of North America have butterflies that survive the winter by seeking cover in sheltered spots. These are the species you sometimes see flying about on a warm winter's day.

In addition to liking flowers and blooming plants that produce nectar, most butterfly species like sunlight. A good way to find butterflies is to seek places that offer a diversity of flowering plants basking in sunlight. If you don't have this natural combination in your own backyard, go find it. Rural roads during the warmest time of the year will surely have an abundance of wildflowers and other flowering plants to which butterflies are attracted.

If you are really desperate to see butterflies, visit your local garden center in the summer. The rows of flowering plants are sure to have some butterflies flitting amongst them. This is also a good way to see which plants are preferred by the butterflies in your area.

Butterfly-viewing optics

Not all birding binoculars are useful for watching butterflies. I have a pair of 10x40 binoculars that are great for bird watching and lousy for butterfly watching. They cannot focus on things that are closer than 15 feet from me. So when I see a butterfly at my feet, I have to back up 15 feet before I can focus on it. This is annoying. The best optics for butterflying are close-focusing, compact models in the 7- to 9-power range. You don't need lots of magnification because most butterflies you look at will be within 20 feet of you. You can get a decent pair of lightweight, compact binoculars starting at about $50. Or you can learn to backpedal a lot. That's what I do.

Name that butterfly

Identifying butterflies, like IDing birds, is easier when you start with the big, obvious species. Monarchs, the members of the swallowtail family, and some of the fritillaries are the easiest species to see and to identify.

The helpful thing about butterflies is that they perch often. And if they find a good nectar source, such as a flowering plant with lots of blossoms, they stick around for awhile. Take advantage of this behavior to get good, long looks at butterflies.

For centuries, the method of butterfly watching involved catching the insects with a net and killing them for easy study in the hand or for mounting in a display case. This parallels the old "shotgun school" of bird watching. Doing this is no longer considered necessary. Many butterfly species are threatened with extinction due primarily to loss of habitat, but it doesn't do the butterfly populations any good when individual specimens are snuffed out by avid butterfliers. Today you can identify and enjoy butterflies from a respectful distance by using small binoculars, much as birders use their optics.

Butterfly field marks

Butterfly ID is similar to bird ID in that you look for key field marks for each species. Most of the key field marks on butterflies are associated with the wings. If you see an unfamiliar butterfly, concentrate on its wing markings and ask yourself these questions:

- ✔ Are there spots, stripes, or bars on the wings?
- ✔ If the wings have spots, stripes, or bars, how many are there, and where on the wings are they located?

Butterfly wings can be quite different when viewed from above (upperwing) and from below (underwing). Be sure to get a look at both sides, if you can. Note the butterfly's overall color, too. Is the butterfly a fast flyer? With these clues, you can get a good idea of the true identity of the butterflies you encounter.

When you encounter the small, drab butterflies known as skippers and duskywings — the fall warblers of the insect world — you need a good butterfly field guide to help you. Several of the best butterfly guides are listed in the Appendix.

Butterfly behavior

You can hang around a candy store and pretty soon you see kids going inside to feed their cravings for sweets. Later on, you can hang around a dentist's office and see many of these same kids.

Butterflies have their food preferences, too. Certain plants are key to the life cycle of each butterfly species. But it's not just plants that attract butterflies. Some species seek mineral nutrients from damp soil, such as that around a mud puddle. In the summer, you may encounter a bunch of butterflies gathered around a moist area of soil. This behavior is called *mud puddling*. Butterflies engaged in this behavior are easy to approach for a close look.

Some other butterfly attractants are rotting fruit and even animal droppings. In both cases, butterflies are attracted by the strong smell. We may not consider stuff like this food, but the butterflies sure do.

You can make your own stinky concoction to attract butterflies. Combine some rotting fruit (apples, plums, pears, bananas, or anything with sweet, sticky juice) with sugar, stale beer, and some molasses. Let this concoction ferment in a jar overnight, or until very smelly, and then place it in a shallow dish in the sunlight. Remember to put it downwind from any open windows.

Flower power

The very best way to attract butterflies is with flowering plants. Butterflies and hummingbirds share a love for flower nectar as a food. For a partial list of nectar-producing flowers, see the hummingbird portion of Chapter 11.

In my yard, the best butterfly plants are butterfly weed, buddleia, Coreopsis, purple coneflower, zinnias, asters, marigolds, and lantana. Our farm fields produce lots of other great butterfly plants, such as wild butterfly weed, wild asters, Joe-Pye weed, ironweed, and several species of goldenrod, among others.

Ask your friendly local garden center operator to recommend the best flowering plants for your region and hardiness zone. It's likely that your yard or property already has some wild plants that butterflies love, but a little augmentation only attracts more butterflies.

A variety of plant species, planted in concentrated beds, can become a butterfly magnet. Butterflies, like hummingbirds, are attracted to large patches of brightly colored flowers.

Pesticide-free is the way to be. Some of the chemicals that gardeners commonly use to control insect pests indiscriminately kill butterfly larvae and eggs. If you can keep even part of your property chemical-free, the butterflies will thank you.

Butterfly feeders and houses

Although many brands and styles of butterfly roosting houses and butterfly feeders are on the market, whether butterflies use them is still a subject of debate. I have never had any luck with either butterfly houses or feeders, but our property has no shortage of shelter or food. I have heard anecdotal evidence that butterflies use houses for roosting, and I have seen one or two using well-stocked feeders (stocked with both rotten banana pieces and hummingbird nectar). I suggest you try one or both items in your backyard to see if they work for your butterflies. Remember, bluebirds didn't always nest in nest boxes, so it is possible that butterflies, over generations, will learn to accept human-offered housing and feeders.

More butterfly info

Several national organizations are devoted to butterfly study. They are:

- ✔ **The North American Butterfly Association (NABA)**
  4 Delaware Road, Morristown, New Jersey 07960

- ✔ **The Xerces Society**
  10 S.W. Ash Street, Portland, Oregon 97204

- ✔ **The Lepidopterists' Society**
  Natural History Museum of Los Angeles County
  900 Exposition Boulevard, Los Angeles, California 90007

Other Flying Insects

An interest in butterflies can lead to an interest in other things that fly and buzz around your yard and garden. Two of the most appealing alternatives to watching birds and butterflies are watching dragonflies and moths.

Dragonflies

A couple of my friends who are deeply into butterflies have told me that the next big craze to hit bird watching will be an interest in dragonflies. I can see what they mean. Dragonflies are beautiful to watch. Their flying skills rival those of hummingbirds. And they are commonly seen during the hot parts of the summer days, when most birds are inactive. But I am not rushing to launch *Dragonfly Watcher's Digest* anytime soon.

The best place to look for dragonflies is around bodies of water, especially ponds, lakes, and pools. Dragonflies need water for egg-laying, and many species spend their entire lives within a short distance of a water source. However, you may also encounter dragonflies and the closely related damselflies in the midst of large meadows or along a woodland path.

One challenge to dragonfly watching is that there is no single continent-wide field-guide source for field identification. Some insect field guides include the common dragonfly species, and some regional guides exist, but no one book covers the more than 450 dragonfly and damselfly species that occur in North America. I am sure this situation will soon be remedied, as the interest in North American dragonflies continues to grow.

Moths

Moths are the mostly nocturnal version of butterflies, and the two insect types are closely related. Although some moths are active during the day, the vast majority are creatures of the night. Most of the more than 100,000 moth species found worldwide have a wing structure that produces a herky-jerky flight pattern, unlike the smooth, graceful flight of most butterflies. In North America alone there are 10,500 species of moths. That's 14 times as many species as there are of butterflies, of which North America has 765 species.

Not all moths are the kinds that fly out of the flour in your kitchen, or that eat holes in your favorite sweater. Some folks think of moths as dull, drab, and ugly. Many moths, such as the silk moths, are bigger and more beautiful than butterflies. I think of moths as more subtly beautiful than butterflies. Moths are also less active than butterflies, especially when they are attracted to a source of light.

You can very easily attract moths for a closer look. Moths love to be around bright lights that shine at night. To lure a mess of moths into your midst, leave an outside light on for a few hours after sunset on a warm summer night. You may attract hundreds of moths in an amazing array of shapes, sizes, and colors.

If you really want to get into moth watching, get a good field guide. Moth species can be frustratingly similar in appearance. In fact, many of the difficult moth ID questions are answered only with long periods of close examination (with a magnifying glass!) of captured specimens. Some moth watchers use small, clear-plastic containers with a lid that is a magnifying lens. Catch a moth, put it inside the container, and gawk at will. These devices (I've seen them for sale at toy and nature stores marketed as "bug bottles") permit you to get a close look at a tiny moth before releasing it.

Bats

Bats are mammals that can really fly, unlike flying squirrels that merely glide. Because bats fly as birds do, eat insects captured in flight, and live near humans, you'd think they'd warrant at least some of the respect that we give to birds. But bats get almost no respect. Why? Because bats have been symbols of mystery, darkness, and evil for centuries. We shouldn't blame these furry creatures for the bad information (and bad acting) presented to us in scores of vampire movies! We should think for ourselves!

The truth about bats

Bats are harmless animals. Not only do they present practically no threat to humans and human health, they actually provide valuable natural services to the environment. Being voracious insect-eaters, as many of our North American species are, bats keep harmful insects such as mosquitoes and many agricultural pests in check. Fruit-eating bats of the tropical forests naturally spread regenerating plant seeds, which helps to keep ecosystems diverse.

As for disease, you stand a greater risk of getting rabies from a rabid dog than you do from a bat bite. Very few bats carry rabies, and most sick bats die without ever coming into contact with any humans.

Bats in your belfry

Bats neither attack nor want to have anything to do with us humans. When a bat finds its way into your house — probably while looking for a safe place to roost such as an attic or chimney — the best way to get rid of it is to open all the windows and sit quietly until it finds its way out. Bats navigate and find food using echolocation, a natural type of radar that helps bats "see" by using their ears. With this technique, bats can find tiny flying insects and so can easily find an open window through which they can exit your house.

If you find you have to capture a bat to remove it from your house, wait until the bat lands, and then place a large can or bucket over it. Slide a piece of cardboard or stiff paper under the container to cover the opening and take the bat outside for release.

A home for bats

These days, many people are anxious to have bats in their yards and gardens, where the bats' insect-controlling help is welcomed. New advances in bat house design have made it possible to host bats quite easily. If you purchase or build a bat house, be sure to place it 15 to 20 feet high on a tree trunk, pole, or building where the sunlight will strike it for several hours each day. In most parts of North America, placing a bat house on a southern exposure does the trick. Bats use artificial housing for roosting, reproduction, and/or nesting, just as birds do.

More batty info

Lots of sources exist for good information about bats, including government extension services and agricultural offices. Three of the continent's most prominent bat organizations are:

- ✓ **The Organization for Bat Conservation**
  2300 Epley Road, Williamston, Michigan 48895

- ✓ **Bat Conservation International**
  P.O. Box 162603, Austin, Texas 78716-2693

- ✓ **Bat Conservation Society of Canada**
  P.O. Box 56042, Airways Postal Outlet, Calgary, Alberta, Canada T2E 8K5

Part VI
The Part of Tens

The 5th Wave   By Rich Tennant

"So far? A finch, a sparrow, a couple of UFOs, but nothing interesting."

In this part . . .

In this part, I get to make some lists of stuff that are both fun and informative — such as when binoculars may not be such a good idea, myths about birds that just won't go away, and my all-time favorite spots to watch birds.

Chapter 27

Ten (+ Ten) Tips for When (And When Not) to Use Your Binoculars

- -

In This Chapter

▶ To have or have not

▶ Honest Officer, I'm BIRD watching!

▶ Lots of birds, no optics

▶ Under the front seat

▶ Looking at the sun

- -

*B*inoculars are the main tool of the trade for a bird watcher. It's mighty difficult to watch birds without them. But even the most ardent bird watcher should understand that there are times — few and far between though they may be — when it isn't intelligent, prudent, proper, or courteous to use your binoculars. The first half of this chapter explains this in detail.

On the other hand, there are times, places, and situations that scream out for your binoculars. The second half of this chapter gives you ten tips for knowing when to be sure and have your binocs at hand.

Places to avoid when using binocs or bird watching

Birds are everywhere, and seeing them is always a thrill. Sometimes, however, you need to curb your bird-tracking impulses and wait for a better time or place (or both) to exercise your bird-watching skills.

✔ **From the bushes near a nudist colony:** Nobody will believe that you're just watching birds.

✔ **Near a missile silo:** I was once almost arrested for using my binocs to look at some burrowing owls. I had absolutely no idea there was a military installment nearby until the security dudes came up and started asking some pointed questions. I tried to show them the owls, but the owls would not cooperate, adding further to the weakness of my excuse for being there.

✔ **During your own wedding (or wedding night):** Unless you're marrying a bird watcher who shares your full-time enthusiasm for feathered creatures, this is one time you may want to leave the bins in the car.

I once saw a bumper sticker that advertised Frank's Fishing Charters. It said "My wife said she'd leave me if I went fishin' one more time . . . Man, I'm gonna miss her." The same is true for lots of bird watchers (of both sexes) that I know. Be sensitive to your non-birding (future) spouse's feelings.

✔ **Any funeral:** Cemeteries are often excellent for bird watching because the habitat is good and the location is quiet and undisturbed. But there are limits to maximizing your birding opportunities. Avoid areas where a funeral is taking place.

✔ **While driving any vehicle:** Bird watching while driving is both dangerous and unwise. And I have the insurance premiums to prove it.

✔ **Underwater:** Snorkeling is my other favorite critter-watching activity. An added bonus is having no expensive optics around your neck.

✔ **Anywhere near a hostile international border:** I went bird watching in the Middle East once. There were lots of places where our guide asked that we not use our binoculars. Before you go birding in a foreign land, it's a good idea to check with the U.S. State Department (or its Canadian equivalent) for any travelers' warnings that may apply.

✔ **On a New York City subway:** I used to take the A-train from Manhattan all the way out to Jamaica Bay National Wildlife Refuge in the farthest reaches of Queens. The train went through some pretty scary areas. Just to be safe, I always tucked my binocs deep inside my coat or backpack.

Then again, binocs can be a good weapon. I once fended off a mugger in Central Park by threatening to conk him over the head with my optics.

✔ **During a solar eclipse:** Just in case you forgot your third-grade teacher's admonition, don't ever look at the sun with your binoculars. Your eyes will fry, and that's no lie, sweetie pie. Try the two-pinholes-in-a-cardboard-box trick instead.

Ten best places to have your binoculars handy

Just as there are times to wait and leave your binocs safely out-of-hand, at other times missing your binocs could mean missing a lifetime opportunity. Following are spots that cry out for binocs-at-the-ready:

- ✔ **By the window that views your feeders:** You never know when something neat may show up. A woman wrote to me at *Bird Watcher's Digest* a few years ago to ask about a two-headed bird she'd seen at her feeders. I didn't believe it until I saw the photographs she sent in a second letter. A two-headed junco, plain as day! This person was prepared! She not only had her binoculars handy, but also had a loaded camera ready to document the moment. And those photos were the only ones we've heard of, of a free-living, two-headed bird: an ornithological first.

- ✔ **In your car:** Many bird watchers have an inexpensive or old pair of binoculars tucked under the front seat. This is very handy for unexpected encounters with birds, or nudist colonies. Just remember to stop the car before you begin birding if you're the driver.

- ✔ **In your briefcase or backpack:** Some of the best birds you may ever get a chance to see will cross your path when you least expect it, so it's a good idea to be ready. Plus, if you have a boring job, you can scan the skies (or neighboring office buildings) out your office window.

- ✔ **In your carry-on luggage:** You'd hate yourself (not to mention the airline) if the airline lost your binocs, along with the other stuff in your suitcase. Having your bins in your personal (carry-on) luggage allows you to start watching birds as soon as the plane hits the runway.

- ✔ **On any boat trip:** I went along with some college buddies on one of those barf-a-minute, all-day, beer-swilling fishing charters off the coast of North Carolina. The day was calm, the sea was flat, the fish were asleep and not biting, and I saw thousands of seabirds. Problem was I didn't have my binoculars. By the time the boat finally docked, I was almost in tears, knowing I'd missed at least ten life birds through sheer stupidity.

- ✔ **On any overseas trip:** "*Perdoname Señor. ¿Donde se puede comprar telescopio para observar pajaros?*"

   Translation: "Excuse me, sir. Where can I buy binoculars for bird watching?"

   This is what you'll be asking total strangers in any tropical Spanish-speaking country in Central or South America if you forget to take your optics. You WILL be seeing lots of birds. You'll be desperate for optical assistance.

✔ **When going to an outdoor picnic, concert, or ballpark:** It's amazing how many birds show up at these things, too. Any outdoor event is bound to have birds flying overhead (or nesting in the rafters). And, optics help if you have crummy seats. Once you've taken binoculars to a concert, you'll never leave them home again. You can watch the lead guitarist's fingers fly or watch the sweat drip off the drummer's brow.

✔ **When walking to the mailbox (compost pile, garage, and so on):** I repeat the *Bird Watching For Dummies* mantra: *You never know when some neat bird will appear.* Okay. Now you say it. . . .

✔ **When you think: "There won't be any birds there; I don't need my binocs."** DEFINITELY take them along. Remember the mantra.

✔ **Anywhere you go during spring or fall bird migration:** Over much of North America, during certain months, birds are their most active and are most numerous. In general terms, these periods are April through June (spring migration and breeding season) and August through October (fall migration and wintering grounds concentrations).

Of course, a blanket statement such as this doesn't encompass all regions — in other words, anywhere is not really anywhere. For example:

- Southern Arizona doesn't really have spring migration *fall-outs* when large numbers of birds pass through in huge waves, comprising thousands of individual birds.

- Florida has lots of wintering birds, but can be somewhat quiet birdwise at midday in mid-summer.

You get the idea. Notice the times of year when birds are most evident in your area, and adjust your binocular-toting accordingly.

Chapter 28
Bill's Ten Favorite Hotspots

- -

In This Chapter

▶ You get 11 for the price of 10

▶ From the stinky to the sublime

▶ Green chile cheeseburgers

▶ Honorable mentions

- -

*O*n the advice of several attorneys, I want to say up front that this chapter contains totally biased selections for my favorite bird watching hotspots in North America. This is NOT an all-inclusive list by any means. You can find your own places of wonderment. These are mine. Each one of these places has yielded great birding delights to me at one time or another.

Here are my fave hotspots, listed in the order of preference.

High Island, Texas

Unbelievable spring migrant fall-outs happen at High Island. Where else can you see a small tree bedecked with painted buntings, indigo buntings, scarlet tanagers, and Baltimore orioles?

From High Island, it's a great thrill to work your way southward down the coast. Birding spots abound in coastal Texas, which is the reason for the recently created Great Texas Coastal Birding Trail, an organized driving tour from one hotspot to the next. You can take a month and not hit half the sites.

Some bird watchers may disagree with my choice of a Texas spot as my number one, but I just love Texas. I've never had a bad trip to the Lone Star state, and I never expect to, either!

Southeastern Arizona

Any place south of Tucson is great for a visiting birder from the North or East. Hummingbirds, hawks, roadrunners, desert species, vagrant birds from Mexico — southern Arizona has them all. I can't pick just one spot to list here because there are so many great ones.

I do recommend that, if you're a first-time visitor to Arizona, start out at the Arizona Sonora Desert Museum, just south of Tucson. Here you can get a feel for the wildlife of Arizona and practice your bird ID skills at the aviaries and environs. Don't miss the hummingbird exhibits.

If you're a serious bird watcher, sooner or later you'll want to make the pilgrimage to Arizona. Tell them I sent you.

Ding Darling National Wildlife Refuge, Sanibel Island, Florida

Ding Darling is the best place to see all the waterbirds at once, and you can do it from the comfort of your own car. Located on beautiful Sanibel Island, along Florida's Gulf coast, Ding is a terrific place to take the entire family.

The great birder Roger Tory Peterson once remarked that people like Ding Darling because they can see all the glamour birds there. The glamour birds are the large, graceful herons, egrets, ibis, and spoonbills that congregate in the refuge's mangrove swamps. Red-shouldered hawks sit within arm's length of your car alongside the refuge roads. These birds are all large and easy to see. And bored kids can find alligators to see. I have heard more than one adult bird watcher mentioning hungry gators to unruly kids at this site.

Point Pelee, Ontario, Canada

Point Pelee is THE place in North America to maximize your spring migrant songbird watching. Birds coming north across Lake Erie look for the first bit of *terra firma,* and this jutting peninsula is it! On amazing fall-out days, you have to watch where you step because the ground may be crawling with warblers, tanagers, thrushes, vireos, and other migrants, exhausted from migration.

Look at Pelee on a map, and you see a vivid example of how geography can determine where birds will end up, thus creating a hotspot. Point Pelee is at the tip of a long peninsula that juts southward into Lake Erie, so it acts as a funnel in the fall (for southbound migrating birds), and as a magnet in the spring (for northbound migrating birds). Better yet, go there and experience it for yourself.

Bonus tip: Nearby Point Pelee is Long Point Provincial Park, another great place for birding during migration. Long Point has just as many birds and a lot fewer people!

Cape May, New Jersey

Equally good in the spring or the fall, but perhaps best-known for its fall hawk flights, Cape May has become the birding mecca of the Northeast. Any weekend in spring or fall, you can't swing your binoculars by the strap without hitting at least two dozen birders. I once joked that it should be against the law in Cape May to yell "vermilion flycatcher!" in a crowded theater because it would get the same response as if you yelled "Fire!"

The guy I was talking to looked at me wide-eyed and said "Where did you see a vermilion flycatcher?"

The Victorian charm of Cape May, beaches, and fishing opportunities are good for distracting non-birding spouses/significant others.

Tied with. . . .

Rocky Mountain National Park, Colorado

My first visit to Colorado was also my first visit to the mountainous West. I'd been to coastal California, but never to a high-altitude spot in the Rocky Mountains. I was blown away! Now I know what John Denver was (and probably still is) singing about.

Lots of high-altitude bird species (ptarmigan, rosy finches, gray jays), plus bighorn sheep, glaciers, and breathtaking (literally and figuratively) scenery. I love nothing more than sitting by a rushing Colorado stream, just waiting for the American dipper to come zooming past. You can't do things like this in Ohio.

Salton Sea, California

This is a gigantic, low-desert lake that draws water-loving species from all over. Ducks, geese, shorebirds, and the occasional vagrant booby make this site worth a visit at any time of year. Take water, sunscreen, and a clothespin for your nose — some parts can get kinda stinky from agricultural runoff. But you can't top the birds!

Plum Island, Massachusetts

One of New England's primo coastal birding spots, these unspoiled coastal dunes and saltmarsh attract many species of waterbirds, especially shore-birds and ducks. When I lived in New York City, I always tried to make at least one trip to Plum Island in the spring and one in the fall or winter. Among the life birds I've seen at Plum Island are Iceland gull (in the winter), roseate tern, and piping plover. Three nice-looking birds!

Bosque del Apache NWR, Socorro, New Mexico

Visit this national wildlife refuge (NWR) in the winter and you can experi-ence the magnificence of wintering sandhill cranes and snow geese by the hundreds of thousands. Also lots of ducks, hawks, and eagles. When you're done looking at birds, visit the nearby Owl Bar and have a green chile cheeseburger. ¡Ay caramba! They're good!

Malheur NWR, Burns, Oregon

Lots of water here means lots of waterbirds. Especially nice are nesting sandhill cranes, long-billed curlews, and trumpeter swans. The drive across Oregon to this place in the southeastern part of the state is a treat too (golden eagles, mountain bluebirds, and more).

Hawk Mountain Sanctuary, Kempton, Pennsylvania

The view from the North Lookout, even without any birds, is worth the long hike up the mountain from the visitor's center. But if you hit it on a fall day when the wind is just right, you'll see a large chunk of the migrant hawks in eastern North America as they fly southward along the Kittatinny Ridge.

Honorable Mention:

Lower Rio Grande Valley, Texas; Southeastern Alaska; Pribilof Islands, Alaska; Cheyenne Bottoms, Kansas; Platte River in Nebraska; Chincoteague NWR in Virginia; Jamaica Bay NWR in New York; Dauphin Island, Alabama; Churchill, Manitoba; Dolly Sods, West Virginia. I could list about 45 others, too. But I think I'll keep a few of them "secret."

Chapter 29

Ten Bird Myths

*J*ust about the time you're ready to consider yourself an intermediate bird watcher, along come people who aren't bird watchers making wildly inaccurate and sweeping statements about birds, and looking to you to confirm their facts — or challenge their accuracy.

This situation puts you in the somewhat squirmy position of having to be an expert on birds. That's human nature: Anyone who knows more about a certain subject than you do must be an expert — and, in this case, you're the expert.

To help you prepare for your transformation into a bird expert, I prepared the following set of tens: The Top Ten Great Bird Myths.

May the farce be with you.

Top Ten Great Bird Myths

Birds are fascinating creatures that live all around us, but there's a lot we think we know about them that isn't so. Sort of like, familiarity breeds fantasy. Here is my list of the top ten myths people believe about birds, along with the facts — and nothing but the facts. So here goes.

Hummingbirds migrate on the backs of geese

How this got started I may never know. But it is one of the most fervently believed myths about birds and nature that there is. Perhaps when Elvis comes out of hiding he can set us straight on the subject. Although it seems logical for hummingbirds to hitch a ride, in reality they have to make it through spring and fall migration on their own two wings.

Take down the feeders so the hummingbirds will migrate

Hey, the hummers leave when the geese do. Those Vs of geese in the sky are actually pointing out for hummingbirds the direction of the nearest hummingbird feeder.

Seriously, though, hummingbirds know instinctively when to migrate. Nothing you do short of capturing them (which is illegal) can keep them longer than they want to stay.

Birds will starve if we stop feeding

This isn't really true. Yes, feeding stations may help more birds survive during extremely harsh winter weather, but birds don't rely exclusively on your feeders for their sustenance. Birds have wings and tend to use them. If there is food within flying distance, most birds can survive just fine.

A baby bird on the ground has always fallen from the nest

Many ground-dwelling species have young that can survive very well on the ground, even before they're able to fly. Killdeer, quail, turkeys, and ducks are among the species that have young which survive for long periods on the ground.

The best thing to do if you find a baby bird on the ground is to leave it where it is. A parent may be taking care of it. Watch from a distance to see if the parents are in attendance. Even if you don't see an adult bird nearby, chances are that the parents are near and the nestling will be fine. Most baby birds leave the nest before they're able to fly very well, so the occasional landing on the ground is perfectly normal. If you're certain the bird has fallen from the nest, but you cannot locate the nest or can't return the bird to it, call a licensed bird rehabilitator for help. Remember, it is illegal to handle or possess native wild birds. You must have a special permit to do so. See Chapter 21 for more information on bird rehabilitators.

Don't touch a baby bird because the mother will smell your scent and abandon it

It's never a good idea to touch or handle a baby bird. But if you do handle a baby bird, you won't doom the youngster to abandonment because birds have almost no sense of smell. Predatory mammals, on the other hand, can smell quite well. What you might be doing by handling a baby bird, or by peering into an active bird nest you have discovered, is laying down a scent path for a hungry raccoon, opossum, skunk, or fox. These mammals know that human scent often means an easy meal. Think about it: dog dishes, compost piles, garbage cans, picnic areas, dumpsters behind fast food restaurants. These human-scented items and places are all positive associations for a hungry mammal.

For this reason I always avoid bird nests, and I try never to touch nestlings or eggs.

Robins are always a sign of spring

In some areas of North America, robins probably are a sign of spring. But robins don't migrate away from cold weather in all areas. They do change their behavior from lawn-hopping earthworm hunters to woodland-dwelling berry eaters.

Some better signs of spring are the first *peent*ing woodcock, the first hummingbird at the garden flowers, or the first bird fighting its reflection in your kitchen window.

Each spring, the swallows return faithfully to Capistrano

Most of the swallows in San Juan de Capistrano, California, are cliff swallows and are mostly resident birds, which means that they don't all go away in the winter. Because they never leave, they cannot return. But it's a great story just the same.

The bald eagle is a fierce predator

In reality, bald eagles are turkey vultures with a press agent. Bald eagles, the symbol of the United States, are more scavengers than fierce killers. They would much rather swoop down to feed on a dead fish than have to get all wet trying actually to catch one. When they hunt, they do a good job of it.

Bald eagles aren't really bald, either. Am I bursting your bubble?

John James Audubon is the father of American bird protection

In reality, Audubon shot birds left and right. In his day, before binoculars, bird watching was done over the sights of a gun. Birds were killed and then carefully examined in the hand. At least Audubon ate most of the birds he killed, and reported in his journals on the relative taste of all of the species upon which he dined.

All vultures are "buzzards." All gulls are "seagulls."

Buzzards are actually European *Buteo* hawks, related to our red-tailed and rough-legged hawks. This term is in common use in Europe, but for some reason is improperly used by non-bird watchers in North America to refer to North American vultures.

Many of our North American gulls live their lives out with only an occasional glimpse of the sea. Although some species are closely associated with salt water, two species that nest well-inland are the Franklin's gull and ring-billed gull. We have Richard Bach's *Jonathan Livingston Seagull* to thank for cementing that one in popular culture.

Appendix

Following is a list of resources helpful to bird watchers.

Audio

Backyard Bird Walk: Bird Walks by Habitat - Volume 1. Lang Elliott. NorthWord Press, 1994. $12.95 (1 cassette), $16.95 (compact disc).

Know Your Bird Sounds, Volume Two: Birds of the Countryside. Lang Elliott. NorthWord Press, 1994. $12.95 (1 cassette), $16.95 (compact disc).

Birding by Ear, Eastern/Central (Peterson Field Guides). Richard K. Walton and Robert W. Lawson. Houghton Mifflin Company, 1989. $35.00 (3 cassettes), $40.00 (compact disc).

More Birding by Ear, Eastern/Central (Peterson Field Guides). Richard K. Walton and Robert W. Lawson. Houghton Mifflin Company, 1994. $35.00 (3 compact discs).

Stokes Field Guide to Bird Songs (Eastern Region). Lang Elliott with Donald and Lillian Stokes. Time Warner AudioBooks, 1997. $29.98 (3 cassettes).

Bird Conservation Information

Bander Training
The Institute for Bird Populations
P.O. Box 1346
Point Reyes Station, CA 94956
415-663-2051

Partners in Flight Information
National Fish and Wildlife Foundation
1120 Connecticut Ave., N.W., Suite 900
Washington, D.C. 20036
202-857-0166

Wings of the Americas
The Nature Conservancy
1815 N. Lynn Street
Arlington, VA 22209
703-841-5300
www.tnc.org

Books for Bird Watchers

1001 Questions Answered About Birds. Allan D. Cruickshank and Helen G. Cruickshank. Dover Publications, Inc., 1976. $6.95 (paperback).

The Audubon Society Encyclopedia of North American Birds. John K. Terres. Alfred A. Knopf, 1980. $75.00 (hardcover).

The Birder's Handbook. Paul R. Ehrlich, David S. Dobkin, and Darryl Wheye. Fireside, Simon & Schuster, 1988. $17.00 (paperback).

Birding for Beginners. Shiela Buff. Lyons and Burford, 1993. $14.95 (paperback).

Birds in Jeopardy: The Imperiled and Extinct Birds of the United States and Canada Including Hawaii and Puerto Rico. Paul R. Ehrlich, David S. Dobkin, and Darryle Wheye. Stanford University Press, 1992. $49.50 (hardcover), $18.95 (paperback).

Birds of the World: A Check List, 4th edition. James F. Clements. Ibis Publishing Company, 1991. $29.95 (hardcover).

Bluebirds Forever. Connie Toops. Voyageur Press, Inc., 1994. $22.95 (paperback).

Bring Back the Birds: What you can do to save threatened species. Russell Greenberg and Jamie Reaser. Stackpole Books, 1995. $19.95 (paperback).

The Complete Birder. Jack Conner. Houghton Mifflin Co., 1987. $8.95 (paperback).

A Complete Guide to Bird Feeding. John V. Dennis. Alfred A. Knopf, 1994. $18.00 (paperback).

The Dictionary of American Bird Names, revised edition. Ernest A. Choate. The Harvard Common Press, 1985. $10.95 (paperback).

Enjoying Bird Feeding More. Julie Zickefoose. Bird Watcher's Digest Press, 1995. $3.95 (paperback).

Enjoying Bluebirds More. Julie Zickefoose. Bird Watcher's Digest Press, 1993. $3.95 (paperback).

Enjoying Hummingbirds More, William H. Thompson, III, editor. Bird Watcher's Digest Press, 1992. $3.95 (paperback).

Enjoying Purple Martins More. Richard A. Wolinski. Bird Watcher's Digest Press, 1995. $3.95 (paperback).

A Guide to Bird Behavior. Stokes Nature Guides. Little, Brown and Company. 1989. $10.95 per volume (3 volumes) (paperback).

A Guide to Bird Homes. Scott Shalaway. Bird Watcher's Digest Press, 1995. $3.95 (paperback).

Guide to the National Wildlife Refuges, revised and expanded. Laura and William Riley. Collier Books, 1997. $16.00 (paperback).

A Guide to Western Bird Feeding. John V. Dennis. Bird Watcher's Digest Press, 1991. $9.95 (paperback).

Hawks in Flight. Pete Dunne, David Sibley, and Clay Sutton. Houghton Mifflin Company, 1988. $11.95 (paperback).

How to Attract Birds. Jessie Wood, editor. Ortho Books, 1983. $9.95 (paperback).

How to Attract Hummingbirds & Butterflies. John V. Dennis and Mathew Tekulsky. Ortho Books, 1991. $9.95 (paperback).

How Birds Fly. John K. Terres. Stackpole Books, 1994. $16.95 (paperback).

How to Choose Binoculars. Alan R. Hale. C & A Publishing, 1991. $14.95 (paperback).

Hummingbird Gardens. Nancy L. Newfield and Barbara Nielsen. Chapters Publishing Ltd., 1996. $19.95 (paperback).

An Illustrated Guide to Attracting Birds. Susan Warton, editor. Sunset Publishing Corporation, 1990. $9.99 (paperback).

Landscaping for Wildlife. Carrol L. Henderson. Minnesota's Bookstore, 1987. $10.95 (paperback).

Lives of North American Birds. Kenn Kaufman. Houghton Mifflin, Co. 1997. $35.00 (cloth).

Nikon Guide to Wildlife Photography. B. "Moose" Peterson. Silver Pixel Press, 1993. $29.95 (paperback).

The Original Birdhouse Book, 8th edition. Don McNeil. Bird Watcher's Digest Press, 1993. $7.95 (paperback).

Ornithology, 2nd edition. Frank B. Gill. W.H. Freeman and Company, 1995. $55.95 (hardcover).

Outdoor Optics. Leif J. Robinson. Lyons & Burford, 1990. $13.95 (paperback).

The Pleasures of Watching Birds. Lola Oberman. Walker & Co., 1986. $12.95 (paperback).

Raptors: The Birds of Prey. Scott Weidensaul. Lyons & Burford, 1996. $40.00 (hardcover).

Songbirds in Your Garden, 5th edition. John K. Terres. Algonquin Books of Chapel Hill, 1994. $14.95 (paperback).

Wild Bird Photography. Tim Gallagher. Lyons & Burford, 1995. $15.95 (paperback).

Books: Field Guides

Field Guide to the Birds of North America, 2nd edition. Jon L. Dunn, Eirik A.T. Blom, chief consultants. The National Geographic Society, 1987. $16.95 (paperback).

All the Birds of North America. Jack L. Griggs. HarperCollins, 1997. $19.95 (paperback).

Stokes Field Guide to Birds: Eastern or Western Region. Donald and Lillian Stokes. Little, Brown and Company, 1996. $16.95 (paperback).

A Field Guide to the Birds East of the Rockies (The Peterson Field Guide Series), 4th edition. Roger Tory Peterson. Houghton Mifflin Company, 1980. $16.95 (hardcover). Other volumes available.

Birds of North America (A Guide to Field Identification), revised edition. Chandler S. Robbins, Bertel Bruun, and Herbert S. Zim. Golden Press, 1983. $14.00 (paperback), $15.96 (hardcover).

Advanced Birding (Peterson Field Guides). Kenn Kaufman. Houghton Mifflin Company, 1990. $15.95 (paperback).

The Audubon Society Field Guide to North American Birds, (Eastern and Western Regions in separate volumes). Miklos D.F. Udvardy. Alfred A. Knopf, 1994. $19.00 (hardcover).

Eastern Birds. James Coe. Golden Press, 1994. $10.95 (hardcover).

Books: Squirrels, Bats, and Butterflies

Butterflies Through Binoculars: A Field Guide to Butterflies in the Boston-New York-Washington Region. Jeffrey Glassberg. Oxford University Press, 1993. $19.95 (paperback).

Enjoying Butterflies More. Jeffrey Glassberg. Bird Watcher's Digest Press, 1995. $3.95 (paperback).

Enjoying Squirrels More (or Less!). Howard Youth. Bird Watcher's Digest Press, 1997. $3.95 (paperback).

Handbook for Butterfly Watchers. Robert Michael Pyle. Houghton Mifflin Company, 1992. $12.95 (paperback).

Understanding Bats. Kim Williams and Rob Mies. Bird Watcher's Digest Press, 1996. $3.95 (paperback).

Listing Software and CD-ROMS

Audubon CD-Rom
Knopf Publishing Group
201 E. 50th Street
New York, NY 10022
212-940-7624

AviSys 4.0/Perceptive Systems, Inc.
P.O. Box 3530
Silverdale, WA 98383
800-354-7755
76506.3100@compuserve.com

BirdBase/BirdArea
Windows
1400 Dover Rd.
Santa Barbara, CA 93103
805-963-4883 (phone and fax)
sbsp@aol.com
Note: Traveling bird watchers can e-mail for free checklists of species endemic to given areas.

BirdBase/Santa Barbara Software, Inc.
1400 Dover Rd
Santa Barbara, CA 93103
805-963-4886

Bird Brain, 3.01/Bird Brain, Jr.
Ideaform, Inc.
908 E. Briggs
Fairfield, IA 52556
800-779-7256
515-472-7256
fax: 515-469-5065
www.birdwatching.com

Birder's Diary, Windows
Thayer Birding Software
P.O. Box 43243
Cincinnati, OH 45243
800-865-2473
513-561-4486
pete@birding.com
www.birding.com

The Birds of North America, Peterson CD-ROM
Houghton Mifflin, Interactive
120 Beacon Street
Somerville, MA 02143
617-503-4800

Easy Bird
9500 170th St.
Hugo, MN 55038
612-439-0891
harlow@mn.uswest.net

Justice Associates "Life Cycles"
Software Division
N3566 Grover Drive
Withee, WI 54498
715-785-7614 (phone and fax)

MacPeregrine, Macintosh
WholeLifeSystems
120 Brown St.
Kennebunk, ME 04043
207-985-3166
www.gwi.net/sing/MacW.html

Ramphastos
P.O. Box 310
Dover, NH 03821
888-221-BIRD

Magazines
Bird Watcher's Digest
P.O. Box 110
Marietta, OH 45750
800-879-2473

Birder's World
44 East 8th St., Suite 410
Holland, MI 49423-3502
800-446-5489

Birding
P.O. Box 6599
Colorado Springs, CO 80934
800-850-2473

Field Notes
700 Broadway
New York, NY 10003
212-979-3000

Living Bird
159 Sapsucker Woods Road
Ithaca, NY 14850
607-254-BIRD

WildBird
P.O. Box 52898
Boulder, CO 80322-2898
800-365-4421

Organizations
The American Birding Association
P.O. Box 6599
Colorado Springs, CO 80934
800-850-2473 or 719-578-1614

The National Audubon Society
700 Broadway
New York, NY 10003
212-979-3000

The Association of Field Ornithologists
Ornithological Society of North America (OSNA) Business Office,
Allen Press
P.O. Box 1897
Lawrence, KS 66044
913-843-1221

Suppliers: Bird Feeders/Houses
Arundale Products
P.O. Box 4637
St. Louis, MO 63108
800-352-9164

C & S Products
Box 848
Fort Dodge, IA 50501
515-955-8513

Duncraft
102 Fisherville Rd
Concord, NH 03303-2086
800-763-7878

Galee Industries
763 Waverly St.
Framingham, MA 01701
800-536-3455

Kempf's
P.O. Box 504
Woonsocket, SD 57385
605-796-4171

Native America (houses)
P.O. Box 5001
Hauppauge, NY 11788
www.nativeamerica.com

Nelson Manufacturing
P.O. Box 636
Cedar Rapids, IA 52406
319-363-2607

Perky Pet Brand Feeders
2201 S. Wabash St.
Denver, CO 80231
800-782-3514

Wild Bill's
Invisible Fence Co., Inc.
Dept. WBDJ
355 Phoenixville Pike
Malvern, PA 19355
800-576-2473

Suppliers: Bird Store Franchises
Wild Birds Unlimited
Suite 146
11711 N. College
Carmel, IN 46032
317-571-7100

Wild Bird Centers of America, Ltd.
7687 MacArthur Blvd.
Cabin John, MD 20818
800-WILDBIRD
www.birdwatcher.com

Wild Bird Marketplace
1891 Santa Barbara Dr.
Suite106, Exec. Park N.
Lancaster, PA 17601

Suppliers: Bird Watching Gear
Birder's Buddy Vest
330 S. Ash Lane
Dept BD
Flagstaff, AZ 86004
800-955-1951

BWD Direct
P.O. Box 110
Marietta, OH 45750
800-879-2473

Scope Pack
21 Jet View Drive
Rochester, NY 14642-4996
800-587-7225

Suppliers: Optics Manufacturers

Bausch & Lomb Binoculars
9200 Cody
Overland Park, KS 66214
800-423-3537

Bushnell Corporation
9200 Cody
Overland Park, KS 66214
813-752-3400

Canon USA, Inc.
1 Canon Plaza
Lake Success, NY 11042-9979
800-OK CANON
www.usa.canon.com

Celestron International
2835 Columbia St.
Torrance, CA 90503
310-328-9560
fax: 310-212-5835

Docter Optics/Bogen
565 E. Crescent Ave.
Ramsey, NJ 07446
201-818-9500

Fujinon, Inc.
10 High Point Dr.
Wayne, NJ 07470
201-633-5600

Kowa Optimed, Inc.
2001 S. Vermont Ave.
Torrance, CA 90502
310-327-1913
800-966-5692
fax: 310-327-4177

Leica Camera, Inc.
156 Ludlow Ave.
Northvale, NJ 07647
800-222-0118

Mirador Optical Corporation
P.O. Box 11614
Marina Del Rey, CA 90295
310-821-5587

Nikon
1300 Walt Whitman Rd.
Melville, NY 11747-3064
516-547-4200

Pentax Corporation
35 Inverness Drive East
Englewood, CO 80112
800-709-2020

Swarovski Optik
One Wholesale Way
Cranston, RI 02920
800-426-3089

Swift Instruments, Inc.
952 Dorchester Ave.
Boston, MA 02125
614-436-2960

Tasco
Box 520080
Miami, FL 33152-0080
305-591-3670

Carl Zeiss Optical, Inc.
1015 Commerce Street
Petersburg, VA 23803
800-338-2984

Suppliers: Optics Retailers (Mail Order)

Camera Corner of Iowa
3523 Eastern Ave.
Davenport, IA 52807
319-391-6851

Christophers, Ltd.
2401 Tee Circle
Norman, OK 73069
800-356-6603
405-364-4898

Eagle Optics
716 S. Whitney Way
Madison, WI 53711
800-289-1132
fax: 608-271-4406

Hazleoptics
757 McNair St.
Hazleton, PA 18201
800-826-1536

National Camera Exchange
9300 Olson Memorial Highway
Golden Valley, MN 55427
800-624-8107

Pocono Mountain Optics
104 NP 502 Plaza #RR-4
Moscow, PA 18444

Redlich Binocular & Optical Co.
711 West Broad St.
Falls Church, VA 22046
800-414-6019

Tour Companies

Bellbird Safaris
19 Old Town Square, Ste 238
Fort Collins, CO 80524
800-726-0656

Bird Treks
115 Peach Bottom Village
Peach Bottom, PA 17563
717-548-3303

Borderland Tours
2550 W. Calle Padilla
Tucson, AZ 85745
800-525-7753

Delaney EcoTours, Ltd.
431 Lafayette Center, Ste. 222
Manchester, MO 63011-3971
314-230-9675

Eagle-Eye Tours, Inc.
P.O. Box 5010
Point Roberts, WA 98281
800-373-5678
birdtours@eagle-eye.com
604-948-9177
fax: 604-948-9085

Field Guides, Inc.
P.O. Box 160723
Austin, TX 78716
800-728-4953

Focus Nature Tours
P.O. Box 21230
St. Petersburg, FL 33742
813-523-3338

Focus Tours
14821 Hillside Lane
Burnsville, MN 55306
612-892-7830

Victor Emanuel Nature Tours
P.O. Box 33008
Austin, TX 78764
800-525-7753

Wings, Inc.
1643 N. Alvernon Way
Tucson, AZ 85712
520-320-9868
Wings@rtd.com

Video

Audubon Society's Butterfly Gardening. MasterVision How to Series, 1997. Master Vision, Inc., 969 Park Ave., New York, NY 10028; 212-879-0448; 92 mins; $24.95.

How to Start Watching Birds. KBRD Video Productions, P.O. Box 1540, Fairfield, IA 52556; 800-779-7256; $39.95 (plus $3.50 s/h).

A Celebration of Birds (With Roger Tory Peterson). Judy Fieth and Michael Male. Bullfrog Films, Inc. Olney, PA 19547; 215-779-8226; 54 mins. $29.95 (plus $5.00 s/h).

Birds, Birds, Birds — Why Bird Watchers Watch.
Maslowski Wildlife Productions; 1219 Eversole,
Cincinnati, OH 45230-3505; 513-231-7301; 44 mins.
$27.45 (includes shipping).

Watching Birds (With Roger Tory Peterson).
Metromedia, Inc. and Houghton Mifflin Company,
1 Beacon St., Boston, MA 02108; 800-225-3362.
$59.95.

Watching Warblers. Michael Male and Judy Fieth.
Blue Earth Video Library, 22-D Hollywood Ave., Ho-
Ho-Kus, NJ 07423; 800-343-5540.

*The National Audubon Society's Up Close Video
Series.* Nature Science Network, Inc. 1989. 55 mins.
each. $33.50 ppd. each: BWD Direct, P.O. Box 110,
Marietta, OH 45750; 800-879-2473.
 Cardinals Up Close
 Owls Up Close
 Hawks Up Close
 Hummingbirds Up Close
 Bluebirds Up Close

Flowers, Vines, Shrubs, and Trees that Provide Nectar for Hummingbirds

Common Name	Latin Name	Annual/Biennial/Perennial	Color
Flowers:			
Bee balm	*Monarda didyma*	P	red, pink
Bleeding heart	*Dicentra spectabilis*	P	rose
Butterfly weed	*Asclepias tuberosa*	P	orange
Cardinal flower	*Lobelia cardinalis*	P	red
Carpet bugle	*Ajuga reptans*	P	blue, purple
Columbines	*Aquilegia spp.*	P	red, pink, yellow, blue, white
Coralbells	*Heuchera sanguinea*	P	red
Dahlia	*Dahlia merckii*	A or P	red, pink, orange, yellow, white
Delphinium or scarlet larkspur	*Delphinium cardinale*	P	red
Four-o-clock	*Mirabilis jalapa*	A or P, depending on climate	red, rose, pink salmon, yellow, white
Foxglove	*Digitalis purpurea*	P or B	purple, red, rose, cream, white
Fuchsia	*Fuchsia 'Riccartonii'*	A or P	red
Gladioli	*Gladiolus spp.*	A or P (tender bulb)	many colors
Jewelweed	*Impatiens capensis*	A	orange
	Impatiens pallida	A	yellow
Nasturtium	*Tropaeolum majus*	A	scarlet, orange, yellow, white
Pestemons or beard-tongues	*Penstemon spp.*	P	purple, scarlet, yellow, white
Petunia	*Petunia spp.*	A	many colors
Phlox	*Phlox drummondii*	A	many colors
	Phlox spp.	P	many colors
Red-hot poker or tritoma	*Kniphofia uvaria*	P	red, yellow
Sage	*Salvia officinalis*	A or P	lavender
Sage, scarlet	*Salvia splendens*	A or P, depending on climate	red

Snapdragon	*Antirrhinum majus*	A	red, pink, white
Spider flower	*Cleome spinosa*	A	rose, pink, white
Sweet William	*Dianthus barbatus*	A or B	red, maroon, rose, pink, white
Tobacco, flowering	*Nicotiana alata*	A or P	many colors
Zinnias	*Zinnia spp.*	A	many colors

Vines:

Honeysuckle, trumpet	*Lonicera sempervirens*	P	red
	Lonicera heckrottii	P	red and yellow
Morning glory	*Ipomoea coccinea*	A	red
	Ipomoea purpurea	A	purple to blue
Scarlet runner bean	*Phaseolus coccineus*	A or P	red
Trumpet creeper	*Campsis radicans*	P	orange, red

Shrubs:

Azaleas	*Rhododendron spp.*	red, pink, white
Beauty bush	*Kolkwitzia amabilis*	pink
Butterfly bush	*Buddleia davidii*	purple, pink, blue, white
Coralberry	*Symphoricarpos orbiculatus*	pink, white
Flowering currant	*Ribes odoratum*	rose, yellow
Hardy fuchsia	*Fuchsia magellanica*	violet and red
Tatarian honeysuckle	*Lonicera tatarica*	red, pink
Flowering quince	*Chaenomeles japonica*	red
Rose of Sharon	*Hibiscus syriacus*	pink, white
Weigela	*Weigela florida*	red, maroon, pink

Trees:

Buckeye or horse chestnut	*Aesculus glabra*	yellow to white
Buckeye, red	*Aesculus carnea*	red
Horse chestnut	*Aesculus hippocastanum*	yellow to white
Black locust	*Robinia pseudoacacia*	white
Chinaberry	*Melia azedarach*	purple to lilac
Flowering crabs	*Malus spp.*	red, rose, pink, white
Hawthorns	*Crataegus spp.*	red, rose, white
Mimosa, silk tree	*Albizia julibrissin*	pink
Siberian pea tree	*Caragana arborescens*	yellow
Tulip poplar	*Liriodendron tulipifera*	yellow with orange markings

Index

(continued)

Art and Photos in Color
Section in order of appearance

Welcome
Birding by Habitat
Garden for Birds
Bird Feeding Station
Seed types
Name that bird:
Downy woodpecker versus hairy woodpecker
Purple finch versus house finch
Cooper's hawk versus sharp-shinned hawk
Separating sparrows
Bill's Top 40 Favorite Birds:
Common loon
Great blue heron
Roseate spoonbill
Blue-winged teal
American avocet
Long-billed curlew
American woodcock
Upland sandpiper

Black skimmer
Atlantic puffin
Cooper's hawk
Red-tailed hawk
California quail
Snowy owl
Eastern screech-owl
Whip-poor-will
Ruby-throated hummingbird
Anna's hummingbird
Red-headed woodpecker
Acorn woodpecker
Scissor-tailed flycatcher
Eastern phoebe
Vermilion flycatcher
Steller's jay
Black-billed magpie
Common raven
Mountain bluebird
Hermit thrush
Gray catbird
American dipper

Mourning warbler
Kentucky warbler
Indigo bunting
Painted bunting
Dark-eyed junco
White-crowned sparrow
Eastern meadowlark
Baltimore oriole
Common redpoll
Evening grosbeak

Receive this **FREE** bird identification guide when you subscribe to

1 year (6 issues) $18.95

AN IDENTIFICATION GUIDE TO COMMON
BACKYARD BIRDS

Know the Birds at Your Feeder!

A SPECIAL PUBLICATION FROM *BIRD WATCHER'S DIGEST*

What is it about bird watching that intrigues you? Unusual birds that visit your feeders? Some species that you can't identify? Heading out early in the morning to join friends at a local nature center? Providing the ideal backyard habitat to attract hummingbirds, chickadees, and woodpeckers?

At *Bird Watcher's Digest* we share your passion for birds and bird watching, as do our writers, photographers, artists, and subscribers. *Bird Watcher's Digest* is like a club where members share their best birding adventures, their top tips for attracting and feeding birds, and their solutions to pesky problems such as trying to keep bees and ants away from a hummingbird feeder.

Bird watching is a voyage of discovery, and *Bird Watcher's Digest* is your map and tour guide . . . as you learn to identify birds by their behavior and song, to keep a yard list, to plan to attend a bird watching festival or maybe to choose a new pair of binoculars. We're bird watchers, and we have faced many of the same challenges. Let us help you, entertain you, and inspire you.

Six times a year *Bird Watcher's Digest* delivers answers to your backyard birding questions, features profiles of 2–3 bird species, explains bird behavior, offers travel tips, and links you to thousands of other bird watchers worldwide.

Now is the perfect time to start your subscription. For just $18.95, you will receive six sparkling issues, and when we receive your payment we will send, free of charge, a copy of *An Identification Guide to Backyard Birds*, a 32-page full-color booklet. *Backyard Birds* (a $3.95 value) contains

more than 80 photographs of the most common backyard visitors from all across North America, along with food preferences, ranges, and field marks of each species.

It's a great value—yours for free!

Let the adventure begin— subscribe to *Bird Watcher's Digest* today!

These pages contain valuable coupons that can save you money on bird-watching gear and products.

Don't miss out on these money-saving offers!

IDG BOOKS WORLDWIDE REGISTRATION CARD

Visit our Web site at http://www.idgbooks.com

ISBN Number: ISBN: 0-7645-5040-3

Title of this book: Bird Watching For Dummies™

My overall rating of this book: ❏ Very good [1] ❏ Good [2] ❏ Satisfactory [3] ❏ Fair [4] ❏ Poor [5]

How I first heard about this book:

❏ Found in bookstore; name: [6] _____   ❏ Book review: [7]

❏ Advertisement: [8]   ❏ Catalog: [9]

❏ Word of mouth; heard about book from friend, co-worker, etc.: [10]   ❏ Other: [11]

What I liked most about this book:

_____
_____
_____

What I would change, add, delete, etc., in future editions of this book:

_____
_____
_____

Other comments:

_____

Number of computer books I purchase in a year: ❏ 1 [12]   ❏ 2-5 [13]   ❏ 6-10 [14]   ❏ More than 10 [15]

I would characterize my computer skills as: ❏ Beginner [16] ❏ Intermediate [17] ❏ Advanced [18] ❏ Professional [19]

I use ❏ DOS [20] ❏ Windows [21] ❏ OS/2 [22] ❏ Unix [23] ❏ Macintosh [24] ❏ Other: [25]_____

(please specify)

I would be interested in new books on the following subjects:

(please check all that apply, and use the spaces provided to identify specific software)

❏ Word processing: [26]   ❏ Spreadsheets: [27]

❏ Data bases: [28]   ❏ Desktop publishing: [29]

❏ File Utilities: [30]   ❏ Money management: [31]

❏ Networking: [32]   ❏ Programming languages: [33]

❏ Other: [34]

I use a PC at (please check all that apply): ❏ home [35] ❏ work [36] ❏ school [37] ❏ other: [38] _____

The disks I prefer to use are ❏ 5.25 [39] ❏ 3.5 [40] ❏ other: [41]_____

I have a CD ROM: ❏ yes [42]   ❏ no [43]

I plan to buy or upgrade computer hardware this year: ❏ yes [44]   ❏ no [45]

I plan to buy or upgrade computer software this year: ❏ yes [46]   ❏ no [47]

Name: _____ Business title: [48] _____ Type of Business: [49] _____

Address (❏ home [50] ❏ work [51]/Company name: _____)

Street/Suite# _____

City [52]/State [53]/Zip code [54]: _____ Country [55] _____

❏ **I liked this book!** You may quote me by name in future
   IDG Books Worldwide promotional materials.

My daytime phone number is _____

IDG BOOKS WORLDWIDE

THE WORLD OF
COMPUTER
KNOWLEDGE®

❏ YES!

Please keep me informed about IDG Books Worldwide's World of Computer Knowledge. Send me your latest catalog.